Assessing Child and
Adolescent Disorders

In memoriam, *pro*
Victoria Pearlman

Assessing Child and Adolescent Disorders

A Practice Manual

Masud Hoghughi

SAGE Publications

London • Newbury Park • New Delhi

First published 1992

 SAGE Publications Ltd
6 Bonhill Street
London EC2A 4PU

SAGE Publications Inc
2455 Teller Road
Newbury Park, California 91320

SAGE Publications India Pvt Ltd
32, M-Block Market
Greater Kailash – I
New Delhi 110 048

British Library Cataloguing in Publication Data

Hoghughi, Masud
    Assessing Child and Adolescent Disorders: A
    Practice Manual
    I. Title
    618.92

    ISBN 0–8039–8296–8
    ISBN 0–8039–8297–6 pbk

Library of Congress catalog card number 92-50135

Typeset by Mayhew Typesetting, Rhayader, Powys
Printed in Great Britain by Biddles Ltd, Guildford, Surrey

Contents

Foreword

In 1980 my book *Assessing Problem Children* (Burnett Books, London) was published. Before long it was out of print. I refused to have it reprinted because the practice of assessment which it advocated had moved on and I felt a new book should reflect it. The early disappearance of the book from the shelves and persistent demands for it confirmed its relevance and accessibility to a large readership which usually shies away from such publications. The present book is a substantially expanded and wholly rewritten update of the subject.

In the interim period, significant changes have taken place in dealing with children and adolescents who have difficulties. The major thrust has been to move away from heavy official intervention, whether in justice, education or social services, towards lighter measures, usually aimed at keeping the child or adolescent in the community. There have been, in the UK, a new Mental Health Act, two new Education Acts, new Children Acts and increasing community dispositions for young offenders.

These moves have blurred the earlier explicit focus on assessment so that there are no longer, for example, many local authority 'Observation and Assessment' centres. This role is now fulfilled as part of a whole approach to children's difficulties which includes some notion of treatment. The underlying attitude change is reflected in the different titles of the two books: from 'problem children' to 'child and adolescent disorders'.

In the past decade, child sexual abuse has emerged as the most prominent preoccupation of all workers with children, at least in the UK. The 'Cleveland Inquiry' into what appeared to be abuse of children on a mass scale put methods of assessment under particular scrutiny and found them wanting. Since then, despite intense interest, the scientific basis of such assessments has remained in some doubt. This illustrates the wider point that the relationship between society's preoccupations and scientific rigour is not straightforward – we do not always have the best information about the areas that most concern us.

This is reflected in the considerable literature on assessment which has burgeoned during the last decade. And yet, with the exception of Lazarus's 'Basic Id', none presents a framework or classification for the *assessment of the whole child*, as 'Problem Profile' does. I have become even more persuaded that whilst DSM and ICD present useful research tools, they are not really suitable frameworks for practical assessments of high quality, other than in very restricted cases. However, my indebtedness to them both, particularly DSM III-R, and to Rutter and Hersov's splendid second edition (1985) of *Child and Adolescent Psychiatry*, should be evident.

To my knowledge, no other book brings together such comprehensive, though unavoidably very brief, information on child and adolescent disorders as the present manual. Inevitably the information is of varied quality, reflecting the state of knowledge in particular areas. Whole books can and have been written about individual topics, which can be pursued from references given. But intensive involvement with a range of assessment activities at a variety of levels persuades me that for most workers with children most of the time, this book will provide as much information as they are likely to need for devising rigorous intervention programmes.

The book aims to avoid jargon, wherever possible. I have also tried to vary the gender of the child to ensure that it is not biassed. If there are more 'he's', it is because the far from resilient and well-endowed male gender seems to suffer most of the disorders.

In deference to the prime purpose of this book as a 'manual' rather than an academic book, I have largely avoided identifying sources with names and dates in the text, but they can nevertheless be pursued in the references given. These consist primarily of books published in the last decade which are, therefore, up to date and easily available for further study.

The National Children's Bureau Library kindly supplied me with some statistical information, as did my colleague Lynda Dunn. Others, including Surya Bhate and Pat Bielby-Smith, commented on chapters which gave me particular trouble. Yet others, such as Lancashire, Newcastle and Aycliffe colleagues, as well as my students at Hull and Durham, have helped sharpen the concepts and affirm the usefulness of the approach in their work. I am most grateful to all of them.

My family's contribution is too varied and fundamental to be easily acknowledged. The same is also true of Doreen Kipling, who has kept pace with my many commitments as well as helped me through many travails. The thanks due to her are many and very special.

Masud Hoghughi

PART I

1

What is Assessment?

The prime aim of every society is to survive. If it does not survive, it can do nothing else and nothing else remains to matter. To survive, it must achieve two fundamental goals – an acceptable level of *order*, and fulfilment of its fundamental *values*. 'Order' is about sequence and predictability. Without predictability of sequence, learning is impossible and, therefore, no cumulative, purposive activity can be undertaken. Values are about what a society considers it important to pursue, both preceding and succeeding the search for order. To achieve order and fulfilment of values in any area of its operation, society needs to fulfil one or more of three other objectives: (1) to promote, enhance and maximize whatever it deems to be 'good'; (2) to maintain the status quo or preserve certain traditions and ways of doing things, not only because they do not need changing, but also because they may be deemed to be good in and of themselves; (3) and to reduce and eventually eliminate whatever it deems to be undesirable, 'unacceptable' or 'bad'.

The social history of every society can be usefully considered in terms of its definition of order and values and how it has sought to pursue these objectives. Each of the objectives is implicit within society's sense of order and values. To this extent 'norms' or 'standards', whether formal or informal, described or prescribed, are an integral part of social functioning. Social control is the mechanism and organization by which the objectives are achieved.

This book is about children as people who present or experience unacceptable conditions, the process of assessing them and the issues which are involved in such a process. Although attempting to control and predict problem behaviour is as old as humanity, 'assessment' as a systematic activity is quite recent. The main meaning assigned to assessment in standard English dictionaries and continued to this day has to do with the 'determination of amount, or scheme of fixing value for the purpose of taxation'.

The professional usage of the term now refers to a 'process of evaluating a person's condition', in an individual or group setting, with a view to determining how the condition should be dealt with. The word is now used by social agencies to mean 'determining the characteristics of an individual or group' for such purposes as school selection, protection from abuse or injury, suicide prevention and any such matters that fall within their professional purview.

Recent developments

Although the idea of assessment as an integrated, purposive activity is new, the practice has major historical antecedents. The oldest systematic practice of assessment is in medicine, which in the course of its development has paid increasing attention to the exact description of signs and symptoms of illness and detailed recording of treatment processes. This approach, based on producing, noting and evaluating evidence, combined with advances in biological and natural sciences, has ensured the development of medicine into the most rigorous discipline, dealing with one area of human problems.

Concern with madness and 'badness' is also old. The former has become, accidentally, the province of psychiatry which draws mainly on the scientific prestige and, only occasionally, the rigour and empiricism of medicine. 'Badness' is mainly a matter of moral judgment; but collective judgments become codified in law and the breach of particular laws in turn defines crime and the 'criminal'. In this context, offenders are assessed on administrative and professional grounds, as a prelude to being allocated to appropriate services – in relation to risk, offence category, length of sentence and similar factors. With juvenile offenders outside penal establishments, assessment is often of the *whole* young person with a view to determining the best or least inappropriate venue of containment and help.

Along with medicine, the most important contribution to the assessment of people has been made by psychology. From its scientific beginnings in the nineteenth century (although general concern with behaviour goes much further back), it has been centrally concerned with the development and evaluation of methods of making relatively stable generalizations about human behaviour. Applications of psychology to problems of living, understanding of human development, and the effect of environmental variables on behaviour now form a major element in any integrated and comprehensive practice of assessment.

Child and adolescent 'disorders', 'problems' or 'difficulties' are all departures and deviations from society's values and sense of order. When a child, for example, fails to thrive it upsets society's view of the appropriate rate of development of children (order) and its sense of what should happen to a normal child (values). Action is taken to investigate the condition as a prelude to remedying it. When an adolescent acts aggressively towards other people, he thereby challenges established values about sanctity of person and provokes intervention. Both order and values can be descriptive ('this is how things *are*', 'this *is* what we value') or prescriptive ('this is how things *should* be', 'this is what we *must* do'). Assessment as a means of identifying a child's condition is a prelude to doing something about it and is, therefore, directly an act of social control.

Problems, needs and related tasks

'Problems', 'difficulties', 'disturbance' and 'disorders' are all variants of something that society, or significant people within it, find undesirable or at worst 'unacceptable'. The condition challenges society's sense of order and values, and, therefore, demands reaction and intervention. In this respect, problems are similar to 'need' which also, by definition, demands fulfilment. If a young child is gasping on a hot day, we say 'he needs water'. If a child is upset because his mother is in hospital, we might say that he suffers from anxiety and he 'needs' mothering. Needs are a pervasive, socially sanctioned means of justifying intervention in other people's lives. However, whereas 'problems' refer to undesirable states, 'needs' can be defined as the 'gap between what is and what should be'. To that extent, needs also invoke social order and values. There are as many varieties of needs (notwithstanding efforts of classify them under a specific number of headings) as there are human experiences of difficulty. Indeed, frequently a difficulty or problem provokes intervention which is legitimized by 'need' as, for example, when an 'unruly' child is deemed to be 'in need of care and control'.

The difficulty with the concept of 'need' is that only a person who experiences or has the need can legitimately and logically correctly assert it. Any other person making a statement about 'x needs y' is making an inference and an attribution which can only be validated by a statement from the person who is said to have the need. Even taking action which removes the original difficulty (e.g. giving a glass of water to a gasping child), does not necessarily show that the original attribution of the 'need for water' was right. Any number of other explanations may be offered as to why the child has stopped gasping. At least in the attribution of *physical needs* we are on reasonably firm ground. After all, human beings have fairly similar physiology and in physical terms, we assume, fairly similar experiences of pain and pleasure. But this is not the case with the less common physical experiences and others which are not physical, e.g. lack of psychological stimulation, absence of control, lack of security. Our ascription of a 'need for security' in a child who has grown up in an unstable home environment, *may be* valid and helpful but there is no satisfactory way of being sure that the child, even if he had the concept and the language to describe it, would agree with us, or that if he did, he would be right.

Thus, although 'need' as a concept seems indispensable, in terms of assessment and treatment of children it should be used with extreme caution, if at all. On the whole, people who give prominence to need terminology as a basis for intervention tend to be predominantly authoritarian, quite often sure of their own ability to identify need and intolerant of search for publicly observable evidence and demands for accountability. Because children are vulnerable to inappropriate adult intervention, they should be protected against any form of practice which is not based on strong, consensually agreed evidence. The term 'need' can be justifiably used to promote action, as long as requirements of evidence and accountability are met.

Strengths are the converse of difficulties and, to some extent, of 'needs'. Children may either have positive strengths such as 'good athletic prowess' or, alternatively, be regarded as strong simply because they do not have a weakness or difficulty in that area. In assessing young people's difficulties, it is important constantly to have an eye to their strengths. Although weaknesses are the focus of intervention, only current or potential strengths can be used to alleviate those weaknesses. Furthermore, identifying and amplifying children's strengths is an important element in building up their sense of self-worth, which is itself an important inoculator against other difficulties.

Assessment as intervention

In the present context, assessment is defined as a continuous *process of identifying problems and determining what should be done about them.* This is a minimal definition which is open-ended and allows for the adoption of a wide variety of approaches and settings in which assessment may be carried out. The continuity and interdependence of assessment and treatment may be best seen in the conceptual map, Figure 1. This map is the distillation of *all types of action* that have to be taken to deal with children's difficulties. The order of concepts indicates the critical path to ensure that all measures are taken in the most efficient, logically coherent manner. The map is *dynamic*, as indicated by two-way arrows, allowing flexible response to changes in the child's condition, including those which arise from any form of intervention.

The core components of the model are as follows:

Referral Before anyone can do anything about children, there has to be a reason, usually a 'negative' condition, which is deemed to justify intervention.

Management Nothing can be done with children until the immediate impact of their problems has been contained or reduced to tolerable levels, so that they are stabilized and the agency can proceed to other tasks.

Care Physical, emotional and social succour are necessary to ensure that children survive and their welfare is assured, so that the agency can safely proceed to carry out its subsequent technical tasks of assessment and treatment.

Assessment This is concerned with describing children's problems and determining what measures should be taken to alleviate them.

Treatment Having described the problems and what should be done to

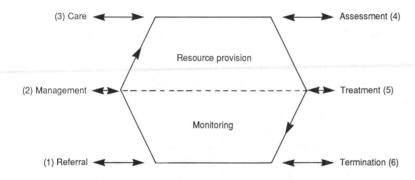

(3) Care — Assessment (4)

Resource provision

(2) Management — Treatment (5)

Monitoring

(1) Referral — Termination (6)

Figure 1 *Tasks with problem children: a conceptual map*

ameliorate them, treatment is concerned with translating the broad objectives into specific actions and implementing those actions so that the problem condition becomes tolerable.

Termination When treatment has been achieved, and the condition is no longer unacceptable, intervention is terminated. As new problems emerge, involvement with children can take new turns through the continuous process of monitoring, reassessment and treatment for the newly identified condition.

Because the determination of treatment measures is largely shaped by the environment in which it takes place, it is more appropriately the subject for a separate discourse on treatment, of which many examples exist. The present book is concerned solely with the identification of children's problems although, as will become clear in Chapter 4, the particular approach adopted has immediate and direct relevance to identifying appropriate treatment.

Conclusions of any assessment relate only to a particular time and place. They are, therefore, variably limited in their predictive potential. In a strictly logical sense, assessment can only be made of *past* (or present) behaviour which may help point to future probability. However, the logical and empirical limitations of the predictive value of assessment do not reduce its indispensability as a basis for undertaking future action. Any *rational* intervention must be based on an assessment of the problem with which it is inextricably bound.

Philosophical aspects

'Assessment' is what philosophers call a 'polymorphous' concept. It is a term whose meaning and related activities depend on the particular context and content. Watching people play a game can be regarded as much an assessment activity as is measuring their skin conductivity, seeing how they react to provocation or asking about their private feelings. Because of this diversity it is neither possible, nor particularly useful, to attempt exhaustively to define assessment. Rather, it is more worthwhile to regard assessment as 'a continuing process aimed at providing information about a person or situation as a guide to the most appropriate response'. Whether what is done is called 'assessment' or not depends on the explicitness of the process and the purpose to which its products are put.

It is commonly assumed that actions following a 'formal' process of assessment have been prescribed by that assessment. But the link between assessment and the actions that follow from it is a matter of preference, expediency and degree, rather that of logical necessity. The same assessment may have different treatment implications, depending on the theoretical orientation and resources of the treatment agent. For example, a child with problems of self-control may be seen to be in need of counselling, behaviour therapy, or both. In practice, the link between assessment and treatment implications for children remains suspect and inadequately worked out, as can be seen from quite different 'treatments of choice' for the same condition.

As a scientific pursuit, the process of assessment is like that of any other *inferential activity*. It starts with the perception of a condition or event which disturbs the observer. The observer has a *hunch* or an idea of what may be wrong and sets about collecting relevant information. The 'causal' hunch and the investigator's attitude (scientific, therapeutic or otherwise) determine the kind and quality of information obtained with which to *describe* or delineate the problem.

The description of the problem leads to greater *understanding* by the observer, who may be sufficiently satisfied with his understanding to regard what he has learned as *the explanation* of what has gone wrong. Alternatively, he may postulate hypothetical explanations of the type 'Johnny threw a tantrum *because* he was told he could not stay up for the late night film' – implying that when Johnny (or anyone else like him) is thwarted, he throws a tantrum. This, however, is an additional logical step. For its validation, it relies on making and testing *predictions* about similar future behaviour. But such testing is impracticable, often unethical and technically impossible in the case of human beings, and even when the behaviour occurs, there are often numerous other possible explanations for it. Although some explanations may be more probable that others, there is logically no way of being certain.

When a behaviour is described, explained and predicted, it may become possible to exercise *control* over it. But just explaining something does not imply that it can be controlled; nor does the ability to control a behaviour imply that it is understood or explained. Successful measures of control deriving from and theoretically related to the explanations simply increase the probability that the explanation *may* be right, but do not allow us to be sure. This means that, in logic and practice, we cannot fully explain human behaviour, however good our assessment may be. We are, at this stage of development of our understanding, better employed in noting regularities of behaviour through rigorous and exhaustive *descriptions* than half-baked attempts at explanation. This point will be further dealt with in Chapters 3 and 4.

The major problem with applying a logical analysis of the concept of assessment to practice is that human beings do not behave logically or consistently. They engage in measures of control which do not follow from adequate descriptions or tested explanations of problems. Further, the same set of problems are often 'explained' by very different and often contradictory hypotheses. And to confound the confusion, the same explanations are used to justify wholly different and often incompatible modes of control. One result is a perceptible degree of scepticism about the utility of formal assessment among those who deal with people with difficulties. At the same time, those very sceptics, by virtue of presumably treating different human beings differently, engage implicitly in some form of assessment. It would, therefore, seem more useful to try and facilitate the process rather than to give up any attempt at rigorous assessment and then proceed as if it had been carried out.

In view of these limitations, it is essential to remember the hypothetical status of assessments. Statements based on an assessment process and the treatment prescriptions to which they lead are limited to the 'here and now' and the circumstances under which the statements are made. Before much can be done to evaluate any assessment in part or as a whole, it is necessary to 'know' the assessment agent, whether an individual or group. Such knowledge helps to determine the broad limits of reliability and validity of the information provided and the degree to which its assessments can be trusted to stand up to changes in time, place and circumstances. In the light of this it is evident that no assessment is ever conclusive. It is, at best, a probable indicator of the state of the assessed person under a range of circumstances. This is not to say that assessment does not remain the basis of valid predictions but rather that such predictive validity cannot be taken for granted as either absolute or self-evident.

Need for assessment

As awareness of and concern for people with problems has grown, various forms of assessment have come into an increasingly central position. Professions have developed to assess and deal with problems. They have, in turn, identified difficulties which make the existence of the professions necessary. Huge social welfare industries have come into existence, of which assessment is the cornerstone. This interdependent, symbiotic relationship of problems and their identifying agencies has political, economic, social and professional aspects which are complex, profound and beyond the scope of this book. In the last resort, however, the consequences of this relationship cannot be wholly divorced from the process of assessment and its products.

In a society with contending priorities, the assessment of people with problems, their need for and 'right to' resources, has become complex and dependent upon specialized knowledge. Despite massive increases in what might be broadly termed 'social welfare' expenditure in the recent decades, the demand for these resources has outstripped their supply, as can be seen in restricting right to welfare benefits, and in the case of children, the choice of 'cheaper' options for long-term treatment. This makes assessment of problem people and their corresponding needs a matter of critical importance.

The necessity to allocate scarce and shrinking resources rationally and efficiently to the most deserving places great demands on assessment. The definition of the 'most deserving' is fraught with political complexities and preferential definitions which may never be resolved beyond dispute. But a democratic society, through the interaction of its political and professional agencies and the operation of 'market forces', eventually establishes a broad spectrum of criteria which enable allocation of resources to be made with a large measure of public acceptability. The assessment of a young person who may be taken into care because of parental abuse, for example, has to be tested in a court of law, thus establishing the 'rightness' of the proposed action and corresponding expenditure of resources.

The expenditure of resources is only part of the total 'cost' and its consequences part of the 'benefits' of assessment. Increasingly important is the consideration of the price paid by society if people with problems are mismanaged. This involves both the notion of risk to the social fabric and damage to those individuals who become subject of socially sanctioned intervention.

This topic has received considerable attention and is likely to remain a major source of social concern. An assessment process based on comprehensive information which takes account of its own limitations and the damages and benefits that may accrue from it, and is open to public scrutiny, is the most rational and ethically acceptable instrument for legitimizing official intervention in the lives of other people. At a fundamental level, no rational action should be taken to alleviate a problem unless the extent and intensity of the problem and its place in the wider context of the individual and society are known. Only when an assessment of the problem has taken place does it become possible to evaluate the results of intervention. Thus, assessment is the cornerstone of *accountability* and *due process*, and is essential to the development of a systematic, evidence-based approach to tackling social problems.

Ultimately, evaluation of an assessment can only be done sensibly in relation to a particular outcome. Obviously, some assessments are not worth the effort, and, equally obviously, others handsomely repay the resources expended. Which is which depends on the circumstances, the potential of the assessment to guide action, and the importance attached to rational intervention. Some of the issues involved in such evaluation are elaborated in the following chapters.

Criteria for evaluating assessment

There are many different types of assessment. To separate the good from the poor, a number of criteria may be applied. These are central concepts in scientific methodology and are treated at length in other texts. They do, however, merit a brief mention here.

Reliability is the first evaluative criterion applied to any form of judgment or measurement. It is primarily an estimate of the dependability, stability and consistency of the measures, their results and the judgments based on them. Reliability is a matter of degree – *every* assessment has some degree of error and it is this error which prevents it from being totally reliable. The more 'factual' and descriptive the assessment, the more reliable it is likely to be. As simple descriptions begin to be superseded by more complex ones and interpretations become ever more abstruse, their reliability begins to tumble, as we see even in medical practice. Reliability forms the indispensable cornerstone of assessment without which no trust can be placed in its outcome.

Different forms of reliability apply to the assessor, tests and measures, the children and the conditions under which they are assessed. Thus each element of a total assessment has its own 'reliability value' but in turn contributes to the reliability of the whole process. Even when a reliable test is used by a reliable tester, the eventual outcome may be unreliable because the test has been used in inappropriate circumstances or the condition of the child may have changed in the interim.

All behaviour is inherently variable and the more complex the behaviour the more variable it is. In view of this, the degree of reliability of a whole assessment process or any individual stage within it should be related to the purpose of assessment. The less important the use to which the outcome of assessment is to be put, the less attention needs to be given to its reliability. In more important cases, such as whether a child should be removed from home or not, the reliability of assessment assumes paramount importance, as endorsed in judicial enquiries into, for example, cases of sexual abuse of children.

In most practical settings, however, it is not feasible to establish the reliability of a total assessment process, given the present stage of development of techniques and resources. For this reason, the most practical immediate solution would appear to be to monitor the consistency of the results of a particular tool, part-process of assessment or the assessment agency over a period of time and determine its reliability in due course. The reliability of the total process can be established incrementally over a period of time, as in medicine, when a disciplined approach has been adopted by practitioners.

Validity is *the* central, most complex and controversial concept in assessment. This is because validity is about 'truth' and the nature of 'reality'. As there is no single truth and there are many realities, it is often difficult to establish validity.

Validity is the answer to such questions as, 'How do you know you are assessing what you think you are assessing?'; 'How far is an IQ a measure of intelligence?'; 'How much weight can be placed on certain emotional expressions as possible predictors of future depression in children?'; 'How do you know that this girl's behaviour indicates that she has been sexually abused?' As these examples illustrate, the validity of any element or process of assessment can be looked at in terms of its content, how much it corresponds with other established facts and truths about a person, the degree to which it fits into an acceptable theory, and its ability to predict certain outcomes.

The difficulty of establishing the validity of any element or the total process of assessment is related to its complexity. It is relatively easy and straightforward to establish that a child who is unhappy does badly at school, or that a truant may be afraid of school. On the other hand, to suggest that difficulties in establishing relationships and maintaining personal equilibrium are symptomatic of a 'borderline personality' disorder is more difficult to validate – even if we know what this diagnosis means! Validity is a matter of degree and depends for its final weight on every element of the assessment process: the assessment tool, its relevance to the subject's condition, the circumstances under which the assessment is carried out, and variables related to the assessor. Although any one of these elements may be valid, ultimate judgment of validity must be based on the criteria of validity being met in the case of each individual element.

Numerous studies of tests, measures, diagnoses and specialized skills of different professional groups have shown acceptable levels of validity to be much more elusive than hoped for or normally assumed. If rigorous criteria of validity were to be applied, not many tests, measures or assessment processes and agents would pass muster. This is no reason for giving up assessment but rather a stimulus towards sharpening up each element of the process. Poor though these may be, they are still better than an undisciplined 'free for all' activity.

For the present, judgments of validity must relate to the degree of consensus which they command among groups of people who, for a variety of reasons, are deemed to be 'knowledgeable'. The judgments they make, however, should be regarded as strictly tentative and open to scrutiny. Because the validity of assessment in the vast majority of circumstances is not adequately established, assessment agents should ensure that their comments are not treated as infallible and that any potentially damaging consequences of their uncertain assessment, such as negative labelling, are minimized.

Efficiency relates to the relationship between the costs and benefits or input and outcome of assessment. Costs include financial outlay, expenditure of resources in terms of personnel and materials, as well as the inevitable price that has to be paid by the child, society, and the assessment agent in order to achieve the benefits of assessment. The efficiency of assessment increases as the cost, in relation to the final outcome, is reduced. The point frequently made by critics of present assessment services, such as local authority 'observation and assessment' centres, is that because they do not have the appropriate resources and organization, they take an inordinately long time to assess a child and thus the payoff is particularly poor in relation to the price paid by the parties involved.

Relevance is an ambiguous notion and one that is not frequently considered in evaluating assessment. 'Pertinence to the matter in hand' as a definition of 'relevance' is a matter of subjective judgment and one which is shaped by the professional training of assessment agents. Clearly it is expected that professionals concerned with assessment of children's problems should throw light on the problem and point to ways of ameliorating them. On this basis, much assessment activity is not relevant. Often, the reordering and renaming of problems (as in much psychiatric diagnosis), fails to identify the circumstances associated with the child's difficulties and what should be done about them. A complicating factor is that what is relevant from the viewpoint of the referral agent, may not be so from the assessor's viewpoint or those of the children and their parents. Given such diversity of views, it makes sense to ensure that assessments are sufficiently comprehensive so as to cover all relevant perspectives.

Usefulness is the overriding consideration in evaluating assessment as an applied activity aimed at alleviating human misery. Ultimately, assessment may be carried out at the highest level of reliability, validity, efficiency and relevance, but if it is not useful to the person who sought the assessment or the child who was deemed to need it, then the effort would have been wasted. As people make different uses of assessment, different criteria of usefulness are employed. In the case of problem children, the objective is to alleviate their problems and it therefore becomes possible to gauge the usefulness of an assessment according to the degree to which it facilitates such an outcome.

The usefulness of an assessment is also dependent on interaction between it and the competence of those who use it. This raises the possibility that the potential of an assessment, however good, may not be realized simply because the people for whom it is intended cannot use it. Although in operational terms such an assessment may not be very useful, it nevertheless has the potential to allow advanced use to be made of it. An example may be of a boy who attacks only when tired and asked to do something when he does not want to. Those who deal with the boy every day may not be able to regulate their own vigilance of the boy to such an extent as to be able to avoid the attack or reduce its occurrence. But if the assessment has met the criteria previously suggested, it obviously reflects more closely the state of the boy than a vague and judgmental statement and can be used as a basis for staff training. The sensible reaction is not to derogate advanced assessment but to try to match up the capability of users to it, provided a deliberate attempt has been made to keep the prescriptive implications of the assessment realistic and practicable.

Constancy and variability of behaviour

Empirical, 'scientific' and evidence-based assessment is concerned not only with the description of present problem behaviour, but also with predicting how it may develop and what should be done to change its course. This concern presumes predictability of human behaviour. In turn, the need for predicting behaviour arises because human beings do not act in ways which are either wholly constant or wholly variable.

Ideas of constancy and variability are at the core of human behaviour and its assessment. Logically, no talk of constancy would be sensible other than by contrasting it with variability. If human behaviour were totally constant it would be totally predictable. On the other hand, if behaviour were wholly variable and at the mercy of chance events, there would be no possibility of predicting it. As it is, different behaviours and personal characteristics can best be construed as falling somewhere along the spectrum of constancy and variability. Even under variable conditions, people can still be differentiated because they tend to behave more one way than another. People also show individual differences in the face of identical environmental circumstances. These relative differences and variabilities persist over time and enable predictions to be made.

All behaviour results from the interaction of *personal* and *environmental* characteristics. In order to discover relative constancies and variabilities of behaviour, the ideal would be systematically to vary the environment in which the individual is placed, to see how the behaviour changes. If, for example, a child behaves aggressively at school, it may be profitable to place him in other settings to see whether, and how much, he continues to behave aggressively. If the behaviour can then be judged (with appropriate safeguards for reliability and validity) as 'aggressive' in the other settings, then it is legitimate to regard that child as having a propensity to behave aggressively.

The more important it is to make accurate predictions about people's behaviour, the more essential it will be systematically to determine how much of their behaviour is due to environmental pulls and pushes and how much due to personal tendencies. Because individual characteristics cannot be easily manipulated (for a whole variety of ethical and technical reasons), the environment is likely to be a more feasible target of change. A child who engages in extensive self-injury at home may have to be removed to another environment for protection. This enables comparisons to be made between that child at home and in the new setting. Her behaviour can be observed in order to discover whether the tendency to self-injury is the reaction to immediate and nearby environmental pressures or rather the result of personal characteristics which perpetuate such behaviour in other settings.

Criticisms of assessment

Such an idea leads naturally on to one of the most frequently voiced criticisms of assessment. It is said that since most formal assessments takes place outside the child's natural setting, in a hospital, clinic, or residential facility, they are invalid and, therefore, by implication, useless. As has been indicated above, if the interest of assessment goes at all beyond the description of the present circumstances, then it is not only desirable but indeed necessary to remove children from their 'natural' setting into a maximally different one in order to discover the degree of variability of their behaviour. Of course, caution should be exercised in evaluating the effects of the new environment on behaviour, but this does not reduce the importance of changing the behavioural setting. Nor is this to minimize the importance of evaluating the costs and benefits of such a removal, as will be considered later.

The criticisms of the setting of assessment are sometimes extended to the idea of assessment itself. Such criticism often gets caught up in notions of objectivity versus subjectivity. As its simplest, the argument suggests that all assessment is to varying degrees subjective and dependent upon the prevailing circumstances and that, therefore, its results cannot be used legitimately as an objective basis for decision-making. This argument, at its most fundamental, is epistemological and relates to the problem of acquiring and communicating knowledge. With human beings, objectivity–subjectivity can be regarded as a continuum denoting the degree of actual or potential agreement among individuals about a piece of information. A pulse rate, though obtained by an individual person, may be regarded as a fairly objective measure, as can an IQ or reading attainment. Such information can be called 'objective', not only because a highly standardized record is available which can be interpreted by a variety of people, but also because the boundaries of interpretation are quite clearly defined. On the other hand, the labelling of a piece of behaviour as 'immoral' or 'aggressive' is subjective because the behaviour is defined in terms of variable and not universally acceptable criteria. Some assessments are more objective than others by virtue of the instruments used to obtain the information. Some people produce more objective assessment because they use criteria which are more easily defined and command wider consensus than others. Ultimately, however, there cannot logically be any such thing as absolute, objective assessment. It is, therefore, misguided to criticize it for this reason. The best that can be done is the adoption of such measures and judgments as may be acceptable to knowledgeable and critical users of assessment.

A more serious criticism of assessment of children with problems is that it results in labels which exceed, in the damage they do, the benefits to the children or those who want to know what can be legitimately done to help them. This argument is powerful and cannot be refuted in general terms. Undoubtedly some forms of assessment produce labels such as 'immoral', 'psychopathic', 'personality disordered', 'delinquent' or 'aggressive', which adversely determine significant people's behaviour to the child for an important part of his life.

At a logical level, every act of perception implies a form of classification (as we shall see in Chapter 3) which in turn involves an act of 'naming' or 'labelling'. The sociological perspective of 'labelling', however, regards it as an act of stigmatization which legitimizes certain negative acts towards the labelled person. But any descriptive evaluation of a person ('This child takes fits'; 'This child is not Christian') may lead to illegitimate negative action. As it is not possible to avoid using such words or their equivalent perceptual classifications, logically the charge of labelling cannot be refuted. In this sense, the argument becomes metaphysical and devoid of any but moral value.

The act of referring for assessment may itself cause the child to be regarded as abnormal. But formal assessment is not the only source of labelling of children with problems, though it may lend power and legitimacy to such labels, according to the status of the agency from which the labels originate. However, the process of labelling goes back a long way and children would not be referred for assessment unless they had already presented problems which, in the eyes of some responsible person, warranted intervention.

Ethics

Most of the above arguments are also related to the ethics of assessment. As a formal, coherent activity or indeed as an informal and haphazard one, assessment is undertaken for a purpose and has consequences both for the assessor and the assessed. The assessor is usually an adult in a position of power and the assessed child is relatively powerless, and in a minority position. It is, therefore, necessary to safeguard the interests of the child against inappropriate use of power in the process of assessment. These safeguards relate not only to questions of whether children should be referred for assessment in the first place and what methods of assessment should be deployed, but also to the consequences of assessment in terms of outcome and prescriptions and the way they are carried out. It is necessary to be satisfied that a child is presenting serious enough problems which, unless curbed, would deteriorate so as to justify assessment at all. If a child is problematic and warrants intervention, the most ethical course of action may be some form of objective assessment which is open to public scrutiny and on which intervention in the child's life may be based.

The methods of assessment may involve subjecting children to practices which are not justified in relation either to the outcome or to the prevailing ethics of the community. To subject children to strong electric shocks, for example, to determine their pain thresholds cannot be justified in terms of the use which could be made of the information, even if it were legally permissible.

The consequences of labelling have already been briefly discussed.

Suffice it to say that labelling has a power which transcends the immediate circumstances warranting it. Labels are frequently used as shorthand ways of legitimizing further action which may not be justified by the evidence available. Clearly, every effort should be made to minimize the use of labels with judgmental overtones. The development of descriptive assessment and alternative approaches to the classification of children's disorders may make the use of labelling unnecessary (see also Chapters 3 and 4). To counteract the effect of labels, not only is it necessary to engage in minimal labelling in the first place but also to ensure that all the labels bear qualifications of time and place which limit their longer range use and applicability.

Much of the information obtained through a process of detailed formal assessment as advocated in this book will have come to light for the first time. Like other information, it is subject to the same requirements of confidentiality and the safeguarding of individual privacy. There is the added constraint that such information can be used to justify measures which may have profound and perhaps adverse long-term consequences for children and their families. Considerable caution should, therefore, be exercised in disseminating confidential information about children, best regulated by the criterion of 'need to know' – those who do not need to have the particular information are not given access to it.

Rights of children

Carrying out assessment is a form of social intervention undertaken by a person who is usually more powerful than the child. As with every other exercise of power, it must be circumscribed by a clear understanding of the rights of the subject and the responsibility of the practitioner. This is not the place to go into the details of juvenile jurisprudence but, undoubtedly, we are now more aware of and ready to endorse the view that children, like adults, have rights and thereby place obligations on those who work with them.

The concept of rights (such as 'ascribed' and 'achieved', 'right to' and 'freedom from') is complex. In the case of children, it is generally accepted that their status as minors bestows rights upon them which should be enforceable in law. The United Nations Charter of Children's Rights and many courts' rulings on the 'human rights' of children are examples of this.

Assessment in the present context presumes the existence of some difficulty and is, therefore, a variety of 'clinical' intervention. As such it places the same requirements on the practitioner as any other form of clinical practice. These can be briefly summarized as follows, in the form of imperatives:

- Give the **child's welfare the highest priority** in everything that you do. That is what the law demands, as does good professional practice.
- **Do not hurt.** Make sure that whatever you do has been filtered and

vetted and the possible unintended consequences have been thought through, to ensure that they do not harm the child.

- **Deal with the child truthfully and honestly.** The fact that a child may only have limited understanding does not absolve you from trying to convey to the child what you are doing. A clear implication of this, particularly in assessment, is not telling the child that your purpose is one thing when in reality it is another.

- **Treat the child as a person.** Even if you do the same job every day with lots of other children, each child is different from others and should be treated as an individual with particular experiences, fears and hopes.

- **Take the child seriously.** Listen to what the child has to say and accord it due weight. This may not be as much as you would give the word of, for example, a respected colleague, but it is not without worth and the child should be able to recognize that you have given it serious attention.

- **Enable the child to participate in decision making.** Wherever possible, give the child voice and choice in eventual decisions. If you are not going to allow the child's choice its full due, do not pretend to give it in the first place.

- **Do not angle the evidence.** Be aware of your own prejudices and their impact on the child, and safeguard against them. As a professional, you should be able to put your 'self' in a separate compartment so that you may do what is right and necessary for the child rather than what you feel like doing.

- **Respect confidentiality** but only in the context of the need to allow free flow of information between yourself and others who are also concerned with the child's welfare. This means you should neither indiscriminately broadcast the child's particulars and statements nor, alternatively, keep them under lock and key and unavailable to others. 'Need to know' is a good principle for determining the extent of confidentiality.

- **Give the child your best.** You may be tired, fed up or otherwise disinclined to exert additional effort. But the children are unlikely to have the benefit of intervention such as yours again and what you say about them is likely to be regarded and used as evidence in justifying further social intervention. This demands that every child should receive your best effort in terms of thoroughness and high standards.

Having considered general issues of assessment, we are now in a position to look at the practice of assessment in a variety of contexts.

Further reading

Becker, H.S. (1963) *Outsiders: Studies in Sociology of Deviance*, New York: Grune and Stratton.
Bewley, B.R., Day, I. and Ide, L. (1973) *Smoking by Children in Great Britain*, London: SSRC.

Coleman, J.C. and Hendry, L. (1990) *The Nature of Adolescence*, 2nd edn, London: Routledge.

Cone, J.D. and Hawkins, R.P. (1977) *Behavioral Assessment*, New York: Brunner Mazel.

Gathercole, C.E. (1969) *Assessment in Clinical Psychology*, Harmondsworth: Penguin.

Gelfand, D.M. and Hartmann, D.P. (1986) *Child Behavior Analysis and Therapy*, 2nd edn, New York: Pergamon.

Haynes, S.N. (1978) *Principles of Behavioral Assessment*, New York: Gardner Press.

Hobbs, N. (1975) *The Future of Children*, San Francisco: Jossey Bass.

Hoghughi, M.S. (1978) *Troubled and Troublesome*, London: Burnett Books/André Deutsch.

Hoghughi, M.S., Dobson, C., Lyons, J., Muckley, A. and Swainston, M.A. (1980) *Assessing Problem Children: Issues and Practice*, London: Burnett Books.

Horrocks, J.E. (1964) *Assessment of Behavior*, Columbus, Ohio: Charles E. Merrill.

Mischel, W. (1968) *Personality and Assessment*, New York: John Wiley.

Morgan, A.J. and Morgan, M.D. (1980) *Manual of Primary Mental Health Care*, Philadelphia: Lippincott.

Morris, R.J. and Kratchowill, T.R. (eds) (1983) *The Practice of Child Therapy*, New York: Pergamon.

Oster, G.D., Caro, J.E., Eagen, D.R. and Lillo, M.A. (1988) *Assessing Adolescents*, New York: Pergamon.

Palmer, J.O. (1983) *The Psychological Assessment of Children*, 2nd edn, New York: John Wiley.

Parfitt, J. (ed) (1971) *Physical and Mental Assessment*, London: NCB.

Popper, K. (1972) *The Logic of Scientific Discovery*, 3rd edn, London: Hutchinson.

Quay, H. and Werry, J.S. (eds) (1986) *Psychopathological Disorders of Childhood*, New York: John Wiley.

Roberts, M.C. (1986) *Pediatric Psychology*, New York: Pergamon.

Rutter, M. (1975) *Helping Troubled Children*, Harmondsworth: Penguin.

Rutter, M. and Hersov, L. (eds) (1985) *Child and Adolescent Psychiatry*, 2nd edn, Oxford: Blackwell Scientific.

Rutter, M., Tuma, A.H., Lann, I.S. (eds) (1988) *Assessment and Diagnosis in Child Psychopathology*, London: David Fulton.

Schwartz, S. and Johnson, J.H. (1985) *Psychopathology of Childhood*, New York: Pergamon.

Social Work Service (1977) *Assessment of Children*, Edinburgh: Scottish Home & Health Dept.

Spitzer, R.L., Gibbon, M., Skodol, A.E., Williams, J.B.W. and First, M.B. (1989) *DSM-IIIR Case Book*, Washington: American Psychiatric Association.

Steinberg, D. (1987) *Basic Adolescent Psychiatry*, Oxford: Blackwell.

2

Assessment in Context

The prime justification for assessment is that it provides appropriate guidance for action. To fulfil their statutory and voluntary duties, many agencies are required to intervene in the lives of children and adolescents. Their work invariably entails some form of assessment, however informal and implicit. These agencies fall under four broad headings of justice, health, education and social services. In this chapter, we shall examine very briefly the role of assessment in each of the major statutory agencies.

The judicial system

The prime purpose of the judicial or law enforcement agencies, in relation to children, is to protect them and their interests, prevent law breaking and respond appropriately when a crime has been committed. These services can be involved with children literally from birth, in cases of paternity and adoption, through such matters as 'matrimonial causes' in the event of break up of the home, to judicial response to law breaking by them. Different courts are designated to deal with particular types of issues. The care and protection functions are predominantly supported and activated by social services, even if a criminal act such as sexual abuse may have been the cause of referral.

In the present context, the concern of the judiciary, and the law enforcement agencies which support them, is limited to determining what to do with young people in order to contain and reduce their propensity to law breaking. So, whether the response is to incapacitate, treat, deter or punish, the prosecution service and the court need to have some idea of the young people's condition and the circumstances of the illegal act, arrive at some judgment of the motivation for law breaking and use this information to evaluate propensity to further offending. This having been done, whatever response and sanction the law enforcement agency determines has to be evaluated in terms of how much and for how long it should be implemented. Each of these steps requires some form of assessment.

The judicial process and the agencies which support it are intricate and proceed usually in steps, seeking information from many sources, such as parents, police, schools, employers and others. The process starts with the first detection of a law breaking act by a member of the public who may report it to the police, who may then decide to caution. If the matter is serious, they may refer it to the prosecution service who also have to decide whether the evidence and gravity of the offence warrant proceeding. The court has then to evaluate the evidence, find guilt and proceed to sentence and disposal. Those with whom the sentence is to be carried out frequently have to evaluate the young person's response and adapt their own views and actions accordingly. This includes whether and when the young person is deemed 'safe' and does not warrant further intervention, unless a fixed penalty is being paid.

This is an extraordinarily complex process, involving multiple layers and types of assessment every step of the way. The assessment is often implicit and informal, carried out according to inadequately defined and tested criteria and processes, often on the basis of subjective (though perhaps experience-based) judgments by members of the public, police prosecution service and lower levels of judiciary. In this, above all other sectors, subjective judgment is the major determinant of action, though there is some attempt to introduce 'menus', 'tariffs' and limitations on measures that may be taken. All of these assessments entail some estimation of risk.

Risk estimation

Risk estimation and the determination of appropriate measures to reduce risk of further law breaking are the cornerstones of assessment in judicial settings. At its best, this is done through intensively evaluating information from social workers, probation officers, psychologists, psychiatrists and counsels for prosecution and defence, as well as other sources of relevant 'expert' information. Probation officers and social workers have broadly similar background and training. Their training rarely includes any explicit exposure to formal or rigorous assessment techniques. More seriously, they do not have a shared classification of problems or conception of what response to them should be. Attempts at systematizing their work are rudimentary, even if often the factual bases of their reports on the child are reasonably accurate and their conclusions seem imbued with 'common sense'.

Magistrates and higher courts not only have to determine guilt but also identify what measures are best suited to curb risk of future anti-social acts, within legally defined limits. The essential elements of this process are identifying (1) the stable and persisting conditions of the youngster and context of offence; (2) specific and transitory elements, which have to be taken into account; and (3) the likelihood of repetition of (1) and/or (2), leading to further offences being committed. 'Conditions of the youngster' include such elements of age, understanding, intellectual level, family factors and anti-social attitudes. 'Offence context' ranges over such matters as whether the offence was solo or in group, planned or opportunistic, common or rare, and where it falls on a scale of 'gravity'. The major concern is with identifying whether the youngster has an anti-social disposition that is likely to be expressed sooner or later in *further law breaking*, although the routes to this conclusion are varied, reflecting experience, professional perspective and personal prejudice of the magistrates and their advisors. A particular concern of these agencies is satisfying public concern that law breaking is being treated with sufficient seriousness. Considerable information is available about risk estimation by different groups of professionals. This shows that the greater the complexity of the case, according to a variety of criteria, the lower the reliability of prediction of recurrence. Although there are variations between professions, the broad thrust is that the younger the child, the less known about the natural history of the disorder and the contextual pulls and pushes, the poorer the prediction of recurrence and risk will be. Although there are theoretical possibilities of developing better and more usable risk estimation measures, there seems to be too much pressure in applied clinical and judicial settings to justify the time and effort entailed in such an activity.

The judicial decision making which underlies the outcome and 'disposal' is sometimes assisted by the existence of a 'tariff' which may or may not be explicit. So, for example, a first-time act of burglary may carry a 'supervision order'. With each repeated offence, the tariff may be raised, although recent British legislation significantly limits the range of disposals.

This is not the place to examine the process of judicial decision making, which is complex, arcane and not readily open to scrutiny or accurate analysis. The major reason for this is that unless an explicit tariff is in operation (and this rarely applies to juveniles) no element of this long judicial process operates by an agreed and universally applied classification of the presenting difficulty, how it should be evaluated in context and what responses it should provoke. The classification systems used are eclectic and bound up with cultural, local, professional and personal biases. In the case of assessment agents involved, predominantly probation officers, social workers and psychiatrists, there is a tendency towards dynamic explanations of behaviour, although increasingly, a behavioural orientation to judgments of law breaking is becoming evident.

Very little is known about reliability and validity of process of assessment in the criminal justice system. The best that can be said is that in an adversarial system such as that in the UK, the defence and prosecution usually examine the facts closely enough for some consensus to emerge, even though they may have different interests in the process.

Criminal responsibility
'Responsibility' is a key concept in judicial processing. It refers to the degree of voluntary or volitional agency in the commission of an act. A person who is not responsible, by reason of age, intellectual handicap, mental condition or other factors, cannot be said to have 'mens rea', and be held guilty and punished. In some cases, as in a child below age 10, no action may be taken on criminal grounds, although the child may become the subject of other intervention. If prosecution proceeds, there may be the need to establish whether the youngster can be held responsible by virtue of his intellectual or mental condition. In the case of adults, these are covered by McNaughton Rules and they apply, by implicit ascription, to juveniles in cases of grave crime.

In the case of young people, assessment of criminal responsibility is determined on the basis of the youngster's understanding that (1) what he did was wrong, (2) it would have certain consequences, and (3) he was in a mental state to be able to make a choice. These are sometimes linked with issues of 'fitness to plead', such as 'being able to instruct counsel', being unable to comprehend legal procedures and being unable to challenge jurors, compounded by such issues as lack of insight due to delusional thinking and inability to understand the sentence. These considerations seem rarely to apply to juveniles. Some of this assessment process is based on psychological and psychiatric procedures for which validity and reliability data may be available (such as in IQ tests and assessment of a child's psychiatric condition). However, outside a relatively limited area where good empirical evidence exists, the eventual outcome depends at least as much on the skills of counsels for prosecution and defence as on the quality of evidence available to them and the court. In these areas, as in others in criminal justice systems, there is little information about the reliability or validity of the process.

Health care

Identification of a disease or disorder and its associated health care is probably as old as humanity. Certainly as an activity, medical diagnosis is the oldest and the most disciplined form of assessment. This is simply because no treatment can be justified unless the physician has some idea of what ails the patient. The fact that diagnoses and their related treatments reflect as much professional and social fashions and more or less limited perceptions of the human condition does not detract from the immense sophistication of medical assessment.

Specialist medical assessment, however, comes at the end of an earlier chain of lay activities. Children have to complain of or be seen to be suffering from discomfort or disease before medical attention is given. Thus, some children and parents fail to identify or refuse to report difficulties, for a variety of reasons ranging from ignorance to deliberate concealment. Even if aware of and willing to report, they may misinterpret signs and symptoms of disorder and respond inappropriately to it. The same process can be repeated at every stage, until it reaches medical specialists. Practice of specialist medical assessment is exceptionally well developed though even here, unreliability and idiosyncrasy increases as we move from the obvious to the subtle, and broadly from the physical towards the psychiatric. Determination of physical ailments is usually followed by identification and implementation of treatment, even if treatment is only theoretical as, for example, in AIDS. Identification of adolescents' difficulties is usually followed by treatment, particularly if the condition is floridly psychiatric, such as schizophrenia, which is susceptible to drug therapy. So, although the majority of the more seriously troubled and troublesome adolescents will receive some form of clinical assessment, many may not receive related treatment, simply because such treatment is not available.

Part of the cause and the effect of advanced medical practice lies in the development and utilization of high-quality diagnostic systems. These, in turn, revolve around rigorous classifications of disorders, as will be described later. The major concern of such diagnostic assessments is the evaluation of 'risk' to the patient and others. Of particular concern in the area of child and adolescent disorders is the contribution of psychiatry.

Psychiatrists are increasingly involved in assessment of children and adolescents even in apparently straightforward paediatric cases, because of the rising awareness of the interdependence of physical and mental functioning. As will be seen in Chapter 3, psychiatric classifications have tended to gather on to themselves a number of conditions of children and adolescents which could not sensibly be regarded as being the purview of psychiatry (such as 'developmental reading disorder'), particularly as any possible treatments do not fall within the competence of psychiatry. For these reasons, and because psychiatrists are a group of specialized, trained and relatively knowledgeable people, they are increasingly involved in assessment of children and adolescents not just in health but also in justice, education and social services sectors.

The core concern of psychiatry, however, remains the determination of mental illness or its older variant, 'madness'. Despite extensive attempts to develop reliable and valid classification and diagnostic systems for mental illness in children, they remain of variable, but on the whole poor, reliability and validity, other than in those conditions where the difficulty is so obvious (such as bedwetting or hyperactivity) as not to require any specialized diagnosis at all, although the 'cause' may need specialist iden- tification. Diagnostic judgments are generally of variable or unknown reliability and validity, as judged by research evidence. Even more significantly, however, we hardly ever know the reliability and validity of an individual clinician's judgments in the case of a particular child, unless controlled treatment and evaluation is carried out – and it hardly ever is.

Despite this, it terms of many of the criteria for good classification systems, psychiatric classifications remain among the best developed. This is in part associated with the importance of medicine which, in its farther reaches, is literally about life and death and has, therefore, attracted extraordinary quality and quantity of human and financial resources for development. In the case of psychiatric assessment, the activity has been massively promoted and supported by the investment of American practi- tioners in private medicine and its linkage to insurance claims and, therefore, payments for good quality practice. In European and other settings where most psychiatrists are employed in the public sector, they remain a dominant group of specialists attempting clinically to promote the welfare of children. The theoretical problems of psychiatry, many of which also pertain to other disciplines, do not diminish their worth and significance.

So far, attention has been exclusively paid to psychiatry, as if this were the only source of assessment of non-physical disorders in children and adolescents. As already indicated, however, the identification of disorder often starts with children and those closest to them – such as parents and teachers. Indeed, the latter's judgments of the children are often as reliable as those of psychiatrists. But within health services, two other groups of assessment agents are prominent in the assessment of children.

Nurses are a trained cadre of usually high-quality and skilled individuals, well able to comment upon and identify children's difficulties in a relatively objective manner, even if their classifications are almost always derived from psychiatry. Indeed, in in-patient and cumulative out-patient 'day-assessment' settings, they are usually the prime providers of information on the child's behaviour to more specialized clinicians.

The other group comprises clinical psychologists who are becoming increasingly prominent in specialized work with children. Compared with both psychiatrists and nurses, psychologists are trained as experimental scientists, capable of setting up clinical contexts for evaluating hypotheses about what may be wrong with a child. Furthermore, they are intensely aware of developmental issues and give them prominence in their assessments. They are also prime designers and developers of tests for use with children and adolescents and are often the only personnel trained appropriately to interpret non-physical test data.

It is primarily due to the influence of psychologists that specialist agencies are turning away from diagnostic labelling towards multivariate, descriptive and behavioural approaches to assessment and non-medicinal forms of treatment. In the most advanced agencies, however, where quality of public service predominates over private profit, psychiatric, nursing and psychological services combine in genuine multi-disciplinary practice. In such settings, a common conceptual framework and vocabulary may operate, utilizing the best features and strengths of each discipline to the greater benefit of the children.

Education

Education, like medicine, is an old activity. The determination of when the child has acquired some basic skills and is, therefore, ready to move on to the next level, demands continuous assessment. Indeed, the class and home work of children is a regular means of assessing their progress and readiness to take on more complex educational tasks. In Western countries, testing for achievement has a long and quite distinguished history but now, because of intense economic competition, is being given even greater prominence. In the UK, for example, the new education law demands assessment of the children's educational competence at 7, 11, 13 and 16 years. Similarly, there is a perceptible return to informal 'streaming' of children according to ability. In the UK also, the concept of 'profiling' children's competence is now an accepted activity. The term is used in the same sense as the problem profile (see Chapter 4) to identify a child's competence in particular areas.

Education services have a long and complex history of development, benefitting from considerable research and resource investment. All teachers are trained and many in special education have specialist qualifications, sometimes extending to specialist educational assessment. Augmented by qualified educational psychologists, they are potentially capable of major contributions to the assessment and wider educational and social welfare of children.

Assessment has a particular place in evaluating the special needs of handicapped, physically disabled or emotionally and behaviourally disordered children. Its purpose is to identify not only the children's difficulties, their extent and manifestations, but also determine what special measures should be taken to ameliorate the difficulties, so as to optimize their educational and social development. This is done through a process of 'statementing', whereby through six stages of assessment involving teachers, parents, psychologists and others, a 'statement of special educational needs' can be made as a basis for specialist response to the child.

The system of 'statementing' is a major legal, professional and administrative means of directing appropriate resources to helping children with special educational needs. There is, therefore, often pressure on educational psychologists not to identify children as having special educational needs unless the education authority has adequate resources to meet them. This is because the 'statement' gives parents the legal right to demand that the local authority provides appropriate services. To this extent, assessment is done *for* allocation of services, but whether and how those services are received remains patchy and questionable. Some recent evidence suggests that in the case of the most difficult young people, particularly the poorer ones, only superficial attention is paid to the implications of statement of special needs.

As has already been intimated, many educational tests are standardized and used by people who are trained to interpret them. This is particularly true of educational psychologists and specialist teachers in many educational support services. Nevertheless, there is no abundance of evidence about the reliability or validity of the *total* process of assessment carried out in educational settings. It is known, for example, that teachers are highly reliable and accurate predictors of children's difficulties. Yet it is not known what use is made of this information for the eventual assessment of children's needs, either scholastic or clinical.

It is also evident that, outside cognitive areas, teachers are no less liable to using idiosyncratic assessment of children's difficulties than many other people. They do not have a common frame of reference or accurate description of children's condition. Nor are these related to particular ameliorative measures. Depending on their personal standards and the rigour of their training, some of these comments also apply to some educational psychologists – hence the high rates of failure of intervention in even moderately complex cases.

Nevertheless, educational assessments can be deemed to be relatively good quality, because they use wide-ranging information, sifted by trained educational psychologists and teachers, who also have to account for their recommendations to parents and others. They are a major resource for the development of good assessment practices with children.

The social services

This is the area where potentially the most complex and difficult assessments take place. Social services receive the failures and rejects of all other services until such time as the children are old enough to become eligible for placement in penal establishments or adult mental hospitals. Furthermore, social services are required by law to ensure that children are given due care and control, literally from birth, under complex conditions which are difficult to assess, particularly as they involve parents, other social agencies and prevailing forces in neighbourhood and culture of the family. Responsibility for service provision continues into adolescence and early adulthood, all relying on the competence of social workers who are the main source of professional expertise within social services departments.

Social services have extensive powers to make a dramatic impact on the lives of children and families because of their ability to remove children from their parents, although this is subject to close regulation and public accountability, recently strengthened under new children's legislation.

Despite extensive and far-reaching responsibilities of social workers, their training is also the most patchy and deficient in concepts and practices of assessing children's difficulties and knowing what to do with them. Much of what goes into social work training is, in reality, 'education' and 'teaching' of certain procedural competencies rather than 'training' in comprehensive assessment or treatment skills. There is no shared conceptual framework of operations other than that established by custom and practice, departmental guidelines and procedures and views laid down by statutory instruments and circulars from government departments.

The deficiencies and potentially disastrous consequences of this state of affairs have been repeatedly noted in reports of committees of inquiry on deaths of children from non-accidental injury, and scandals about child sexual abuse. These have been reinforced by public and government anxieties concerning social workers' alleged ideological approach to young offenders and inappropriate, woolly measures taken to curb their anti-social behaviour. Extensive regulations and guidelines have, therefore, been developed to ensure adequate minimal standards in some areas, such as operation of 'child protection panels' which are essentially concerned with estimation of risk to children. These are now being extended to encompass a wide range of other matters relating to children and young people, as well as other client groups.

Despite these, huge variations in practice remain. This is unlikely to change as long as social services do not adopt a coherent conceptual framework, common classification of disorders and ways of assessing children on the basis of evidence, as has happened in medicine and education. In the absence of empirical procedures, social workers are likely to continue to work through largely personal intuition, even when it is guided by experience and instances of good empirical knowledge. There is a prevalent ideological bias among social workers and probation officers reinforced by recent legislation against formal intervention in the lives of children, of which assessment is a part. This is often compounded by financial constraints. Comprehensive and perhaps specialist assessments are seen as heavy or overkill interventions which are not invoked other than in cases of serious abuse or extremely troublesome behaviour which cannot otherwise be contained. This is evident, for example, in the general disregard of sexually abusive behaviour in adolescents because 'minimum intervention is best' and the young person is 'likely to grow out of it'. This results in a tendency to refrain from formal, coherent and multi-faceted assessment, until things go seriously awry and social workers have no choice but to resort to 'residential' or psychiatric facilities (both of which are thought to label and stigmatize the child), often when chances of amelioration are significantly impaired by ineffective previous intervention.

Social services utilize a range of assessment settings for children and adolescents. These include assessment in the home and the community, assessment fostering, placement in small facilities and larger specialized establishments for specific assessment of children's general condition and risk of deterioration. Young people with difficulties have quite dramatically varying access to such facilities because of the individual policies of social services departments and the variability of orientation among their workers, even within the same departments.

The new Children Act 1989 is likely to place considerably new pressures on social services for accurate and action-related assessment of children. In any compulsory measures to be taken with a child, social services will be required to assess and present supportive evidence for:

- ascertainable wishes and feelings of the child;
- child's physical, emotional and educational needs;
- likely effect on the child of any changes in his or her circumstances;
- any relevant characteristics of the child, such as age and sex;
- any harm the child has suffered or is at risk of suffering;
- capability of parents or any other person to meet child's needs.

It is difficult to evaluate assessments of children and young people in social services. There is little information to suggest that they are reliable or valid or that they are often much more than ways of legitimizing access to or placement in particular agencies. There is undoubtedly some excellent practice, for example in specialized fostering for difficult or abused adolescents and handicapped children. But there is also evidence of extensive failure of every social work action with children and young people, reflecting the quality of the assessment from which the action flows and its subsequent implementation.

Given the new legal safeguards and standards in intervening in children's lives, social services are likely to require, as an early priority, a common framework of assessment, which they do not at present possess.

As may be seen from this brief outline, assessment is an integral and inalienable part of the operation of all the major areas of social policy and intervention. The fact that it is not always formally administered, evaluated and tracked does not reduce the significance of the activity. However, because the four major sectors have no shared classification of children's difficulties, nor shared frames of reference in terms of corresponding tasks, priorities or ways of evaluating their assessments, they tend to fragment both the children and ways of helping them. They also dramatically undermine efficient and effective intervention. The most conspicuous need of the day-to-day 'coalface' workers in these agencies is, therefore, for a *usable* format and system of assessment.

The purpose of this book is to provide such a framework of assessment. The approach propounded in this book can be directly adopted by *all* workers and *all* service agencies with a considerable degree of evident reliability, validity, efficiency, relevance and usefulness. The adoption of the approach across different services would bring together the response to what is after all an *integrated child* and to whom services must be directed as an integrated, networked whole, if they are to have any chance of success.

Further reading

Bevan, H.K. (1973) *The Law relating to Children*, London: Butterworth.

Black, D., Wolkind, S. and Hendriks, J.H. (eds) (1989) *Child Psychiatry and the Law*, London: Royal College of Psychiatrists/Gaskell.

British Dyslexia Association/Dept of Health (undated) *Dyslexia Early Identification*, Reading, Berks.

Cooper, J. (1983) *The Creation of the British Personal Social Services 1962–74*, London: Heinemann.

Hoghughi, M.S., Lyons, J., Muckley, A. and Swainston, M.A. (1988) *Treating Problem Children: Issues, Methods and Practice*, London: Sage.

University of Leicester and Department of Health (1990) *Children in Need and Their Families – a New Approach*. Leicester: Leicester School of Social Work.

Warnock, H.M. (Chairman) (1978) *The Warnock Report – Special Education Needs – Report of the Committee of Enquiry into the Education of Handicapped Children and Young People*, London: HMSO.

White, R., Carr, P. and Lowe, N. (1990) *A Guide to the Children Act*, London: Butterworth.

Zander, M. (1981) *Social Workers, Their Clients and the Law*, 3rd edn, London: Sweet & Maxwell.

3

Approaches to Assessment

The purpose of assessing children is to identify their difficulties and potentials and determine what should be done with them. Any form of identification is based on differentiating one condition from another, according to some systems of naming, categorizing or 'classifying'. Some form of classification is involved in all purposive human activity from pruning roses ('this is a dead head, this is a new bud'), or ordinary life ('traffic light is red so I cannot drive on') to specialist activity ('this child has been hit, not fallen downstairs').

Assessment, classification and taxonomy

Assessment is the process of identifying the difficulties and strengths of the child. Clearly, the condition of one child (or the same child in a different state) cannot be differentiated from another unless the condition and its components can be classified – such as 'This child is very fearful', 'This child is very aggressive.' No assessment is, therefore possible without classification.

However, classification can be done according to a wide range of criteria such as 'cause', impact, usefulness, legal requirements and many, many others. So a child may be classified as being 'in need of care and control' according to some legal definition, or a group of tests may be deemed 'useful' for intellectual assessment. Classification criteria can be 'external' to the condition (as in the above examples) or 'internal' – as, for example, 'all depressed children look unhappy and are likely to cry easily'. Taxonomy, on the other hand, always refers to the 'internal' similarities of conditions as in the 'depressed' example above. Classification is, therefore, a wider concept than 'taxonomy' which it encompasses. Whilst distinguishing between classification and taxonomy is worthwhile in academic discussions, the broader term, classification, will be used in the present context as being familiar and useful to most people who are likely to engage in assessment as an applied activity.

Classifications come in all shapes and sizes, with varying degrees of complexity, breadth of coverage and dependence on particular theoretical orientations. As we shall see, these factors dramatically determine the kind of assessment that is carried out, simply because any assessment process has to use one or more classifications to generate information. In practical terms, therefore, we cannot satisfactorily separate assessment from the classification(s) on which it is based.

Similarly, we should note that the kind of assessment or classification carried out is determined by the *purpose* of the activity, which may be different from just identifying the child's difficulty – collecting data for a study, disproving a hypothesis or keeping troublesome parents quiet would be examples of other purposes. This distinction is important because it alerts us to one reason why diverse approaches are adopted with apparently similar children. Assessment in our context might be regarded as a comprehensive form of classification aimed at producing a basis for the amelioration of a person's difficulties. How good the classification is will, to a large extent, determine how good the assessment outcome will be in terms of the criteria set out in Chapter 1. This point cannot be over-emphasized, and accounts for the difficulties associated with, for example, psychodynamic principles or traditional ways of diagnosing non-physical problems in children.

Function of classifications

In the area of human disorders, classifications fulfil the following functions:

- providing a basis for understanding, explaining and theory formation;
- describing a condition and guiding/helping collect information about it;
- providing a common vocabulary and system of names or labels for objects, events and collections of signs and symptoms;
- identifying relationship between life events and disordered conditions;
- identifying antecedents and consequences of the condition and helping determine what treatment should be given;
- dependent on adequacy of such understanding of condition, enabling predictions to be made and control exercised.

Approaches to assessment

Because some form of assessment underlies all purposive action and there are many kinds of action, a wide variety of different forms of assessment are employed. Of necessity and predating concern with scientific rigour, the oldest and most common approach is a descriptive one simply stating 'X is the difficulty', presumably followed by 'I must do Y'. As disciplined and professional enquiry into the human condition has intensified, so approaches to assessment have proliferated.

Surveying texts on assessment gives the impression that there are many fundamentally different kinds of assessment. So we encounter such terms as 'behavioural', 'diagnostic', 'observational', 'rating scale', 'multivari-ate', 'empirical', 'group' and 'psychodynamic' assessment. Proponents and critics make claims and counter-claims for each of them in relation to others. The claims are understandable, arising from the same impulse that drives all artistic and scientific endeavour towards creating something new and different.

In reality, however, the differences between these 'methods' are largely in the terminology and *medium* through which the assessment is carried out, and do not constitute fundamentally different kinds of assessment. As we shall see in Chapter 6, all information can be grouped as deriving from questions or interview, observations of one sort of other, and test data. Particular forms of assessment such as group dynamic or family therapy may use a combination of one or more sources of information. This is best exemplified in multi-axial psychiatric assessment which may combine the results of neurological, biochemical and physical examination together with cognitive and personality tests, observations of group and family dynamics and a range of other sources of information. The broad base of such an assessment does not make it conceptually different from another that may use only one source of information – such as an interview. It is essentially the scientific *belief system* underlying the assessment which differentiates one *approach* from another.

According to this criterion, we can only distinguish three main types of assessment, irrespective of the medium of information they utilize. These are the *descriptive*, *diagnostic* and *multivariate approaches*. In considering each of these for purposes of assessing child and family disorders, it is helpful first to have some idea of the criteria against which classifications, and the assessment on which they are based, may be judged.

Criteria for evaluating classifications

Classifications fulfil a wide array of functions and can be judged in general terms. However, there are also some criteria which come into play prominently in the field of child and adolescent disorders. The greater the number and the rigour of the criteria fulfilled, the better will be the classification. *No* classification in the field of child and adolescent disorders fulfils all or even most of these criteria and it may be that, depending on the purpose of assessment, different criteria will be given different weights.

In general terms classifications should:

- provide a clear *description* or *definition* of the category or class of phenomena being addressed;
- provide a clear demonstration that *items* within each class are *related* with a high level of recurrence;
- enable phenomena to be reliably categorized, as judged by different observers, and remain *stable* over a period of time;
- show that there is coherent and sensible relationship between the items within the category and other items which are not used to define them in the first place, i.e. the classification should be *valid*;
- be capable of as many forms of validation as possible;
- be complete and *comprehensive*, i.e. preferably cover the total area of child's functioning;
- be *parsimonious* in using the smallest number of classes to describe the phenomena comprehensively;
- ensure that one class of phenomena is *independent* of and mutually excludes other classes;

- be based on systematic, validated information and remain open to changing personal and social circumstances of the child;
- allow for developmental and organic changes, i.e. respond to relative constancy and variability of behaviour in interaction with different environments;
- be *usable* by a wide range of people both inside and outside a profession and thus make sense to a wide audience;
- allow for *detailed gradations* of judgment according to specialized needs and competence of its users;
- be capable of incorporating *new findings* regarding children's disorders;
- not be a disguise for personal or cultural derogation;
- take account of fundamental differences between adults and children and different cultural milieux, and give due weight to the different significance of disorders according to the social context;
- take account of different levels of response from normal to the seriously disordered in each functional area, i.e. be 'multi-axial';
- not give prominence to one aspect of functioning at the expense of the integrated whole;
- not be so theory-bound as to exclude its use by those who do not subscribe to the theory;
- have direct and clear implications for treatment but allow for the use of a variety of methods;
- be recordable in detail to allow research, refinement and use for teaching.

Descriptive approaches

Description is the oldest and most elemental approach to classifying phenomena and assessing their importance and implications for action. However, because it is so old and pervasive, it is not usually identified as a distinct approach to assessment in the professional literature. In the context of child and adolescent disorders, such an approach to assessment would lie simply in stating what a young person's difficulty is.

Every culture has its own terminology for describing young people's difficulties, arising in a complex way from its own preoccupations. Cultural usage and the fact that a word has become common part of the descriptive language suggest that the classification employed is 'useful' in that culture. We see this, for example, when a shaman speaks of a child's delirious fever as being 'devil's possession' or early descriptions of epilepsy being 'St Vitus's Dance'. In implying an underlying 'cause', such descriptions are in reality akin to our more recent diagnostic statements.

The complexity of such 'informal' classifications is clearly related to the level of sophistication of the culture. Whatever the level, the basic description of the condition in ordinary language, however, is usually quite sound, e.g. 'this child is shaking all over', even though subsequent causal explanations may not be. Such descriptions are the basic element from which all other classifications are made. Without descriptions which are commonly recognizable, there can be no identification of a difficulty.

Most professions concerned with human disorders, other than medicine, some parts of psychology and education, operate by relatively simple descriptive terms which may be incorporated into their professional procedures. These eventually acquire force or importance through custom and practice. For example, probation or social worker reports give a description of background and present circumstances of a youngster and some idea of how these are likely to change. On this basis they make recommendations for treatment or disposal of the case. Such reports may include technical terms which are not part of the ordinary language, betraying a particular orientation, but this is infrequent. The majority are fairly straightforward descriptions of the client's condition and are usually regarded as adequate.

As an activity becomes more professional and sometimes more disciplined, so the 'descriptors' become more complex, refined and abstract. In children's disorders, partly because of the many professions which are concerned with them, there is no uniform or procedurally universal terminology. Nor are there any shared frames of reference linking the condition to treatment, hence the immense difficulties which arise from the use of different classifications by different professions dealing with the same children. One aspect of this difficulty is that children are, in essence, *fragmented* between different professions, each with its own terminology and possible disposal routes but little regard to the *integrated* nature of the children, their disorders and treatment needs. An illuminative example of this is in some investigations of child sexual abuse, as in the 'Cleveland Affair', where paediatricians, social workers, police and the courts adopted quite different stances in assessing the condition of the *same* children. These differences arose from their different frames of reference and the implied classification systems that underlay them.

The advantages of culturally common descriptive approaches to assessment lie in their familiarity, extraordinary wealth of diversity, cultural pervasiveness and usefulness. Disadvantages lie in their very diversity, idiosyncratic usages, cultural overlap both within and between different approaches, tendency to fragment young people and their disorders and unusability as a basis for a discipline of assessment.

The 'balance sheet' of descriptive assessments is quite a complex one, if only because there are so many different forms. We can only sensibly evaluate this approach when some attempt has been made to systematize it, as will be seen in detail in Chapter 6. A major scientific form of descriptive assessment is behavioural assessment.

Behavioural assessment
This approach is inextricably bound up with the development of behaviour therapy and the theoretical perspective that most behaviour is learned through its associations and consequences. Rather than adopting a particular classification system, it takes as its starting point accurate

description of the child's difficulties, and through observation and other data collection forms a *hypothesis* concerning the nature and 'causes' of the difficulty, and the effects of various treatments. It is associated with names such as Bellack, Gelfand, Hartmann, Hersen, Mash and Terdal.

The cornerstone of behavioural assessment is belief in the unique individuality of the child. Although common terms, dimensions or 'traits' may be utilized, any treatment is geared to the individual child and must, therefore, use information which points to what makes a child and the organization of his behaviour under different circumstances unique. Associated with this, there are a number of other marks which distinguish this approach from traditional, often diagnostic, approaches:

- behaviour is shaped significantly by the situation in which it occurs;
- there is both consistency *and* variability of behaviour over time, though this is clearly dependent both on the child and the condition;
- behaviour is more determined by its concurrent controlling variables than by historical 'causes';
- prime area of intervention is the behaviour, not its 'causes';
- behavioural assessors are interested in direct methods, such as observation, rather than indirect ones, such as interviews;
- information obtained is directly relevant to the difficulty in question and its treatment, rather than diagnosis or prognosis;
- behavioural assessment data are not massively 'interpreted';
- assessment is bound up with treatment and both are subject to continuous review and monitoring of accuracy and effectiveness.

Application of behavioural assessment to children's disorders continues to develop apace, specifying ever-increasing conceptual and empirical frameworks for its practice. Compared with other approaches, it particularly recognizes children's developmental peculiarities, the need for careful normative judgments; the wide-ranging behaviours implicated in most children's disorders; the wide-ranging situations in which children's difficulties are manifest and, therefore, the need for guidelines for selection of the relevant target behaviours, to ensure efficient and effective assessment and treatment.

It is not, in general, possible to compare behavioural assessment with the other more traditional approaches in terms of reliability, validity, usability, efficiency and other relevant criteria. The comparative research information is not available, although there is a considerable body of writing, almost exclusively psychological, which supports the contention that behavioural assessment is likely to be superior to diagnostic and multivariate approaches on almost every count. The very nature and methodology of behavioural assessment is more likely to lead to this conclusion on a priori grounds.

The difficulty is that good behavioural assessment is carried out almost exclusively by psychologists or others trained in experimental method, who are capable of setting up and testing problem-related hypotheses. Such people are not plentiful or likely to be able to deal with a lot of cases in busy clinics and institutions. Furthermore, the emphasis on the presenting problem, if exclusively and rigorously pursued, is likely to present a very lopsided picture of the child and the wider difficulties which, though not prominent, are likely to be part of the wider ecology of a child's difficulties. The approach, however, presents an ideal to which all assessments would, at their best, approximate.

Diagnostic approaches

This is the major scientific and professional approach to assessment of child and adolescent disorders. 'Diagnosis' derives from two Greek words which mean 'differentiating' or 'knowing between'. It has its origins in the practice of physical medicine where clinical conditions can be usually identified and differentiated from others. Difficulties comprise a series of *signs* (condition seen by the clinician) and *symptoms* (complaints by the patient). These are evaluated against the clinician's knowledge and experience of similar cases, where a number of signs and symptoms 'co-vary' or occur together ('syndrome'). Having been satisfied about what these signs and symptoms signify, the clinician proceeds to give it a name or label which differentiates it from other (similar) conditions. Many conditions bear the name of the person who first identified it, such as 'Down's', 'Kleinfelter's', or 'Tourette's' syndromes. Through use, the clusters eventually assume the status of *real* entities – 'reified' or 'thinged' – taking on a life of their own. Listening to or reading clinicians' reports, it is often difficult to remember that these labels are, at best, no more than convenient abstractions and only tenuously refer to real entities, particularly in non-physical disorders.

This approach is usually referred to as 'Kraeplinian', after the great German physician Emil Kraeplin, who published perhaps the most influential of classifications of psychiatric disorders with a heavy physical bias. In due course, this was expanded to take in 'psychogenic' disorders and has formed the basis of all diagnostic classifications which are currently in existence, including those specifically related to children's disorders – see Further Reading at the end of this chapter.

Diagnosis entails making an affirmative statement about a condition with a degree of probability of correctness that is dependent on how much is independently and empirically known about the condition. Although there are many different types of validating diagnostic statements, ultimately they rely on making testable predictions – where the test is the treatment. So when we say 'this girl is depressed' we are stating at best a highly probable hypothesis that can only be confirmed (or more accurately, fail to be disconfirmed) by the relevant treatment.

When we set diagnosis in the order of the comprehensive stages that have to be covered to treat a patient, we see that it requires a significant list of antecedents and successors to make full sense of it. These encompass:

- *description* of the 'pathogenesis' or aetiology of the condition – identifying how the condition (probably) originated;
- stating the probable *course* of development of the condition;
- *diagnosis* – making a statement that 'this is what is wrong with this patient';
- *identifying* the *treatment* to be undertaken to ameliorate it;
- projecting how the condition is likely to develop with or without particular forms of treatment – that is, giving a *prognosis*;
- carrying out the appropriate *treatment*; and, lastly
- *evaluating* the diagnosis through evaluating the outcome.

Clearly not all of these are undertaken when a diagnosis is made, often because we are not and cannot be even moderately confident of such matters as the aetiology of a persistent difficulty – such as 'conduct disorder'. Furthermore, even if we were, few disorders have generally accepted even theoretical treatments, as in 'autism'. Even when a treatment may exist in theory, diagnosticians do not always or often undertake the kind of treatment that may be indicated by the diagnosis in order to validate it, as again in 'conduct disorders'. Nevertheless, to give some idea of the range and sophistication of diagnostic systems, a brief outline of the two most important systems is in order.

DSM III (1980), DSM III–R (1985)
The DSM (*Diagnostic and Statistical Manual* of the American Psychiatric Association, different versions) is the most famous and rigorously developed diagnostic system for identifying child and adolescent problems (though less well than those of adults). Over the period of years, it has become increasingly sophisticated, dropping some conditions and adding others, and being constantly refined in the process. Its structure and terminology derive from extensive discussions among clinicians (almost exclusively American) and some research. A major driving force behind the development of this system (as of others in the US) is to enable rapid and accurate reimbursement of clinical costs by insurance and federal agencies.

The DSM is a 'multi-axial' system, each axis intended to cover one area of functioning, which is meant to be statistically and conceptually distinct from others. The axes are as follows:

Axis I   Syndromes
Axis II   Minor disorders
Axis III Physical disorders
Axis IV   Associated stresses
Axis V   Level of functioning before disorder set in

Child and adolescent disorders are described in Axis I, although any adult diagnostic label (such as 'depression') may also be used to diagnose the child's condition. These diagnostic categories are set out in Table 1.

Table 1   **Main disorders of infancy, childhood and adolescence (DSM III–R) (abridged descriptions)**

1   Mental retardation

1 *Mild mental retardation*   significantly below average intelligence but can cope with normal social demands (IQ 50–70)
2 *Moderate mental retardation*   significantly below average (IQ 35–55) but capable of being trained
3 *Severe mental retardation*   grossly impaired (IQ 20–35); learning ability only for the most basic material
4 *Profound mental retardation*   immeasurable IQ; need basic life support

2   Pervasive developmental disorder (PDD)

1 *Autistic disorder*   lack of responsiveness to others, gross impairment in communication skills, profound disturbance in social relations and multiple oddities of behaviour, developing before 30 months of age
2 *Pervasive developmental disorder* (not otherwise specified)   as above but where full criteria are not met

3   Specific developmental disorders

Academic skills disorders
1 *Developmental arithmetic disorder*   poor arithmetic skills not accounted for by mental retardation or other factors
2 *Developmental expressive writing disorder*   poor writing skills, as above
3 *Developmental reading disorder*   poor reading ability and other difficulties, as above

Language and speech disorders
4 *Developmental articulation disorder*   poor articulation of sounds, not accounted for by any other clinical condition
5 *Developmental expressive language disorder*   poor ability to express, as above
6 *Developmental receptive language disorder*   poor ability to understand speech, as above

Motor skills disorders
7 *Developmental co-ordination disorder*   poor ability to co-ordinate movement, as above
8 *Specific developmental disorder*   any others not otherwise specified

4   Disruptive behaviour disorders

1 *Attention deficit hyperactivity disorder*   developmentally inappropriate inattention, impulsivity and hyperactivity
2 *Conduct disorders*   persistent pattern of conduct disorder in which rights of others and major social norms are persistently breached; occurs in *group*, *solitary aggressive* and *undifferentiated* types
3 *Oppositional defiant disorder*   general pattern of negative and disruptive behaviour without major law breaking

5 Anxiety disorders of childhood and adolescence

1 *Separation anxiety disorder* inappropriate level or kind of anxiety about separation from parent or other person
2 *Avoidant disorder of childhood or adolescence* excessive avoidance of contact with others, so as to affect relationships
3 *Overanxious disorder* excessive or inappropriate anxiety

6 Eating disorders

1 *Anorexia nervosa* refusal to maintain, and intense fear of gaining, bodily weight
2 *Bulimia nervosa* binge eating and deliberate vomiting to avoid weight gain
3 *Pica* persistent eating of non-foods
4 *Rumination disorder of infancy* repeated regurgitation of food and loss of weight
5 *Eating disorders* not otherwise specified

7 Gender identity disorders

1 *Gender identity disorder of childhood* intense distress about gender and desire to change
2 *Transsexualism* intense discomfort and persistent desire to change sex in adolescence
3 *Variants on the above*
4 *Gender identity disorders not otherwise specified*

8 Tic disorders

1 *Tourette's disorder* multiple motor and vocal tics
2 *Chronic motor or vocal tic disorder* either motor or vocal tics but not both
3 *Transient tic disorder* as above but not lasting beyond 12 months
4 *Tic disorders not otherwise specified*

9 Elimination disorders

1 *Functional encopresis* repeated involuntary passing of faeces
2 *Functional enuresis* repeated involuntary passing of urine

10 Speech disorders not elsewhere classified

1 *Cluttering* abnormally rapid and irregular speech rhythm
2 *Stuttering* frequent repetition, halting or prolongation of sounds or syllables

11 Other disorders of infancy, childhood and adolescence

1 *Elective mutism* persistent refusal to talk in one or more social situation
2 *Identity disorder* severe subjective distress about aspects of self
3 *Reactive attachment disorder of infancy or early childhood* marked difficulty in relating to others, starting before age five and not due to other clinical conditions
4 *Stereotype/habit disorder* repetitive, intentional behaviour which serves no understandable or socially acceptable purpose
5 *Undifferentiated attention deficit disorder* a residual category for any other form of inattentive behaviour

International Classification of Diseases (ICD–9)
With the DSM, this is the other major diagnostic classification, sponsored by the World Health Organization. It is primarily associated with the name of Rutter, leading an international group of psychiatrists. Since its inception it has been very influential. Indeed, part of the reason for the latest revision of DSM (III–R) is to incorporate some of the features of ICD–9.

This system is similar to DSM in also employing five axes for fully describing a child's psychiatric state – clinical psychiatric syndrome; specific delays in development; intellectual level; medical condition; associated abnormal psychosocial condition. It presents nine subtypes of neurotic disorders, eight special symptoms or syndromes including most of those listed under specific developmental disorders of DSM, and nine categories of transient adjustment disorders. There are a further three categories of 'Disturbance of Conduct', 'Child or Adolescent Emotional Disturbance' and 'Hyperkinetic Syndrome of Childhood'.

The ICD is also similar to DSM in relying on subjective judgments of clinicians to identify particular disorders and bring together the symptoms which support them. However, these are later subjected to a variety of statistical analyses to discover their discriminating ability, reliability and a variety of other factors under different circumstances.

Recent work on ICD has sought to refine the reliability of broad- and narrow-range diagnosis and answer thornier questions about 'mixed syndromes'. It has evolved seven diagnostic 'umbrellas' which cover a range of symptoms. These are set out in Table 2.

Table 2   *Umbrella categories of ICD–9*

Umbrella 1   Adaptation reaction

308	Acute reaction to stress
309	Adjustment reaction

Umbrella 2   Conduct disorder

301.3	Personality disorders – explosive
301.7	Personality disorders – sociopathic
309.3	Adjustment reaction – conduct disturbance
312.0	Disturbance of conduct – unsocialized
312.1	Disturbance of conduct – socialized
312.2	Disturbance of conduct – compulsive
312.8	Disturbance of conduct – other
312.9	Disturbance of conduct – unspecified
314.2	Hyperkinetic – conduct disorder

Umbrella 3   Emotional disorder

300	Neurotic disorders
313	Disturbance of emotions
311	Depressive disorder

308.0	Acute reaction to stress – disturbance of emotions
309.0	Adjustment reaction – brief depressive reaction
309.1	Adjustment reaction – prolonged depressive reaction
309.2	Adjustment reaction – disturbance of other emotions
309.8	Adjustment reactions – other

Umbrella 4 Depressive

296	Affective psychoses
311	Depressive disorder
298.0	Other nonorganic psychoses – depressive type
300.4	Neurotic disorders – depression
309.0	Adjustment reaction – brief depressive reaction
309.1	Adjustment reaction – prolonged depressive reaction
313.1	Disturbance of emotions – with misery and unhappiness

Umbrella 5 Mixed

309.4	Adjustment reaction – mixed
312.3	Disturbance of conduct – mixed
308.4	Acute reaction to stress – mixed

Umbrella 6 Anxiety

300.0	Neurotic disorders – anxiety
300.2	Neurotic disorders – phobic
309.2	Adjustment reaction – other emotions
313.0	Disturbance of emotions – anxiety
313.2	Disturbance of emotions – sensitivity

Umbrella 7 Mixed psychosis

295	Schizophrenic psychoses
297	Paranoid states
298*	Other nonorganic psychoses (except depressive type)

* Except 298.0.

Source: Gould et al., 1988

The common elements of these two classifications are attention deficit disorder (with or without hyperkinesis), aggressive conduct disorders, anxiety and general unhappiness. There are, however, considerable differences in the number and content of special categories in each. For example, both hyperactivity and attention deficit are quite differently subcategorized by the two systems. The classification of anxiety and unhappiness is even more markedly different, with many more sub-categories in the ICD than in the DSM, and both more than can be justified by reliability or validity data. Such comparisons can be multiplied, presenting a puzzle as to how relatively similar child and adolescent conditions can be so differently categorized in US and European cultures. And yet these very cultural differences, subsuming economic, social and even scientific orientations, may account for the divergent end products. Nevertheless, the similarities of these diagnostic classifications are greater than their differences and they also present broadly the same advantages and disadvantages for assessment, and it is to these that we now turn.

Advantages
These can be briefly set out as:

- *Complexity* Because of the wide range of conditions described, they allow for quite detailed differentiations to be made in the condition of children.
- *Common vocabulary* These classifications provide a highly detailed vocabulary through which a mutually understood and identified scrutiny of children's conditions can be provided.
- *Reliability* Studies have shown that some conditions, such as attention deficit disorder with hyperkinesis, can be distinguished at a high degree of reliability.
- *Cross-cultural application* Extensive usage by clinicians across cultures has allowed collection of comparable information for research, refinement of practice and identifying prevalence of particular clusters which have warranted attention.

Disadvantages
The disadvantages of diagnostic systems considerably outweigh their advantages.

- There is very poor interrater reliability for most conditions, including some which occur commonly, such as anxiety disorders.
- Many of the conditions specified in diagnostic systems have no information on their reliability at all.
- When a condition is obvious, such as 'attention deficit disorder with hyperkinesis', reliability is good, but when it becomes less obvious, such as 'attention deficit disorder without hyperkinesis', its reliability suffers.
- The same stricture applies to many other diagnostic conditions. On the whole when a condition is so obvious that it does not require a great deal of diagnostic subtlety, it can be established with good reliability, but the moment it begins to diverge from the obvious, reliability takes a nose-dive. This is particularly the case when 'narrow range' (e.g. 'disturbance of emotion with misery') as opposed to broad diagnoses (e.g. depression) are made. This suggests that clinicians' ability finely to differentiate diagnostic states is unlikely to be better than lay people's.
- Although diagnostic systems use broadly similar categories and originate from similar cultural backgrounds, they are not strictly comparable and their similarities are not supported by shared data. Although they use similar terms (e.g. anxiety), they seem to refer to different states, suggesting that there may be something fundamentally awry about the conceptualization.

- There is hardly any information about the stability of the diagnoses of child and adolescent disorders over time. Although there is a methodological difficulty about reconciling stability in diagnoses with variability and development of the children's condition over time, nevertheless diagnostic systems should be susceptible to such examination. In practice, they have not been found to be so.
- Many of the diagnoses use 'Latinized' or jargonized versions of common terms, masquerading as diagnoses, e.g. 'episodic dyscontrol syndrome' which simply means periodic severe loss of temper. Psychiatric diagnoses are riddled with such terminology.
- The use of diagnostic terminology tends to pathologize a condition even when it is not pathological, such as the DSM's 'developmental reading disorder'.
- Judged by criteria of 'usefulness', many diagnoses are not clearly related to a form of management or treatment. They fail to identify what should be done with the particular condition, often even in theory, as in conduct disorders. They therefore raise the issue of why the diagnosis was made at all.
- Diagnostic labels emanate from relatively powerful people. As such, they tend to restrict views of the child's condition and what should be done with the difficulty, often to the child's detriment.
- Diagnostic systems have a tendency to tramline the condition so that it fits into a diagnostic category, when the diversity of young people and their circumstances render this difficult and of dubious utility. Not only is this not necessary (apart from providing research data), in reality, very few children present textbook clusters and most present mixed conditions and fall between various diagnostic categories. Research diagnosticians are aware of this but simply see it as a source of low reliability data to be improved or eliminated. This low reliability is because categorical (either/or) assessments are less accurate or helpful than those which adopt a dimensional (more or less) approach.
- By the use of specialized terminology, diagnoses exclude other people from making equally valid and powerful statements about the child and thus reinforce the position of the clinician as the only person to use it. In reality, however, given the above comments about reliability and complex conditions, most diagnoses are simple and straightforward and many other people can (and do) make them with perceptibly no less reliability.
- Diagnoses are partial, emphasizing the major 'syndrome' and despite the availability of other axes, do not and cannot result in a comprehensive assessment of the child.
- Critical diagnostic labels are devoid of time and place qualifications, thus implying that the child's condition is permanent.
- They do not incorporate a developmental perspective or, readily, cultural and social diversity.
- Despite appearances to the contrary, in daily practice only a small

minority of psychiatrists seem to follow the strict criteria for diagnosis of clinical conditions, unless engaged in research. Most use the terminology in personally modified forms, so that even the relatively poor reliability data from research studies cannot be sustained.

Multivariate approaches

Multivariate approaches use a variety of statistical analyses to identify the major *clusters of conditions* and their common features drawn from a variety of sources. These sources include case histories, research studies, clinical descriptions and any other material which bears on the condition. This approach, therefore, does not rely on clinical 'hunch', or even on expert opinion about what is entailed in a condition, but rather on cold statistics to extract the main features shown to prevail in the clinical condition of children and adolescents.

Although this approach has not led to classification systems similar to those of diagnosticians, nevertheless it has over the years identified two broad dimensions or over-arching clusters of children's disorders. These may be broadly categorized as (1) 'behaviour' problems, which are essentially outwardly directed difficulties, and (2) 'personality' problems, which entail self-directed difficulties. 'Behaviour' problems have also been called 'externalized' and associated with 'aggression'. 'Personality' problems have been regarded as 'internalized' and associated with 'withdrawal' or anxious type behaviour. The two broad clusters, therefore, seem to be as follows:

'Behaviour'	**'Personality'**
Aggression	Withdrawal
'Externalized'	'Internalized'

The multivariate approach, which is associated with the names of Hewitt and Jenkins, Quay and Werry, Aschenbach and his colleagues, was started in the 1940s, as a psychological reaction to psychiatric theory-building. From the hesitant beginnings of only two clusters, the number has gradually expanded until it now encompasses eight clusters, which are remarkably constant both within and across cultures.

The eight clusters of conditions which are statistically associated are set out below in descending order of their prevalence and pervasiveness among disordered children. These could be regarded as empirically derived 'syndromes' but are not often in practice used or named as such. Within each cluster, the descriptions are presented in descending order of the degree of empirical support, so that earliest descriptions in each category have the greatest degree of empirical support.

1 *Under-socialized aggressive conduct disorder*
fights; hits; assaults;

disobeys; defies; throws temper tantrums; disrupts;
impertinent; impudent; unco-operative; resists;
seeks attention; bullies and threatens;
interrupts; noisy; irritates; negative;
restless; dishonest; lies; overactive

2 *Socialized aggressive conduct disorder*
undesirable companions; truants; runs away;
steals with others; belongs to a gang; delinquent friends;
stays out late; steals from home; cheats

3 *Attention deficit disorder*
poor concentration; short span of attention; distractibility;
daydreams; clumsy; poor co-ordination; 'not with it';
stares into space; passive; lacks initiative; easily led;
fidgets; restless; does not finish jobs; gives up easily;
sluggish; impulsive; easily bored; overactive; drowsy

4 *Anxiety/withdrawal/unhappiness*
anxious; fearful; tense;
shy; timid; depressed;
sad; disturbed; depressed;
over-sensitive; easily hurt;
feels inferior; worthless;
self-conscious; easily impressed;
lacks self-confidence;
easily frustrated and confused;
cries frequently; 'loner';
worries

5 *'Schizoid'/unresponsiveness*
will not talk;
withdrawn;
shy; timid; bashful;
cold and unresponsive;
lacks interest;
sad;
stares blankly;
confused;
secretive;
'loner'

6 *Social ineptness*
poor peer relations;
'loner';
teased and picked on;
prefers younger companions;

shy and timid;
stays with adults; ignored by peers

7   *Psychotic disorder*
incoherent;
repetitive speech;
bizarre; odd; peculiar;
visual hallucinations;
auditory hallucinations;
strange ideas and behaviour

8   *Motor overactivity*
restless, overactive;
excitable, impulsive; cannot wait;
jittery;
over-talkative;
makes odd noises

Advantages
- This approach shows those conditions which have been repeatedly identified by clinicians and, therefore, what 'really exists', not what is hypothesized or imagined.
- Built into a rating instrument, it allows relatively reliable measurement of how far a child diverges from the norm.
- It allows the disorder to be seen in the context of its different facets so that unusualness can be easily identified.
- Produces data most useful for constructing scales, for including what is important and, therefore, best as the minimum necessary set of items for evaluating children's clinical condition.

Disadvantages
- Because multivariate approaches are based on descriptive studies, they bear all the weakness and variability of their sources, such as reliability and validity. They *cannot* generate or identify conditions which have not occurred in those studies with sufficient frequency to be identified as a 'variable', such as deliberate self-harm.
- The outcome depends on the specificity of the condition and degree to which correlated behaviours have been identified, that is, some form of 'syndrome'.
- The dimensions of *behaviour* as identified above do not help in identifying the type of *individual* who is the subject of clinical concern. Given that usual checklists are based on discovered dimensions and themselves contribute to multivariate studies, it is often difficult to identify the total condition of the individual. So, for example, it is not possible to identify a brain-damaged child according to such an approach, and yet clearly such children exist and their condition must be identified.
- The disordered behaviour depends on the specific circumstances in

which it was identified. Results obtained in one setting and using one set of data may not be strictly comparable with another, even though they may look alike.

- The approach is complex and user unfriendly.
- The approach demands use of terminology similar to that from which the data were derived.
- Critically, multivariate approaches are not in any shape or form treatment-related, particularly as general dimensions of behaviour. Even if they allow a child to be uniquely located on a series of behavioural dimensions (which they may not), they do not allow for unique treatment.

Empirical assessment

This is essentially a variant and elaboration of the multivariate approach associated mainly with the names of Achenbach, Edelbrock and McConaughy. The preferential use of the term 'empirical' is interesting in that it seeks to single out this approach from a range of others, such as behavioural assessment which is infinitely more evidence-based and, therefore, 'empirical'. The process demands identifying a child's condition on a *predetermined scale* which is based on multivariate data of the type described above. However, the fact that a person rates a child on a scale with quantifiable results and a graph of the child's condition does not make it empirical, if this means that such identification is valid and based on evidence.

This approach explicitly uses 'psychometric' principles which demand that:

- assessment should follow standard procedures;
- multiple sources of information should be used on every aspect of the child;
- items should yield quantitative data;
- scores should indicate how each individual compares with relevant groups;
- developmental factors should be taken into account;
- assessment should produce good evidence of reliability and validity.

These criteria are generally accepted and are aimed at by all classification and assessment systems. The extension of the multivariate approach to designing and applying rating scales and behaviour checklists does not, of itself, fulfil the above requirements.

This approach is also said to be multi-axial. However, here the five axes refer to:

Axis I   Parents
Axis II   Teachers
Axis III   Cognitive assessment
Axis IV   Physical assessment
Axis V   'Direct' assessment of child

This is a confusing use of the term 'axis' because there is no evidence in the published material to show that these are or produce statistically independent information. The use of the terminology is, therefore, questionable. The process of assessment itself is a complex one encompassing (1) data collection leading to (2) identification of the child's similarities and differences with others of the comparable group as judged by a behaviour checklist, leading to (3) 'formulating case dynamics' – 'causes' and goals leading to (4) selecting targets for change. These steps are essentially no more than an uneconomic description of *any* assessment process.

This is a complex and time-consuming process of assessment which pretends to rigour that it does not possess. No relationship is shown between this complexity of input and usefulness of outcome. Reliability for many of the conditions described is rather poor although still significant. The case history material employed in the main writings demonstrates that a considerably easier approach could have been adopted with identical conclusions. Indeed, the case conclusions very often could have been reached on the basis of quite simple data and do not bear any logical or empirical relationship to the condition cited. There is little evidence to show that in use this approach is much different from diagnostic systems in apparently making statements about the child which bear many of the same difficulties, even though the basic data may have been derived from empirically developed tools. The major contributions of this approach lie in translating the results of multivariate research into readily usable and empirically derived checklists, with relatively wide applicability. The use of quantitative data from such checklists allows accurately locating children with their age group and showing continuities from childhood to adolescence. The advantages of this approach to assessment are shared by the Problem Profile Approach described in the next chapter, without many of the difficulties.

Overall evaluation of the different approaches

None of the three main approaches and the classification systems which they follow or produce are perfect. They have different strengths and weaknesses which achieve significance in particular contexts. It is, therefore, unproductive and irrational to push one against the others.

However, for the majority of young people presenting or experiencing mixed difficulties, neither diagnostic nor multivariate assessment would be *useful*, given the number and range of problems and the need for rapid response.

There are clearly exceptions to this as, for example, in the case of psychotic, brain-damaged or hyperkinetic children where accurate diagnoses are possible, highly desirable and associated with some reasonable treatments. But these are not the children who present the majority of difficulties (as seen in the clusters of multivariate analysis) and who demand urgent intervention, if for no other reason than that no straightforward treatments are available in the majority of cases. Indeed, as the above example indicates, diagnosis is most suitable in cases with a known or highly probable physical basis, where the necessary antecedents of diagnosis, as set out earlier, can be satisfied. Furthermore, such 'physical' cases also have comparatively the least ambiguous epidemiological and experimental data to support them, very much as in physical medicine.

Furthermore, while DSM or ICD approaches may be suitable vehicles for research and some high-level clinical practice, it is unlikely that they will reach a level of respectable reliability and validity sufficient to warrant their widespread clinical usage. Compared with the criteria for classifications, they are limited and stigmatizing, cannot be used by anyone but psychiatrists and clinical psychologists, and do not take adequate account of children's development or the situational specificity of much behaviour.

Multivariate approaches provide a scientifically rigorous basis for assessment but suffer from the shortcomings indicated earlier. They also seem at present best suited to research and where treatment response is not of the essence. In clinical practice, there is little reason to believe that they significantly improve assessment or treatment. They do, however, provide a necessary empirical underpinning for assessing many *aspects* of functioning in an individual child.

Overall, therefore, the question is not one of either/or with these approaches but rather which of them is most useful and in what context. On the basis of available evidence and considerable attempts by a variety of practitioners to use them, the following conclusions may be tentatively drawn:

- diagnostic and multivariate approaches are both suitable for the development of a discipline of clinical child psychology and psychiatry;
- multivariate approaches are much more reliable and productive for research purposes;
- multivariate approaches are more effective in accurate placing of children's difficulties in relation to others, provided that appropriate empirically derived tools and norms are available;
- descriptive approaches, whether behavioural or otherwise, are the most usable for comprehensive assessment, with closely allied open-ended treatment indications.

We are, therefore, left with descriptive assessment as *potentially* the most accurate and responsive approach to children's difficulties. This has not been rigorously pursued because its value in scientific terms has not been deemed to be as great as the others. However, its daily usage by the whole of humanity, including highly competent clinicians (though they may wrap it up in other terms) indicates its massive face validity as an approach to identifying children's difficulties. As most people *will* use descriptive and culturally established taxonomies or clusters, we might as well expend some effort on making this approach more systematic and disciplined.

The next chapter will describe in detail the most developed of these descriptive approaches.

Further reading

Achenbach, T.M. (1985) *Assessment and Taxonomy of Child and Adolescent Psychopathology*, London: Sage.

Achenbach, T.M. and McConaughy, S.H. (1987) *Empirically Based Assessment of Child and Adolescent Psychopathology*, London: Sage.

Bijou, S.M. and Baer, D.M. (1978) *Behavior Analysis of Child Development*, Englewood Cliffs: Prentice Hall.

British Association of Social Workers (1977) *The Social Work Task*, Birmingham: BASW.

Cone, J.D. and Hawkins, R.P. (eds) (1977) *Behavioral Assessment – New Directions in Clinical Psychology*, New York: Brunner Mazel.

Gelder, M., Gath, D. and Mayou, R. (1989) *Oxford Textbook of Psychiatry*, 2nd edn, Oxford: Oxford Medical Publications.

Gelfand, D.M. and Hartmann, D.P. (1986) *Child Behavior Analysis and Therapy*, 2nd edn, New York: Pergamon.

Gould, M.S. et al. (1988) 'U.K./W.H.O. Study of ICD-9', in Rutter, M., Tuma, A.H. and Lann, I.S. (eds), *Assessment and Diagnosis in Child Psychopathology*, London: David Fulton.

Herbert, M. (1991) *Clinical Child Psychology*, Chichester: John Wiley.

Hersen, M. and Bellack, A.S. (eds) (1976) *Behavioral Assessment: a Practical Handbook*, Oxford and New York: Pergamon.

Hersen, M. and Van Hassett, V.B. (1987) *Behavior Therapy with Children and Adolescents*, New York: John Wiley.

Hobbs, N. (ed) (1975) *Issues in the Classification of Children*. San Francisco: Jossey Bass.

Hoghughi, M.S. (1978) *Troubled and Troublesome*, London: Burnett Books/André Deutsch.

Hoghughi, M.S., Dobson, C., Lyons, J., Muckley, A., and Swainston, M.A. (1980) *Assessing Problem Children: Issues and Practice*, London: Burnett Books.

Lazarus, A.A. et al. (1976) *Multimodal Behaviour Therapy*, New York: Springer Publications.

Mash, B.J. and Terdal, G. (eds) (1981) *Behavioral Assessment of Childhood Disorders*, New York: John Wiley.

Nay, W.R. (1979) *Multimethod Clinical Assessment*, New York: Gardner Press.

Ollendick, T.H. and Hersen, M. (1984) *Child Behavioral Assessment*, New York: Pergamon.

Quay, H.C. and Werry, J.S. (eds) (1986) *Psychopathological Disorders of Childhood*, New York: John Wiley.

Rakoff, V.M., Stancer, H.C. and Kedward, H.B. (eds) (1977) *Psychiatric Diagnosis*, New York: Brunner Mazel.

Rutter, M. and Hersov, L. (eds) (1985) *Child and Adolescent Psychiatry*, 2nd edn, Oxford: Blackwell Scientific.

Spitzer, R.L. and Williams, J.B. (eds) (1987) *DSM III–R*, 3rd edn, Washington: American Psychiatric Association.

4

The Problem Profile Approach

This approach originates in the common attempts to make sense of disturbed and delinquent youngsters. It evolved in an environment specifically devoted to assessment and treatment of their difficulties. It was first published in 1969 and it has been subsequently tried out in thousands of cases, and subjected to professional scrutiny in a variety of settings.

The concept of 'problem'

This term has diverse meanings depending on the context. It is usually regarded as a puzzle, difficulty or quandary which needs solving or resolving.

As we saw in Chapter 1, striving after order and values demands that events and experiences should be regarded as falling somewhere along the spectrum of good, indifferent, bad. Our concern here is with those conditions which fall at the negative end of the dimension because this is usually why young people are referred for help and the legal basis for official intervention. However, problems can only be understood in the context of the total condition of children, including strengths, which become particularly pertinent when treatment commences.

In the present context, problem is defined as *unacceptable condition*. In any language, it simply means that the condition cannot be allowed to continue – that it is beyond 'latitude of tolerance'. This concept, in turn, means that there is a range or band of behaviour around the central average, mode or norm, outside of which the behaviour or condition provokes either positive or negative reaction. At the negative end of this spectrum, a condition which becomes increasingly 'undesirable' as it moves away from the middle begins to be 'intolerable' or 'unacceptable'.

Human behaviour is evaluated on a dimension ranging from totally unacceptable to highly prized, and everything else in between. In most human characteristics this variation is *normally distributed*, which means that there are as many good as there are bad features either side of the average band. Most people cluster around the average mark while others, in ever smaller numbers, verge towards either end. Most people change their position on any dimension such as 'kind–cruel' to some degree depending on the circumstances. However, in relation to other people, they also manifest some degree of constancy of behaviour, which underlines our ability to speak of 'personality' or 'attitudes' and to predict others' reactions in particular circumstances.

As we begin to go further from the middle towards the negative end, so, increasingly, the condition disturbs our sense of 'what is right' and, therefore, acceptable. When it passes a point when we can no longer put up with it and demand or engage in some action, then we have reached the 'unacceptable condition'. Therefore, some things may be undesirable but still tolerable enough and thus not a problem warranting intervention. So a child may be often unhappy but we may well not intervene unless he takes an overdose. When a condition becomes intolerable, it is a 'problem'. Alternatively, anything negative that is subjected to intervention is implicitly unacceptable, such as when we give aspirins for a headache or a glass of water for thirst. An unacceptable condition, therefore, does not have to be extreme but rather anything that warrants intervention.

Problems are a matter of degree, which is why we can speak of 'serious' or 'mild' problems. So even a serious difficulty, such as persistent deliberate self-harm or temper tantrums, may be tolerated because the cost of intervention may be too high to be acceptable. This is akin to examples in medicine where even a serious condition may have to be tolerated because of the risks entailed in treatment. The implication here is that anything that is a problem demands intervention. So if no intervention is contemplated, at least in theory, and if resources were available, the condition should not be defined as a 'problem'. This is a necessary caution to many professionals and lay people alike who define a condition as a problem even though they have no intention of doing anything about it.

Latitude of tolerance depends on:

- *culture*   different societies operate by different criteria of order and value, depending on their wider condition and priorities. So child prostitution may be acceptable in one country but not another;
- *generation*   within cultures, criteria of propriety of order and values change and what may be acceptable to one generation is not to another. Child abuse was accepted by an earlier generation of professionals but is not by this one. Conversely, sexual experimentation among youngsters was not acceptable to an older generation but is to the present;
- *age*   there are strong cultural presumptions of age-appropriate behaviour and dramatic departures are made the subject of intervention. Alcoholic intoxication is tolerated in teenagers but not in primary school children. Conversely, bedwetting is more acceptable in young children than adolescents;
- *visibility*   of the condition: the more socially obvious and conspicuous the condition, the more likely it is to provoke intervention. Emotional abuse of children is hardly ever mentioned and even less reacted to than physical and sexual abuse;
- *impact*   this is in part an extension of the concept of 'visibility'. If we do not know about a condition, we are unlikely to be aware of *its* impact on the child and are ourselves less likely to be distressed by the breach of our standards that it represents.

Fact and judgment

An important implication of the concept of latitude of tolerance is that a problem is not a 'fact' but a *fact* plus a *judgment*. That a girl of six may be sexually abused is a fact, as is that a boy of 14 may have committed murder. But why should they not? They should not, because they dramatically breach prevailing cultural norms, whether these simply describe things as they *are* or as they *should* be. Those norms themselves are not a fact but rather a sum of judgments which is enforced by those in power. This in turn indicates a power relationship between the person who judges the condition and the person whose behaviour is judged. This is particularly important to remember because of the tendency of professionals to speak of 'problems' as if they were facts, and not properly disputable by anyone with a different point of view. Indeed, as in laws, professional perspectives and prevailing standards, problems are disputable as judgments, which they would not be as facts. It is questionable whether the incidence or prevalence of childhood disorders has very much changed in the past few decades. And yet we have quite different preoccupations now compared with a couple of decades earlier, and are both more ready to assert some things as facts (e.g. child abuse) and less ready to assert others (e.g. that sexual experimentation is bad for young people).

The term 'problem' can refer to unacceptable conditions which are *presented* or *suffered* by children. Anti-social behaviour may be regarded as an example of the former and being abused as of the latter. This is the active–passive dimension, necessary in order to include the many difficulties to which children are subjected and are prominent when they themselves present problems.

Profile

In painting and sculpture, this is usually regarded as 'outline', 'contour' or 'side view' representation of the main characteristics of a person in graph or sketch form. Other meanings include a sketch or highlights of a person's characteristics according to test results or other sources of information. This is the meaning employed here, but intended to be irrespective of the amount of detail, from the merest outline to an extended account of a person's history and current state.

The term is adopted here in relation to problems because of its unique quality, derived from the origin of the Latin word 'profilare' – to draw a light sketch. Profiles look different according to the relative positions of the observer and the observed. If we may use a sculptural analogy: a statue looks different from different angles as the viewer walks around it. Alternatively, if the viewer stands still and the sculpture is turned around, so its profile changes.

Applied to problems, the term 'profile' incorporates the idea of *change* which is, perhaps, the most fundamental aspect of children's conditions. It recognizes that children change in different contexts and their behaviour can be judged to be problematic or not according to who is judging them – as in behavioural assessment. When the observer or the context of the child's behaviour changes, so may the problem. If the problem persists, we can then begin to regard it more confidently as a persisting characteristic of the child.

Approach is a way of getting close to or reaching an area. In this context, approach simply means a way of looking at and clustering difficulties and unacceptable conditions in a child. It is not a model, theory or method but a descriptive view of problems. It is theoretically unbiassed and open-ended and can be used by anyone, irrespective of theoretical orientation.

Classification of problems

The classification adopted in this approach arises from the common distinctions made in the linguistic culture of most countries. There is no pretence either of diagnostic/causal analysis or that it is rigorously or empirically derived. But it has already been suggested that this approach is the most pervasive both within and outside professions. Professional classifications are simply refinements or elaborations of those states and labels which are identified in ordinary language and experience.

A major difference between professional classification of human problems and common terminology is the many varieties and gradings of labelling used in the former. So, in common language, we may say someone is 'mentally ill' or has 'difficulty in speaking'. A mental health professional or speech therapist, on the other hand, would use a more finely focussed range of descriptors, not only identifying the particular form of disorder but also its severity, urgency of need for action and probably the way it should be tackled.

The classification contains six categories of problems which encompass all the difficulties presented or experienced by children and adolescents.

Problem areas

Physical This area includes all disorders, dysfunctions and deficits concerning the body as a whole or any of its subsystems, whether hereditary or acquired during the child's lifetime from, say, colour deficiency and epilepsy, through diabetes and poor hearing, to undescended testicles. It also includes the psychoses, as well as psychophysiological, autonomic and visceral disorders.

The inclusion of pervasive developmental disorders, psychoses, drug abuse and 'psychosomatic' disorders in the area of physical problems may be surprising. The reason, however, is straightforward. To suggest that they are not 'physical' presumes a theoretical bias that is not supported by the available evidence. That evidence would suggest that some of these disorders have a strong genetic or physiological basis (as in psychoses and PDD); primarily affect physiological functioning (as in drug abuse or psychosomatic disorders) or are susceptible primarily to pharmaceutical intervention (as in psychoses). They are, therefore, more appropriately placed in this problem area than in any other.

Cognitive   This category is concerned with children's ability to cope with the intellectual demands of daily life, particularly in school and work settings. The area also encompasses cognitive problems such as illiteracy, which may arise for many reasons, such as intellectual deficit or persistent truancy. In this sense, not being able to read and write fall within the cognitive problem area and are functionally equivalent to difficulties arising from intellectual deficit, although clearly leaving the potential to learn unimpaired. The problem can be general, such as mental retardation, or specific, such as difficulty in synthesizing words. Interest in school or work is included, partly because it is often associated with cognitive difficulties, but also because the assessor often wishes to evaluate it in the context of cognitive functioning.

Home and family   This is the largest and the most complex category of problems associated with disordered youngsters. In tackling such a large area there is a danger of regress into infinite detail and, therefore, the limits of how far and wide the problems should be described depend on the specific requirements of the investigator. Problems can be traced back and sideways as far as necessary if they seem to be part of the difficulties presented by the family.

Family problems encompass the background of the parents; their socio-economic status; the neighbourhood they inhabit; the home; their individual characteristics at a variety of levels of analysis; the pattern, content and emotional tone of their interaction with each other and with their children, both together and singly; the style and method of upbringing of children including forms of communication, guidance and control; quality of involvement and emotional bonds; children's relationships with their parents and one another, and aspects of abuse, both within family and wider social context.

Social skills   These encompass the difficulties and conflicts of children in coping with the growing demands of social interaction with both peers and adults. They refer to peculiarities of self-presentation; difficulties in basic interaction; conversation skills; assertiveness; perception of social cues and the ability to relate to others, reciprocate and engage in co-operative activity; amenability and response to social pressure; attitude to other children and adults, and specific situational difficulties.

Anti-social behaviour   Next to physical disorders, more children are referred for assessment of difficulties in this area than any other. It includes infractions of laws, rules, customs and rituals of behaviour in the wider social (as opposed to small group) settings. It comprises all offences and encroachments against person and property as well as 'victimless' offences, such as drug taking and soliciting. In addition, it includes acts which, although not strictly offences, such as self-destructive gestures, temper tantrums, truancy and absconding and odd sexual proclivities, are nevertheless seriously disruptive and frequently provoke strong reaction in other people. Attitudes to anti-social acts are included as a major area of concern in assessing risk.

Psychological This area covers three distinct but closely interrelated aspects: deviation in stable personal attributes; emotional development, tone, adaption, and control; and identity or self-concept, best described as a child's difficulty in answering such questions as 'Who am I?', 'What am I?', 'Who cares for me?', 'What am I worth?' Traditionally, most clinicians have confined themselves to the first two categories. The third, however, is regarded as fundamental to the understanding of the way children make sense of their lives, and determine how they should behave under different conditions, insofar as their behaviour is purposive.

The detailed Master Code is set out in Part II.

Levels of analysis

The present classification recognizes the need for finely focussed descriptions, substantially beyond what is provided by or possible in the other current classifications, with the exception of some physical and cognitive disorders. Three levels of analysis are employed, ranging from the most general to the most specific. Logically an infinite number of levels of analysis is possible, although the three levels would meet more than the usually necessary requirements in conducting a comprehensive and detailed assessment of a child.

Problem areas This is the broadest category of information about children's difficulties. Areas are divided because in our current culture and scientific community we distinguish them as being qualitatively different from each other. The six areas are the minimum necessary and sufficient to cover the total information about a child. Because of their face validity, shared in part by diagnostic classifications (multivariate classifications are not concerned with the whole child), there is no need to do a statistical analysis to show that the areas are accurately defined in this manner.

Problem attributes These cover the next more detailed level of specificity. They identify the full range of difficulties *within* each problem area. They are the most common way of distinguishing individuals *within* and *between* problem areas, e.g. 'this is an epileptic child', 'this is a fire raiser' where both descriptions differentiate the child's condition from other physical or anti-social difficulties. Although usually such broad spectrum conditions justify social intervention, they usually need more detailed definition before focussed action can be taken, though this depends on how advanced the treatment methodology is. A physician may need to know no more than the child is anxious in order to prescribe anti-anxiety medication. A psychologist may, on the other hand, need to know much more about the many forms of anxiety-related behaviour in order to select the appropriate treatment technique from the wide range available.

Problem 'behaviour' This is the most detailed level of analysis, referred to sometimes as 'signs' and 'symptoms'. 'Signs' are unacceptable conditions or indicators of other unacceptable conditions detected by the observer. 'Symptoms' are those of which the child complains. So a child may be seen to be tense, drawn and unhappy-looking and says that he is afraid of going to sleep. The first three would be 'signs' and the latter a 'symptom' of depression or anxiety. This is the level of description required by behavioural assessment.

In the absence of broad spectrum treatments (as in pharmaceutical treatment of anxiety) it is the behaviour which must become the focus of treatment, particularly in conduct disorders and other behavioural problems. Every behaviour can be further detailed, depending on the state of knowledge about both its assessment and treatment.

The six areas are exhaustive of all the unacceptable conditions that can be found in children and adolescents. There is simply nothing else that a child can present or experience which could be deemed problematic and which would fall outside these areas. Attributes and behaviours, on the other hand, are not exhaustive. Further ones can always be added according to new discoveries (the original version of this classification paper in 1967 did not speak of 'child abuse') or, alternatively, according to the needs of the environment or characteristics of the particular population being assessed. This is why every problem attribute and behaviour includes the category 'other' to ensure that the assessor remains alert to problems not identified in this book.

Parameters for evaluating problems

If all children presented or suffered from the same difficulties, it would be difficult to differentiate them from one another. But they do not. We distinguish them not only as bearers of certain personal features but also on the basis of their problem profiles. These profiles are clinically distinguished from each other on evaluative parameters that are set out in the acronym EIDU – **extent, intensity, duration, urgency**.

Extent refers to the *number* of problems. The greater the number, the more problematic a child is, and the greater the spread and range of problems within and between different areas, the greater the complexity of the child's problem. A child with 50 problems is twice as problematic as one with 25, other things being equal. A child with difficulties in four areas will present a more complex treatment task than one with problems only in two.

The larger the cluster of problems in any one area, the more likely we are to identify that as the primary focus of difficulty. A child who presents a large number of physical difficulties, by comparison with those in home and family or social skills areas, is likely to be seen as a predominantly physical problem, whereas one presenting more anti-social difficulties than any others is likely to be seen as predominantly anti-social.

Extent or number is arrived at by simple counting. However, counting by itself does not get us very far because it is often the intensity of particular problems which warrants intervention rather than a wide range of low-level difficulties which may be undesirable but would not be serious enough to become intolerable.

Intensity is a measure of *severity* of disorder. A totally deaf child is more seriously problematic than a partially hearing one; one who is suicidal is more severely problematic than one who engages in deliberate self-harm for attention-seeking. Severity of a problem is the major trigger to action. So, for example, a child who is frequently but mildly punished by father *may* not warrant intervention but one who has received a severe beating, leaving bruises and welts, does. It is this criterion which usually pushes us beyond the latitude of tolerance.

Intensity relates to the presumed *depth* of a problem. The more intense the problem is judged, the more severe it will be. For example, the girl who mopes and says 'I am fed up' is less of a 'problem' than one who is clinically depressed. Evaluation of intensity can be done either subjectively by an individual, through consensus by an assessment group, or through the use of an objective measure in any of the generally accepted ways. Intensity is rated 1 = mild; 2 = moderate; 3 = severe.

Duration can be seen as a major contributor to judgments of intensity. It refers to the *length of time* a problem has been manifest. This is an important measure, particularly in professional assessments of disorder, because:

- the longer the pre-morbid history, the more serious the disorder is likely to be, because it suggests deeper impact and more complex development of disorder;
- human beings are adaptive organisms who try to come to terms with their problems. Therefore, the longer a problem has been going on, the more it is likely to have resulted in maladaptive accommodation or assimilation which may also need treatment.

In clinical diagnoses (as in DSM III–R) fairly arbitrary (if sometimes consensual) time periods are used for the determination of a disorder. As a rule of thumb, duration can also be rated as 1 = within 3 months; 2 = within 1 year; 3 = longer than 1 year. These indicate a probable ascending order of difficulty in delivering successful treatment, other parameters being equal, though they can be varied if the assessor has good reason for doing so.

Urgency is how quickly *action* has to be taken to ameliorate the unacceptable condition. It is essentially a measure of 'action potential' of a disorder. In the end, all the other three parameters of extent, intensity and duration lead to and are summed up in this.

Even in the case of a child with serious difficulties, not all problems are of equal urgency. Some behaviours with the same profile are likely to provoke action more quickly than others. Serious self-harm or a burst appendix demand more urgent attention than drug abuse. Similarly, when a number of children are being considered for treatments which take up scarce resources, the relative urgency of each child's most serious problems will determine which will be treated first. Urgency can be rated as 1 = mild; 2 = moderate; 3 = critical.

Urgency allows the assessment agent to rank problems in order of priority warranting intervention. Different criteria may be used for this type of ranking, such as the social impact of the problem or its consequences for the child. Whatever other criteria are considered, 'urgency' is likely to be the most influential in determining priorities. This involves subjective judgment, whether individual or group based, regarding the possible consequences of *not* taking certain measures. It can also be based on an understanding of the hierarchical order of problems, such as 'unless we reduce her anxiety, we cannot bring the rest of her behaviour under control'.

Between them, the Problem Profile and the four evaluative parameters provide a uniquely individualized assessment of the child's condition. As an example, 'John has been epileptic since childhood but his condition is now fairly well controlled. He is mildly educationally retarded, comes from a good home, has poor social skills, has been moderately disruptive at school and is quite introverted, moody and negative.' In this case, John seems to have five problems (counting the psychological ones as one), none of which warrants a greater intensity rating than 2, with at least one condition of lifelong duration, therefore $d = 3$, and none which warrants urgent intervention, therefore $u = 1$. Contrasting middle-class out-patient referrals with young people in in-patient clinic or institutional settings provides another example of how such profiles may vary in terms of extent, intensity, duration and urgency of their problems – in a much more objectively rigorous way than any alternative classification system can provide.

The method of carrying out assessments according to the Problem Profile is set out in this book. It essentially entails identifying the difficulties and disorders of children and adolescents, drawing on as many sources as possible, where the resulting information is agreed on by most people who know the child. Disagreements are quickly identified and usually ironed out between sources of information, as they are between child's history and current state. The results of the child's profile may be entered on a *Child and Adolescent Problem Profile (CAPP)* (based on the Master Code in this book) which also provides a short form of assessment as set out in Appendix 1. The longer and more complex method results in an assessment report of the type set out in Appendix 2.

Evaluating the Problem Profile Approach

The PPA was developed in a multi-disciplinary setting concerned with the assessment and treatment of severely disordered youngsters. It is an attempt to establish a rigorous, non-stigmatizing, generally usable system for the description of children's problems. With its associated concepts, it provides a systematic guide to those areas of a child's functioning which warrant intervention.

By eliciting reliable, broadly based and potentially validated information, it enables the development of complex and dynamic typologies of children's attributes and their responsiveness to particular treatments, both for single elements and sets of problems. It does not remove the eventual need for diagnostic systems but provides a more coherent basis on which they may be developed. Over the period of time the PP has been in use, its advantages, compared with other commonly available classifications of children's disorders, have become evident. It may be worthwhile to set these out, particularly in relation to the previously presented criteria.

The six problem areas encompass the totality of difficulties experienced or presented by the child. Each area can be treated at the level of detail and comprehensiveness that the complexity of the child's problems and the resources of the assessment agency warrant. An individual social worker on first acquaintance with a child may use it as a handy checklist for a superficial scanning of the range of the child's possible problems. Equally, a specialized agency may probe each element of the same checklist or an expanded one at high levels of specialism until the full complexity of the child's problems has been established.

Information is derived from three main sources (see Chapter 6). Because the information obtained relates to the same problem areas, such as physical functioning or social skills, it becomes possible to determine the consistency and weight of opinion regarding the child's problems. Emphasis on multiple sources of information ensures that, even at its lowest level, it is likely to be more reliable and valid than alternative approaches which use a narrower range of information, e.g. from an interview.

The reliability of the items is, on the face of it, 100 per cent or near, since all problems are identified according to consensus or a respondent's own perception of what the difficulties are. Studies have produced reliabilities in the range of $r = .68$ for 'presentation' to $r = .98$ for epilepsy. As with diagnostic approaches, the more physical and publicly recorded events (including home and family features), the higher the reliability of the information recorded. However, the need for consensual assessment even puts these low reliabilities in context. In practice the low reliability of 'presentation' simply indicates people's different understanding of whether a particular presentation is odd or not according to their own cultural and personal criteria.

Unless assessment agents are omniscient, their reliance on multiple sources of information encourages participation of others in the child's assessment, and hence decision making about what to do with him. As will be argued later (Chapter 7), the more serious the child's actual or potential problems, the more necessary it will be to carry out team, as opposed to individual, assessment. This classification is particularly appropriate to a team or multi-disciplinary approach because it does not presume a particular professional background. This is especially important in the case of a difficult and anxiety-producing minority, such as disordered children, who may be given questionable labels which legitimize empirically and ethically marginal treatments. The wider the decision-making base, the less idiosyncratic it is likely to be.

Problem Profile assessment does provide a quantitative score for extent, intensity, duration and urgency, if desired. The quantitative scores would not only accurately reflect the child's problem profile but also priorities in each area. However, this concern with numbers (which, contrary to claims, is *not* an indispensable requirement of psychometric precepts), is not very helpful in most applied (as opposed to research) situations. In the American context generally, there is something akin to obsession with numbers. In the British and European context, discursive and broadly agreed judgments are more often the norm.

Although the strictest psychometric approach suggests that scores should be translated into norms for comparison, this is seriously questionable in most forms of assessment other than, for example, cognitive, where moderately reliable norms exist. As comprehensive assessment is intended to help towards treatment of the child and each child is unique, scores and norms do not make sense and are wholly unnecessary as a prelude to action. Even when a physician sees a highly abnormal cardiogram, she simply uses that as confirmatory evidence for her original suspicion that there may be something wrong with the child's heart which must be treated. For the same reason, age norms should only be used if necessary but, as already indicated, they frequently are not. The definition of a 'problem' as an 'unacceptable condition' in an individual case, e.g. stunted growth, already presumes age comparisons.

The Problem Profile has considerable face validity because it does not posit any theoretical entities and simply seeks to describe that which has already been deemed problematic against its cultural background, as confirmed by questions, observations and possible test data. Because it does not depend on hypotheses or inferential labels, problems of validity do not arise. It is essentially as reliable and valid as the information on which it is based and the language which describes the condition. Additional validation can be obtained according to diagnostic or multivariate approaches, but these are not appropriate because PPA does not stipulate 'syndromes' or diagnostic entities as does DSM or ICD.

The approach uses a language of problems which is almost universal and enables easier communication than can be achieved with any other classification between different levels of expertise and professional points of view. Because learning about functional areas is part of any normally intelligent citizen's upbringing, *everybody* can contribute usefully to the determination of each of the problem areas. The descriptive language is common English (or Hebrew or Cantonese or whatever) and as such demystifies the disorder of the child. This is an important consideration, bearing in mind that most classifications achieve professional status at the expense of mystifying the many non-specialists concerned with the welfare of children and anxious to understand their problems.

The definition of 'problem', on which this approach is based, relates to the interaction of children and their environment, including the time and the place in which the condition is found to be 'unacceptable'. Thus, the approach is dynamic and allows for the fluid and rapidly developing nature of children's conditions. Such fluidity results not only from the ebb and flow of the children's problems but also the shifting perspectives of those who deal with them.

The PPA does not depend on the use of derogating and empirically questionable labels such as 'psychopath'. The detailed description of problems transmits maximum information with minimum distortion and makes such labels unnecessary. The description provides the profile of a unique individual whose similarity to another individual is only to the extent of overlapping problems. This is quite different from the use of syndromic labels such as 'psychopathic' which suggest, at least superficially, that all who bear the label are alike, when this is at best dubious and a matter for empirical enquiry and at worst, damagingly untrue.

In this approach, the description of disorder does not presume common aetiological factors. This is one of the major limitations of diagnostic classifications, arising from the paucity of established and accepted evidence regarding the roots of disorders. The present approach allows for wholly different aetiologies to be associated with the same pattern of disorder. This is in keeping with common clinical experience. For example, one girl's wrist-cutting may be a guilt reaction to incest with her father and her mother's suicide attempt, another's a learnt, manipulatory ploy. Each of the 'causal' inferences here would themselves *constitute*, and be described separately, as, *problems* if they are ascertained as such.

An associated advantage is that the PPA is not bound to any particular theoretical orientation such as the psychoanalytic or the behaviourist. It leaves open the possible use of such orientations but only insofar as they enable the identification of particular problems and open them to detailed description and evaluation.

Likewise, the approach makes diagnoses largely redundant. The function of diagnosis (other than in a research context) is to differentiate and facilitate relevant treatment. The configuration of one child's problems, particularly against the evaluative criteria of extent, intensity, duration and urgency, amply does this. Going beyond such a description is not necessary other than for purposes of developing an empirical taxonomy.

That activity can be carried out separately as research and should not, ethically, become mixed up with the alleviation of the child's problem. Bearing in mind the dynamic nature of most child and adolescent problems and the changing circumstances associated with them, diagnoses, with their implications of fixity, limit the range of treatments that should be offered from one age and circumstance to another, even though the diagnostic label remains the same. The changing profile does not have the same problem. In this approach, because diagnoses are not necessary, there will be no search for 'syndromes' accompanied by the attempts to collect together as many syndromic signs and symptoms as possible. As few individuals present 'textbook' pictures of disorders and many fall uncomfortably between several syndromes, it may make more sense and be more true to human diversity if attempts were not made to squeeze them into a few doubtful categories, but rather allowed each their unique configuration of attributes. In this sense, the PPA allows for a more complex and sophisticated view of human problems than any of the other approaches. Because individuals are not diagnosed in terms of syndromes, this obviates the need to change diagnoses in the course of treatment. Treatment is instead geared to each element of the configuration of problems as it emerges.

This is not to say that certain collections of attributes are not regularly present and thereby lead to the identification of syndromes, such as 'simple schizophrenia'. Rather, the contention is that, in each human being, the diversity of problems is at least as great as the similarities and, unless empirically established broad-spectrum treatments are available (as, for example, in schizophrenias), it may be more productive to concentrate on the differences in the problem profile than on the similarity of particular elements. This is in any case forced on us by the inevitably unique profile of the whole child's problems.

The acid test, ultimately, of any classification system, is the degree to which it guides action, in this case the treatment of problem children. Despite the formal connection between diagnosis and treatment, rarely, even in physical medicine, is total configuration of problems susceptible to only one form of treatment. Rather, in almost all cases, there is the need for a variety of approaches not only to deal with a particular problem but also to mobilize diverse resources to cope with side-effects of treatment and related issues. Traditional approaches to children's problems are beset by doubts and ambiguities about how to bridge the gap between assessment and treatment.

By contrast, the PPA has direct pointers to treatment. Because the description is elemental rather than holistic, it focusses attention on the use of methods of treatment suitable to each problem. This does not, however, rule out the use of one medium or method which may have a wider impact, such as wide-spectrum anti-anxiety medication which may alleviate several problems at one stroke. The treatment options are not foreclosed by diagnosis – they are left open in all their diversity – and, therefore, allow a multi-modal approach to a disordered youngster. For example, family problems may indicate the use of intensive casework, while the youngster's aggressive behaviour may be modified by operant techniques and his anxiety reduced by psychotherapy or medication. If a specific technique does not work with a particular problem, then only that one technique needs to be changed rather than the whole treatment. While this approach demands greater sophistication in treatment, it is likely to be more efficient than any diagnostically holistic approach and lead to more successful long-term alleviation of problems.

The PPA is particularly useful for purposes of training in the field of children with problems. The small number of problem areas and comprehensive nature of the classification makes it easy to remember and use, even by the least experienced practitioners. At succeeding levels of sophistication, more complex description of children's problems can be provided without recourse to specialist barriers to acquisition of such knowledge. This is a far cry from the self-defeating complications of diagnostic approaches which are used in their full range only in research studies.

Traditional classification of children's disorders are frequently partial. They emphasize one aspect of the child's functioning and, by implication, underplay the importance of other functional areas in the genesis of the child's disorders. They are also difficult to record in adequate detail other than in research settings. For these reasons, it is currently difficult, with a few exceptions, to adduce rigorous and methodologically sound evidence regarding how children's problems change and respond to treatment in the inescapable context of their total functioning or even as single attributes. The elemental and comprehensive nature of the PPA, on the other hand, is specially suited to recording and research. Through relatively straightforward research designs, it is possible to determine changes in the extent and intensity of children's difficulties and the efficacy of particular treatment measures in relation to single (and clusters of) problems. Such an approach enhances the possibility of establishing an empirical discipline of treating problem children.

This approach has been put forward throughout as 'descriptive' rather than explanatory. This is because knowledge of the origins and circumstances associated with the development and continuation of problems is scant, patchy, inconsistent and inadequately established. There are, therefore, no generally acceptable explanations for children's non-physical disorders. Rather, there are many theories, typologies and sets of explanations each with their adherents. Because of the difficulties, both ethical and practical, of controlling human behaviour and the circumstances that impinge on it, certain forms of external validation demanded by diagnoses remain logically and technically impossible.

In view of this, it would be more rational and ethical if all treatment were to be tied to a rigorous and detailed description of problems rather than to inevitably hypothetical explanations. The choice of a treatment technique may presume an explanatory hypothesis on the part of the treatment agent, but in a multi-disciplinary team, such a choice would remain limited to one functional area of one child, and could be tested as a short-range hypothesis.

In a number of important treatment applications, the potential of the PPA for complex, individual treatment of severely disordered children has been recognized and utilized. The results confirm the conceptual soundness and operational utility of the system.

It is hoped that the PPA, with its potential for comprehensive, multi-disciplinary assessment and action orientation, will form the basis of a new discipline of empirical assessment and treatment of disordered children and, when suitably developed, of other groups.

A note on positive attributes

The definition of problem adopted in this book – an 'unacceptable condition presented or experienced by children' – is deliberately negative. It may, therefore, suggest that the assessment of children entails only the description and evaluation of their negative interactions with the environment. In an important sense this is true, because this is most often what brings children to the attention of helping agencies.

But, like all other human beings, problem children possess a mixture of 'positive' and 'negative' characteristics. In coping with them and enhancing their potential for improvement and increasing self-help, it is crucial to know as much about their strengths as it is to know about their difficulties. Positive characteristics also fall under the same functional headings as do problems. For example, a child can be described as a strong gymnast; particularly good at a school subject; having concerned and competent parents; being capable of generating good feelings in others; socially adept or particularly resilient.

Evaluation of children's strengths is of concern in planning how to ameliorate their problems. In any such treatment planning a wide range of resources should be evaluated, of which children's own competencies and strengths are the major element. But, since this book limits itself to assessment only, the evaluation of positive attributes will not be separately treated.

5

Special Considerations in Assessing Children

Assessing children has much in common with that of adults, but nevertheless there are significant differences between them because of age, developmental variables and their particular responses to different types of difficulty. Because of the greater vulnerability of children to inappropriate decisions, it is worthwhile setting out certain of the special factors affecting their assessment in brief outline. Every topic covered here can be pursued in much greater detail in the Further Reading sections of Chapters 8–13.

Developmental change

This is the most fundamental characteristic of children. Children's development is both rapid and uneven. This fact complicates any judgment that may be made. Assessment of children implicitly involves comparisons with norms and developmental milestones. Although solid information on these is available, they begin to become less useful and more subjective as we move from the physical and the younger children towards more psychological problems and older children. So it is relatively easy to identify the difficulties of an epileptic child of 8 who is having school problems but more difficult to assess a 15-year-old who is often weepy and drunk. The more complex the condition, the fewer the norms for comparison.

The developmental perspective clearly applies to physical factors including growth, height and weight, and differences between boys and girls and their 'body images' at different stages of development, particularly in adolescence where preoccupation with the body becomes paramount. Cognitive development takes place also according to a pattern and sequence which is well researched. Recognizing the level of language development is particularly crucial in determining the young person's ability to make sense of the environment, achieving cognitive mastery and avoiding trouble. Social development encompasses the growth of ability to make and maintain relationships with parents, early peers, other adults and later on with persons of the opposite sex. As children move from puberty to adolescence, so in general their sense of 'self' becomes better established – involving ideas of 'who am I?', 'what/who is important to me?', 'what do I want to do with my life?' This includes also moral and social development, where recognition of general principles of social conduct and sense of personal responsibility begin to emerge.

Age factors

Although age is related to development, it raises its own issues of whether any special measures have to be taken to deal with children of different ages in terms of assessment. For the youngest children, the environment for assessment would seem to be most suitably a playroom with appropriate play equipment, whether or not the child's play is being variously 'interpreted'. Although the scientific basis of interpretations may be dubious, there is little doubt that many practitioners use children's play for this purpose. This has been recently much encouraged by play with anatomically correct dolls in cases of suspected sexual abuse, where a child's response is interpreted in terms of inappropriate sexual knowledge. With older children, the environment seems to matter less as long as it does not give the distorted perception of the purpose of assessment (such as a hospital with lots of white-coated people for a youngster with mood disorders). The important factor is the degree of ease and trust generated between the child and the assessor, particularly as children do not usually ask to be assessed but rather are persuaded or coerced into receiving help. Because they do not volunteer, greater effort needs to be made to establish a non-coercive relationship to trust with them. With adolescents, this becomes even more crucial because of their greater uncertainties about themselves and their usually greater anxiety about how they are perceived by others.

Trust or its absence deeply affects the quality of the assessment. The greater the trust, the less the degree of structure that needs to be employed in interviewing, and the less the need to cross-check and validate the information with other sources. As with all other sources of information, children's reliability varies because of their own qualities (such as ability to understand the question) and their perception of the purpose of the interview. In general, the more factual the questions, the older the children and the less sensitive the area being probed, the higher is the likelihood of reliability.

In all dealings with children, it is necessary to create a gentle, unoppressive atmosphere. The more sensitive and the older the child, the more critical this will be.

The areas covered in interviews with children would include everything in the problem profile and/or specific corroborative data, if a particular disorder is suspected. There is little information about how comprehensively interviews are conducted before particular professionals arrive at their conclusions concerning the child. It is accepted that the more comprehensive and probing these are, the more reliable will be the assessment based upon them, although this is still more conjecture than fact.

Response to environment

All behaviour has a social context and develops according to however best a person can survive. Thus, abnormality can be the result of a person with abnormal propensities (such as psychosis) attempting to adapt to a *normal environment* or a person with normal features attempting to adapt to an *abnormal environment* (such as abusive parents).

This is why it is crucial to place as much emphasis on identifying and evaluating the characteristics of the environment as it is to expend effort on determining the child's peculiarities. Unfortunately, in most professional assessments, such as those by psychologists and psychiatrists, this is not the case. Much greater emphasis and professional weight is given to diagnosis of the major and minor clinical condition (Axes 1 and 2 on DSM III) than on 'psychosocial stressors' (Axis 4) which are more ambiguously, less systematically and, therefore, much less comprehensively covered, and without the aid of a checklist.

This is done partly in the belief that others concerned with the child's 'psychosocial' environment will have carried out and be able to provide the clinician with the relevant quantity and quality of information on which to base a rounded clinical judgment. This is, however, rarely the case. To our knowledge, the Problem Profile Approach is the only formalized system of assessment which demands the same comprehensive (and prompted) coverage of the environment of the children as their clinical condition.

Children from cultural and ethnic minorities

Culture, as the embodiment of a sense of order and values, is an overarching source of influence on behaviour. Its influence, however, is inadequately understood unless the behaviour being dealt with is highly explicit and well documented. It provides children with a series of stimuli to which they react and sets down the boundaries of what is an appropriate response. In increasingly multi-valued and multi-racial societies, we need to be aware of the different power structures at work, and the propensity of the more powerful group to subvert the racially and culturally less powerful by negatively evaluating behaviour and characteristics which are appropriate in their own culture. Any cultural or racial minority, if it can be so identified at all, is at risk of such negative evaluation, as we know from reactions to particular religions, colour, and levels of income or difficulty by particular sections of society.

Awareness of cultural factors demands understanding what is proper and normal in that particular culture, in order to evaluate the normality of children's behaviour, as suggested above under response to environment. It also demands awareness of the appropriate terminology, so that derogatory labels and unintentionally negative measures are not applied. The results of assessment must then be checked to ensure that it is free of unintended slurs and loaded value judgments.

Both behavioural norms and our knowledge of them are a matter of degree. The more 'invisible' the culture and the less your knowledge about its general norms, the more difficult it will be to interpret the child's abnormality. In this context, given the normal variations of a family even within one sub-culture, we can begin to see how cautious we must be in the assessment of abnormality. So, for example, if a family are used to incantations and divinations as a way of communing with ancestral spirits, then the child's incantations in response to a sign which may not be immediately apparent to the clinician can seem like an hallucination. The degree of ease or difficulty of interpreting the impact of the culture is, in part, related to the degree to which a sub-culture is integrated within the wider prevailing culture. But the impact even of such integration is a matter of conjecture rather than of fact.

Cultural norms seem to be more applicable to 'social' behaviour, e.g. stealing, sexual promiscuity, than to the more florid psychopathological disorders such as psychoses. There are, however, grey areas, e.g. in affective disorders which have a strong cultural component in self-evaluation.

It is important to respect the different views of a racial minority, however divergent they may be, and not to make judgmental comments about them. The clinician should ask for help from a member of the culture or the sub-culture in identifying the abnormality and seeking information about the prevailing norms from referral sources, parents and the children themselves. A particularly important point in relation to adolescents from racial and cultural minorities is that some or much of the abnormality may be best understood in terms of self-perceptions of prejudice, mistreatment, and what may be legitimate responses to them.

Anti-social children

Such children and adolescents may or may not present any other abnormality than their anti-social behaviour. They are likely to come to attention after a history of more or less well established anti-social behaviour, associated with negative and resistive attitudes to authority. From considerable research information, we also know that the parents and wider social contexts of such children are also likely to be anti-social in attitudes and behaviour and, therefore, to have instilled in their children considerable suspicion of authority figures who are likely to be involved in their assessment. By the time a young person reaches specialists, she or he also has a history of probable past interventions which have failed, thus reinforcing the young person's difficulty with adult figures.

A major task of such adults is, therefore, deciding how to present themselves to the child – whether as an advocate for the child, someone who is trying to do a dispassionate job or an authority figure. Although each of these approaches has its merits (with the dispassionate stance being the response of choice), nevertheless the others may have to be adopted depending on the young person and the circumstances at hand. All clinicians have their own favourite repertory of responses to anti-social young people and developed means of communicating with them.

Given the background of youngsters, however, establishing rapport is as important as it is often difficult, since often a broadly unco-operative, defensive, denying response pattern from the young person is likely.

It seems, therefore, important to adopt a straightforward, always truthful stance to the young person, which says effectively, 'I have been asked to give an opinion about why you do . . . and suggest what should be done with you, so I'd welcome your help to make sure that I do not make any big mistakes in what I say about you.'

On occasions, it may be appropriate to 'paradox' the young person in order to bring out a truthful response. So the clinician can say to the young person, 'If I seem to be getting to anything sensitive you don't want to talk about, just say "I don't know".' Such paradoxing, however, only works with young people who are not bright enough to understand its purpose and who are yet alert enough to separate it from the more traditional shoulder shrugging, indifferent responses.

Explicit questions about known offences and attitudes to them may provoke truthful answers because usually they cannot be denied. However, such youngsters frequently and through long practice with various authority figures, have a standard 'I don't know' response and other denial tendencies which become more prevalent and persistent the more sensitive the probed area becomes. It is thus well known that young people suspected of sexual abuse, as perpetrators (and often as victims), are likely to continue denying that they have committed any offences over an extended period until they are left with no alternative through carefully wrought confronting.

Confronting is not the same as having confrontation. Particularly with older, stronger, potentially more aggressive youngsters, the clinician has clearly to weigh up the advantages of deeper probing against the disadvantages of increasingly angering the young person who may react by verbal and physical violence. It is in this area that circular questioning in the form of 'What do you think your best/worst friends/parents/police/people here would say about you?' may come in handy.

Just in case the above comments place the 'negative' onus of these issues on the young people, the clinician should be equally chary of information from the police and others with a vested interest in the outcome of clinical assessment. Information from these sources should be treated with caution and tested against what the young person says.

In this context the clinician would wish to ascertain:

- *known* offence history
- any offences not recorded
- when started and why carried on
- ABC of the offences
- whether in groups or solo
- whether opportunistic or planned
- perception of payoff
- who is to blame for the offences

- perception of impact on self and others
- any compunctions about offending
- general attitude to offending
- evaluation of prospects

Sexually abusive adolescents

As already indicated, such young people show a high level of defensiveness which may mask whatever other personality and intellectual difficulties they may have. Indeed, the ease, nonchalance or underhandedness of the responses to probing are themselves germane to the grossness of disorder. It is usually young people with very poor social sensitivity, superficial fellow feeling or shallow emotional responses who tend to give easy and unconcerned answers. On the other hand, reluctance to answer cannot be directly interpreted as embarrassment or depth of affect, for the reasons indicated above.

However, in both child victim and adult rape cases, there is considerable denial of offences or, if not offence then of personal responsibility for it. Unless the young person is seriously mentally handicapped or suffers from gross conduct disorder and total lack of sensitivity, considerable denial is likely.

The aim of assessment of such young people is to identify the extent and kind of disorder, its complexity and meaning for the adolescent, pervasiveness and preoccupation with the behaviour in the young person's psychological make up, all with a view to estimating possible risk and need for special treatment. A similar structure and content of questioning to that indicated above would be relevant. Additionally the following focal areas may be addressed:

- onset and type of sexual abusing
- antecedents of offending
- consequences of offending
- use of aggressive/violent/sadistic behaviour
- opportunistic/premeditated behaviour
- age and sex of victim/relationship to offender
- attitude towards victim/perception of victim's experience
- victim behaviour
- attitude to offence
- onset and type of deviant sexual experiences
- attitudes and feelings towards deviant sexual experiences
- exposure to deviant sexual role models/learning
- experience of physical/sexual abuse
- exposure to pornography
- onset and types of non-deviant sexual experiences
- attitudes and feelings towards non-deviant sexual experiences
- sexual identity and preferences
- level and sources of sexual knowledge

- heterosexual skills
- attitudes to women
- offence fantasies/sexual fantasies
- sexual anxieties
- sexual dysfunctions
- nature and extent of self-disclosure
- insight into sexual problems/attitude to treatment

Sensorily impaired children

These are usually children with visual and/or auditory impairment ranging in seriousness from total blindness and deafness to relatively small degrees of impairment. Specialist examination to determine the extent and severity of such impairment is usually a specialist job and will not, therefore, be covered in this book. Our concern is with those children where impairment occurs in association with other difficulties, the assessment of which should take such impairment into account. A major difficulty in determining the role of impairment in children's disorders is that, other than in explicit cases (of for example, developmental retardation), the relationship cannot be specified with any degree of certainty. The clinician should, therefore, consider how much resource should be expended on attempting to evaluate it.

Visually impaired children
The main difference of these children from others is that they cannot respond to visual cues and are less likely to do well with a largely visual language and environment, particularly at the younger ages. Otherwise questions and other interview material should be the same as for other children. Indeed, in certain visually impaired children, particularly the brighter and older ones, an acute ear, both for content and nuance, seems to function. Therefore, there should be no general problem in assessing such children as long as no recourse has to be made to visual material.

Inevitably, there will be major reliance on other sources of information than the children, which is why behavioural assessment and its ability to produce relatively objective information is particularly important in assessing them. The reason is that children themselves cannot account for visually determinable antecedents (e.g. being bullied by a bigger boy) and consequences. Their response, therefore, must be shaped by auditory or other stimulation and internal conceptualization of events. Even though those events cannot be seen, they mediate the child's responses. They therefore merit serious consideration even if they should be checked against other information.

Hearing impaired and non-communicating children
The above point is even more acute in the area of hearing impaired children. Available evidence suggests that hearing impairment is more often associated with behaviour disorders than visual handicap. This is

because of the critical role of language in cognitive and social development of the child. A hearing impaired child is likely both to fail to acquire concepts and to acquire idiosyncratic ones, particularly if brought up with parents who are themselves hearing impaired. There is, for example, a suggestion that hearing impaired children are more often subject to sexual abuse because of their inability to pick up relevant social cues about the unacceptability of abuse, to disclose it and identify the perpetrators. The difficulty indicated here is that many deaf children also have major speech problems. The normal forms of communicating with the child cannot, therefore, be utilized. Because we are often unsure of how the hearing impaired child may be conceptualizing events, we are unable to interpret their reactions.

To deal appropriately with this difficulty, it is evident that information from the child can only be obtained by a signer who is not only good at this skill but is sufficiently expert in psychopathology to interpret what is being said. Given the generally poor services for the hearing impaired, particularly at the specialist level, this is likely to present a major difficulty. However, once such communication has been established, normal assessment can be carried out, paying due regard to the cautions sounded above.

Many children suffering from pervasive developmental disorders, such as autism, are also non-communicating. There is, on the whole, little effort made to interview them. Information is usually gleaned from other sources which helps to establish quickly the extent of the disorder, as is evident from high-level interrater reliability in the diagnosis of this disorder.

Children who are 'electively mute' present similar difficulties to other non-communicating children. Depending on the time-scale involved and the urgency of the assessment, such young people can be placed in a highly nurturant and emotionally caring environment which usually unfreezes them in order to allow verbal communication. If, however, this is not possible then the clinician must rely on observational data and detailed questions to referral agents, parents and others who have known the child. The degree of interpretation of data is usually considerable and the reliability of the assessment is not usually known. However, if diagnosis is avoided and emphasis is laid instead on a descriptive assessment of the problem profile type, then there is little danger of unreliable labelling of a child unwilling to communicate.

Sexually abused children

This is an area of major concern for professionals and is being increasingly presented for assessment. In this brief note, our concern is not to provide a guide to what to look for in order to corroborate or rule out the probability of abuse but rather to alert the clinician to particular considerations in the process of assessment. These arise from the complex of reactions surrounding sexual abuse of children and young people – in the children themselves, the family, social agencies and the public. The older the child being interviewed, the greater the frequency of the abuse, the longer the duration of abusive events and the more recent the abuse, the greater will be the child's sense of betrayal, powerlessness, and guilt.

To an abused child everyone, including the clinician, is potentially suspect because children (like everyone else) generalize perceptual phenomena which, in this case, include generalization from the non-protecting or abusive adult to the assessor.

The chief purpose of assessment of such children is to enable them to disclose and to establish whether abuse has taken place. Rapport is, therefore, crucially important and places considerable demands on the clinician for achieving it with different age groups. So drawing materials and anatomical dolls may be necessary in a non-distracting atmosphere for evaluating the reactions of a very young child. These materials are not appropriate to an adolescent who, over and above considerable privacy and confidentiality, requires different ways of relating to and being empowered by the investigator to disclose the dimensions and consequences of abuse.

There is some professional controversy about whether the investigator should be of the same gender as the abused child or different. Strong arguments have been propounded for both. There is still no consensus. However, the balance of argument seems to lean towards suggesting that the interviewer's ability and skill, including establishing non-threatening rapport and drawing out accurate information from the child, is more important than gender. In any case, *co-working* not just with the child but also others involved, including family and other professionals, is the preferred mode of operation in investigating sexual abuse, for the protection of the assessor and cross-validation of the work. It can thus ensure a gender mix to optimize the child's responses. We do not yet know enough about this phenomenon (despite enormous activity) to be categorical.

In this area of assessment, the investigator's concern is not just with facts but also with the child's thoughts, feelings and extent of traumatization, particularly associated with force and hurt. From the evidence available it appears that the satisfactoriness of the child's relationship with the non-abusive parent (almost always the mother) and relationship with her is often most important in predicting long-range responses. The better the relationship between the mother and the child, the less traumatic the long-term consequences are seen to be. Finding out about family relationships seems, therefore, to be germane to the total assessment of abuse.

Given the public reaction and children's often observed confusion and guilt in relation to sexual abuse, it is crucial to frame question in an open-ended way which does not suggest or reinforce the child's sense of guilt or imply complicity in the abuse. The older the child and the more complex the circumstances of the abuse, the more important this is likely to be.

With adolescents, all these issues take on much greater and more urgent weight. Adolescents are generally less ready to disclose. This is particularly true of boys whose sense of shame and powerlessness is more deeply rooted in a male-dominated culture and leads, therefore, to their greater unwillingness to disclose. With adolescents the approach to exploration of the abuse has to be much more gentle and tangential. The investigator has to be alert to the implications of what is said, non-verbal cues, refusals to discuss as well as expressions of direct denial, anger and explosive reactions.

Issues become much more fraught and complex if the adolescent has done something which has provoked a coercive reaction, such as taking an overdose and ending up in a hospital, or committing vengeful arson, which has resulted in being locked up. The young person's anger at this fate compounds and confuses those of the abuse, from which it must be unravelled and separated. In the case of troublesome adolescents particularly, it is likely that anti-social behaviour may mask reactions to previous and current sexual abuse, thus appearing as anti-social conduct disorder. Evidence suggests that much behaviour of this kind may be a form of long-range, adaptive anger to sexual abuse which, in the case of boys, has been externalized.

It may, therefore, be worthwhile to plan a series of interviews with the young person which proceed gradually from the relatively simple and unprovocative to the more complex and sensitive material. The Problem Profile Approach provides a good structure for either sequential planning or serially more complex probings.

Investigators should also be aware that with the greater prominence given to sexual abuse and the currently accepted view that any disclosure should be accepted at face value, some young people are likely to claim sexual abuse as an excusatory, explanatory reason for their anti-social behaviour. The investigator is clearly in a dilemma as to how much weight to place on such a disclosure. There are no surefire guidelines available. The only thing that can be done is to ensure that a detailed enough history has been taken to allow the identification of the particular pattern of the behaviour, the factors and contexts surrounding it and whether and how much it can be more parsimoniously explained by other factors. Many of these factors are entailed in the process of collecting information already outlined and the organization of assessment to which we now turn.

6

Information for Assessment

The amount and kind of information and the way it is used are the major determinants of the quality of assessment carried out. 'Information', in our context, is a general term which covers everything that is or may become known about a person. Information is communicated and set out in the form of questions and statements, whether 'opinions' or 'facts', which describe persons or events and have different probabilities of being *false*. The significance of this qualification is that no statement about a human being, however objective and rigorous, can be said to be 'true', with the implicit assertion 'certainly'. Statements are made about one set of people by another who, given their different backgrounds, education, orientation and interests, are likely to be more or less off the mark. It is possible to evaluate information and determine its degree of error according to the same criteria as assessments, mainly reliability and validity.

Sources of information

In general terms, information for assessment is gleaned from one or more of three main kinds of source: referral, proximal and specialist.

Referral sources
These sources include all those persons and agencies who have identified and defined a child as having problems which warrant intervention. The referral agency, whether a parent, the police, family doctor or anyone else, must have perceived an unacceptable condition (for example, temper tantrums, offending, unexplained injuries) to have referred the child. This 'unacceptable condition' can be further defined by the official agency which is at any time dealing with the child according to its own standard procedures and can often provide additional information about the history and development of the child from its own particular viewpoint. This information may relate not only to the child's contact with that particular agency, but also other aspects of background and current status. The amount and quality of information available from referral sources is dependent on the degree and quality of contact between them and the subject as well as their willingness to part with that information.

The agency or person who has referred the child for assessment may or may not have a great deal of information but at least would know why the referral has been made and what the purpose of assessment should be. Depending on the amount of information available, the referral source can be asked questions following the six problem areas. This may include other elements set out in a standardized form, as below.

Referral interview prompts

1 Biographical information, such as name, age, current family state, schooling.
2 Reason for referral. If many reasons, what order of importance from the referral agent's point of view.
3 Examples of each of the problems; the most severe and recent.
4 What does referral source believe started the problem(s) and what is sustaining or exacerbating it/them? Is there a particular pattern of association with time, place, people and events?
5 What are the immediate known consequences of the problem (behaviour)? Are they broadly negative or positive? How? Who mediates or produces the consequences?
6 What is the history of previous intervention and with what consequences?
7 What does the referral agent want from the referral?
8 What strengths may be utilized in the child, family, community and others to help resolve the difficulties?
9 What particular difficulties does the referral source believe militate against satisfactory treatment of child?

Proximal sources

These include all other agencies and persons who have had contact with the child and who may be able to provide information about specific areas and contexts of functioning. These persons and agencies are potentially numerous though the depth to which any one may be explored can vary from the simplest to the most complex. In assessment, the child, family (both nuclear and extended), neighbours, school, police, clergy, voluntary and statutory agencies which have been involved, as well as friends of the family and any other concerned persons, may provide information regarding the child's development, and express views regarding the extent, depth, source and the course of the problems. Information from parents and schools is of particular significance in highlighting the child's problems because of their close and prolonged involvement. A search should be made to find out whether there is a person or an agency which has had particularly close contact with the family and who may be able to provide a different perspective on the child's problems.

Clearly the information will vary in content, perspective and detail. But more importantly, it will vary in terms of reliability, validity, usefulness and other criteria. In general terms and from the research evidence, it is not possible to state categorically that one source of information is 'better' than the others, if for no other reason than that the degree and kind of involvement with the child may well shape the information given. For example, whilst parents are most knowledgeable about their children, the extent of this knowledge is determined by the level and quality of their involvement with the child. If the child is suspected of being abused by them or is drifting into trouble because of their poor supervision, the information they give is likely to be less than wholly accurate. Here, as elsewhere, perceptions of why the information is being sought and the use to which it will be put, i.e. concern with 'social desirability', will to an (unknown) extent determine the responses given.

Specialist sources

These include all those persons who may provide information regarding one particular area of functioning in which they have some form of expertise. Physicians and allied personnel would provide information about aspects of physical functioning; psychologists and specialist teachers about cognitive performance; social workers, experienced case workers, and those who work with families about its structure and dynamics; psychologists and others, trained to observe and assess small group behaviour, can evaluate social competence; a wide range of people who work with problem children, but particularly psychiatrists, psychologists, intermediate treatment and residential workers can provide a measure of the child's potential for committing anti-social acts and present an appropriately complex picture of personality structure and levels of emotionality and control.

It is important to remember that even the specialists using the most rigorous techniques operate within a margin of error. The size of the error varies according to individual competence and the potential of the methods used to obtain the information and is almost always unknown. Professional reputation may be a guide to reliable and useful information but has, nevertheless, to be treated with considerable caution. This is particularly important if there is information contradicting expert opinion or when the expert pronouncements are likely to have particularly serious implications for the child. As always, consensual views arrived at through *open* assessment by a group of knowledgeable people exercising reasonably equal power are likely to be the best safeguard against idiosyncratic judgments. Organization of assessment is discussed in Chapter 7.

However, despite any ambiguities of information, the risk presented by or to the child may be so great that even dubious information has to be treated as if it were 'certain fact', but such a situation should only arise in exceptional and emergency conditions, e.g. if the child may have been sexually abused. As soon as the crisis has been dealt with it should be possible to try and establish the limits of the acceptability of information. There are new safeguards built into recent British legislation, demanding open accountability in a judicial context for coercive measures taken with children and their parents.

Children's perceptions

People do not see the world and what happens in it in uniform ways but, rather, according to their own background and expectations. Although these may be similar, they may also be divergent from each other in important details. A person caught up in a stressful situation is likely to perceive the event differently from another who is watching the event from afar. Further, a particular person's reasons for committing an act may be different from the reasons perceived by someone else. It is not possible to establish the truth of one set of perceptions against the other in any satisfactory way other than through the use of 'consensus'. But consensus reflects power and authority, whether individual or collective, rather than necessarily the validity of individual perspectives.

In the context of assessment, children's views of what has happened to them are rarely sought and are frequently discounted on the grounds that children have neither the maturity nor the intellectual competence to make valid judgments about their experiences. There is little empirical evidence to support such a contention. Depending on their intellectual and mental state and how secure they feel, children are capable of giving accurate information about themselves, matching that given by parents, teachers and others.

Aside from the relative validity of such observations, it is important to discover children's views of both their past and current state because these are additional and central sources of information regarding *their reasons* for behaving in particular ways. A variety of techniques can be used to help them describe those aspects of reality which impinge on them and shape the way they behave. Some aspects of this are discussed further in the next chapter.

Medium of information

All the information on a child can only be obtained through one or more of three activities: through asking questions of the child and a whole variety of other persons (questionnaire and interview data); observing and noting events (life data); and using specialized tests and measures (test data). These three types of activity – talking, watching and testing – provide *all* the information that may be used for constructing a comprehensive picture of children and their problems. In this book, considerably more space is devoted to observations and factors associated with them. This is because, as will be seen, observations are the basis of all other forms of assessment and many of the conditions applying to them are equally pertinent to other media of assessment. I discuss talking and watching here and address more formal testing at the end of the chapter.

Questionnaires and interviews

Talking is the most distinctive human activity. Questions can be the most efficient way of eliciting information from children about those aspects of their life of which they can be expected to be aware. Talking can be structured in a form which ranges from paper and pencil questionnaires (as substitute for asking questions out loud) through formal interviews to free floating conversation in a natural setting. The criteria applied to all forms of assessment, such as reliability, validity, usefulness and rigour, are relevant to the form of such questioning and the degree of structure that may be imposed on it.

Questionnaires   In order to elicit factual information, questionnaires may be developed which are applied under standard conditions so that standard data may be obtained. The design of questionnaires, their administration and responses to them are complex subjects which will not be pursued here. It is, however, important to remember that the greater the structure in the form of questioning, the more easily its reliability can be established, but at the price of more restricted information and creating an 'official' atmosphere which is not conducive to an appropriate relationship outside research and coercive settings. There are ways of mitigating such an impact by the way the questionnaire is introduced and help with its completion given.

There are numerous questionnaires available which cover almost every field. The Further Reading section for this chapter and subsequent ones in Part II provide a starting point for further exploration of the field.

Interviews   Interviewing has been described as 'conversation with a purpose'. The purpose of the conversation is normally to obtain information which relates to facts about the child (such as age and school history), descriptions and evaluations of development (e.g. peer relationships) and highly interpretative accounts of child's attitudes and perceptions. The degree of interpretation involved applies both to the subject and to the interviewer and accounts for the large margin of error in both the reliability and validity of interviewing as a technique.

Interviews can be conducted either on a dimension of structure which ranges from a detailed 'interview schedule' (a predetermined format and wording of questions) to a broad discussion which eventually covers the area of concern in an unstructured manner. On the whole, interview schedules are thought to be more satisfactory because they ensure that an area is totally covered and the questions are asked in a standard fashion which enables the comparison of one child with others in a relatively rigorous way. Interview schedules can be geared to factual information ('How many children are there in your family?'), fixed alternative questions ('Do you like your father?'), or open-ended questions ('What do you think will happen to you?').

As with all other forms of assessment, the questions asked in an interview are shaped by their setting and purpose. These aspects also determine the level and complexity of the interview and the degree of rigour brought to bear on it. Thus, the interviewing of a young person for purposes of 'sectioning' under the Mental Health Act would be more exhaustive and rigorous (one hopes) than one which seeks to establish whether a child wishes to pursue one career rather than another.

The advantages of interviewing lie in the fact that it is the easiest and most natural form of obtaining information from and about children. It is flexible, capable of being adapted to individual circumstances of particular children, and can produce information about areas of child's functioning, such as his hopes and anxieties, which may not be open to scrutiny by other methods. It is a particularly useful tool for the assessment of children, especially those who, for intellectual or other reasons, are put off by formal situations. It also has the advantage of allowing direct comparison of the statements about a child among the various assessors, and enables probing into reasons for and contexts of a child's behaviour without which both observations and test results are deficient and arid.

The difficulties of interviewing lie in achieving adequate levels of reliability and validity, reducing the potentially large error margin in the perception of both questions and answers, and the inherent variability of these answers according to child's mood, circumstances and expectations of the outcome of the interview. Interviewing requires high levels of training, skill and other personal characteristics such as sensitivity, warmth and empathy. It is costly in terms of both time and specialized personnel. There are, therefore, also significant restrictions on who can use it to advantage.

With the importance attached to verbal communication, its currency among all groups of people concerned with problem children, interviewing is the most immediately appealing and culturally acceptable method of obtaining information and one that can be rigorously pursued. Its advantages can be maximized through the use of interview schedules which, at the same time, take account of the unspoken words such as silences, facial expressions and emphases with which speech is interspersed. Investing in its good quality use is likely to pay handsome dividends.

Observation of behaviour

Observation encompasses the full range of activities concerned with watching or witnessing the behaviour of another person actively or passively, directly or otherwise, and under a variety of circumstances with varying degrees of predetermined structure. Much observation takes place incidentally and without particular purpose. Deliberate observation, however, is undertaken in an attempt to identify, describe, explain and suggest possible solutions for problems presented or experienced by a youngster. Behaviour to be observed covers the full range of appearance, speech, mannerisms, moods, interactions with and acts towards the self and others, in other words how the individual behaves. In the end, even the most powerful questionnaires and tests have to be validated against what a child *does*. Observation is, therefore, the cornerstone of all assessment.

In the present context, observation can be seen as ranging on a continuum from the external and the visible to the internal and the inferred. All human behaviour is or can be watched and then described by an adverb, such as 'intelligently' or 'selfishly'. The adverb is then used as a basis for attributing a quality to the person ('intelligent', 'selfish') which in turn becomes the basis for inferring a general characteristic of the person such as 'intelligence', 'selfishness'. There are major complications, both theoretical and practical, in this process which are outside the scope of this book to pursue.

On the surface, observation implies no theoretical bias in that it 'simply notes' the behaviour. It can be used equally as a basis for explanations and interventions which range from one extreme of psychoanalysis to the other of behaviour modification. However, it is now clear that on both philosophical and technical grounds, no observation of behaviour is wholly 'atheoretical'. Every observation has to utilize a system of 'naming' or 'classification' which, in turn, presumes a particular focus of interest and perhaps theoretical orientation. This recognition has received a major impetus from the development of behavioural assessment and other forms of behavioural intervention based on learning theory which, in turn, emphasize observable behaviour. This has led to more rigorous behavioural observations, whose chief features are: a close association between assessment and intervention; emphasis on detailed specification of variables; emphasis on quantification; emphasis on current environmental 'cause and effect' linkages; individual differences in behavioural characteristics and determinants; emphasis on publicly observable events; emphasis on observation of behaviour in the natural environment; evaluation of assessment procedures and carrying out treatment alongside continuous assessment as an integrated 'self-correcting' system.

Many of the elements above apply to all observations, though they are conceptually and practically usually closely linked with rigorous psychological intervention, particularly behaviour modification. The emphasis on observable and current behaviour is an important and necessary corrective to the tendency of dynamically orientated professionals who claim to 'notice' and in some other ways infer unobservable characteristics of their patients or clients. It should, however, be noted that such detailed, highly specific observations require extensive skilled resources which are available only in either research projects or highly specialized settings where the treatment sophistication warrants the necessary effort.

Functional analysis

Such behavioural approach has led to specification of behaviour for purposes of intervention, which is fundamentally useful in any approach to difficulties presented or experienced by children. The basic premise is that although any *behaviour* may be *triggered* by any number of factors, its *probability of being repeated* is determined by whether the child is *rewarded* or *punished* by (likes or dislikes) the outcome.

This demands breaking down the behavioural sequence into (1) *antecedents*, (2) *behaviour* and (3) *consequences*. This provides the ABC of 'functional analysis'. Antecedents include the children's fundamental characteristics, such as genetic and physiological make up, intelligence, personality, past experiences, propensity to particular behaviours and perceptions of the desirability of the outcome. They also include similar features of all the other people interacting with the child, as well as the 'natural history' of events and circumstances in which the child may get caught up – such as gang violence or an abusive family.

Behaviour simply refers to what the child does in a particular set of circumstances, specified in more detail below. Consequences range from the most relevant, visible and salient features of what follows on the behaviour, such as material rewards, particular experiences and other people's reactions. The critical factor is the child's evaluation of whether the outcome was good or bad, worth repeating on not. In the shaping of any behaviour (covering all but strictly physical and physiological features of child's life), such a functional analysis is indispensable.

The behavioural environment

The focus of all observations is behaviour, and all behaviour occurs in an environment. The 'reality' of that environment includes all elements which impinge on children and to which, at any given time, they respond. This reality has a number of components each of which, depending on circumstances, may assume particular importance. The more important of these are:

The self This is the collection of experiences, expectations and attitudes of the child, her particular make up, previous experiences of stress and coping, perceptions of what is happening to her now and expectations of what is likely to happen if she behaves in particular ways. This is the major element of what has been referred to as 'antecedents'.

The peer group Much research evidence suggests that in group settings children's behaviour is affected much more by their peers than by adults. The composition of the peer group, its dynamics and the way it impinges on a child at any given time, the norms of group behaviour and child's perception of these norms, and how they may be enforced, affect the way the child is likely to behave in that particular environment. Many problem behaviours are generated and maintained by peer-group pressure, just as the reverse may become true depending on the prevailing circumstances. Children, because of their diverse 'selves', respond differently to prevailing group climates. In assessing children it is, therefore, important to consider the effect of the group in which they operate.

The adults Adults are in a position of authority, and control much of the (more obvious) rewards and punishments that the child is likely to receive from the environment. They are, therefore, powerful determinants of the child's behaviour. Additionally, children's past experiences of adults, and current perceptions and expectations of them, determine how they are likely to respond which, in turn, will affect adult behaviour toward them. Frequently, adults in a position of observing children are unaware of the image they project, the complexity of their interaction, and the degree to which this determines children's behaviour towards them and the wider environment.

Another aspect of adults' interactions with children, disordered or otherwise, is their view of themselves, how they see their task in relation to the children and their personal values and goals. An adult who does not like, is threatened by and intolerant of ups and downs in children's behaviour is more likely to behave in an oppressive and derogatory fashion towards them. This may provoke antagonistic behaviour which he will then describe as the 'child's problem'. We should always be careful in analysing adults' statements about children and consider how much of what is said reflects their own particular views, rather than children's persistent characteristics.

The physical environment   There is little systematic knowledge about the effect of physical environment on behaviour. Apart from certain features such as temperature, humidity, amount and quality of space and colours, the most that can be said is that the effect of the environment depends on children's past associations with it and their current perceptions of its purpose and impact.

This aspect is usually given little prominence in evaluating children's (or for that matter, adults') behaviour. Increasing research, however, shows that certain factors, such as overcrowding and with it the invasion of children's personal space, are important determinants of behaviour, though to what extent and in what manner is not yet established. In the present state of knowledge, little can be done other than looking at the physical environment and noting any unusual environmental features which *may* be associated with problem behaviour.

Assessment in structured environments

Most children, even when they present problems, live in their homes. Their problems can be investigated while they continue to live at home. Most workers who visit the family or see the child on a day-to-day basis are carrying out an assessment of this sort. However, specialist staff, such as psychologists and psychiatrists, are in short supply and the economics of organization frequently dictate that the child should be taken to them. Any environment in which specialists operate – school, clinic, or day centre – is of necessity a 'structured environment'.

The term 'structured' is ambiguous. It is not always clear whether those who use it intend to denote physical limits to and regulation of behaviour, or to the formality of relationship with the children and the process to which they are subjected. In this context a structured environment means one which is not wholly fluid or variable according to the wishes of the children and others who live with them, but one that is intended to fulfil a particular task and produce a specified end product. In this respect a child guidance clinic, a surgery, a day centre, are all instances of a structured environment.

The reasons for seeking a structured environment are often that the appropriate personnel are not available to carry out the assessment in an unstructured setting (such as the child's home); a child's behaviour cannot be systematically assessed in the natural environment (because there are too many distracting variables); the target behaviour may not be manifested frequently enough in a natural environment to warrant the expenditure of resources. The child is, therefore, assessed in a structured setting in which the target behaviour (such as temper tantrums or aggressiveness) can be precipitated, and environmental characteristics and stimuli can be systematically varied and controlled.

There may be other overriding reasons for removing the child from the normal setting than gaining better assessments. The most common reason is that they are likely to suffer other physical or psychological harm if they stay where they are. Alternatively, they may present the public, the family or other children with such risk that protection of others may warrant their removal from the normal setting.

'Structure' is a matter of degree and as such it can be varied to resemble more or less the child's natural setting, depending on the requirements of the assessment. The important consideration is to ensure that the new environment is sufficiently sensitive and flexible to be able to discriminate between relatively stable behavioural characteristics of the child and those which are stimulated by the new environment.

Numerous studies of children and their parents in a variety of structured settings have shown that such settings do not hinder good assessment. In general terms, there is little research or other evidence to suggest that the requirements of assessment and structure are incompatible or that the results of such assessment are less reliable and valid than they would be elsewhere. Validity of assessment in structured settings is particularly difficult to determine as they must elicit the same range of behaviours as appears in the normal environment of the child to be able to make sensible judgments. Because the range of behaviour in the normal environment is not known, it is not possible to see how such a requirement may be satisfied. If a child's behaviour is significantly different in the two settings, all that can be inferred is that the behaviour is more responsive to environmental stimuli than to stable personality characteristics. Such an inference would not mean that the assessment in one setting is more valid than the other. Depending on the seriousness and desired rigour of assessment, it may be necessary to vary environmental features systematically to discover which features stimulate what behaviours.

The behavioural environment is a complex of elements which interact and which together constrain and shape children's behaviour. Each factor must be taken into account, both separately and in interaction with others, in order to allow an understanding of the behaviour. In theory, this would be so onerous both conceptually and practically that no useful observations would be made. In practice, however, this is not as difficult as it sounds because a competent practitioner or agency dealing with the assessment of children is likely to build up a store of knowledge, intuitive or empirical, of the baselines of behaviour of a variety of children which have emerged from the interactions of all the above factors. It then becomes possible to make statements with varying degrees of probability, implicit or explicit, that for example 'this child is more aggressive than the normal run of children' or 'this child is more withdrawn than others in the same circumstances'. Such observations can and often are considered alongside other sources of information.

Observer variables
The meaning that observers place on children's behaviour enables them to make sense of that behaviour. Thus, some interpretation is involved in all observations. The observers' own predispositions and expectations through training and role perception are the major determinants of what interpretation they will place on the observed behaviour. These expectations provide the structure and format of observations. Who observes the behaviour is determined by considerations of economy, efficiency, involvement, reliability and validity of the outcome. Observers known to the child have obvious advantages in the ease with which they can observe familiar behaviour which might possibly change in reaction to an unfamiliar observer. But the closeness of observers to children does not necessarily increase the reliability or validity of their observations. Indeed, particularly in the case of problem children, those who are most familiar with them (such as parents) provoke and perceive behaviours which are part of continuing problem interactions. Furthermore, the information may be distorted in particular ways, even though it is an essential part of the total assessment. It is useful to remain aware of the effects of inter-personal perception on behaviour and arrive at an acceptable balance of familiarity and distance in determining who should do the observation.

The observer is like a measuring instrument, liable to make either constant or variable error. As such, the observer may interpret a child's behaviour too leniently – where 'bullying and intimidation' are described as 'teasing' – or too strictly – where a mild scrap is described as an 'act of violence'. One way of overcoming this is through the use of non-interpretive, micro-descriptions of behaviours; another is through using a wide range of observers.

An extension of observer error is termed the 'halo effect'. The behaviour of a child who is said or expected to be 'aggressive', 'depressed', or 'attention seeking' is more likely to be interpreted as falling into these categories than if child were not so labelled. The 'halo effect' cannot be eliminated, though it can be much reduced by having multiple observers, because most professionals take their interpretive cues from one another. The only satisfactory solution is to be aware of the force of such haloes and be ready to counteract them through seeking independent corroboration.

The point has already been made that every observation must be placed in the frame of reference of the assessor who is operating against a background of greater or lesser discipline and expertise. Physical acts such as seizures, bedwetting or stuttering are unusual because they are often involuntary and their interpretation may be relatively straightforward. In behaviour, on the other hand, there is little that is unpurposive to an observer and even less that is 'irrational'. What may be regarded as such by the observer may have a perfectly sound explanation, if the subject could or would give it. Furthermore, perceptions of intention, purpose and outcome of the same behaviour can be dramatically different according to who is the observer and who the observed.

All these factors are part of the complexity of human behaviour, which, though inconvenient from the viewpoint of scientific rigour, give it its unique fascination and flavour. The difficulties in categorizing behaviour cannot be logically overcome. However, the use of uniform frames of reference by groups of observers with uniform training, frequent cross-checking of the frames of reference, and shared cultural propensities by the observer and the observed can reduce the divergence to acceptable levels.

Sampling

Although attempts have been made to observe the 'totality' of children's behaviour, these have to be restricted to short periods because of the tremendous demands made on observers. In any case, no observation, however comprehensive, can be said to be exhaustive, because it is always possible to give examples of behaviours which had not been observed. All observations, therefore, relate to *samples* of behaviour. Such samples or portions of behaviour should be as representative as possible to enable appropriate inferences to be made about a child's behavioural characteristics. 'Representativeness' is a matter of degree, and can only be evaluated in relation to the time, duration, place and circumstances of the observation.

Sampling can be done according to either *time periods* during which the number of occurrences of a particular behaviour is noted or the specific *behaviour* (event) which can be observed as it occurs in due course. Each form of sampling has its own advantages and disadvantages. In general, time sampling is more useful where the target behaviours are relatively frequent and trained observers are available to record the occurrences of the behaviour.

Event sampling is more appropriate when the target behaviours are relatively infrequent and are not likely to occur at predictable intervals. Most of the more serious problem behaviours of children, such as self-destructiveness, aggression, depression and anti-social behaviour, are of the latter variety. Event sampling demands that a child's behaviour should be watched sufficiently closely so that such occurrences can be noted. In this respect, residential assessment in a clinic or other setting where children can be closely observed for long periods and under a wide set of conditions has a more useful role to play.

The frequently noted 'behavioural slopes' of systematic changes over time of a particular behaviour, can be regarded as resulting from the habituation or adjustment of the children to the observer and assessment environment. In order to ensure that behaviour is adequately sampled children must be observed in a variety of situations and in comparison with other children so that the relative frequencies of behaviour can be established.

Observation frames
Observations can be carried out either in general terms and subsequently divided into specific areas, or vice versa. As observation of behaviour can potentially cover the totality of human acts, it is not possible to provide an exhaustive list of categories of behaviour. Depending on the observer's frame of reference, particular behaviours will be observed. Specific observations related to the assessment of individual attributes will be presented in Part II of this book. At this stage it may be worthwhile to set out two different general formats of observation which encompass the larger part of children's behaviour and which may be found to be of particular value in observing them in groups. Detailed observation prompts pertaining to particular areas of difficulty are set out under each attribute in Part II.

Frame I
General behaviour Facial expressions, mannerisms, gait, manner of speech; Reaction to frustration, ability to tolerate frustration, reaction to levels of frustration; Expressed fantasy, day-dreams, expressions of goals and ambitions, any role play; Particular fears, unusually strong interest or avoidance in some particular activity, striking habits which appear peculiar or out of the ordinary; How much control over behaviour? Does control break down under certain conditions? What are the conditions? What is his self-image? What does he think are his assets and liabilities? What does he see as his biggest problem? What do you think of these? How often does he express and cope with hurt, anger, sadness, joy? Is he on the whole a happy or sad child? Is his anger shown by irritability or blow up, or is it kept in check?

Response to peers What sort of response does she seek from peers? What does she do to get it? How successfully? How does she react when she gets the response she has sought? What does she do when response is denied? Does she seek dominance or popularity or is she unconcerned about/untouched by the group? To what types of peers does she seem closest? Which does she avoid? How friendly is she with the others? How does she express friendliness? Whom does she come into conflict with? How does she express it? Is she good at judging the other children and regulating her own behaviour towards them? Does she seem to need the other children? Is she content to be alone? How often and under what conditions? How do the other children react to her? Is she popular, respected, disliked, feared, ignored? Is there a consensus of opinion about her? Is there any sexual interest in peers? How is it expressed? Attracted to any particular sub-groups? What are they like? How good is she at getting on with the other children? Does she get on better in large or small groups?

Response to adults Which of the above observations with peers also apply here? How often does he seek help, encouragement, affection? What form does it take? Does he get on with particular kinds of adults better or worse – male, female, older, younger, tougher, softer? Generally obedient or defiant? How does he show it? How often does he show aggression and in what form? How often sulky, worried, hostile, friendly, etc? How do adults here feel about him? Can he manipulate adult reactions? How accurately does he understand adult intentions and instructions?

Response to management What management techniques seem to work best to get her to comply? Which seem to reduce defiance? How does she respond to insight-giving discussions? Is she interested in discussions? What is her reaction to threat or implementation of sanctions? Does discussion or peer-group pressure help regulate her behaviour? How does she respond to limits set? Does it make a difference whether limits are obeyed by the rest of the group? In general, how does she respond to the structure of the day: rules, routines and activities? Do any particular rules, routines or activities give trouble?

Frame II
This frame is more appropriate to a residential setting, particularly with adolescents.

Physical Brief physical description: noise level, shouts a lot? Quiet? Activity level: never sits still; very lethargic?

Hygiene and dress Observations of what she does in this area, how much prompting needed to wash, how fussy about clothes; does she complain about clothes? does she mind what clothes she wears? Does she seem able to make her bed and keep her space tidy? Sleeping and eating – anything unusual?

Intellectual Thoughtful or not? Does he read much, and what does he choose to read? Does he produce ideas and suggestions which seem independent from the crowd or does he simply echo what has been said? Does he give constructive solutions to problems which arise or does he withdraw and look to others for the answer? What comments does he make about school work and classroom sessions? How does he react with games which require longer periods of concentration?

Language Is speech clear and distinct? Does he appear to have a reasonable vocabulary for his age? Can he describe his ideas adequately?

Does he resort to clichés and meaningless verbal substitutes? Can he converse? What about? Is there much repetitive content in his conversation?

Group behaviour   Has she proved constantly appealing to others? What does she do to gain popularity? Is it important to her to get group acceptance? What does she do when left out of things? Does she make friends quickly? What kind of children does she associate with? Does she restrict or ration her friendship? Does she help to introduce people to each other, or help with other children? Does she appear strongly attached to a peer-group culture and, as such, opposed to staff or adult ideas? If she falls out with a friend what follows on? Does she prefer to remain on her own? If influenced by peers will her behaviour change from previous characteristic levels of self-control, obedience, maturity, etc.? Can she be seen to be imitating other children?

Aggression–subversion   Does he fight much? What prompts him to hit others? Does he seek to establish a position of dominance? Does he swear at others or call them names? Does he plant stories, etc., and stir up conflict between others? Does he refuse to back down voluntarily from conflict situations? Are other children frightened or wary of him? Is he deliberately slow to carry out or understand staff instructions? Does he set up other children to annoy staff? Does he answer back a lot? Does he play up in front of others? Does he refuse to do as asked? Does he show overt aggression to adults and under what circumstances?

Sexual   Does she show special interest or embarrassment when sexual topics are discussed? Has she engaged in any mutual sex play? Does she discuss girl/boy friends or sex? Is she shy when undressing?

Social conformity   Does there appear to be deliberate over-conformity to staff wishes? Does he volunteer too much? Is he always too prompt in doing as told? Does he frequently mention reports and adults' views of him? Does he seek confirmation about how well he is doing?

Handling and authority   What is his reaction to various kinds of handling? Does he take advantage of slackness? Does he respond aggressively to directive management? Does he succumb to threat of sanctions? Can he function acceptably if treated as an 'adult'? Do environmental factors enter into his response to handling in a noticeable way? When surrounded by peers, or in an outside environment, does his response differ? Does he seem to respond well to a sympathetic approach? Is he easily reduced to tears, and if so, how? Does he appear to play adults off against each other? Does he actively try to get adult decisions changed by persuasion or non-co-operation? How far does he push his resistance, and how does this vary from person to person?

Emotional Tearful? Easily upset? Initial mood on first contact or arrival? How about mood changes? Does she get angry quickly? Does she calm down quickly? Does she laugh much? Is her mood infectious to other people? Is her face expressive of feelings or is everything hidden behind a mask? How does she react when she is clearly upset? Does she become hostile? Does she seek support and if so from whom? Does she appear to forget about the problem and divert attention elsewhere? Does she have temper tantrums?

General self-presentation Does he avoid being looked at? Does he look at people when he is talking? Is he secretive? Does he seem concerned about what people think of him? Is he unusually careful about his possessions? What are his reactions to self-criticism?

In evaluating the information in the above areas, it is necessary to recognize that individual behaviours have 'meaning' for the child and others in an integrated complex and are, in turn, triggered off by simple or complex stimuli. The stimuli may be observable or not. The behaviour may be recurrent or episodic, intense or low level, with varying degrees of active direction by the child. It is as important to note what terminates a particular behaviour as it is to note what triggers it off.

The behavioural environment in which a child is observed is capable of manipulation in order to determine the constancy or variability of the child's response to particular circumstances. The section on management in Frame I is an illustration of this. The child is deliberately subjected to various forms of management from soft to hard, fair to unfair, firm to indecisive, in order to note particular reactions. Such systematic variation of the behavioural environment is often not practicable in natural settings unless the adults are able and willing to adopt such roles.

Observational information is only as good as the accuracy with which it is placed in context, communicated and used for formulating problems and modes of alleviating them. It may, therefore, be necessary to develop and use specific observation sheets coded for particular children and/or specific behaviours as a way of providing reliable information if the circumstances allow and warrant it. Numerous observation schedules are available in both research literature and in commercial form.

Tests

Tests are collections of standardized items or measures intended to yield quantitative data. Their purpose is to differentiate between human beings in a structured, repeatable manner which reduces observer error and subjective judgments.

There is a wide array of tests covering many aspects of human behaviour – most aspects of physical functioning, intelligence, attainment, vocational aptitudes, social relationships, personality, attitudes and values.

Theoretically, the merits of tests lie in their relative objectivity: different users are able to get roughly the same response from the same subject. They can be specific to particular aspects of functioning, such as creativity or anxiety reaction; they are easy to validate against not only other tests but observable events; and they yield numerical results which can be easily computed and communicated. Their disadvantages lie in the tendency to glorify and lend weight to some highly dubious conclusions; susceptibility to distortion by the subjects based on perceived purpose of the test; tendency to 'reify' (give substance or make 'real') the often abstracted characteristic they measure; openness to vagaries of both tester and subject; assumption that significant words in a test mean the same to all children; and frequently poor validity against external criteria.

From a practical point of view, they have the advantage of structuring observations and yielding a great deal of information about a child. Their major limitation lies in the amount of training and skill needed to administer tests and interpret results and the consequent restrictions on their use. Frequently, the more valid and potentially significant a test, the greater are the restrictions on its use by unqualified personnel. Both the British Psychological Society and the American Psychological Association classify availability of tests according to the kind of persons who can use them. Most of the better validated tests fall into the most restricted category which can be used only by specially trained and accredited psychologists.

These limitations severely restrict the use of tests in the majority of assessment settings where the appropriately qualified persons are not available. For this reason, we have not cited particular tests for the assessment of problem areas. These may be pursued through the Further Reading lists in this book and by contacting test publishers.

Sequence of information

All information has a temporal context, past, present or future, even though in some languages the 'tense' may be disguised in particular constructions. Furthermore, we tend to see events as 'strings', 'chains' or sequences in order to make sense, predict and perhaps control them.

History

In order to make sense of the children's *current* condition, we often feel we need to see them against their background in order to establish a pattern which allows us to see the continuity, duration, developmental milestones and the stability of their behaviour in different contexts. The personal history also allows us to identify the children's response to different events and, therefore, become better able to predict their behaviour.

The exactness with which such complex historical information is elicited and utilized varies according to the type of assessment and the use to which it is being put. In psychoanalysis, for example, the child's history and experiences of parenting are a critical source of information, not only for identifying the child's disorder but also what should be done about it. In behaviour modification, on the other hand, less emphasis is placed on history, but more on the child's current condition. Even so, history is important in determining how well established or over-learned a pattern of behaviour is, in order to devise an appropriate treatment programme. Ascertaining the history of disorder should be seen strictly as an aid to determining the seriousness of the child's problem rather than as a major end in itself.

Personal history, which provides detailed information about significant events in a child's life, is an important source of material and can be obtained under the following headings:

Family list Members of the immediate family as well as other persons in the home.

Family setting Geographical setting, physical state of home and neighbourhood; economic status, standing in the community.

'Mother' and 'Father' Background: Origin, family life, education, job, employment stability
Personal characteristics and behaviour; intelligence, personality features, attitudes to authority and society; personal problems
Attitude and behaviour towards child; involvement with child; attitude to problem behaviour; methods of coping with problem behaviour; quality and degree of communication, support, guidance and affection; any evidence of physical, emotional and sexual abuse.

Parental relationships Stability of family life, strength of emotional bond, harmony, dominance and decision-making patterns; modes of coping with each other's problems; extent and quality of conflict and their consequences.

Siblings Extent, severity and pattern of problems; significant features; influence on child; rivalry and scapegoating; quality of emotional bond.

Child's development and behaviour Though main focus is on the onset, source and development of problem behaviour, it is also important to describe any notable positive events and characteristics.

Each section should bring out the response by the relevant people to child's problem behaviour and his reaction to intervention. Each section, therefore, comprises two parts, the second one of which will be devoted to the child's account and interpretation of *what happened and why*. This will emerge from comprehensive interviews with the child. Such interviews can be usefully structured in the following manner:

Child's physical state

School history from school(s), parents and child's view.

In the community from available sources of information and child's view.

Anti-social behaviour, if any (with dates and some indication of seriousness) and child's view.

Specialized intervention and its effects by whom; for how long. This deals with the child's view of referrals to and action by specialized agencies, such as school psychological services, medical and psychiatric services, court, probation, social services, and others.

These sections provide comprehensive information from referral and proximal sources to which specialist comments can be added as a result of the use of interviews, observations and tests.

Current state
This is the main concern of assessment, although as soon as it has been carried out, it itself becomes historical. Current state is determined according to whatever assessment framework is used, ranging from general superficial scan to deep probings of a particular part.

The need for and purpose of determining the current state depend in turn on the wider purpose of assessment. Different formats are used for current assessment, including mental state examination in psychiatry, PPA or other forms of professional assessment.

A major, and by now well-established, mode of determining the child's current state, particularly in a clinical setting, is the mental state or present state examination (MSE or PSE).

General schema for mental state examination
This schema has been specifically developed for psychiatric examination but it is, in general terms, no less relevant to others. Its chief utility is to 'here and now' as a background for interpreting presenting problems and impact of known history of disorder. It highlights the need for evaluating the child's state at several levels simultaneously, e.g. content, coherence, tone of verbal statements, correspondence with non-verbal signs, changes in response to the subject matter and a variety of others. To carry out such a complex task demands:

- minimum distraction for the interviewer and the child;
- some idea of what areas to cover and how to approach each area, and, therefore, the need for considerable preparation on the basis of referral information;
- simultaneous recording of questions and answers *at the time*, lest they should be forgotten.

The information gleaned is subject to distortion in recall and unobtrusive note-taking is difficult, even though children eventually get used to it. The increasing use of audio-visual techniques make this somewhat easier but such measures are highly time-consuming, which is why detailed MSE/PSE is used mainly for research or special assessment purposes, as for example in child sexual abuse cases or where the outcome is likely to be serious.

An outline of MSE is set out below:

Presentation	size, dress, grooming, posture, facial expressions eye contact;
Motor activity	general level, ability to sit still, fidgetiness, involuntary movements, lassitude, fine and gross co-ordination unusual gait;
Physical state	any evident sign or symptom of abnormal physical state including vision and hearing
Cognitive	general impression of intellectual level orientation in time and space knowledge about self level of general information distractibility attention span inquisitiveness
Speech	quantity and quality volume vocabulary rhythm clarity complexity
Thought content	readily forthcoming/has to be pulled out suspicious, fearful, cautious preoccupation, worries, fears hopes and wishes loves and hates fantasies and daydreams systematic distortions/hallucinations/delusions belonging/alienation view of self fluid, negative, unrealistic, positive
Emotional response	observable tension anxiety: general and specific sadness, wretchedness, despair

tearful – quiet/noisy weeping
anger, aggressiveness
embarrassment, shame
emotional warmth/involvement in topics
emotional range and complexity in relation to topics

Social response   reserve/expansiveness
confidence/shyness
friendliness/hostility
co-operativeness/resistance
change over the examination period and topics

Overall judgment of the examination

Evaluation of prospects

The identification of sequence in the development of children's difficulties is implicitly intended to identify the *trend* in their behaviour, thus throwing light on their prospects and the likely course of the risk they present or experience. In normal circumstances, prospects can be identified by 'extrapolating' or projecting forward what is known about the development of children's difficulties over a period of time. This process is, however, immensely complicated by not only the developmental trend of different forms of behaviour (some *usually* get better and some worse as we can see under each of the attributes in Part II), but also the considerable variability within each behaviour and child, depending often on unforeseen circumstances (e.g. the detection and departure of an abusing father, or mother finding a new partner).

Nevertheless, the difficulty of identifying trends and prospects is a matter of degree rather than of kind. Here also, the likelihood of prospects has a probability of error, as in the area of history and current state. It is important to give it at least the same rigorous attention as the others, because its acceptance provides the justification for whatever action may be taken concerning the child.

Having considered the central matter of information for assessment, we are now in a position to consider some of the issues that arise in relation to assessing children with particular problems.

Further reading

Barker, P. (1990) *Clinical Interviews with Children and Adolescents*, New York: Norton & Co. Inc.

Fiske, D.W. (1971) *Measuring the Concepts of Personality*, Chicago: Aldine.

Johnson, O.G. and Bommarito, J.W. (1971) *Tests and Measurements in Child Development: a Handbook*, San Francisco: Jossey Bass.

Jones, D.P. and McQuiston, M.G. (1988) *Interviewing the Sexually Abused Child*, London: Royal College of Psychiatrists/Gaskell.

McReynolds, P. (ed.) (1975) *Advances in Psychological Assessment*, San Francisco: Jossey Bass.

Othmer, E. and Othmer, S.C. (1989) *The Clinical Interview using DSM–IIIR*, Washington: Americal Psychiatric Press.

Savage, R.B. (1968) *Psychometric Assessment of the Individual Child*, Harmondsworth: Penguin.

Shouksmith, G. (1968) *Assessment Through Interviewing*, London: Pergamon Press.

Spitzer, R.L., Gibbon, M., Skodol, A.E., Williams, J.B.W. and First, M.B. (1989) *DSM–IIIR Case Book*, Washington: American Psychiatric Association.

7

Organization of Assessment

Assessment is a co-ordinated, purposive activity which involves different people and resources. To meet the objective of providing assessments efficiently, its resources and tasks must be organized. This chapter addresses some of the main issues in conducting assessment as a co-ordinated activity in professional settings, even if few facilities and services are now set up purely for purposes of assessment.

Resources

Material resources

These comprise, broadly speaking, buildings and equipment. Little is known about the specific building requirements for residential or centre-based day assessment, apart from such details as rooms with one-way mirrors for watching children at play or family therapy, and various specialist examination rooms. It is, nowadays, unlikely that buildings will be put up just for purposes of assessment or that these would be very different from many others designed to house children and those who look after them. The major consideration, therefore, should be to provide an environment for the adequate management and care of children. These include facilities for living (and sleeping), working, education and recreation. Adequate provision can usually be made for meeting these needs in warm, comfortable and attractive surroundings.

Additionally, care considerations demand that while children should be at all times observable, they should also be able to withdraw from this pressure in order to replenish personal reserves, if appropriate. In clinics and institutional settings a range of environments from open to closed areas, multi-purpose spaces such as common rooms, and factors such as different colours, textures and spatial complexities are required to stimulate a range of behaviours which may influence a child's behaviour and aid the final assessment.

The relationship of specific types of environment to behaviour patterns is unknown. Experience suggests that children, even those from very poor homes, respond favourably to civilized surroundings which are comfortable and aesthetically pleasing though not so extravagant as to frighten and alienate them. The need for durability of fabric and finish is a crucial aspect in the design of the environment to prevent rapid and accelerating deterioration of otherwise acceptable surroundings, particularly in facilities which deal with anti-social boys – girls seem less prone to vandalizing the environment.

The extent and diversity of material resources provided depends on the level at which the assessment is to be carried out. The creation of a 'normal' caring environment demands that children should have access to appropriate playthings and recreational equipment.

Need for assessment materials is dictated by the particular source of information being tapped. Tests, questionnaires, simulators and measuring instruments are available to make particular forms of assessment possible, though these are most likely to be utilized in restricted medical, educational and psychological arenas. Depending on the complexity of the organization, facilities may also be required for storage and retrieval of information.

Aspects of security

Secure accommodation is required for curbing the movement of those children who put themselves at severe risk or present unacceptable risk to the public or who, by persistent absconding, render any assessment impractical. Such provision raises complex legal, ethical and professional issues which are outside the purview of this book.

Strictly in terms of assessment, however, security raises particular difficulties. It may either arouse or dampen anxieties in young people (in the UK, children under 13 may not be placed in secure accommodation) which affect their behaviour in unpredictable ways. They may, for example, bend all their efforts on escaping from the facility. In the course of this they may, for example, engage in generalized or specific aggressive and destructive acts which may lead staff to believe that they are always like this and describe them in these terms, without recognizing the situational specificity of the behaviour. There is, inevitably, some degree of 'artificiality' in such a setting, but exactly how it affects assessment of behaviour depends on the particular circumstances, the skills of assessors and measures taken to counter the adverse consequences of security.

Staff also have particular and shifting priorities in relation to the assessment and management of children in security. These affect their views of children as sources of risk. Such views may, in turn, create and spread a 'halo effect' on their interpretation of the child's attributes. A child who presents risks of persistent absconding or other disruptive acts is likely to be described in generally more adverse terms.

More specifically, the inevitably structured environment of a secure setting restricts the range of stimuli to which young people can respond. Most young people behave in a *less disordered* fashion under secure conditions than in the 'outside world', simply because they are exposed to a narrower range of events and experiences. This makes it difficult for the staff to evaluate the full range and depth of their difficulties. It therefore becomes necessary to take special care to ensure that the young people have the opportunity to respond to a wide array of stimuli, stressful and otherwise. The greater the similarity of behaviours in different circumstances, the more valid the conclusions are likely to be about the stability of the young people's attributes.

Human resources

These encompass not only the specific assessment staff but also all other persons who are required to care for and help provide information on the children and their problems. As has already been indicated, adults are a critical component of the behavioural environment of children, and the assessment team is crucial in determining behaviour in the facility and making decisions about the children. Their diversity and ability to take on different roles in relation to the children will be an important source of information about the latter's response to different behavioural environments.

Qualities of staff

These are the *fundamental* characteristics of staff – usually those with which they are born and which consistently shape, and are expressed by, their behaviour. They include intelligence, sensitivity, warmth, ability to empathize, maturity, stability, compassion, resilience and many others. The demands made on these are probably no greater in an assessment setting than they are in any other that deals with problem children. However, the technical demands of assessment specially emphasize the need for intelligence and sensitivity. Children undergoing assessment for negative reasons (and sometimes even those in positive contexts, such as a gymnastic competition) are likely to suffer from anxiety, distress and a range of other demanding and distressing adaptive reactions. These all call for considerable awareness of the children's difficulties and the kind of empathy that would enable the assessor to see the reason for their behaviour. The requirement to communicate the results of assessment calls, additionally, for articulateness and literacy.

One thing that an assessment setting does not need is 'relationships' in the emotional sense used in dynamic psychology and social work. The necessary components of trust, affection, dependence and predictable reciprocity do not have the chance to become established in the usual short period of acquaintance of the subject and the assessor. Nor is there any reason to suppose that if the assessment period were lengthened it would enable the development of a relationship which might make assessment 'better'. The give and take of any relationship brings a new dimension to the interactive behaviours involved, further complicating an already complex situation. This is one reason why special caution should be exercised in interpreting the evidence of those who do have a relationship with the child, such as parents, neighbours and others. Additionally, in an assessment facility which is intended to have only temporary contact with the child, the necessary severance of ties due to moving on may create additional difficulties for an already problematic child, unless the assessment were to lead on to treatment by the same people, as is often the case.

It is also morally questionable to establish a relationship *in order* to get information out of the child. In practice, children react positively to the open and honest statement that they are being assessed as an aid to resolving their problems. Such openness seems better than leaving the purpose of assessment either hidden or to the child's imagination. Given a fundamentally decent and positive attitude to children, it is surprising how much frankness they can tolerate.

None of this is intended to imply that it is not crucially important to establish a caring and settled environment for the children in which the difficulties of interaction with a new group of adults do not exacerbate their anxieties and often the very problems that brought them to attention. The development of some sort of relationship with the child is in any case inevitable. Difficulties arise mainly when the assessment agency sees it as an essential part of its task to establish relationships with the children and seeks to arrive at its assessment through such relationships.

Specialist staff

Specialists (such as psychologists, psychiatrists, teaching and social work staff) are the most scarce resource in the total assessment process. It is important to know how best to make use of them. This depends to a large extent on the organizational rigour of the assessment agency and even more centrally on the competence and personal characteristics of the specialists. Particular individuals may have skills which considerably transcend their specialism. A psychologist may, for example, act more as a resource for staff training and development than as a direct child assessor. In view of this, it is not particularly helpful to define the contribution that each speciality can make. In any case, the unequal geographical distribution and availability of specialists to individual assessment services make this into a somewhat academic exercise. This fact by itself makes it imperative to utilize specialist staff efficiently. It is, for example, not very sensible to utilize a psychiatrist to obtain the basic personal history information from a child, even though she would frequently wish to cross-check this information with the child.

A further and more fundamental aspect of utilizing specialist (and, indeed, any other professional staff) is knowing what the agency requires of them and ensuring that this fits in efficiently with the agency's overall function. Few things are more irritating and wasteful of scarce resources than chaotic, laissez-faire interactions of staff and not knowing what to do with the information provided by them.

Considerations of care

No work with children should be undertaken unless their primary care requirements are met. These encompass provisions for *physical care*: adequate feeding, clothing, sleeping and shelter; *emotional care*: support to achieve a reasonably stable frame of mind and some degree of happiness; and *social care*: protection and encouragement as an aid to acceptability and satisfaction in peer interaction. Standards of care vary from place to place but there is some cultural consensus about acceptable minima which should guarantee an adequate level of care.

In an assessment setting, the purpose of providing care is to bring about a level of behavioural and psychological stability against which the child's behavioural baseline may be established. A child who is abnormally cold, unhappy or rejected by age mates is likely to behave in an abnormal fashion. Any information gained about behaviour in such circumstances is likely to be only of benefit in indicating how he behaves when he is upset and would be of little value in predicting his behaviour under other conditions.

This abnormality is exacerbated in the case of those children whose problems are so great that they have to be removed from home and placed in some form of residential provision. The removal from home and the anxiety of separation from a familiar environment as well as the need to adjust to the new and potentially threatening setting may induce panicky responses and other forms of transient disorder.

Although these may be of value in providing unusual information about a child, they are also likely to increase the error in evaluating the child's normal response patterns and behaviour, other than under those specific circumstances. In view of this, the priority task of any assessment facility should be to stabilize the children and familiarize them with the new environment until they have become basically stable and confident, before the proper programme of assessment gets under way. With some children this task may be so difficult and protracted as to take several months. With the majority, however, it is achieved in a matter of hours or days if the environment is caring and competent enough to ensure that the child is welcomed and minimally stressed in the new setting. The length of time each child takes to settle down is a valuable guide to her adaptive ability, provided staff efforts to this end are relatively constant. Given the cumulative nature of interview, observational and test data in assessment, special heed should be paid to interpreting and placing in context particularly maladaptive and disruptive behaviour to ensure that it is not given undue prominence.

Who does the assessment?

As indicated, there are several sources of information for assessment. Under normal circumstances such information is provided by individuals who follow particular assessment objectives and adopt different viewpoints. There is, therefore, no good reason to believe that the focus of these differently orientated persons on the same child will produce an integrated view of his problems. The use of apparently the same language, and identical words such as 'aggressive' or 'withdrawn', does not necessarily imply that specific referents of (or features associated with) those words are understood uniformly and hence likely to lead to similar actions. In any case, because much assessment by individuals is frequently done in isolation and in the absence of comprehensive briefing and consultation among them, there is much duplication and wasted effort in the assessment of children.

In the case of children with wide-ranging problems, this approach is likely to be of little use as it fragments the child and does not provide a coherent focus for action. People capable of bringing the various strands of assessment together and drawing out their treatment implications require such high levels of knowledge, understanding and integrative skills that they are not likely to be in over-abundant supply.

Because of this, it is preferable to refer the more problematic children for assessment to integrated multi-disciplinary teams who are capable of providing coherent information at different but interlocking levels of expertise. These teams, by virtue of learning through working together, are more likely to acquire a basic understanding of each other's language and areas of concern. By concentrating together on children they are more likely to provide an integrated view of their problems than isolated individuals. They are also normally organized in a manner that specifies how the information provided by each of them is to be integrated into the whole and who is to draw together into a coherent pattern the different strands of assessment.

Such a pattern is likely to be of considerably more use than discrete bits of information. Teams, by virtue of belonging to the same organization, can potentially provide a more rapid and efficient service because they can short-cut the necessity of transmitting the information from one place to another and bringing together, if necessary, the various persons to share in the discussion and decision-making. The organization of an assessment team is subject to the same constraints and possibilities as any other organization and has no implications about where they should be based.

Judged by this, there are special problems in youngsters being assessed by individuals of *any* discipline, particularly in such areas as social work, probation, general teaching and fostering. This latter is particularly problematic in the case of 'assessment fostering' (variably used by some British social services departments, where the children are sufficiently disordered to have been removed from home). Whilst foster parents can usually provide a good level of care and many a reasonably articulate and valuable view of children, they are unlikely to be able to provide the rigour of co-ordinated assessment which a trained and focussed team can. However, as with so much else in social work, the reasons for seeking (and finding) a particular facility for the child are not always founded on premises of rigour, long-term efficiency, reliability and validity.

Where to assess?

The initial reason for assessment is that the child is presenting a problem which is deemed to be sufficiently serious to warrant intervention. Depending on the risk factors involved, consideration should be given to whether the child's environment should be changed for purposes of assessment. The vast majority of children who present problems are assessed by people of various levels of expertise while they continue to live at home. Visits to the hospital or clinic or visits by a health visitor or a school psychologist take place while the child's normal routine is continued. This happens usually when the problem presented by the child, such as difficulties in reading or sleeping or onset of offending, are so mild as not to present 'major' risk either to the child or to the surroundings. Any such risk is weighed against the disadvantages of removing the child from home, such as intolerable stress to the parents or the child, or subsequent difficulties of re-integration into the normal setting.

Costs and benefits of intervention

In any intervention in children's lives, a price has to be paid which includes not only the expenditure of scarce human and material resources but also potential damage to the children and/or their environment and the risks arising from either taking or failing to take a particular course of action. Taking an action presumes that the benefits of the outcome will probably outweigh its costs. All practitioners have some intuitive grasp of contending pressures in their work with children and their actions follow, even if confusedly, from their evaluations of the reasons for and against alternative courses of action. In practice, referral for assessment is determined by a worker's access to services, governed increasingly by financial and other resource constraints, balanced by the severity of the risk presented to or by the child.

Access to services depends on the worker's knowledge of those services (and not even all professionals are up-to-date or all-knowing), what they can and cannot do, and how far they are likely to help particular children, insofar as their knowledge (and prejudices) go. These are shaped in both individual and collective responses by a 'calculus' made up of such elements as cost, geographical distance, reputation, availability, waiting lists and other even less clear yardsticks.

Official agencies, such as education and social services and workers within them, have, if they are knowledgeable, a notion of a hierarchy of assessment services related to the seriousness of the problems of an individual child. These notions are often inexplicit and vague, more so in the case of those workers who have a few difficult children and who need to use explicit assessment services only on rare occasions. The knowledge of facilities is more often passed by word of mouth and agency attitudes than by hard and valid information.

Evaluation of *risk* arises from the worker's perception of the condition of the child. In this sense, some form of 'pre-assessment', however vague and intuitive, is an inevitable and logically necessary aspect of any form of social intervention of which referral for formal assessment is one example.

The risks presented to or by the children warranting intervention are laid down in the various laws specific to each country. In general terms and with some variations, they include hindrance of physical and psychological development; physical, emotional or sexual abuse; truancy; exposure to 'moral danger'; being beyond control; offending and psychological breakdown. A judgment is made of the extent, intensity, duration and urgency of such problems, enabling the worker to come to a decision as to 'how bad' the problem is. This then leads to a judgment of how these conditions are likely to develop and with what consequences to the child, the community, the official agency and the worker. The collective name for this often implicit process is 'risk estimation', shown (in Chapter 2) as characterizing all agencies' work.

The above elements interact to produce a balance of reasons for and against a course of action. Such actions are of an ascending order of 'seriousness' in response to what the referral agent sees as the problem. The more serious the condition, the more serious the action taken. A child who is periodically absent from school may provoke the Head Teacher to contact the parents, one who is more persistently absent may warrant the intervention of an Education Welfare Officer or Educational Psychologist and the most persistent truant is likely to be taken to court and subjected to more rigorous sanctions.

But such decision making is rarely carried out in an explicit or logical manner. Because of its ambiguities and frequent miscalculations, it results in much avoidable damage to any deterioration of children's condition. This is in part dictated by a current 'minimalist' ethos of social agencies increasingly driven by scarce financial and personnel resources. This ethos revolves around a set of beliefs and feelings (rather than established facts) that 'minimum intervention is best' – for ethical, professional and resource reasons. This is wholly admirable and usually successful, but by definition only in those cases where the intervention curbs and ameliorates the child's problems. Its failure in many cases, particularly where multiple social and psychological difficulties affect the children, leads inescapably to more serious and far-reaching interventions, with greater costs to the children and agencies responsible for them. To ensure that this does not happen warrants using the best assessment resources, at the start of a child's difficulties, to allow pre-empting deterioration due to inadequate assessment.

To remove or not to remove
Other than in those medical cases where diagnosis and treatment have, of necessity, to be carried out in a hospital setting, children are removed from their normal settings only when they present or experience serious behavioural difficulties, such as offending or being abused. The case for medical diagnosis in a 'residential' hospital setting arises from the complexity of the case and the need for specialized procedures. The removal of children for 'social' reasons, on the other hand, is much more linked to perceptions of risk to the child and its outcome for the workers. To this extent, residential disposal of children has a strong element of 'insurance policy' for both the child and the agency. This is best illustrated in many contested and notorious cases of social workers removing children suspected of being abused. In these cases, social workers' commitment to children has been fuelled by their fear of repercussions if they are not seen to have acted with due haste. The fact that they are likely to be castigated for *whatever* they do does not improve their powers

of cool, dispassionate judgment but seems to have the contrary effect.

The worker's task in balancing the pros and cons is, therefore, one of achieving the 'best fit' between the child and the appropriate level and venue of assessment in terms of a desired outcome. Against this background, and with a clear appreciation of its shortcomings, a *tentative* list of classes of reasons for and against removal for assessment (or management, care and treatment) is presented below. It should, however, be remembered that 'assessment' is rarely the pure objective. It is often overlaid by the need to *curb* and *contain* the risk presented or experienced by the child.

For removal

The child
- Are problems not likely to improve if child stays at home (or in normal setting)?
- Are problems likely to get worse?
- Is child likely to be at risk from family and/or others?
- Are the problems such that an available day agency such as outpatient hospital service, child or adolescent psychiatric unit, school psychological service, social services day assessment centre or peripatetic teams *cannot* cope? Have you checked?
- Are these agencies not interested or available in the time or manner required?
- Is there a particular assessment service with additional facilities and attributes which would benefit the child but is not available at home?

The community
- Is the community likely to feel it is at risk, if the child remains at home?
- Is the community likely to be concerned that the child has not been removed from normal setting?

The organization
- Is your organization likely to be criticized if the child stays at home?
- Is it the organization's policy that children subject to certain risks should be removed from normal environment?
- Does this child fall into that category?
- Does the organization only take certain actions when an external assessment has been carried out?

The referral agent
- Are you likely to be censured or otherwise at risk if you do not remove the child?
- Do you need a certain type of service that you can get from a particular agency only when child is away from home?

Affirmative answers to any of the above may indicate the need for removing the child. The higher the number of affirmatives, the stronger the indication for removal, which is now required as evidence by recent legislation.

Against removal

The child
- Are the child's problems likely to get worse if removed from home (or natural setting)?
- Which problem is most likely to deteriorate?
- Are there likely to be serious consequences for child's ties and support systems – such as the family?
- Is child likely to suffer from particular problems if removed to a particular facility?
- Is child likely to be stigmatized or emerge with more problems than he started with?
- Is the removal likely to have adverse consequences for child's resettlement at home (or in normal setting)?

The organization
- Is removal too expensive in time and money and in terms of its probable outcome?
- Is the outcome likely to be unhelpful in determining what you should do with this child and others like him?

The referral agent
- Are you likely to be censured or otherwise at risk if you remove this child for assessment?
- Are you likely to end up as a result of such assessment with having to do more than you can or want to do with the child?

Affirmative answers to one or more of the above questions would contra-indicate removal of child. It is at present difficult to formulate and solve such equations of contending factors but it is possible to make reasonably informed guesses about them which can in due course be tightened to form the basis of research and provide empirical guidelines for future action. As observed throughout this book, we strongly believe that intervention in the lives of children is capable of disciplined approach and evaluation. It does not have to remain in the present morass of partial knowledge and mythical belief which places powerless children with problems at the mercy of inconstant feelings of those who deal with them.

Presentation of information
Information can be conveyed with varying degrees of efficiency and accuracy which ranges from the one extreme of ambiguity to the other of exactness. The medium of presenting information can also vary from

words to visual materials such as graphs, curves and tracings, auditory and visual recordings to numerical data. Specialized measures produce all of such basic data which can be and usually are translated into words.

Words are the normal medium of social communication. They vary in complexity, exactness and nuance. As such they can communicate not only factual information but also considerable emotional and social overtones regarding the state of the child and the assessor. But these virtues also constitute the major shortcomings of verbal communication. Even common words such as 'disordered', 'anxious' and 'withdrawn' have different meanings to different people and professional groups. Words are difficult to store and because of the diversity of their meanings they are difficult to use as sources of information for research purposes, unless the key words are used according to a glossary, as in for example, DSM, ICD, or Problem Profile.

But whatever the difficulties, it is not possible to dispense with words. Numbers, as the only other alternative, are inappropriate for communicating information about problem children. They are, however, particularly useful for codifying assessment information for purposes of subsequent research.

Assessment meetings

The whole process of assessment is intended to describe the child's problems as a prelude to alleviating them. In order to do this, assessment data are evaluated, placed in a coherent structure and used as a basis for decision making. Where separate reports are obtained from different sources, the task of integrating and making sense of the reports falls upon whoever has been responsible for initiating the search for information. Difficulties inherent in this approach have already been outlined. Other than in physical medicine and some parts of cognitive psychology, there are currently no established methods of comprehensively evaluating information from discrete sources and unifying it in a manner which points to specific treatments. It is, therefore, particularly difficult for a single person from any discipline to bring the reports together, sort out the essential from the less so, reconcile different points of view, translate the problems and the recommendations into an action programme and give individual components their order of priority and then refer to or implement the necessary treatment.

Contrary to prevailing attitudes, assessment of an even moderately problematic child is too complex to be carried out by an individual person, be it a psychiatrist, a psychologist or a social worker. It is, therefore, preferable to present the assessment information in a group setting with an explicit decision-making focus, mode of presenting information, and recording decisions. An 'assessment meeting', appropriately chaired, which brings together the persons most knowledgeable about and involved with the child, is the best medium for processing such information.

There is some controversy about whether children and their parents should participate in assessment meetings. The uncertainties have centred on whether sharing the information and decision making is a 'right' and how this should be reconciled with notions of confidentiality and the legal responsibilities of agencies such as education or social services departments. The issues are too complex to be elaborated here and relate, in any case, to all other forms of social control than just assessment. The subject of 'children's rights' is too recent to have become an established part of jurisprudence. Any arguments would, therefore, be at best tentative, although recent British legislation demands ascertaining wishes of children and parents before finalizing decisions, and parents will remain partners throughout a child's care career.

It may, therefore, be more useful to adopt a pragmatic approach to this issue. If the participation of the child and parents in the assessment meeting is likely to enhance either the process or its outcome, or conversely, if there are no 'good and urgent' reasons why the parents should not participate, then they should be asked to do so. Such participation is likely to enable them to understand the problem and the reasons for a particular course of action, and thereby help the treatment process. This should, however, be set against costs of a potentially less efficient and satisfactory assessment meeting, if it inhibits free and open communication among its members.

Considerable experience of assessing seriously disordered adolescents, with them and their families in serious crisis, in meetings where they are all present and share *all* the information, would suggest that parental participation is both possible and desirable. This is even the case where one or both parents are abusive, hostile or rejecting. Clearly, however, such meetings and their underlying processes demand very sensitive and yet firm handling if they are not to degenerate into damaging experiences for any of the parties.

Whether the assessment report is prepared in an integral form by an assessment team or brought together from a variety of sources, experience suggests that it may be best if individual participants in the meeting present the report in the following order: the child's particulars and reason for referral and the six problem areas in terms of history and current state, with child's own views providing a coda to all the 'official' information. The person chairing the meeting would then summarize the problems and cross-check the summary for comprehensiveness and accuracy with the rest of the group. Problems can be specified at a level felt to be desirable for the *users* of the assessment report. The chairperson would then proceed to make treatment recommendations which directly correspond to the problems highlighted. Each stage would be discussed with the participants towards seeking consensus.

Having summarized the problems and specified the treatment recommendations, it then becomes necessary to consider *where* best, and *by whom*, individual components or the total *treatment* programme may be carried out, over what sort of time span, with what kinds of resources and expected outcome, and the method of *monitoring* which should be employed throughout the process. The determination of the venue of treatment can range from the general, such as the child's home, 'a special school', to the naming of a specific agency or person who may undertake the treatment of the problem. The meeting will be concluded by recommending when the child's condition should be reviewed. Increasingly (and in children's law) a three- to six-month review interval is deemed appropriate, although an earlier one may be necessary.

Such a structure for the meeting recognizes the need for intensive and free interchange of information between participants. However, it also recognizes that an assessment meeting has a *purpose* which can be fulfilled with varying degrees of efficiency. There is sometimes a tendency on the part of the participants at assessment meetings to use the venue as a platform for ventilation of feelings about the child and other matters which may be of dubious relevance to either the identification of child's problems or the determination of methods of alleviating them. Thus, a high degree of *structure* in such meetings is desirable, conducive to concentrated and efficient information processing and reduction of errors related to the personal feelings of participants. Information may not be accurate in the first place but there is little sense in increasing its inaccuracy by allowing it to become confused with people's feelings unless those very feelings are part of the problems.

Skills of chairing

Taking accurate information for granted, the chairperson ('chair' for short, as is now often preferred) of the meeting is the most significant determinant of the quality of the end product of assessment – the summary of problems, treatment recommendations and identification of appropriate treatment venue. However good the assessment information, it would be wasted if it cannot be adequately, accurately and efficiently transmitted to users. Anyone entrusted with this task must, therefore, possess the necessary qualities to ensure that the task is adequately achieved. The following attributes appear central to this task.

Considerable knowledge of the structure of assessment and its sources of information are required. It is not necessary for the chair to know the child, because all the relevant information is presented at the meeting and in the reports. Indeed, there may be some merit in the chair not knowing the child so as to be able to arrive at an impartial synthesis of information.

The chair must have sufficient technical knowledge to be able to question the content and quality of the reports presented including, where appropriate, those from specialists. She should be sufficiently sensitive and sympathetic to detect overtones and draw out double meanings and misgivings that participants may hesitate to express. At the same time she must be sufficiently firm to resist attempts by anyone to swamp and sway the meeting with idiosyncratic views of the child and the required treatment.

This raises the whole issue of the power relationships in assessment meetings. As the purpose and need for structure already mentioned indicate, the chair is the leader and pilot of the meeting. Whether the leadership is expressed through 'democratic' (one person, one vote!) or other styles depends on the proclivities of the leader. There is, however, little question that unless the chair manages the meeting authoritatively, it is likely to be rambling, wasteful and unproductive. A crucial aspect of this is ensuring that all parties to the meeting, particularly those who are likely to feel powerless (such as child and parents), have the opportunity to make their views known and are not further disempowered by the assessment process and conduct of the meeting.

The chair should have considerable analytical ability to be able to discern from the mass of information the most important elements and to synthesize them in a pattern of problems which is comprehensive, relevant and makes sense to the participants. For this reason, she must also be literate and articulate.

She should have knowledge of general treatment approaches and facilities and be sufficiently authoritative and persuasive to arrive at a consensus about what should be done with the child.

The chair must, besides, have those elusive qualities which induce in the participants the feeling that their views have been valued and a satisfactory job has been done. Many of these qualities are personal and inborn but they can be enhanced by training, experience, recording techniques and decision-making aids. To this end, summary sheets of the information presented, checklists of problems and treatment are of considerable help.

Monitoring assessment

Sensible comments about a child's attributes can only be made in relation to a reference population, whose characteristics are known. It is, therefore, necessary to establish *baselines* about critical attributes of children both in general and in a variety of specialized settings. For example, in order to know whether the child is undersize and underweight, it is necessary to have general norms about the size and the weight of children in different age groups. The same criteria apply to other aspects of physical and intellectual functioning, though less readily to other areas such as family structure, social relationships, social behaviour and personal circumstances. This is where applications of 'empirical assessment', outlined earlier, are particularly valuable.

Information about criteria of 'adequate functioning' in physical and cognitive areas is generally available. This is in stark contrast to other problem areas, such as family dynamics, social relationships, anti-social behaviour and personal conditions (other than sometimes in relation to specific tests) or research studies. It is difficult to see what might be regarded as the 'norm' in these areas. It is, therefore, necessary (and possible) to establish specific agency baselines, such as averages, percentages and distributions against which the state of a child may be evaluated. Whilst the scientific value of such baselines may not be very great, they are, nevertheless, better than making what are, in reality, blind comparative judgments, as if they were absolutes. It is necessary to have, even at a basic level, enough solid comparative information in order to differentiate one child from others. For this reason it is important to record and store assessment information for all children referred. The extent and detail of information collected varies according to the resources and requirements of the agency. This requirement becomes crucial in the case of seriously disordered children who, by virtue of their dramatic behaviour, create a 'halo effect' which renders them liable to blanket, frequently damning judgments. In reality, they may be no different from most other children in critical respects. Fortunately, as this book and a number of other recent publications indicate, there is now widespread recognition of the need for solid information, which is being increasingly accumulated and made available for assessment.

Research and training

The comments so far have pointed up the considerable ambiguity that surrounds almost every aspect of assessment, its use and organization. Bearing in mind the extensive investment of human and material resources in assessment services of one sort or another, the importance attached to it and the price paid by society and children for a process which may or may not be useful, it is surprising that not many attempts have been made either to systematize the process or to subject it to empirical research. This is a matter of some importance and urgency and one which is likely to pay early dividends by ensuring a better service.

Any survey of assessment services for children shows that considerable uncertainty surrounds the following topics on which research might concentrate:

- The process of referral: who is referred, for what kind of assessment, on what grounds, to what sort of services;
- What determines the form of assessment, the main sources of information utilized, the sequence of processes and their relation to outcome;
- The reliability and validity of individual elements and whole processes of assessment in relation to particular groups as well as relevance and utility of different assessment reports;
- The effects of context – structure, physical security, different sizes and mixtures of peer and adult groups and professional orientations on children's behaviour;
- Who uses assessment reports, for what purpose and with what results;
- Do different assessment processes lead to different outcomes and forms of treatment? Are types of assessment reports differentially related to processes and forms of treatment?

Every stage of the assessment process from 'pre-assessment' and referral to the final writing and utilization of assessment reports suggested by the above questions requires training for practitioners. Such training should be aimed not only at increasing the levels of expertise in managing, caring and assessing but also at rational evidence-based decision making in assessment and monitoring of its outcome. All practitioners should be taught to do some critical analysis of their own assessment activities, so that they become ideally practitioner-researchers.

There is already some fragmented training in assessment. Medicine's focus of activity in diagnosis and treatment is at the core of training its practitioners, including psychiatrists. Psychologists and some teachers acquire assessment skills as part of further, specialized training. Social work training, on the other hand, pays hardly any systematic attention at all to either the issues or practice of assessment. And yet, paradoxically, it is the social workers who are likely to be lumbered with the most complex, disordered children in need of systematic assessment. Even setting this aside, none of the professions are usually trained to carry out team assessment, which is increasingly recognized as the preferred option. Inadequate and damaging assessment in social work has been particularly criticised in many cases of child abuse, both in cases of 'over-zealous' interventions and tragic failure to evaluate risks to children appropriately. All indications are that to meet new legal criteria, it needs massively to upgrade and systematize its assessment activities with children.

Part of the difficulty lies in the absence so far of a unifying assessment orientation which would make such training possible. The Problem Profile Approach, as presented here, can provide such a unified basis for training, particularly of teams which are required to carry out integrated assessment of the child. Without training, no disciplined approach to assessment can be developed. Without such discipline, assessment of problem children will remain an unfamiliar terrain from which some children will be guided on to a safe path, others will emerge bruised, and yet others irrevocably lost.

PART II

How to Use Part II

This part of the book is concerned with the *practice of assessment*. It is about how a judgment can be made of the extent, complexity and severity of each of the six *problem areas* of physical, cognitive, home and family, social skills, anti-social and psychological disorders.

Each problem area is divided into its constituent *attributes*, set out in bold letters, with a preceding four-digit number. The first two digits – from **01** to **06** indicate the problem area, and the latter two digits the number of the attribute – so that **0107**, for example, refers to 'epilepsy'. Each attribute is broken down into its constituent elements – the *behaviour*, set out in the box. Each element has a two-digit identifying number so that, for example, **010704** refers to 'simple fits'. These digits enable encoding for purposes of computer storage and retrieval. The category 'other' is meant to encompass any other features that may be felt or discovered to be associated with this attribute. The specific difficulty can be pinpointed in the Master Code that follows.

The information about each attribute is presented broadly in the format adopted by the American Psychiatric Association for DSM III–R. This format enables presentation of otherwise complex and confusing information in a readily identifiable and quick reference form. The DSM format, however, has been modified to provide a logically more coherent form (e.g. 'prevalence' before 'impairment') and shortened to avoid, where possible, unnecessary duplication in an area not replete with detailed information.

The information contained under each heading is the best that is available from the published research and other authoritative sources. Sometimes these sources themselves reproduce what can only be 'guess-timates' but every figure presented is based on published evidence. Many (but not all) of the sources are cited in Further Reading at the end of the chapters. As this book is not a methodological critique of research information in child and adolescent disorders, the information has been reproduced without such methodological filtering. It is, however, obvious that much of the information is not of utmost reliability and validity – even though it may be the best that is available.

There is little doubt that some specialist readers would disagree with some of the 'facts and figures' produced here. This is to be expected, as there is little agreement, even in authoritative sources, about what these facts and figures are. One would have to be extraordinarily unsophisticated, narrowly read and inexperienced not to recognize the very sandy foundations of much of what appears to be solidly built evidence in this area.

This same reservation applies to the qualitative commentary on various aspects of disorders in children and adolescents, set out under different headings. The fact that someone is bound to disagree with some of the comments simply points to the wide diversity (and often divergence) of opinion in this area. Though the situation is improving, many researchers have their favourite descriptions and explanations of a disorder. To ensure that this book is not theoretically biassed, the major explanations and descriptions have been presented in briefest outline. In general, it is best to be cautious, open-minded and undogmatic about pretty well all the material concerning children and the assessment of their disorders, summarized in this part.

Definition of terms used

The information about each disorder is presented under a number of headings, which assessors are likely to find useful. They are as follows:

Description indicates what the disorder and its main features are. It also seeks to place the disorder in a wider context, where appropriate.

Associated features refers to the *secondary characteristics* usually found together with the main elements outlined under 'description'.

Prevalence is concerned with the extent of a problem among young people. It is presented as a proportion of the total population of children and adolescents who are found at some time or other in their lives to present or experience this condition. Because estimates vary and are dependent on the number of children of the appropriate age for a disorder, the prevalence is presented as a range – such as 5–7 per cent or as '1.5 in 10,000'. Reference to 'clinical and institutional' population denotes those youngsters who are seen in child and adolescent clinics, psychological services and in residential facilities for disordered children and adolescents, be they in justice, health, education or social service sectors. When alternative sources are not available, some of the information is drawn from researches at Aycliffe, where a particularly distilled population of disordered adolescents receive treatment. When hard data are not available, a statement is made based on clinical experience of the author and other colleagues, or inference is drawn about the likely distribution of a condition. The *sex ratios*, where information is available, are presented together with the prevalance to which they refer. Wherever available, the prevalence data relate to British samples. The information in this section is the least reliable and most variable, since it is only as good as the latest findings and sophistication of the research designs used.

Onset and course refers to the age at which a disorder became apparent and the way it usually develops.

Predisposing factors are features of the person or the environment which place a child at a higher risk of the particular disorder and which can be identified *before* the disorder has become apparent. Sometimes these factors are very similar to those cited under Associated features. Familial patterns and continuities are cited under this heading.

Complications are difficulties that arise as a consequence of a disorder, such as neurological damage arising from intense solvent abuse. They also refer to any particular difficulties encountered in the course of assessment.

Impairment refers to the disadvantaging and adverse consequences of a disorder in physical, social and psychological terms. Sometimes the differences between complications and impairment are marginal.

Prompts refer to questions and observations which provide the basic information for the determination of the disorder. They are, of necessity, often an elaboration of the elements of the disordered condition, seeking to establish duration, pervasiveness, severity and other aspects. They are broadly set out from prompts about history to those about current condition, covering both questions and observations. They are not in any order of importance, though clearly replies to some are more revealing and significant than others in indicating future risk.

Prompts are *not* exhaustive but cover the main elements of the disorder. Different clinicians may have prompts which are different from those cited in this book. No pretence is made, unlike the DSM, that a particular number of prompts (and the conditions to which they refer) have to be positively answered before a child can be deemed to present the particular disorder. This is because other factors, such as intensity, duration and urgency of the difficulty have also to be considered in order to arrive at a basis for intervention. Clearly, the greater the weight and convergence of the answers to the prompts, the greater the likely reliability of the conclusions will be. Judgments of *severity* vary in each disorder, associated as they are with extent, intensity and duration of a problem in individual cases. Clearly, the higher each of these factors, the more severe is the condition likely to be.

Action is simply a broad judgment of the seriousness of the problem based on available information, containing some indication of whether and how easily the condition may be tackled. The specific treatments that can be utilized for each condition are set out in the companion volume *Treating Problem Children*, and many others.

It should again be emphasized that the graver the risk associated with the condition, the more thoroughly must it be investigated, utilizing specialist measures and personnel which are beyond the scope of this book.

The Master Code

01 PHYSICAL PROBLEMS

0101 Birth circumstances

0102 Developmental milestones

0103 Physical condition

01 Poor physical condition
02 Poor personal hygiene
03 Hygiene-related infections
04 Frequent minor ailments
05 Emaciation
06 Obesity
07 Other

0104 Pervasive developmental disorder (PDD)

01 Poor or abnormal social development
02 Deviant language development
03 Severely restricted activities or routines
04 Onset of difficulties before 30 months
05 Other

0105 Psychoses

01 Impairment of intellectual functioning
02 Impairment of cognitive functioning
03 Language disorder
04 Delusions
05 Hallucinations
06 Mood swings
07 Social withdrawal
08 Attention interference
09 Loss of pleasure

10 Loss of insight
11 Loss of personal identity
12 Ideas of reference
13 Other

0106 Brain damage

01 Impairment of memory
02 Motor inco-ordination
03 Overactivity
04 Impulsivity
05 Emotional instability
06 Other

0107 Epilepsy

01 Major fits ('Grand Mal', clonic)
02 Muscle jerks (myoclonic)
03 Absences ('Petit Mal')
04 Simple (focal) motor or sensory fits
05 Complex fits, accompanied by sensory, emotional or behavioural consequences
06 Other

0108 Motor disorders

01 Tics, twitches, muscle jerks
02 Bizarre postures
03 Poor fine or gross co-ordination
04 Unprovoked grunts, barks, swearing, sniffing, throat clearing (Tourette's)
05 Other

0109 Sight

01 Blindness
02 Defective vision
03 Squint (strabismus)
04 Colour deficiency
05 Other

0110 Hearing

```
01  Profound hearing loss
02  Partial hearing loss
03  Other
```

0111 Speech

```
01  Stammer
02  Lisp
03  Other articulatory defect
04  Aphasia
05  Other
```

0112 Eating disorders

```
01  Anorexia nervosa
02  Bulimia nervosa
03  Pica
04  Food fads
05  Other
```

0113 Elimination disorders

```
01  Nocturnal enuresis
02  Diurnal enuresis
03  Nocturnal encopresis
04  Diurnal encopresis
05  Retention of faeces
06  Other
```

0114 Menstrual disorders

```
01  Menstrual pain
02  Cessation of periods
03  Irregular periods
04  Other
```

0115 Substance abuse

> 01 Medical drug abuse
> 02 Non-medical drug abuse
> 03 Alcohol abuse
> 04 Excessive smoking
> 05 Solvent abuse
> 06 Other

0116 Sleep disorders

> 01 Difficulty in going to sleep
> 02 Periodic waking up in the night
> 03 Over-sleepiness
> 04 Night terrors
> 05 Sleep walking
> 06 Other

0117 Psychosomatic disorders

> 01 Bronchial asthma
> 02 Overbreathing
> 03 Alopecia
> 04 Eczema
> 05 Nettle rash
> 06 Psoriasis
> 07 Other

02 INTELLECTUAL AND EDUCATIONAL PROBLEMS

0201 Intellectual disorders

> 01 Mental retardation
> 02 Verbal skills deficit
> 03 Practical skills deficit
> 04 Functioning well below potential
> 05 Other

0202 Attention deficit disorder (ADD)

> 01 Fidgety and restless
> 02 Easily distracted
> 03 Difficulty in sustaining attention
> 04 Rapid shifting from one activity to another
> 05 Impulsive activity without thought for consequences
> 06 Passive, day-dreaming, bored
> 07 Other

0203 Specific learning disorders

> 01 Developmental reading disorder
> 02 Developmental writing disorder
> 03 Developmental arithmetic disorder
> 04 Other

0204 Memory

> 01 Short-term memory deficit
> 02 Long-term memory deficit
> 03 Auditory memory deficit
> 04 Visual memory deficit
> 05 Other

0205 Reading

> 01 Inability to read
> 02 Severely retarded reading
> 03 Poor comprehension of written material
> 04 Inadequate vocabulary
> 05 Poor word-building skills
> 06 Other

0206 Spelling

> 01 Severely retarded spelling
> 02 Retarded phonic skills
> 03 Reverses letters/words in writing
> 04 Other

0207 Written communication

01 Illegible handwriting
02 Poor written expression
03 Punctuation problem
04 Distorted grammar
05 Other

0208 Arithmetic

01 Severely retarded arithmetic
02 Cannot count
03 Cannot measure
04 Other

0209 Language disorder

01 Poor articulation of speech sounds
02 Poor expressive language
03 Idiosyncratic speech
04 Confused speech
05 Poor language comprehension
06 Other

0210 Interest in school or work

01 Avoidance of school
02 Embarrassed by poor skills
03 Disinterest in school
04 Expectation of failure
05 Other

03   HOME AND FAMILY PROBLEMS

0301   No home base

01   No parents or whereabouts unknown
02   Parents homeless/scheduled accommodation
03   Parents unwilling/unable/inappropriate to accommodate
04   No appropriate relative willing to accommodate
05   Other

0302   Locality

01   Development area
02   Poor amenities
03   Delinquent area
04   Culture contrary to family's
05   Other

0303   Status in neighbourhood

01   Stigmatized
02   Ostracized
03   Victimized
04   Other

0304   Material condition

01   Substandard housing
02   Overcrowding
03   Gas and/or electricity cut off
04   Parents on Social Security benefits
05   Insufficient food/clothing
06   Lack of personal possessions
07   Other

0305 Child's status

01 Illegitimate
02 Adopted
03 Fostered
04 Does not know parent
05 Other

0306 Parents

01 Parent dead
02 Single-parent family
03 Divorced
04 Separated
05 Living apart
06 Child unsure which parent to live with
07 Other

0307 Family instability

01 Parental separations
02 Short-term cohabitations
03 Other disturbing person in house
04 Other

0308 Adverse parental factors

01 Physical illness/defect
02 Mental disorder
03 Alcoholic/drug user
04 Gambler
05 Offender
06 Violent/cruel
07 Rigid/authoritarian
08 Anti-authority attitudes
09 Unemployment
10 Prostitution
11 Attempted suicide
12 Other

0309   Parental coping ability

```
01   Physical difficulty
02   Intellectual difficulty
03   Coping with each other
04   Coping with children
05   Other
```

0310   Family harmony

```
01   Marital disharmony
02   Physical conflict
03   Parental conflict with children
04   Conflict between children
05   Other
```

0311   Family involvement

```
01   Parental over-protection
02   Parent–child indifference
03   Parent–child rejection
04   Sibling–child indifference or
     rejection
05   Other
```

0312   Emotional relationship

```
01   Loose emotional ties
02   Lack of emotional support
03   Emotional detachment
04   Other
```

0313   Parental guidance

```
01   Inadequate
02   Inconsistent
03   Deviant
04   Other
```

0314 Family communications

```
01  Inadequate
02  Superficial
03  Deviant
04  Other
```

0315 Parental control

```
01  Inadequate
02  Inconsistent
03  Harsh
04  Through bribes
05  Through collusion against other
    parent/authority
06  Other
```

0316 Child abuse

```
01  Pawn between parents
02  Scapegoat
03  Physical abuse
04  Sexual abuse
05  Emotional abuse
06  Other
```

0317 Adverse sibling factors

```
01  Physical defect
02  Mental disorder
03  Alcoholism/heavy drinking
04  Prostitution
05  Special education
06  Offender
07  In alternative care
08  Penal establishment
09  Other
```

04   SOCIAL SKILLS PROBLEMS

0401   Presentation

01	Dirtiness, smelliness
02	Odd body movement or posture
03	Odd facial features
04	Odd speech rate/volume
05	Poor eating habits
06	Other

0402   Interaction skills

01	Odd visual contact
02	Misuse of facial expression
03	Inappropriate use of gesture
04	Standing too close/too far
05	Touching people inappropriately
06	Other

0403   Conversation skills

01	Making noises while others speak
02	Interrupting
03	Persistent, irrelevant questioning
04	Constantly whining
05	Other

0404   Assertiveness

01	Not making demands or requests
02	Giving in quickly when challenged
03	Generally pushed around
04	Making demands petulantly or incompetently
05	Making demands aggressively
06	Shyness and uneasiness
07	Easily embarrassed
08	Avoiding social contact
09	Showing anxiety in interaction
10	Inept attempts at making friends
11	Other

0405 Sensitivity

> 01 Undersensitivity to cues
> 02 Misinterpretation of cues
> 03 Ignoring cues
> 04 Not altering behaviour to fit social environment
> 05 Other

0406 Fellow-feeling

> 01 Failing to help others
> 02 Not saying kind things about others
> 03 Not showing appreciation
> 04 Not showing affection
> 05 Unsupportive when others are troubled
> 06 Showing no interest in others
> 07 Not sharing things
> 08 Not conceding
> 09 Not co-operating
> 10 Other

0407 Social integration

> 01 Ignoring by others
> 02 Disliking by others
> 03 Bullying by others
> 04 Scapegoating or taunting by others
> 05 Social isolating
> 06 No friends
> 07 Other

0408 Attitude to other children

> 01 Antagonism to others
> 02 Domineering tendencies
> 03 Manipulatoriness
> 04 Over-dependence
> 05 Submissiveness
> 06 Other

0409 Attitude to adults

01 Hostility
02 Defiance
03 Untrustingness
04 Over-familiarity
05 Over-dependence
06 Other

0410 Specific situational skills

01 Getting service in shops and cafés
02 Using the telephone
03 Relating to opposite sex peers
04 Joining clubs and organizations
05 Interviews
06 Seeking and getting jobs
07 Other

05 ANTI-SOCIAL BEHAVIOUR

0501 Disruptiveness

01 Stirring up trouble
02 Making allegations
03 Temper tantrums
04 Disturbing others
05 Making odd/inappropriate noises
06 Other

0502 Response to control

01 Defying adults
02 Testing out limits
03 Forcing confrontation
04 Unreasonably seeking attention
05 Demanding counselling/medication/
   services for no good reason
06 Provoking frequent conflicts
07 Wearing out adults
08 Other

0503 Truancy

01	School refusal
02	Not attending school – persistent
03	Not attending school – occasionally
04	Other

0504 Running away

01	Running away from adults
02	Planning and executing attacks on property to escape
03	Hanging around doors and attempting to run out
04	Encouraging others to run away
05	Running away from home and other placements
06	Other

0505 Deliberate self-harm (DSH)

01	Serious attempted suicide
02	Taking overdoses or poisons
03	Inflicting wounds on self
04	Attempting to obtain harmful materials
05	Tattoos
06	Other

0506 Verbal aggression

01	Criticizing
02	Antagonizing
03	Threatening
04	Swearing
05	Gesturing/snarling
06	Screaming abuse
07	Other

0507 Physical aggression

01 Nipping/biting
02 Hitting/punching/kicking/head butting
03 Using objects to hurt
04 Bullying
05 Injuring others deliberately
06 Violence to animals
07 Other

0508 Sexual disorder

01 Cross-dressing
02 Fetishism
03 Exhibitionism/public masturbation
04 Homosexuality under age
05 Interest in little children
06 Sex with hurting or being hurt
07 Attempting non-consenting sexual activity
08 Soliciting
09 Unusual interest in pornography
10 Other

0509 Sexual offences

01 Indecent exposure
02 Indecent assault
03 Buggery
04 Unlawful sexual intercourse
05 Attempted rape
06 Rape
07 Other

0510 Property offences

> 01 Aiding and abetting
> 02 Theft
> 03 Taking and driving without owner's consent
> 04 Burglary
> 05 Robbery
> 06 Robbery with violence
> 07 Destroying/damaging property
> 08 Other

0511 Fire setting

> 01 Lighting fires
> 02 Setting fires to destroy
> 03 Preoccupation with fire and fire setting materials
> 04 Other

0512 Offences against person

> 01 Aggravated robbery
> 02 Bodily harm, actual or grievous
> 03 Attempted murder
> 04 Manslaughter or murder
> 05 Other

0513 Attitude to anti-social acts

> 01 Denial
> 02 Distortion of reasons for acts
> 03 Projecting of blame
> 04 Lacking or poor insight
> 05 Boasting or uncaring
> 06 Other

06 PSYCHOLOGICAL PROBLEMS

0601 Maturity

01 Preferring company of younger children
02 Emotional reactions inappropriate for age
03 Social reactions inappropriate for age
04 Engaging in behaviour appropriate to a younger child
05 Engaging in behaviour appropriate to an older child
06 Other

0602 Self-centredness

01 Interest primarily in self
02 Using others for own ends
03 Seeking to achieve personal superiority
04 Greediness, over-demanding
05 Enviousness
06 Not helping others
07 Indifference to others' feelings
08 Other

0603 Frustration tolerance

01 Lacking patience
02 Inability to tolerate delay of gratification
03 Showing tantrums/aggression if does not get own way
04 Easy to disappoint
05 Giving up on tasks easily
06 Other

0604 Impulse control

01	Acting without apparent thought, volition or deliberation
02	Not trying to control self
03	Bored easily
04	Poor resistance to temptation
05	Other

0605 Conduct disorders

01	High level self-centredness
02	Emotional coldness
03	Lacking feeling for others
04	Calculating and manipulatory behaviour
05	Callousness and cruelty
06	Little or no remorse or guilt
07	Not learning from mistakes
08	Abnormal search for excitement and variety
09	Difficulty in delaying gratification
10	Lacking inhibition
11	Becoming hostile easily
12	Cheating/lying
13	Viewing others as enemies or objects to be used
14	Other

0606 Emotional response

01	Crying/laughing easily
02	Getting over-excited inappropriately
03	Sulkiness, petulance
04	Over-reacting to stress
05	Pronounced mood swings
06	Bland or rare emotional expressions
07	Superficial or shallow emotions
08	Other

0607   Anxiety

01 Tension or inability to relax 02 Restlessness 03 Overactivity 04 Apprehensiveness 05 Indecisiveness 06 Needing constant reassurance 07 Irritability, jumpiness 08 Tics and tremors 09 Feelings of impending disaster 10 Sleep disturbance 11 Palpitations or pallor 12 Excessive perspiration 13 Nausea or other bodily discomfort/   pain 14 Constipation or bedwetting 15 Apparent imperviousness to stress 16 Other

0608   Anxiety-related disorders

Hypochondriasis
01 Exaggerated concern with physical
      and/or mental health
02 Frequent complaining of minor
      ailments
03 Frequent demands for medical
      attention
'Hysteria'
01 Loss or disorder of sensory or
      motor functions
02 Loss of voice
03 Sleepwalking
04 Loss of memory
Obsessive-compulsive disorder
01 Rigid conformist and orderly
      behaviour
02 Intolerance or inflexibility
03 Doing the same things over and
      over again
04 Complaining of persistent, irrational
      thoughts, impulses and actions
05 Other

0609 Phobic reaction

01	Abnormal fear of animals and insects
02	of situations
03	of persons
04	of places
05	of objects
06	of injury
07	Other

0610 Depression

01	Excessive and continual unhappiness
02	Lack of attention to others
03	Self deprecation and pity
04	Sleep or appetite disturbance
05	Preoccupation with self
06	Persistent lethargy and apathy
07	Weeping with little or no provocation
08	Guilt feelings
09	Suicidal ideas
10	Depression alternating with periods of exaggerated, elevated mood
11	Other

0611 View of self

01	Disagreement with others' view of self
02	Unrealistic
03	Inflated
04	Confused
05	Controlled by outside events
06	Negative or deviant
07	Other

0612 Moral development

01	Inability to identify right and wrong
02	'Wrong' defined by probable punishment
03	Minimal concern for the impact of behaviour on others
04	Ignoring rules/obligations
05	Identifying with and emulating delinquent standards
06	Anti-authority attitudes and proclivities
07	No guilt or shame
08	Other

8

Physical Problems

This area contains a wide range of difficulties resulting from physical disorders or deficits. These may have their origins in genetic or hereditary factors, trauma during pregnancy, or as a result of accidents and illnesses in later life. The area represents problems concerning the whole body, or any of its organs or subsystems. It is thus very wide, covering diseases such as diabetes and epilepsy; congenital or acquired conditions leading to, for example, visual, hearing or speech abnormalities, 'psychosomatic' disorders such as alopecia, asthma and skin rashes; and other disorders such as bedwetting, incontinence and eating disorders. Pervasive developmental disorders and psychosis are included in this section, because of their presumed physical bases.

Because the human organism is an integrated entity, physical problems may lead to difficulties in other areas. Speech, hearing or visual defects can result in intellectual retardation and learning difficulties as well as social and personality impairment. As an example, a severe hearing deficit could impair the appropriate learning of language and speech, retard conceptual development and reading ability, lead to social embarrassment and withdrawal, and result in the development of a paranoid and prickly personality.

This book, however, is not concerned with the vast array of possible physical problems from which children suffer and which are the purview of medicine. We will not, for instance, catalogue and describe those 'purely' medical problems such as appendicitis and pneumonia which are appropriately and effectively dealt with by medical practitioners and whose assessment and treatment causes no confusion or difficulty, particularly as such physical difficulties are not as conspicuously associated with other disorders as those cited in this book.

A number of physical problems, however, do not have such a clear-cut medical basis, purely physical consequences or procedures. Frequently, those concerned with a child's overall assessment may not be aware of a physical problem, or know how to formulate it, or when to refer the child for further specialist assessment. There are also problems with a known physical basis such as brain damage, which have a direct impact on the wider problems of the child and for the diagnosis of which a medical specialist may need additional information from the assessment agency. For these reasons, this book offers a framework for the minimal assessment of those physical problems which are usually presented by children in any assessment setting and of which adults should be aware.

0101   Birth circumstances

This heading is simply meant to alert the assessor to consider whether the physical circumstances of the child's birth were normal or not. If there are abnormalities, this may raise or corroborate the possibility of perinatal damage and longer term consequences for the child's development, as well as mother's views of and relationship with the child. A particularly difficult or fraught birth may 'bond' the mother very closely to the child or, alternatively, identify him as 'troublesome' from the beginning.

Mother's health
- Had mother been fit and healthy up to and including the time of birth?
- Had she had any accidents or serious illnesses whilst carrying the baby?
- Was the baby on time, premature or overdue?
- Was delivery normal?
- If not, was the baby 'breech', 'Caesarean', 'forceps or other abnormal delivery'?

The child
- Was the child normally born?
- Was the child a 'blue baby'?
- Were there any abnormal features apparent shortly after birth?

0102   Developmental milestones

Though each child is unique, all children go through recognizable and fairly universal developmental stages – if they are normal. There are some children who show a marked abnormality such as late speech, but who are otherwise normal and go on to develop into healthy youngsters.

For this reason, and despite the existence of developmental norms, any examiner is best advised to be cautious when examining children who appear to be developmentally retarded or otherwise outside the norms. Unless the abnormality is gross, developmental norms are best judged as abnormal in *retrospect* than at the time of the examination. Nevertheless, and despite this caution, knowledge of the child's development is helpful in identifying possible continuities in difficult behaviour or parents' response to child's abnormal development.

- Walking: at what age and how easily achieved?
- Talking: at what age and how easily achieved?
- Toilet training: at what age and how easily achieved?
- Response to food: easy or difficult; faddy?
- Response to cuddling: receptive or rejecting?
- Sleep patterns: sound sleeper or disturbed; short or long spells?
- Amount of movement

0103   Physical condition

01	Poor physical condition
02	Poor personal hygiene
03	Hygiene-related infections
04	Frequent minor ailments
05	Emaciation
06	Obesity
07	Other

Description

This attribute refers to abnormalities of physical condition in children.

Bodily health is difficult to define and the concept of an 'average healthy' boy or girl proves mythical and elusive. Physical condition is determined by a number of factors such as weight, height and progress in development and freedom from disease and infection. Wide variations exist in the weights and heights of healthy children. There are many reasons why a child may be too short or too tall, too fat or too thin. A common and natural cause of shortness is heredity. Small parents are likely to have small children.

Growth may be retarded by poor nutrition, physical ailments, hormonal abnormalities or seriously adverse psychological experiences. Occasionally, the use of drugs or other treatments may have an adverse effect on growth. Some children's heights and weights are below the normal range because they are developing more slowly than usual. They will eventually reach normal proportions as adults but they will take longer to do this.

If children are very tall, this is most commonly due to heredity, although there are certain rare diseases which cause excessive growth. Many children who are very tall are simply early maturers who as adults will be within the normal range of stature. Children as a whole are getting taller.

When children are too fat, the cause is almost always over-eating. Obesity in children as a result of disease or glandular malfunction is very rare. Poor physical condition through under-nutrition and inappropriate diet may lead to frequent ailments and infections, and, if prolonged, will produce emaciation. Poor physical hygiene under these circumstances will contribute to the risk of infections and ailments.

Associated features

General sickliness suggesting poor endowment or postnatal difficulties. Otherwise, difficulties are usually associated with poverty, poor health care and parenting.

Prevalence
Considerable, as attested by heavy demands on paediatricians and GPs. Cannot be sensibly put into percentages. Applies to both boys and girls, though boys seem to suffer from more physical disorders than girls and present greater incidence of obesity.

One in three of British children are said to be overweight. Emaciated children are much more likely to be found in countries where some people suffer from starvation.

Onset and course
Any age. No particular course, apart from progressive obviousness in emaciation and obesity.

Predisposing factors
Poor genetic endowment, perinatal or postnatal difficulties or poor parenting. Continuities of physical disadvantage have been established through extensive research.

Complications
Any number, depending on the exact form of poor physical condition. Emaciation and its associated factors leave child open to infective and other diseases. All the above conditions can lead to social difficulties and adversely affect children's view of themselves.

Impairment
Depends on the severity of the condition from little to life-threatening.

Prompts
Does child's weight and height fall within the normal range?
In unusually tall, short, thin or stockily built children, is the body build similar to that of the parents?
Does child have a normal appetite and is his diet normal?
Did child pass through his developmental milestones early, normally or late?
Does the obese child eat abnormally?
Any abnormality that is evident on examination.

Action
Depending on severity, may warrant referring to GP, but more usually requires improving hygiene habits and encouraging child to normalize weight.

0104 Pervasive developmental disorder (PDD)

01	Poor or abnormal social development
02	Deviant language development
03	Severely restricted activities or routines
04	Onset of difficulties before 30 months
05	Other

Description

This is a profound disorder of the total social and psychological functioning of the child, becoming evident in early infancy and continuing to affect functioning throughout the individual's lifespan.

In the past many terms, such as 'childhood psychosis', 'atypical development', 'childhood schizophrenia' and a number of others, were used to describe this condition. However, it is now widely accepted that this condition is different from psychoses which typically arise later in childhood and during adolescence.

The core and fundamental example of this condition is *infantile autism* which is characterized by the above features. The condition is traditionally thought to be different from a number of other pervasive disorders, such as mental retardation. As the general term (PDD) indicates, the disorder affects certain crucial aspects of the child's development in ways which are qualitatively even more severe than and distinct from other conditions, such as mental handicap. Some of the features become less evident with age (e.g. inability to discriminate between strangers and familiar people), but others may become accentuated (e.g. inability to make friends). The prompts below show the range of abnormalities, some of which have a well-established course of development but others which are idiosyncratic and wholly individual.

Associated features

This disorder is often associated with other abnormalities such as mental retardation throughout life and epilepsy, particularly during adolescence. Extensive and sometimes high-quality researches have failed to show any associations with social class, family pathology or neurological abnormalities. There are many hypothesized diagnostic conditions associated with autism, such as Asperger's 'autistic' or 'schizoid psychopathy' but there is little good empirical evidence to support them.

Prevalence

The condition occurs in between 4 and 13 in every 10,000 children. In the UK the prevalence is of the order of 3 per 10,000 but the rate increases to as high as 20 in 10,000 when mental retardation is present. This condition is more prevalent among boys than girls, in the order of roughly 3:1.

Some research suggests that girls presenting this condition are more seriously disordered than boys, with more severe (anti-)social problems.

Onset and course
Evident in infancy, below around 2½ years, by which time abnormalities of language, play and social relationships become evident. It is, however, generally accepted (though without adequate evidence) that the condition must be genetic and, therefore, present from birth. The condition remains evident throughout the lifespan. The child is highly likely to remain severely handicapped and unable to look after himself. Some features, such as language and ability to play, may improve but others, such as complex social relationships, will remain impaired and sometimes grow worse with growing up. The extent of impairment is often positively correlated with the extent of associated intellectual and language difficulties.

Predisposing factors
Extensive and high-quality research in this area has produced quite different conclusions about predisposing factors. However, there are no good theoretical models of how the disorder may come about and remain so pervasive through lifespan.

Complications
Epilepsy, particularly around adolescence, is more prevalent among this group than in the general population. Mental handicap is the commonest feature associated with autism, whether as a primary feature in its own right or as a functional consequence of this disorder. Families often have immense difficulty in coping with the range of difficulties presented by autistic children, particularly as the child grows older and could be normally expected to make friends and receive enjoyment from life. In rare cases there may be anti-social behaviour, such as soliciting by girls and fire setting by boys, but these are much less common than in the 'normal' population. Clinical difficulties are simply accentuations of the primary features, sometimes complicated by secondary and not necessarily correlated difficulties, such as 'psychopathic' behaviour in older adolescents. Very few autistic adults marry or produce children.

Impairment
Extensive, severe, pervasive and lifelong, though each dependent on the gravity of individual condition. In other words, even autism is a matter of *degree* and although there will be some, probably serious, impairment it need not be debilitating, as shown in studies of reasonable coping ability in some individuals.

Prompts

Social relationships
Does the young child:

- recognize parents or other close caretakers?
- show any evidence of specific attachment?
- discriminate between close caretakers and others?
- seek comfort from anyone and close caretakers in particular?
- show distress or happiness at caretakers leaving it or returning to it?
- use eye-to-eye contact as a social signal, accompanying its other behaviour, e.g. wanting something?
- engage in normal give and take in a social group?
- engage in social play?
- seem to spend a lot of time doing nothing?
- behave as if he or others have no feelings?

Language skills
Does the young child:

- seem unable to imitate early speech patterns, such as 'da da' and 'bye bye'?
- seem to have difficulty in using toys or other objects for their normal use, such as spoon goes into the ear rather than the mouth?
- seem to have difficulty in understanding spoken language at the level appropriate for his age?
- seem to be unable to make faces and mime with close caretakers?
- seem prone to reversing I–you in sentences, so 'you want drink'?
- seem to speak in an abnormal rhythm and using unusual words?
- seem to have difficulty in following instructions?

Does the older child:

- speak much less than normal for age?
- have difficulty in engaging in the normal give and take of a conversation?
- speak in a flat tone, devoid of much facial and vocal emotion?
- seem not to relate current conversation to previous events or hopes and imaginings for the future?
- seem able to shift topic of conversation as you would expect a normal child?

Play
Does child's play seem to be stereotyped, unimaginative, routine and not accompanied by expressions of pleasure?
Is child preoccupied with only one activity?
Does child's play seem to be characterized by collecting old or useless objects which he then carries around with him and resists having to give up?

Does child's play seem to be unresponsive to new stimulation or provision of new games and play objects?

Does child seem distressed with changes in its immediate environment such as playing in another room?

Does child seem to use playthings in an odd or unusual manner, e.g. for smelling, rubbing or putting in mouth, rather than playing?

Do child's bodily movements associated with play seem odd or unusual?

Are there any other unusual features about the child, such as expression of emotions, eating or sleeping difficulties?

Action

Intensive, long-term and wide-ranging action is required to alleviate the child's difficulties in areas of social responsiveness, language use, other associated difficulties and parents' distress. The child is likely to require lifelong support, depending on the severity of disorder.

0105   Psychoses

01	Impairment of intellectual functioning
02	Impairment of cognitive functioning
03	Language disorder
04	Delusions
05	Hallucinations
06	Mood swings
07	Social withdrawal
08	Attention interference
09	Loss of pleasure
10	Loss of insight
11	Loss of personal identity
12	Ideas of reference
13	Other

Description

Psychoses refer to the most serious forms of mental disorder in a child, alongside PDD, which generally cannot be understood as an extension or exaggeration of ordinary experience.

Psychoses can conveniently be divided into two groups, 'functional' and 'organic'. Functional psychoses are those in which an organic pathology is not shown. They comprise schizophrenia, including paranoid states, psychotic depression and mania.

Organic psychoses are those which are a primary result of disturbance of brain function, for instance following disease, poisoning, accidents, degeneration or deficiency. Frequently, in organic psychoses there will be some impairment of memory, orientation, intellectual functioning and judgment with shallow, rapidly changing emotional expressions.

Functional psychoses (schizophrenia and manic depressive psychosis) occur only very rarely before puberty. With the onset of adolescence, psychoses are more frequently manifested and by late adolescence, the peak age for the presentation of schizophrenic symptoms has been reached. Characteristic of psychoses are loss of contact with reality, delusions, hallucinations, social withdrawal, bizarre language, poor insight and loss of identity. These and other symptoms may exist separately or coexist to varying degrees.

There is considerable controversy regarding the status of psychoses. Whatever theoretical view is adopted, it is evident that the behaviours associated with this condition result in the most serious impairment in functioning. It is included in the area of 'physical' problems not because of a particular theoretical orientation, but because, so far at least, the only accepted and generally available remedies for psychotic behaviour are varieties of anti-psychotic medication, which affect the physical organs of the body, such as the brain.

The criteria by which psychoses are recognized in childhood are necessarily different from those in adult life. In the case of a very young child, it is not usually possible to decide confidently whether there is reduced contact with reality or insight is lacking. The difference from autism cannot often be clearly established other than by careful history taking. A child who shows clear evidence of deterioration (as opposed to failure to progress) may possibly be suffering from brain disease. In such circumstances, medical referral should be made without delay.

Psychotic states can vary between social withdrawal and difficulty in experiencing feelings of pleasure to gross disturbance in psychological functioning, resulting in an inability to meet the ordinary demands of life. Often, a progressive rise in frequency and intensity of problems occurs.

The most common psychotic state in adolescents is schizophrenia. Other psychoses such as depressive, 'bipolar' or manic depressive psychoses are rare in this age group. Other hypothesized psychotic states, such as 'borderline personality disorder' characterized by behaviour problems, poor social relationships and intense mood swings and transient, apparently psychotic episodes, cannot be reliably regarded as psychotic and can be more usefully seen as extreme forms of particular disorders which occasionally present in a cluster. To call them 'psychotic' adds little to our understanding or ability to treat the young people.

Associated features

Almost any of the features of psychosis can be present, in any combination, with different elements presented at differing degrees of intensity. In the case of adolescents, depressed or flattened mood may be accompanied by odd mannerisms and speech (in a way that does not make sense even in that idiosyncratic and colourful culture), intense expressions of conviction or total muteness, agitated movements or apathetic immobility, self-inflicted harm, bizarre behaviour (such as public masturbation or eating plucked hair) and any number of other oddities of speech, behaviour or mood.

Prevalence
The condition occurs in about 1 per cent of adolescents referred for out-patient and about 5 per cent of those referred for in-patient help. Of these, about 3/5 are likely to be schizophrenic. The prevalence in the general population, is therefore, likely to be of the order of 0.02 per cent of the population. Boys and girls are equally susceptible to this condition, though the former are more likely to manifest anti-social features.

Onset and course
Not usually (setting aside PDDs) before puberty, but around puberty and gradually growing to a peak in late adolescence or early adulthood. Onset in boys is earlier than in girls. The features associated with psychoses must have been present for at least six months before a diagnosis can reliably be made. Even so, non-psychotic (though relatively long-lasting) adolescent disturbance is so prevalent that it is difficult to be sure what the significance of the condition is. However, often in clinical practice one feature (such as delusions and thought disorders) may be so serious as to lead to a diagnosis of schizophrenia, even though other features may be absent and the condition may be quite recent.

The active phase of schizophrenia is preceded by a *prodromal phase* in which oddness of speech, unusual severity or variety of moods or emotional expressions, apathy or agitated states or odd and exaggerated ideas become apparent so that those close to the youngster say he is a 'changed' person. The earlier the onset and the longer this phase, the worse the outcome is likely to be.

The *active phase* itself, which may be set off by an unusual or stressful event, is marked by a combination of the main features of serious enough intensity to make it impossible for the young person to operate in a social context or for his caretakers to be able to manage him.

After the intensity of this phase which may last from one week to several, the symptoms subside, although some flattening of emotional reaction and milder forms of some other symptoms may remain. A return to some reasonable level of adaptation so that the individual can live in a normal social context is not unusual, particularly with good care and close clinical oversight. However, a high probability of recurrence remains, particularly in the turbulent years of adolescence. The long-term outcome depends on the age of onset, presence of other disadvantages and disorder and crucially, the level of family, social and clinical support. The incidence of mortality among schizophrenics is higher than in the general population.

Predisposing factors
There is increasing evidence that heredity and, therefore, genetic abnor-mality may play a part in psychotic disorders (schizophrenia in

particular), although the basis of heritability has not yet been identified. There is significantly greater prevalence of this disorder in families where a biologically related member is also psychotic. Twins of psychotic youngsters also have a greater chance of becoming psychotic. The relationship is not constant, thus showing the importance of environmental factors such as adverse life experiences in this disorder.

There is a greater incidence of schizophrenia in working-class youngsters, though apart from greater chronic stress there are no good explanations of why this should be so.

There is also a great deal of hypothesizing about particular family dynamics and patterns of communication, particularly affective, which are said to characterize psychotic youngsters. The evidence, however, is ambiguous. The differences noted may be the *consequences* of families attempting to adapt to the usually introverted, intense or apathetic and odd youngster even before the condition has become fully apparent.

Impairment

Depending on the stage of illness, it may range from mild to severe and life-threatening, both to the young person and others in any one or more of the primary areas of disturbance. Response to the illness is usually determined by seriousness of the episode and where the necessary protective and therapeutic measures can be best taken.

Complications

These depend on the ability of the young person's family and social context to take protective (against self-harm or risk to others) measures during the psychotic episode. Equally important are treatment measures (such as medication) and social support for the youngster to ensure that the more serious consequences of the condition are mitigated until the active phase passes.

Prompts

Is child exhibiting vagueness in speech? Does his speech convey a lack of information?

Does his speech lack coherence and display a paucity of ideas?

Do others say this of him?

Is child's speech reduced or absent as compared with previous patterns of speech?

Is child's speech continuous? Is it difficult to break into conversation?

Is speech inappropriate?

Does he use one theme or phrase continuously and out of context?

Has child shown a propensity to repeat questions or final words of the questioner?

Has child shown a tendency to make up new words?

Does child hold odd or distorted beliefs? If so, what?

Are they systematic or disjointed?

Are they unusual for a child of his age, background and ability?

Does child ever behave as if he is hearing or seeing something which others do not?

Are these associated with going to sleep or waking?

Do they occur at other special times and places?

Are you satisfied that the child does not have a straightforward visual or auditory problem?

Are you satisfied that the child is not conning you?

Are mood swings extreme and beyond what can be considered normal?

Are feelings experienced in the absence of any apparent causes?

Has child demonstrated a loss of interest in external matters recently?

Has he shown a reduction in his emotional responses?

Has he shown an unreasonable lack of affection for family and friends?

Is he unusually preoccupied with himself?

Is he apathetic?

Does child possess poorly developed social skills?

Has child shown a deterioration in his social involvement?

Has child shown a marked loss of concentration and attention recently?

Does he show difficulty in directing his attention to a particular topic?

Does child express doubts about his beliefs and perceptions?

Does he talk to others about what he feels and why?

If others talk to him about his state, does he seem to understand?

Does the child have a 'big chip' on his shoulder?

Does he ever unreasonably accuse others of acts against him?

Does he pick out particular people or is he indiscriminate?

Is he generally very suspicious?

Does the child appear inactive or withdrawn?

How does he respond to stimulation?

Does he participate in games or other activities?

Is his face blank? Or gloomy?

Does he behave in an exaggerated or reckless fashion?

Does he babble and go from one topic or activity to another?

Is he easily irritated?

Questions to child

Do you feel as though thoughts have been put into your head from outside?

Are you able to think clearly or is there any interference with your thoughts?

Do your thoughts get mixed up and sluggish?

Do people read your mind?

Are you aware of anything like telepathy going on?

Do you feel particularly close to God? Does He communicate with you? How?

Can you communicate with others without actually speaking?

How do you explain what is happening?

Are there any things like radio waves, laser beams, transmitters affecting you?

Do you think that some people are saying things about you behind your back?

Are people following you about?

Do you ever see anything in the papers or TV that has a special meaning for you?

Do you think someone is helping you or protecting you?

Do you have any special qualities or powers?

Are you important or are you related to someone very important?

Is anything wrong with your mind or body?

Do you ever hear noises or voices that you can't explain?

Do you ever hear noises like talking, murmuring or music?

Do the voices threaten you or say bad things to you?

Have you had visions or seen things that other people couldn't see?

Do you see these things with your eyes or in your mind?

Were you sleeping or fully awake at the time?

What time of the day did it occur?

How would you explain what you saw?

Do you feel reasonable or have you been feeling depressed or miserable recently?

Have you felt that life wasn't worth living?

Have you felt especially cheerful and enthusiastic without any particular reason recently?

Is there anything that you like doing at present?

Is there something you used to get pleasure from but don't any longer?

Can you tell me something that amuses you?

If someone told a funny joke do you think you would laugh easily?

Do you consider that you are a serious person?

Even when you feel convinced of what you are hearing and/or seeing, do you ever think at the back of your mind that you may just be imagining things?

When you are not actually feeling depressed, do you think that you understand why you feel unhappy at times?

What do you think about the way you feel?

Do you feel that some power or force other than yourself is able to control you?

Does this force or power make you do things against your will?

What are the sorts of things it makes you do?

What sorts of things can it not make you do?

Do you think other people are like you in this respect or different?

Do you ever think you might be dissolved into someone else or just disappear?

Do you think that things are specially arranged to harm you? What?

Do you think that certain people are disapproving of you? Who and why?

Are some people making accusations against you?

Do you think anybody is trying to get you? Who?

Action

Psychosis of any type, but particularly frank and florid schizophrenia, is a seriously disabling and socially disruptive condition. It requires urgent and specialist psychiatric help, but may be managed in the community. Once the condition has been identified, extended support is needed to guard against and forewarn of its recurrence, in order to give possibly pre-emptive help.

0106   Brain damage

```
01   Impairment of memory
02   Motor inco-ordination
03   Overactivity
04   Impulsivity
05   Emotional instability
06   Other
```

Description

This condition refers to difficulties which may be associated with brain dysfunction.

The brain is the central, most complex and important organ of the body. What happens in the brain determines the functioning and co-ordination of almost everything else in the body. For this reason, a number of researchers have attributed the wider problems of children, including their anti-social behaviour, to various forms of brain dysfunction, even though research results have rarely supported these views. There is, however, general consensus about the importance of a healthy brain as a necessary but not sufficient prerequisite of normal functioning in every other area of living.

The brain may be adversely affected by oxygen deficiency (as in birth asphyxia), mechanical trauma (as in forceps delivery), headblows or penetrating injuries, meningitis or particular forms of poisoning, including severe substance misuse. Brain injuries may affect directly the emotional stability of the child as well as his motor and sensory functions. In addition, a direct result of brain dysfunction, such as overactivity, may lead to other secondary problems such as difficulties of social learning and behaviour. The groups of signs which may describe the child with brain damage includes overactivity, motor inco-ordination, distractibility, impulsiveness and perceptual disorders. The term 'minimal brain dysfunction' has been used in preference to brain damage when describing this group of difficulties. The group of signs described may occur in children whose intelligence is about or above average. The characteristics mentioned are most common in brain-damaged children but they may also occur as isolated problems in otherwise normal children and in disordered children free of brain damage.

Associated features

The range and severity of features is dependent on the site, extent and age at which damage is sustained. Associated behaviours may range from epilepsy and intellectual impairment through difficulty in sustaining attention, overactivity, serious anti-social behaviour, temper tantrums and mood disorders.

Prevalence

Superficial scalp injury is a common occurrence in childhood, affecting perhaps as much as 15 per cent. However, serious head injuries resulting in long-term dysfunction are much rarer but still between 3 and 5 per cent of the population. Evidence about sex ratio is mixed. There are on the whole more boys with brain damage. However, the evidence about associated disturbance is also mixed, some claiming that brain-damaged boys are more impaired and others that there is no difference.

Onset and course

Can occur at any age. Allowing for differences in extent and site, the later the damage the worse seem to be its consequences, though the evidence for this is mixed. Depending on locus and extent of damage, sensory or motor impairment may be immediate. Depending on the response to the child's brain injury, the child's adaptation may improve, thus diminishing the adverse effect, or increase until other aspects also begin to suffer.

Predisposing factors

None that can be identified consistently. Perinatal injury, accidental head injury during childhood and neurological damage due to infections, poisoning and substance misuse are all common among the more disadvantaged children, but these are not 'predisposing' in the technical sense. There is no constant familial pattern.

Complications

Most serious is epilepsy, not because it cannot be controlled but often because of inappropriate and inadequate response to the child. Evidence consistently shows that head-injured children who have been in a coma have a significantly higher rate of psychiatric disorder than normal children, and that these disorders are worse than the physical consequences.

Impairment

Occurs primarily in the area of *senses*, such as seeing and hearing, and motor behaviour, such as spasticity and poor co-ordination. Extent of impairment depends on the severity and site of the damage. Some impairment is directly due to inadequate or inappropriate responses to the brain-damaged child.

Prompts

Were there any birth difficulties?

Is there any evidence that oxygen deficiency may have occurred during birth?

Was he a blue baby?

Did child require mechanical assistance during birth?

Has child ever had a head injury?

Has child ever been poisoned?

Has child ever had a serious illness or one which involved the brain?

Is child overactive or clumsy?

Is motor inco-ordination or distractibility evident?

Is child impulsive?

Does child have difficulty in seeing or hearing?

Has child demonstrated any specific learning difficulties?

Does child's mood change quickly and with little provocation?

Are mood expressions extreme?

Action

Brain damage itself cannot be repaired and made good but its consequences can be modified with specialist help. A difficult task requiring a good deal of specialist help and patience.

0107 Epilepsy

01	Major fits ('Grand Mal', clonic)
02	Muscle jerks (myoclonic)
03	Absences ('Petit Mal')
04	Simple (focal) motor or sensory fits
05	Complex fits, accompanied by sensory, emotional or behavioural consequences
06	Other

Description

This condition covers a wide variety of fits or paroxysmal behaviours, generally accompanied by loss or alteration of consciousness.

This is associated with brain dysfunction, characterized by abnormal EEG (electroencephalogram) patterns of brain activity. It is not in itself a disease, as its features, course and prognosis depend upon the conditions underlying it. These may include brain damage or tumours, metabolic disorders, infections and toxic conditions. In general, epilepsy is now categorized into 'generalized', which involve both brain hemispheres, and 'partial' seizures, which emanate from a particular area of the brain.

In a 'Grand Mal' seizure, the child may fall to the ground unconscious, making no attempt to save himself. He becomes rigid with hands clenched and feet extended and often with eyes rotated to one side. His chest is fixed, breathing is difficult and he becomes blue. After a few seconds, he passes into a second stage when he begins to twitch, the face, the eyes and limbs all involved; he may bite his tongue or pass urine and froth at the mouth. The second stage may last for a few minutes when the shaking stops, leaving the person in a coma. He may then sleep for a while or return to consciousness a little confused and complaining of a headache. Some children suffer from multiple epileptic seizures – so called 'cluster fits'. Children who are in a constant fit ('status epilepticus') are much less common and do not survive for long.

'Petit Mal' seizures generally begin during childhood and only rarely start after puberty. They are characterized by a sudden, transitory loss of consciousness. This lasts for about five to ten seconds and may be accompanied by small muscular twitches about the face and in the upper limbs. There is no warning and the fit may pass unnoticed by those around, for the child does not fall and resumes whatever activity he is engaged in, possibly after shaking his head as though to reorientate himself. Some variation occurs in the length of time or the frequency of the attacks. When the attacks last longer than five or ten seconds, complex motor activities may be noticed, such as lip smacking or chewing. At other times, the only clear-cut abnormality is in the EEG recordings, the subject showing no outward evidence of alteration in consciousness.

Minor seizures include those where complex or partial loss of consciousness is not accompanied by convulsions, and many other varieties whose differentiation is a complex, specialist task.

Associated features

Generally greater prevalence of most forms of behavioural and emotional disorder is found amongst epileptic children, including poor adjustment to school, poor social relationships, anger and temper tantrums and sometimes anti-social behaviour.

Prevalence

About 4 in 1,000 children, with about 1.5 persisting into adolescence. The data are mixed but on the whole there appear to be more epileptic boys than girls.

Onset and course

Epilepsy can start at any age, dependent on the reason, such as infection of the central nervous system or head injury. Epileptic fits follow a fairly regular pattern, as described above. The course of becoming epileptic depends on the cause (infection, poisoning or injury), extent and intensity. In some cases, the condition improves with age and the greater maturation of the brain. In others, it becomes worse, for reasons which are not always clear. The incidence of mortality in epileptics is higher than the general population.

Predisposing factors
There seems to be a hereditary element in epilepsy which is not a direct result of injury or infection, though the mechanisms for this are not known. Otherwise as for brain damage (q.v.). There is some evidence of greater incidence of 'idiopathic' epilepsy, where the cause is not known. This suggests that fits are a function of how low the 'threshold of fits' is – some people's is higher than others and this may be genetically transmitted in, as yet, unknown ways.

Complications
These are dependent on the cause and severity. The more frequent and severe the fits, the more the child is likely to suffer from physical injury and intellectual impairment – if allowances are made for the ambiguous effects of age.

Impairment
Massively dependent on the severity of the condition and the response of parents, school and others to it. Anti-convulsant drugs create their own complications. On the whole, severe epilepsy is associated with poor school performance and a range of social and emotional difficulties, particularly aggressive behaviour.

Prompts
Is there any previous history of seizures, faints or unaccountable falling?
Is there any history of head injury?
Is there any particular activity or behaviour associated with the seizure?
Does child say he notices anything before the seizure, such as flashes of light or odd sensations?
Is child under medical surveillance for seizures and is he receiving medication?
Does child make any noise or cry just prior to the onset of the seizure?
Does he lose consciousness and fall?
Does he show rigidity of muscles (hands clenched, feet extended)?
Does he show any twitching or convulsions? Does he bite his tongue or froth at the mouth?
Does he wet or mess himself?
Are you sure he is not conning?

Action
Potentially life-threatening and cause of serious disadvantage. Epilepsy should be assessed by a specialist and a programme developed for controlling the fits and compensating for/countering its adverse emotional, social and adaptive consequences.

0108 Motor disorders

01	Tics, twitches, muscle jerks
02	Bizarre postures
03	Poor fine or gross co-ordination
04	Unprovoked grunts, barks, swearing, sniffing, throat clearing (Tourette's)
05	Other

Description

This condition concerns a range of disorders of neurological control of movement.

Motor disturbances are varied and occur commonly with mental disorders or are present on their own. These disturbances may include psychomotor slowing down (as in depression), rapid, exaggerated movements (in manic states), restless and repetitive movements (in agitated depression), limited repetitive movements (as encountered in tics), tremors and habit spasms. Bizarre postures, stiffness and oddness of bearing, grimacing, mannerisms of gesture, twitchings, rituals and sudden impulsive actions may be indicators of possible psychoses such as schizophrenia.

Poor co-ordination in the form of clumsiness, coarse and fine tremors, may be organic, psychological, or the side-effects of drug treatment.

Repetitive, involuntary jerky movements of the body are quite common in childhood and usually take the form of blinking or sideways movements of the head. Tics in childhood are usually mild and generally disappear if ignored. However, tics accompanied by loud, apparently involuntary barking, swearing, spitting and other socially disruptive behaviours may warrant attention.

Associated features

Generally a high level of tension or anxiety, not necessarily but often associated with other behavioural or emotional difficulties, particularly after stressful experiences. Poor co-ordination may be associated with mental or neurological impairments. Behaviours under (04) above, associated with the name Gilles de la Tourette, usually occur in youngsters with a wide range of other social and behavioural difficulties.

Prevalence

Estimates vary between 10 and 24 per cent of children showing some motor disorder at some time, with the more serious Tourette's being evident somewhere between 0.01 and 1.6 per cent of the population. Sex ratio is roughly 3:1 of boys to girls. Tourette's is particularly uncommon in girls, though varieties of poor co-ordination seem to be equally distributed.

Onset and course

This condition is more frequent in younger children from 2 to 15, though Tourette's occurs later. Tics, twitches and jerks occur commonly in childhood and most duly disappear. Bizarre postures are likely to be associated with other difficulties. Poor co-ordination generally improves with age. Tourette's normally starts with simple tics and gets worse as child grows older.

Predisposing factors

There are strong indications of greater incidence of tics and other involuntary actions in families, ranging from 15 to 30 per cent of families showing some form of motor disorder. This may be related to an inherited level of tension, impulse control and obsessive-compulsive tendency which may be genetically transmitted but whose mechanisms are not known. As already indicated, substantially greater prevalence of these disorders exist in families, though whether for genetic or social modelling reasons is not clear. Tourette's, which is generally regarded as a neurological disorder, can in fact be more usefully seen to be associated with poor socialization and wider difficulties of impulse control.

Complications

These are on the whole few, unless associated with other neurological or physical disorders. Complications may arise from the inability of the school or wider social context to tolerate the more severe cases of involuntary vocal or muscle tics.

Impairment

Not great, though this depends on the range and severity of the disorder. Impairment is primarily social, because the child is easily identified and often stigmatized by other children and adults. Co-ordination difficulties have significant implications for scholastic, social and vocational activities, depending on how severe they are.

Prompts

Do parents and others report tics and twitches?
Do they or others complain of clumsiness or the fact that he has accidents, etc?
Do they say he cannot do things with his hands expected of his age?
Is child aware of these problems? How does he react to and explain them?
Does child show any abnormality of movement?
Is this because he moves too much, too little or what he does is odd?
Does he seem to be able to co-ordinate his movements?
Is he more gawky or clumsy than other children of his age or state?
Does he bump into things, drop objects or show difficulty in playing games?
Is he on any medication which has such a side-effect?
How frequently do these problems occur?

What are the child's reactions to them?

Does child swear, bark, clear his throat or make other peculiar noises, apparently involuntarily?

Is there anything else indicating difficulties in impulse control?

Action

This depends on whether the behaviour can be tolerated and accommodated or not. If not, referral should be made so that a range of drug treatment, behaviour therapy, relaxation and other measures may be tried.

0109   Sight

01	Blindness
02	Defective vision
03	Squint (strabismus)
04	Colour deficiency
05	Other

Description

This condition concerns serious difficulties in seeing.

Human beings rely more on their sight for social living than on any other of their senses. In the case of children, sight is even more crucial than in adults because they are still, intellectually and socially, in their formative years. Total or partial blindness may be congenital or result partially from accident or damage to eye or the nervous system.

Visual defects are usually related to long or short sight, asymmetry in the curvature of the cornea (astigmatism), failure to control the movement of the eye (squint) and disturbances of colour vision where a particular or whole spectrum of colour may not be perceived by the individual. Most visual defects are quite common, to the extent that in mild cases many people are not even aware of them. Most are also easy to correct, particularly if they are detected early.

Associated features

In blindness, there may be ante- or perinatal trauma affecting mother and child (such as rubella); later accident or disease; severe mental retardation or physical handicap. In other conditions no special pattern of features is evident.

Prevalence

In the British population, about 2,500 people up to age 18 were registered blind and about 2,200 partially sighted in 1989. The numbers with defective vision requiring attention vastly exceed these numbers, affecting seemingly more males than females. No statistics are available on prevalence of squints but they are thought to affect well under 1 per cent of the population and are rapidly treated. Depending on the kind and severity of colour deficiency, prevalence rates range from under 1 per cent to over 5 per cent of the population.

Onset and course
Blindness may occur at any age, as might defective vision. Colour deficiency is present from birth and squints become apparent soon after. Total blindness may either be the end product of a process of gradual (though variously rapid) deterioration or present from birth. Partial sight may become better or worse in individual cases. Colour deficiency is present in its full state probably from birth and throughout life. Squints usually become more apparent as child grows older, though mild squints become better.

Predisposing factors
Blindness may be congenital and inherited from parents. Partial sight and defective vision also seem to be more prevalent in certain families, as is colour deficiency. The latter is the result of straightforward genetic transmission, but the mechanisms for inherited blindness are inadequately understood. There is no apparent pattern of predisposition to squints.

Complications
None significant *arising from* these conditions.

Impairment
Total blindness is a major disability and source of risk to the child. Unless compensatory measures are taken, the child's intellectual and social development are likely seriously to suffer. Defective vision can also impair a child's schooling and peer relationship if serious and uncorrected. Colour deficiency is not a source of major impairment in normal development. Squint is a visible stigma which may result in ridicule and social isolation. Blind children are at greater risk of abuse.

Prompts
Has child been assessed as blind or partially sighted?
If so, what is the reason?
Do parents or others report visual difficulties?
Does child himself?
Has he ever been referred to an optician or ophthalmic surgeon?
Does child have difficulty in focussing on near or distant objects?
Does child screw up his eyes when trying to focus on words or objects?
Does he confuse similar objects of different colours?

Action
Any child suffering from the above conditions is likely to become intellectually and socially disadvantaged unless compensatory measures are

taken. Child should be referred for appropriate attention, although colour deficiency need not impair and cannot usually be corrected.

0110   Hearing

01	Profound hearing loss
02	Partial hearing loss
03	Other

Description

This condition refers to hearing deficiency in children.

Hearing appears to be even more vital to intellectual, social and emotional development of the child than vision. The ability to name objects and experiences and test them out in communication is at the core of intellectual development. Social interaction and concepts are specially sensitive to symbolic representation. Speech development is, in turn, dependent on the ability to hear and reproduce sound patterns. Hearing impairment is, therefore, likely to have profound consequences for the child's intellectual, social and psychological development, unless identified and adequately dealt with at an early age. Many deaf and hard-of-hearing children are treated as if they are mentally impaired.

Forms of deafness are commonly classified according to the site of the pathological condition believed to underlie the deafness. The three major types are conductive, sensory and nerve deafness. Each type of deafness is evaluated in terms of severity (total or partial) and duration (temporary or permanent).

Associated features

Ante- or perinatal trauma to mother and child (such as rubella); severe mental or physical handicap; ear infections or accidents.

Prevalence

Some level of hearing disorder affects about 0.6 per cent of children. There are more deaf than hard-of-hearing and more who are deaf and have no speech then those who have some speech. More exact statistics about type and severity are not available. There seems to be a slightly greater incidence in boys.

Onset and course

From birth or later, though early onset is difficult to detect and may be confused with mental handicap or other developmental disorders. Course is usually gradual and gradually noticeable. Can be slow or rapid, depending on the case. The deterioration may stop at a particular age or result in total deafness.

Predisposing factors
There is a greater likelihood of deaf parent(s) producing a deaf child. Some families have other members with a hearing disorder, suggesting a genetic link.

Complications
There are few physical complications apart from lack or disorder of speech. Social and psychological complications are highly probable and potentially serious unless early, intensive and high-quality measures are taken to compensate for the condition.

Impairment
Potentially severe in every area of life, but particularly intellectual and social development because of child's inability to hear. Usually associated with inability to speak, thus compounding social difficulties. Such children are potentially subject of considerable physical, emotional and sexual abuse because of their relatively greater powerlessness and ability to communicate with and complain about abusers.

Prompts
Do parents or others report that he does not seem to hear?
Does the subject present any speech or language difficulties?
Has child been ascertained as hard-of-hearing or deaf?
Does child behave as if he does not hear well?
Does he turn his head to one side when listening?
Does he still seem to be hard-of-hearing when you quietly talk to him
　　about something nice?

Action
Urgent action is required to compensate for, or if possible correct, child's hearing deficiency to ward off or minimize its adverse effects.

0111　Speech

01　Stammer
02　Lisp
03　Other articulatory defect
04　Aphasia
05　Other

Description
This condition refers to a range of disorders of speech.
　　Speech disorders seldom arise from any single cause. Speech development is highly complex, a number of systems being involved in its production. A defect in any part of the long chain can produce a speech

disorder, and defects may be present at any site from the speech centre to the vocal apparatus itself. Hearing defects may be overlooked and can produce speech delay or other problems. Emotional disturbance may both cause and result from speech disorders. Speech disorders are usually classified as arising from *receptive* (such as hearing) and *expressive* difficulties (such as malformed voice box).

Common speech disorders include stammer, stutter and lisp as well as a variety of articulatory expressive and receptive disorders. Basically, stammering consists of difficulty in commencing or completing words and is characterized by abrupt interruption of the flow of speech or by the repetition of sounds of syllables. Stuttering is the condition in which the even flow of speech is interrupted by hesitations and repetition of particular words. Both stammering and stuttering occur in normal people from time to time, particularly under stress.

Articulatory defects are more frequently caused by difficulties in co-ordinating the complicated movements of the tongue, on which clear speech depends.

Lisp usually refers to the substitution of 'th' for 's' or 'w' for 'r' sounds, 'yeth' for 'yes' and 'wubbish' for 'rubbish'. Sometimes articulatory defects sound so like the correct sound, like 'f' for 'th' as in 'fumb' for 'thumb', that there is no difficulty in understanding.

Aphasia literally means the loss of speech but it is also used in a wider sense to refer to whole or partial loss of expression or comprehension in speech, writing or gesture. Reference here is made only to impairment of production of spoken language. Aphasia may be suspected when spontaneous or elicited speech is inappropriate or disjointed or ungrammatical when taking into account the intellectual, educational and social background of the child. Allowance should be made for local dialect and idiosyncratic responses.

Associated features
Other developmental disorders, including language, reading and other motor functions, are usually present. There may also be a delay in reaching normal milestones. Bedwetting and emotional problems such as withdrawal and behaviour difficulties may also be present.

Prevalence
Estimates range from 3 to 10 per cent of school-age children who suffer from one or more of these conditions. The prevalence of aphasia, particularly of the more severe form, is around 2 to 4 per cent of the population, associated with a range of other disorders. Both boys and girls suffer from this disorder, though there seems to be a somewhat higher incidence in boys.

Onset and course
Usually apparent before 3 or 4 years. Other less severe forms, associated with emotional difficulties, may not become apparent until adolescence.

Most affected children eventually improve, particularly with good speech therapy and parental persistence in good speech modelling. Lisp may persist in many cases as would more serious cases of loss of speech.

Predisposing factors
Mental retardation or pervasive development disorder seem to predispose to this condition. These difficulties are more likely to occur in families where a first-degree biological relative suffers from a language disorder.

Complications
These are usually associated with schooling and peer relationships, but other than in severe cases, probably associated with other difficulties (such as brain damage or pervasive development disorder), there are usually no complications.

Impairment
Speech is an essential tool of communication. Its absence or abnormality in a child creates frustration, anger, isolation and perhaps some stigma. Good compensatory and corrective help, however, is usually available and effective. The residual impairment in most cases is barely detectable.

Prompts
Does child stammer or stutter? If yes, under particular conditions or generally?

Is there any obvious association between these and fatigue or distress?

Does any member of the child's family lisp or show other speech disorders?

Does her difficulty improve when she is speaking slowly with only one person, or singing?

Does child speak spontaneously?

Is spontaneous speech inappropriate?

Is speech ungrammatical?

Does child convey a sense of confusion by her speech?

Has child ever been referred to a speech therapist?

Action
Aphasias require urgent detailed investigation and treatment. Because of their intellectual, social and emotional consequences, the other speech defects also warrant early attention.

0112   Eating disorders

```
01   Anorexia nervosa
02   Bulimia nervosa
03   Pica
04   Food fads
05   Other
```

Description

This group of conditions is associated with serious disturbances of eating in children and adolescents.

Most children present some dietary problems in the course of their growth. Most grow out of their difficulties as they reach adolescence or at least the difficulties are not serious enough to cause anxiety.

Of all these, anorexia gives the greatest cause for worry, because of the risk of the adolescent's weight reaching and dipping below the critical level (around 75 to 85 per cent of normal weight) where the condition becomes life-threatening.

Bulimia is a condition where binge eating gross quantities of food is followed by self-induced vomiting, taking laxatives or other pharmaceutical agents to get rid of the food and keep the weight down. Pica is the persistent eating of non-foods, becoming more serious when the preferred material (e.g. hair) is likely to cause severe physical complications. Aversion or preference for particular foods are widespread and become unacceptable only when coupled with other disorders.

Associated features

In anorexia, the young person has fear of unacceptable weight gain and severely restricts eating in order to remain within a 'safety margin'. Continuous under-eating is less common, in most cases this condition being interrupted by periods of binge eating. The anorectic patient is typically a thin girl whose weight loss is self-induced, has distorted ideals of weight and whose periods have ceased. Depression and other psychological disorders may also be present.

In bulimia, the usually older girl may not be thin, be a secret eater, remain preoccupied with ideals of size and weight and engaged in finding ways of counteracting 'fattening' of body. Pica has no regularly associated features apart from possibly severe personality or incipient psychotic problems. Food fads are common but tend to be more frequently found in anxious and otherwise temperamental children.

Prevalence

Estimates of prevalence of anorexia range from 0.25 to 1 per cent of the schoolgirl population, rising with age and social class. Bulimia is more common, up to four times as much as anorexia. Pica as a serious enough disorder to be referred to specialists (and hence become part of statistics), is very rare. Severe food fads that may feature in general pictures of psychological disorder occur in up to 10 per cent of the adolescent population. Both anorexia and bulimia, though present, are much rarer and usually occur with more serious difficulties. Over 95 per cent of anorectics are female. Bulimia is similarly much more common in young women than men. The information on pica is mixed and that on food fads suggests that they occur equally in both sexes.

Onset and course

Pica starts in infancy and is usually apparent by two years. It may occur later, particularly when the preferred food is deemed to be culturally unusual (e.g. hair, faeces). Food fads may start also in early infancy and either disappear with growing up or become more pronounced.

Anorexia typically starts in girls 14–18 but can sometimes arise in girls between 8 and 12, who may not have even reached puberty. Bulimia usually starts at a later date than anorexia and may well not become evident until late adolescence or early adulthood.

Predisposing factors

Anorexia is more common in families when another sister is also anorectic and even more common among identical twins. The genetic data are, however, inconclusive and may point to a general vulnerability which is sometimes manifested in the disorder. There is also a greater incidence of depression and other serious affective disorders in biological relatives of anorectics. There is considerable speculation, supported by some evidence, that the family 'systems' may be faulty – with middle-class, well-off and over-achieving parents communicating a 'perfect' picture to the girl who tries to measure up to it. The girl usually feels helpless and over-dependent on parents' evaluation. She therefore either takes their expectations too far, becoming fearful of letting up with eating as a symbolic measure of success, or she may use her eating as a powerful means of achieving control over family dynamics. The fact that anorexia is an almost exclusively white, female condition among largely the better off suggests strong social determination of this condition.

Earlier history of anorexia would make subsequent bulimia much more likely. There is no evidence about predisposition to pica. Food fads are also more likely in better-off families, where choice is available, and in temperamentally tense children. Eating disorders have been more recently cited as one long-term consequence of sexual abuse.

Complications

Anorexia is almost invariably associated with cessation of menstrual periods, serious thyroid disorders, emaciation and depriving the body of essential energy and other nutrients. It is, thus, potentially life-threatening, particularly as it makes the girl more liable to infections, illness and possible adverse peer pressure. Depression and serious anxiety may be present both as a precursor and consequence of anorexia. In bulimia, the main complications arise from damage to mouth, teeth and throat, due to attempts to induce vomiting and possible long-term effects of laxatives and other pharmaceutical agents on the gastrointestinal system.

Impairment

Severe weight loss is life-threatening and demands hospital treatment. In bulimia, body systems may be disturbed and lead to dehydration and, in severe cases, cardiac disorders and, as in anorexia, death. The impact of pica depends on what is eaten and how easily it can be ingested or expelled by the body. Food fads are often only a nuisance, unless they threaten a balanced diet.

Prompts

Is girl abnormally thin or emaciated?
Does she come from a well-off family?
Are parents apparently 'perfectionists'?
What is girl's view of her family situation?
Have there been any recent untoward events?
What is her view of the ideal shape and weight?
How else has she tried to control her weight?
What is parental and peer response to her condition?
Is there any evidence of hoarding food, secreting or throwing away?
Is there any evidence of binge eating?
How does girl control her weight?
Are her attempts at disgorging food unobtrusive or demonstrative?
What non-food material is eaten, when, how often?
Associated with any particular events and conditions?
Can the food fads be accommodated?
Is emotional or sexual abuse suspected?

Action

If either anorexia or bulimia become life-threatening, clearly urgent action is warranted. Short of this, and if there is no risk of serious deterioration, action should be aimed at identifying and correcting the associated cognitive and family distortions and shaping better adaptive responses.

0113   Elimination disorders

01	Nocturnal enuresis
02	Diurnal enuresis
03	Nocturnal encopresis
04	Diurnal encopresis
05	Retention of faeces
06	Other

Description
This condition refers to problems of continence.

Bedwetting is a common problem among children. In most, bladder control is achieved by about the age of two but in a small proportion, bedwetting continues for some considerable time.

Involuntary urination during the day (diurnal enuresis) is much less common than nocturnal enuresis and, when it occurs, is usually associated with nocturnal enuresis. Bladder control during waking hours is achieved before control in sleep. Occasional involuntary urination during the day following the development of effective control may be associated with serious stress or upset. Continuing diurnal enuresis and failure to develop primary control may indicate physical abnormality. Excessive urination may be associated with certain diseases or physical conditions such as diabetes and infections of the bladder and urinary tract.

Abnormalities of the bladder, urethra and genitalia usually result from defects during the antenatal period. Some of these defects may predispose to infection or enuresis.

Encopresis or faecal soiling is much less common than enuresis. It is a major source of discomfort to the child and of distress and anger to those who have to deal with him. Soiling during the day is more common that at night and encopresis is generally more associated with psychiatric and psychological disturbances than enuresis. In some cases, its origin may lie in physical disorders.

Three types of encopresis are broadly recognized. First, there is in the younger child a failure to gain control over his bowels. The soiling is frequently associated with urination, and faeces are passed wherever the child is at the time he needs to defecate. A second type is where there is blockage of the bowel by hard faeces and secondary overflow with loose motions. Thirdly, encopresis may take place in a child who has gained control of defecation but then starts soiling as part of a more wide-ranging disturbance.

Associated features
Enuresis which is not the result of physical disorder is usually found in children who display a range of other emotional and behavioural difficulties. Soiling and other faecal problems are associated with more serious psychological disorders.

Prevalence
Primary enuresis gradually declines with age so that by age 5, roughly 5 per cent of boys and 3 per cent of girls present this difficulty; at age 10, 3 per cent and 2 per cent respectively; at 18 about 1 per cent of males and hardly any females. Primary encopresis is present in about 1 per cent of 5 year olds. Both disorders are more common in boys than girls.

Onset and course
Bedwetting may either continue from early failure to establish continence or start after a period of dryness – sometimes years later. Wetting and soiling may start in later childhood and early adolescence sporadically after at least one year of continence (called primary) and gradually become persistent (more than three episodes per week). Alternatively and particularly when early toilet training has not been fully successful, they may continue persistently (secondary) and gradually become sporadic, depending on wider adjustment of the child. Urination disorders usually disappear by early adulthood, but in some cases wetting may well persist or recur later.

Predisposing factors
In primary form, these disorders may be present because of inadequate physical development of the related muscles or other medical problems. More commonly they are associated with poor toilet training and parenting in socially adverse circumstances. In secondary form, they are usually associated with psychological stress in the child, such as going to or change of school, illness and episodes of sexual abuse – particularly in girls. Primary enuresis is more common in families when another sibling is also likely to be enuretic.

Complications
These are predominantly in terms of personal and social adaptation, unless the elimination disorder has a physical basis. Unless adequate hygiene counter-measures are taken, the child is likely to develop rashes, soreness and a persistent clinging smell that will be a social handicap. Children with these disorders are also likely to develop problems of body image and negative self-concept.

Impairment
Adequate toilet habits are essential prerequisites of social adjustment. Their absence or disorder is socially stigmatizing and personally onerous because of the labour and expense of changing bedding. Problems of habit control during the day have much wider and more serious social consequences than nightly ones because of their greater visibility by and impact on others.

Prompts
Was child toilet trained by about the age of three years?
If not, when was adequate bladder control achieved?
Is the present problem a continuation of wetting since infancy or of recent origin?
Has child's enuresis given cause for concern before?
Have there been any previous attempts at treatment?
If yes, with what results?
Does child wet himself only in bed or also out of it?

Is wetting associated with particular states such as stress due to change of circumstances or illness?

Is child obviously distressed by the wetting?

Has he done anything to control it or asked for help?

Had child developed control of defecation by age 5?

Has there been a continuous history since childhood or is the encopresis episodic?

Is failure of bowel control associated with urination?

Does he have any control over defecation? Is he able to delay defecation for any length of time after he feels the need to defecate?

Do episodes occur randomly or is there a pattern?

Are episodes associated with any obvious events or upset?

Is child very upset at his state?

Have there been any previous attempts at treatment? If yes, with what results?

Action

Because of the social stigma and personal derogation associated with these disorders, early intervention is indicated. However, the need to involve the wider family or caretaker network may make this more difficult than indicated by the reasonably uncomplicated treatment methods available.

0114   Menstrual disorders

01	Menstrual pain
02	Cessation of periods
03	Irregular periods
04	Other

Description

This condition refers to difficulties associated with monthly periods in girls.

Most girls cope reasonably well with their menstruation, its uncomfortable corollaries, and whatever else menstruation itself may signify. It is, however, known that the menstrual cycle is particularly sensitive and vulnerable to any upsets which a girl may experience. For this reason, girls with other difficulties seem to have rather more menstrual complaints than others, though the exact nature of the association is not known.

The most common menstrual disorders are excessive pain associated with periods (dysmenorrhoea), cessation of periods (amenorrhoea) and irregular periods. Cessation of periods does not cause any concern apart from its usual association with pregnancy or other serious physical and psychological disorders.

Associated features
These conditions often occur as single difficulties with no other problems. Increasingly, however, they are thought to be associated with girls' anxiety and difficulties in the area of body image and 'self-concept'. There is considerable recent suspicion that they may be associated in certain cases with physical, emotional and sexual abuse.

Prevalence
Estimates of prevalence of these disorders range from 3 to 15 per cent of women as a whole. Though specific statistics for adolescents do not exist, given the turbulence of this age, the rates are likely not to be much lower.

Onset and course
These difficulties occur from menarche onwards. Cessation of periods may occur from mid to late adolescence. For many girls, pain and irregularity eventually disappear in late adolescence and early adulthood. In some, however, it continues well into middle age. Cessation of periods, apart from pregnancy, is usually associated with other serious and perhaps life-threatening conditions (e.g. anorexia) and may well remit when those conditions improve.

Predisposing factors
As a straight gynaecological condition, none of these are thought to have predisposing factors. Anxiety, susceptibility to and experience of stress in personally adverse circumstances, accompanied by poor hygiene and food intake, may predispose to these conditions. There does not appear to be a family pattern in these disorders.

Complications
None important, these conditions being themselves usually the consequence of other difficulties.

Impairment
Other than in the case of pain, none serious.

Prompts
Has girl begun to menstruate?
Is onset of periods associated with pain and obvious discomfort?
Has this always been a problem?
If periods have stopped, is pregnancy suspected?
Have there been previous stoppages?
Is stoppage or irregularity associated with any obvious changes in
    circumstances or stress?
Does girl complain of her condition?
How does she show the distress?
What help does she seek?
Is abuse suspected?

Action

Medical help should be sought to reduce pain and evaluate need for referral to gynaecologist. If associated with other stress, counselling and other help may be necessary.

0115   Substance abuse

01   Medical drug abuse
02   Non-medical drug abuse
03   Alcohol abuse
04   Excessive smoking
05   Solvent abuse
06   Other

Description

This condition refers to a range of difficulties arising from excessive or misuse of drugs.

To the general public a drug is a medicine or a substance used in the treatment of a disease. However, a more complete definition of a drug is any substance, other than food, which alters physical or psychological functioning. Some medical drugs are mild and harmless, others are dangerous if not (or even when) taken as prescribed. The use of certain dangerous drugs is controlled by law.

In recent years, there has been considerable public alarm at media accounts of drug taking by youngsters. While there seemed to be an upsurge in some forms of drug abuse, public attention has abated with and switched to other problems presented by youngsters. Nevertheless, there is understandable concern at the risk presented to children as a result of drug taking which may escalate to other harmful pursuits.

With the repeated use of any mood-modifying or behaviour-changing (psychotropic) drug, an individual may develop physical or psychological dependence. The drug assumes an increasingly important role in his subjective life, whether his body requires increasing doses of the drug or not. This applies equally to medical and non-medical drugs, alcohol, cigarette nicotine and solvents, such as petrol and glue.

Medical drug abuse refers to the use of medically prescribed drugs, usually psychotropic medicines, for other than medical purposes. In considering drug abuse and dependence, a number of drugs can be identified, including depressants, stimulants and hallucinogenics. Non-medical drugs include such substances as cannabis, cocaine, 'magic mushrooms' and a wide array of others, used to bring about mood changes.

Alcohol is a universally available and used means of altering mood. Children and adolescents are by law prohibited from buying and consuming it – something which they widely ignore. Smoking is similar to alcohol in its prohibition but is even more widely ignored. Solvents provide a relatively recent form of substance misuse, essentially limited to young people with other major social and psychological problems. It entails inhalation of petrol or petrol-derived vapours and aerosol contents to create intoxicating effects.

Associated features

Substance misuse of all forms in the young is associated with poor parenting, even in families which are financially well off. It entails failure by the parents to recognize and instil in the growing child the dangers of substance misuse and alternative modes of stimulation. Whilst alcohol may be socially drunk at home, its use and that of tobacco outside the home (other than occasionally) and in peer groups is often associated with other anti-social and behavioural difficulties. The misuse of both medical and non-medical drugs is normally associated with more serious forms of breakdown in family and social controls.

Prevalence

Estimates of prevalence vary widely. Medical drug abuse is said to occur between 1 and 3 per cent of the adolescent population; non-medical drug abuse up to 5 per cent. In a recent British survey up to 25 per cent of adolescents claim regularly to drink alcohol, as do about 11 per cent of 11–16 year olds. Smoking is even more prevalent, affecting about 50 per cent of the population at some time. Solvent abuse affects less than 5 per cent, although it is said to account for more deaths than all the other drugs put together – around two young people per week in the UK. The main difficulty in estimating prevalence lies in the ambiguities of when a socially proscribed but nonetheless common activity becomes serious enough to warrant attention. Substance misuse is almost four times more common in males than females. However, in all areas of drug taking the gap between the sexes is narrowing, and the age of misuse coming down as the extent is increasing.

Onset and course

Illicit, occasional and experimental smoking and drinking may start before 10 in all children but more persistently those from disorganized families. Solvent abuse comes around puberty, and drug misuse during adolescence and later, if at all. Almost all drug taking starts slowly (the exception being rare, single incident addiction to 'hard' drugs) and gradually builds up if the young person likes the experience and the family and peer group context allow, fail to curb or encourage it.

Predisposing factors

There is great paucity of genetic data on substance abuse in childhood and adolescence. However, if genetic continuity through development is assumed (reasonably), adult data on various forms of substance misuse would suggest the strong possibility of such predisposition in younger persons. The greater the intensity or unusualness of the misuse, the greater this influence seems to be – on need to affect normal levels of arousal and the tendency to establish dependence.

More obviously, an early peak intake of or experimentation with drugs is characteristic of adolescence – a developmental stage which is more turbulent, is associated with more anxiety and depression and an age when identity is at its most unstable.

But experimentation is not the same as dependence. The latter is more often associated with serious family and psychological disorganization and adversity as well as a range of anti-social behaviour patterns. There is also some suggestion from research that persistent drug abusers are seeking to ameliorate personal difficulties and that gullible persons may be more susceptible to dependence than those of a more robust personality. The high association between all forms of drug use and delinquency is part evidence of this.

Complications

Although psychological and social stimuli are important in bringing about desired drug effects, these are primarily manifested in changed biochemistry of the nervous system. There is little evidence to show that small dosages or episodic uses of drugs do any major damage – though this clearly depends on the age and vulnerability of the young person, the dosage and the drug involved.

The major complications include transient or permanent damage to the nervous system, psychotic episodes, depression commencing with withdrawal, agitation and aggression in anticipation of the next 'fix' and a range of other difficulties. Excessive alcohol intake may lead to poisoning as will the intake of a number of other drugs, particularly in unregulated combination. Alcohol intake is also associated with aggressive and anti-social behaviour, while other drugs such as amphetamines and solvents may lead to high-risk behaviours which may endanger the young person. Choking on vomit after solvent abuse and in other cases of serious intoxication is a real possibility. The more seriously damaging complications of smoking do not become apparent until later adulthood.

Impairment

The evidence concerning long-term effects of substance misuse is patchy and mixed. Extended use of medical drugs (when not seeking to correct the condition for which they were intended) can cause damage to the nervous and digestive systems. Dependence on any drug will inevitably impair adaptation and lead to a range of compensatory/anticipatory acts which may undermine physical, social and psychological functioning. Apart from nicotine intake which has a long-term pernicious effect, the other drugs also increase morbidity from accidents and other high-risk events, such as asphyxia and cardiac arrest when under influence.

Prompts

Are there any members of family, including child, on medication for a mental state?

Is child suspected of having taken drugs prescribed for others?

How did suspicion arise?

Has child ever been suspected by police or others that he may have associated with drug takers?

Is there any evidence that he may have taken non-medical drugs?

Does any member of the family drink excessively?

Has child been suspected of drinking by parents, teachers or others?

On the basis of what evidence?

Do parents sanction smoking by the child?

Is there any evidence of craving for cigarettes? Long standing or of recent origin?

Have parents, police or teachers suspected glue or other solvent sniffing?

If yes, for how long and on what evidence?

Has child ever been referred because of drug abuse problems?

Do random checks of child's hiding places reveal any drugs or materials indicative of drug abuse?

Does child become restless in a cyclical fashion and appear to return to a state of tranquillity after an absence?

Have other reasonable alternative explanations been ruled out?

Does child show any evidence of undue lethargy and apathy after absences?

Does child ever have an unusual breath smell?

Do his eyes water, or does his skin seem irritated?

Does he have any abrasions or needle marks on the forearm or inside of elbow?

Can he adequately account for the use of his income?

Does his breath smell of alcohol?

Does he cadge or procure cigarettes and cigarette ends?

Does he become agitated if deprived of cigarettes?

How would he react to a solvent container 'accidentally' left around?

Does the fact that he may be observed make any difference?

Action

The need for action depends on the severity of the condition, arising from its age of onset, frequency, solo or group nature and the specific drug(s) used. Treatment is complex and dependent on personal characteristics of the child and the quality of parental and environmental support. In serious cases, the young person may have to be removed from his or her normal setting for treatment.

0116   Sleep disorders

01   Difficulty in going to sleep
02   Periodic waking up in the night
03   Over-sleepiness
04   Night terrors
05   Sleep walking
06   Other

Description
These conditions are associated with difficulties of sleeping in children.

Sleep disturbances are a common feature of childhood, though the presenting problem changes in the course of growth from early infancy to adolescence and beyond. They are all concerned with the failure satisfactorily to complete a night's sleep – through not going to sleep, waking up, sleep walking or being anxious about sleeping. These difficulties are usually classified as 'dyssomnias' – difficulties of going to or remaining in sleep – or 'parasomnias' associated with abnormal events occurring during sleep. The important criterion for this disorder is, therefore, subjective discomfort and complaint.

Associated features
Sleep disorders rarely present as the single complaint. They are most often associated with other physical (such as attention deficit disorder) or psychological difficulties (such as depression, anxiety). Most children are robust and use enough energy to fall and remain in sleep even when upset. When sleep is seriously disturbed over a prolonged period, in terms of its amount, timing or quality, it can be taken as indicative of serious difficulty.

Prevalence
About 15 per cent of the adult population complain of sleep disorders for which some seek professional help. The prevalence in children, as an independent disorder, is not known. However, taking the full clinical picture, the prevalence varies from about 1 per cent for night terrors, less for sleep walking. Problems of sleeping are difficult to estimate reliably but may affect the same proportion as adults, becoming worse during adolescence. Boys complain more of this disorder than girls, though in adulthood the picture is reversed.

Onset and course
Some children never learn to sleep during normal periods. Early parental anxiety and tendency to indulge a child with food or play during 'normal' sleeping hours may result in an odd sleep/waking pattern. Sleep disorders can occur at any age but generally get worse with growing up. Sleep

walking and nightmares occur and disappear earlier. Difficulties of going to and remaining in sleep occur later and gradually get worse with ageing.

Predisposing factors

Some people seem to 'need' less and have more difficulty in going to and remaining in sleep than others. This may be related to a nervous system which is easily aroused and stimulated into wakefulness, either by stress or its own spontaneous activity. All forms of susceptibility to stress, whether physical, social or psychological, at whatever age, are likely to predispose to disturbances of sleep.

Complications

These are primarily associated with consequences of fatigue and response to any external stressors with which sleep disturbance is associated. Appetite and school work may be affected. The child may become more irritable and, therefore, behave in an anti-social manner. Sleep walking may place the child at physical risk, and night terrors are distressing and may result in distressed or angry reactions in parents and others. Further complications may arise if medication is used which has side-effects.

Impairment

Not much beyond child's fatigue, tendency to wandering attention and falling asleep. Parent and child irritability may impede good social relations and make the child susceptible to other maladaptive response.

Prompts

Difficulty in going to sleep or complaints of this?
Fatigue after apparently good night's sleep?
Happens more than three times a week and for at least a month?
Excessively sleepy during the day even after a good night's sleep?
Falls asleep when engaged in activity?
Schedule of waking/sleeping abnormal?
Repeatedly (on same or different nights) wakes up after frightening dreams?
Distressed at the recall of those dreams or at prospect of going to sleep?
Child wakens with a scream and seems difficult to comfort?
Engages in sleep walking?
Unaware of this when woken up?
Is this put on? Does child do anything that he then excuses by saying he was asleep?

Action

Only warranted if child is at direct risk or suffers or makes others suffer unduly. Primary concern would be to rule out possibility of other and more serious disorders.

0117 Psychosomatic disorders

01	Bronchial asthma
02	Overbreathing
03	Alopecia
04	Eczema
05	Nettle rash
06	Psoriasis
07	Other

Description

Psychosomatic disorders are those in which psychological distress is believed to 'cause' physical ailments.

These disorders are included in this problem area because the problem, regardless of its origin, is physically manifested. The list of disorders subsumed under this heading at some time or other is very long and of dubious utility. We have included here only a short list of those disorders which are most commonly encountered in children with other problems and which cannot be directly attributed to physical causes.

Emotional factors have an effect on the respiratory system, notably in bronchial asthma and overbreathing (hyperventilation). Asthma is characterized by episodes of wheezing and struggling for breath. Anxiety or stress play a part in precipitating this condition. Hyper-ventilation consists of either an increase in breathing rate with frequent sighing, or in its severe form, rapid, shallow breathing which may lead to light-headedness and dizziness. Loss of hair (alopecia), eczema, nettle rash (urticaria) and psoriasis are all skin disorders in which emotional factors and stress are thought to play a considerable part both in onset and in perpetuating the conditions. Alopecia is a sudden, patchy loss of hair without obvious physical cause. Chronic eczema is a persistent, patchy, mild, itchy inflammation of the skin. Nettle rash or hives (urticaria) is an eruption of weals on the skin which are red, itchy and clearly demarcated. Psoriasis is a disorder manifested by red blotches covered with silvery scales, occurring most often on the scalp, back and arms.

Associated features

These conditions are almost invariably accompanied by an evident level of anxiety, tension and apprehension in a child who is more often than not shy and socially retiring. Each condition is seriously distressing (and, in the case of asthma, sometimes life-threatening) and seems to occur in the absence of any obvious physical causes, such as allergies and infections.

Prevalence

The prevalence rates vary from 0.40 per cent for asthma, and less for eczema and psoriasis. The prevalence of other disorders is not known. All the disorders seem to be more common in boys than girls.

Onset and course
Asthma usually begins to be manifest after two years of age, though it may occur earlier. It gradually gets worse, unless the condition is mild and is skilfully treated, and peaks around adolescence. Overbreathing is not uncommon in very young children and usually disappears, unless it is established as a maladaptive response in an adolescent. Eczema can become manifest from an early age and continue into adulthood. Nettle rash and psoriasis start usually in adolescence and may continue into adulthood.

Predisposing factors
All these conditions are more common in children who have a biologically related close relative with the same or similar disorder. Whether this is because of some physiological susceptibility or the possibility that they live in similarly polluted, allergenic, infective or stressful environments is not known. Another aspect of this is that persons subject to these disorders are usually shy and introverted, socially ill at ease, anxious and subject to frequent or abnormally strong tensions and these may have a genetic component.

Complications
Asthma is very distressing. Both the condition and its treatment may lead to social inhibition, isolation, fear and susceptibility to bullying and consequences of over-protectiveness by parents. The other disorders are also distressing because of their irritating and visibly stigmatizing effects on the child. Their presence accentuates the child's normal difficulties and is likely to lead to uncommunicably intense misery which may scar the child emotionally well into adulthood.

Impairment
The signs of impairment are very similar to and derive from the above complications. The child with these conditions is not only distressed but also causes distress in others. Schools are likely to feel readier than usual to overlook the child's propensity to be absent from school, with the result that child's educational progress will suffer.

Prompts
Are disorders obvious?
Are they of recent origin? If so, associated with obvious events or stress?
Have there been any previous treatments? With what effect?
Are overbreathing or asthmatic attacks a means of avoiding difficulty?
Are there asthmatic attacks even when no obvious gains are to be made?
Is child able to neutralize distress?
Is there any evidence of guilt, shame or other adverse reactions?
What are the consequences for child's social and scholastic attainments?

Action
Apart from overbreathing, which will probably disappear if ignored, these are all conditions with good physical treatments which should be tried to alleviate stress to the child at an early date.

Further reading

Abraham, S. and Jones, D.L. (1987) *Eating Disorders: the Facts*, London: Oxford University Press.

Agras, W.S. (1987) *Eating Disorders*, New York: Pergamon.

Assn for All Speech Impaired Children (1987) *Specific Speech and Language Disorders in Children: First International Symposium Proceedings*, London: Whurr Publications.

Assn for All Speech Impaired Children (1991) *Second International Symposium Proceedings*, London: Whurr Publications.

Bartimole, C.R. and Bartimole, J.E. (1987) *Teenage Alcoholism and Substance Abuse: Causes, Cures and Consequences*, London: Compact Books.

Beschner, G.M. and Friedman, A.S. (ed) (1979) *Youth Drug Abuse: Problems, Issues and Treatment*, Lexington, Mass.: Lexington Books.

Billard, J. and Nettelbeck, T. (1989) *Bedwetting – a Treatment Manual for Professional Staff*, London: Chapman & Hall.

Birdwood, G. (1969) *Willing Victim: a Parent's Guide to Drug Abuse*, New York: Haworth Press.

Brain, Lord (1961) *Speech Disorders*, London: Butterworth.

Brook, J.S. (ed) (1985) *Alcohol and Substance Abuse in Adolescence*, New York: Haworth Press.

Browne, T.R. (1983) *Epilepsy Diagnosis and Management*, Boston: Little, Brown.

Bruch, H. (1973) *Eating Disorders*, London: Routledge, Kegan Paul.

Brumberg, J.J. (1988) *Fasting Girls: Emergence of Anorexia Nervosa as a Modern Disease*, Cambridge, Mass.: Harvard University Press.

Brush, M.G. and Goudsmit, E.M. (1988) *Functional Disorders of the Menstrual Cycle*, New York: John Wiley.

Butler, R.J. (1987) *Nocturnal Enuresis: Psychological Perspectives*, Bristol: Wright.

Cameron, J. (1988) *Solvent Abuse: a Guide for the Carer*, London: Croom Helm.

Coggans, N. and Davies, J. *Adolescent Drug Addiction*, London: Cassell.

Coombs, R.N. (ed) (1988) *Family Context of Adolescent Drug Abuse*, New York: Haworth Press.

Cruickshank, W.M. (1967) *The Brain-Injured Child in Home, School and Community*, New York: Pitman.

Darby, J.K. (ed) (1985) *Speech and Language Evaluation in Neurology*, New York: Grune & Stratton.

David, K. and Cowley, J. (1980) *Pastoral Care in Schools and Colleges: with Specific References to Health Education and Drugs, Alcohol and Smoking*, Sevenoaks: E. Arnold.

Dinnage, R. (ed) (1986) *Child with Epilepsy*, NCB bibliographies, Windsor: NFER.

Dobree, J.H. (1982) *Blindness and Visual Handicap: the Facts*, London: Oxford UP.

Duker, M. and Slade, R. (1988) *Anorexia Nervosa and Bulimia: How to Help*, Milton Keynes: Open University Press.

Eisonson, J. (1986) *Language and Speech Disorders in Children*, New York: Pergamon.

Family Service Units (1982) *Enuresis in School Children*, London: FSU.

Felsted, C.M. (ed) (1986) *Youth Alcohol Abuse: Readings and Resources*, New York: Oryx Press.

Field, H.L. and Domangue, B.B. (eds) (1988) *Eating Disorders throughout the Life Span*, New York: Praeger.

Gadow, K.D. (1986) *Children on Medication, Vol. 2, Epilepsy, Emotional Disturbance and Adolescent Disorders*, London: Taylor & Francis.

Garrison, W.T. and McQuiston, S. (1989) *Chronic Illness during Childhood and Adolescence*, Newbury Park, Calif: Sage.

Garron, L.R. (1985) *Menstrual Disorders and Menopause*, New York: Praeger.

Ghodse, M. and Maxwell, D. (1990) *Substance Abuse and Dependence*, London: Macmillan Press.

Grunwell, P. (1990) *Developmental Speech Disorders: Clinical Issues and Practical Implications*, London: Churchill Livingstone.

Gullick, W.L. (1971) *Hearing, Physiology and Psychology*, London: Oxford University Press.

Haynes, S.N. (1982) *Psychosomatic Disorders*, New York: Praeger.

Hofman, F.G. (1975) *A Handbook in Drug and Alcohol Abuse*, London: Oxford University Press.

Hollins, M. (1989) *Understanding Blindness: an Integrative Approach*, Hillsdale, NJ: L. Erlbaum.

Hopkins, A. (ed) (1987) *Epilepsy*, London: Chapman & Hall.

Hurlock, E.B. (1973) *Adolescent Development*, 4th edn, New York: McGraw Hill.

Hynd, G. and Obrzut, J.E. (1981) *Neuropsychological Assessment and the School-Age Child*, New York: Allyn & Bacon.

Ives, R. (1986) *Solvent Misuse in Context*, London: NCB.

Kaplan, D.W. (1986) *Eating Disorders: Obesity, Anorexia Nervosa and Bulimia in Childhood and Adolescence*, Basel: Karger.

Kaplan, D.W. (ed) (1990) *Sleep Disorders in Childhood and Adolescence*, Basel: Karger.

Kirschenbaum, D.S., Johnson, W.G. and Stalonas, P.M. (1987) *Treating Childhood and Adolescent Obesity*, New York: Pergamon.

Klemz, A. (1977) *Blindness and Partial Sight*, Cambridge: Woodhead-Faulkner.

Kolvin, I. et al. (eds) (1973) *Bladder Control and Enuresis: Clinics in Developmental Medicine*, London: MacKeith Press.

Lachman, S.J. (1972) *Psychosomatic Disorders: a Behavioral Interpretation*, New York: John Wiley.

Lacks, P. (1987) *Behavioral Treatment for Persistent Insomnia*, New York: Pergamon.

Laidlaw, J. and Richens, A. (1988) *Textbook of Epilepsy*, London: Churchill Livingstone.

Laidlaw, M.V. and Laidlaw, J. (1980) *Epilepsy Explained*, London: Churchill Livingstone.

Lechtenberg, R. (1985) *Diagnosis and Treatment of Epilepsy*, New York: Collier.

Lechtenberg, R. (1985) *Epilepsy and the Family*, Cambridge, Mass.: Harvard University Press.

Lezak, M.D. (1976) *Neuropsychological Assessment*, New York: Oxford University Press.

Ludlow, C. and Cooper, J.A. (1983) *Genetic Aspects of Speech and Language Disorders*, London: Academic Press.

Martin, M. and Grover, B. (1986) *Hearing Loss: Causes, Treatment and Advice*, London: Churchill Livingstone.

Mencher, G.T. (1976) *Early Identification of Hearing Loss*, Basel: Karger.

Merrill, E. (1985) *Sniffing Solvents*, Birmingham: Pepar Publications.

Meyerhoff, W.L. (1984) *Diagnosis and Management of Hearing Loss*, Philadelphia: W.B. Saunders.

Mittler, P.J. (ed) (1970) *The Psychological Assessment of Mental and Physical Handicaps*, London: Methuen.

Moorcroft, W.H. (1989) *Sleep, Dreaming and Sleep Disorders: an Introduction*, New York: University Press of America.

Moses, D. and Burger, R. (1975) *Are you Driving your Children to Drink? Coping with Teenage Drug and Alcohol Abuse*, New York: Van Nostrand Reinhold.

Newcomb, M.D. and Bentler, P.M. (1988) *Consequences of Adolescent Drug Use*, Beverly Hills: Sage.

Norris, M. et al. (1957) *Blindness in Children*, Chicago: University of Chicago Press.

Nowinski, J. *Substance Abuse in Adolescents and Young Adults*, New York: W.W. Norton.

O'Connor, D. (1984) *Glue Sniffing and Volatile Substance Abuse*, Aldershot: Gower Publishing.

Oyer, H.J. et al. (1987) *Speech, Language and Hearing Disorders: a guide for the Classroom Teacher*, London: Taylor & Francis.

Peterson, H.A. and Marquardt, T.P. (1989) *Appraisal and Diagnosis of Speech and Language Disorders*, Englewood Cliffs, NJ: Prentice Hall.

Powell, D.J. (1980) *Clinical Supervision: Skills for Substance Abuse Counsellors – Trainees Workbook*, New York: Human Science Press.

Renfrew, C.E. (1972) *Speech Disorders in Children*, New York: Pergamon.

Retterstol, N. and Dahl, A. (1986) *Functional Psychoses: Classification and Prognosis*, Basel: Karger.

Rhodes, J.E. and Jason, L.A. (1988) *Preventing Substance Abuse among Children and Adolescents*, New York: Pergamon.

Rodger, J. et al. (eds) (1985) *Epileptic Syndromes in Infancy, Childhood and Adolescence*, London: S.J. Libbey.

Rogan, P.J. (1986) *Epilepsy: a Teacher's Handbook*, Liverpool: Roby Educational.

Ross, E. and Reynolds, E. (1985) *Paediatric Perspectives on Epilepsy*, Chichester: John Wiley.

Ross, E.R. et al. (1987) *Epilepsy in Young People*, Chichester: John Wiley.

Schaefer, C.E. (1979) *Childhood Encopresis and Enuresis: Causes and Therapy*, New York: Van Nostrand Reinhold.

Schaffer, C.E. (1979) *Therapies for Psychosomatic Disorders in Children*, San Francisco: Jossey Bass.

Schlundt, D.G. and Johnson, W.G. (1990) *Eating Disorders: Assessment and Treatment*, New York: Allyn & Bacon.

Scottish Health Council (no date) *Solvent Abuse*, Edinburgh: ITRC Education Group.

Senay, E.C. (1983) *Substance Abuse Disorders in Clinical Practice*, Bristol: Wright.

Slade, R. (1984) *Anorexia Nervosa Reference Book*, New York: Harper & Row.

Thomas, A.J. (1985) *Acquired Hearing Loss: Psychological and Psychosocial Implications*, London: Academic Press.

Trimble, M.R. and Reynolds, E. (1988) *Epilepsy Behaviour and Cognitive Function*, Chichester: John Wiley.

Twist, C. (1989) *Inhalants and Solvent Abuse*, London: Gloucester Press.

Ward, B. (1986) *Smoking and Health*, London: F. Watts.

Watson, J.M. (1990) *Solvent Abuse: Adolescent Epidemic?* London: Croom Helm.

Watson, R.R. (ed) (1989) *Diagnosis of Alcohol Abuse*, London: CSC Press.

Wellbourne, J. and Purgold, J. (1984) *The Eating Sickness*, New York: Allyn & Bacon.

Whitman, S. and Hermann, B.P. (eds) (1986) *Psychopathology in Epilepsy: Social Dimensions*, London: Oxford University Press.

Williams, R.L., Karcan, I. and Moore, C.A. (1988) *Sleep Disorders: Diagnosis and Treatment*, New York: John Wiley.

Williamson, D.A. (1990) *Assessment of Eating Disorders: Obesity, Anorexia and Bulimia Nervosa*, New York: Pergamon.

Wilson, C.P. and Mintz, I.L. (eds) (1989) *Psychosomatic Symptoms: their Underlying Personality Disorders and the Technique of Psychotherapy*, New York: J. Aronson.

9

Intellectual and Educational Problems

People's ability to perceive, understand and solve problems is the key to how they function in almost every area of life. Any deficiencies are important not only as possible problems in their own right but also in generating others. Thus, for example, individuals of very low intellectual competence have difficulty in acquiring the self-help skills necessary for survival, are usually a massive drain on their families, and may become incapable of forming social relationships. They may also present and be subjected to major social risk because of their inability to predict the consequences of their behaviour. 'Intelligence' is the core of all this.

Psychologists' view of what constitutes intelligence has become increasingly complex and cautious. It is now widely accepted that, other than for narrow academic purposes, it is not very sensible to talk of people's intelligence or intellectual potential in isolation from their other attributes. This is because what people can do with their potential depends on their personality, interests and the demands made on them. For this reason, it is becoming much less common to ask 'What is this child's IQ?' and expect a sensible answer.

Alongside the theoretical changes in the concept of intelligence, its measurement has also become increasingly sophisticated and subject to reservations and qualifications. Tests of intelligence elicit only restricted *samples* of children's intellectual competence and tend to emphasize certain cultural preoccupations. As such they are not wholly 'fair' to children from subcultures where values and concerns may be different.

Many intelligence tests in common use today still test *acquired* or learned knowledge in addition to skills of a more *innate* variety. What children have learned may well be a good guide to their present functional level, but not necessarily an indication of their *potential* capacity for learning. Children from home environments which are intellectually deprived or unstimulating frequently have marked deficits in such areas as 'general knowledge', yet they are able to perform relatively much better at more abstract practical tasks. They obtain low scores on verbal intelligence tests, yet many do reasonably well at more practical, non-verbal items, such as computer games. Caution must, therefore, be exercised in the interpreting of test results.

There is considerable controversy about the origins of intelligence. It is the traditional battlefield of the contending nature–nurture armies and has of recent years acquired an extra dimension of political significance. Arguments on both sides are complex and incapable of being wholly settled by research evidence. A balanced view would hold that people are born with a given intellectual capacity or potential, but for this potential to be realized, they need a great deal of stimulation and a wide range of opportunities for learning. In this sense, we never fully *know* the limits of a person's potential.

Intellectually limited children may, therefore, have a poor endowment. Alternatively, they may have been brought up in intellectually unstimulating environments. In either case, it is worthwhile to attempt improving their intellectual skills, though in both cases there will be practical limits to how much can be achieved. The question is how soon those limits will be (judged to have been) reached – and that can only be answered by trying.

Deficits in verbal skills may result from a lack of stimulation, but when this explanation is ruled out, other causes of a more specific nature, such as a poor auditory memory or difficulty with certain practical tasks, such areas as visual memory and specific perceptual abilities, should receive detailed investigation. Detailed findings are only useful insofar as they lead to treatment recommendations, and lengthy reports full of impressive findings rich in psychological jargon are often of little practical value.

Distinction is usually drawn between 'backwardness' and 'retardation' in educational attainments. The concept of 'backwardness' relates to children of limited ability who, primarily for this reason, are poor at basic attainments. 'Retardation', on the other hand, relates to children who are not deficient in intellectual potential but who have fallen behind significantly in basic attainments. The use of attainment tests yielding standardized scores enables a direct comparison to be made between intelligence and attainments, in a way that is not readily possible with tests yielding age equivalents.

Many intellectual and educational problems of children are connected with unrewarding school experiences. Which is the 'cause' and which the 'effect' is an unresolvable question. It is clear, however, that many of these problems would be tolerated and alleviated in a stimulating school environment which is concerned with the total social competence of the child. Teachers are, therefore, in the best position not only to assess but also to alleviate the problem. However, because of the specialized nature of much of the (more advanced) assessment, close liaison with psychological facilities would seem essential.

0201   Intellectual disorders

01	Mental retardation
02	Verbal skills deficit
03	Practical skills deficit
04	Functioning well below potential
05	Other

Description

These conditions relate to a range of difficulties concerned with intellectual functioning.

The essential feature of this condition is that the individual operates at significantly below the level of intellectual functioning of the general population, resulting in difficulties of problem solving and adaptation over a wide area. Verbal and practical skills deficits are only subvarieties of the general retardation. Under-achievement, in the present context, is applied to a child who behaves at the level of a mentally retarded child but is not retarded in terms of measured intellectual potential.

Judgment of intellectual disorder must, therefore, be based on rigorous intellectual assessment, using relevant and valid tests, carefully interpreted to allow for the child's physical, emotional, motivational and social features. Wider perspectives are needed to evaluate the child's effectiveness in such areas as survival, communication, daily living skills and ability to operate effectively according to age and relevant cultural group norms, outside standardized intellectual tests.

Associated features

Mental retardation is frequently associated with Down's Syndrome ('Mongolism'), autism, attention deficit and hyperactivity. The more severe the retardation the more likely will be other associated physical problems, such as epilepsy. There may also be a range of behavioural and emotional difficulties, such as anti-social behaviour, temper tantrums, aggression and self-stimulation, although some of these may be attributable to learned behaviour rather than retardation.

Verbal and practical skills deficit are more often evident in test scores than in daily behaviour, unless the deficit is gross. In the latter case there is usually a history or other evidence of probable organic damage or other serious disorder.

Prevalence

Mental retardation affects about 3 per 1,000 of the child population severely and about 2 per cent in a mild form, though the rate is higher in certain localities and sections of the population. It affects boys rather more than girls in a ratio of 1.5:1. Verbal skills deficit are much more prevalent among working-class children to as much as 10–12 per cent and primarily in boys. Practical skills deficits occur in about 1 per cent of children.

Onset and course

Primary mental retardation (congenital) is by definition present at the time of birth. Secondary retardation – resulting from damage at birth (e.g. forceps delivery) or subsequently – will be dated from the event. Verbal skills deficits are particularly affected by inadequate environmental stimulation and poor schooling. They may, therefore, not become apparent until puberty. Practical skills deficit may be present from infancy onwards or may become noticeable after illnesses, such as meningitis, or other trauma, such as accidents. Under-achievement is not usually noted until third or fourth year of schooling.

The course of mental retardation is dependent on its origin, profundity and level of environmental stimulation. In progressive physical disorders, such as epilepsy, the associated retardation will also increase. However, in other forms, the course of retardation is significantly slowed with high quality care, stimulation and support. Most mentally retarded children can now operate in non-institutional settings, and those with mild to moderate retardation in normal schools. Verbal and practical deficits also usually improve with growing older, unless associated with degenerative disorders.

Predisposing factors
The larger proportion of the mentally retarded and particularly the severe and profound, suffer from genetic abnormalities of many different kinds. The causes of the abnormalities are only inadequately understood. Some biological traumas, such as rubella, lead poisoning and certain diseases and deficiencies in the mother are more common in poorer families.

Complications
Numerous physical disorders may be associated with severe retardation, both as 'cause' and effect. The effects of institutional treatment may further complicate the assessment of seriously retarded children, as would their treatment in social and vocational settings.

Impairment
Intellectual capacity is an indispensable element of daily living and normal scholastic and social problem-solving. In profound or severe retardation, ordinary living and personal survival skills are so severely limited that irrespective of age, the child will require 'baby' treatment. In moderate and mild retardation, the slower rate of learning of skills rather than absolute inability marks out the child. Nevertheless a retarded child will continue to require some protection against intellectual and social demands that he cannot understand and fulfil. Such children are also much more at risk of physical and sexual exploitation as well as varieties of abuse. The level of handicap resulting from verbal and practical skills deficits depends on the degree of deficit.

Prompts
The quickest and most accurate source of information in this area is careful assessment of intelligence by a suitably qualified psychologist. Answers to the following prompts would, however, serve to fill in the picture and pinpoint particular areas of difficulty.

Does child have any general knowledge of the world around him?
Does child have a basic fund of knowledge, such as coinage,

hours/minutes of time, the calendar, immediate neighbourhood (one-mile radius), general locality (up to, say, five miles)?

Is child able to look after his own basic everyday needs, such as going to toilet, washing, dressing and eating?

Has child developed competence in freedom of movement?

Does he venture a reasonable distance from home without becoming lost?

Can he make and receive telephone calls, including the use of a public call box?

Can he catch buses and find his own way to places outside the immediate locality?

Can he do simple shopping?

Does child know his own name and date of birth/age?

Does he know his address, and how to locate it?

Is child able to tell the time quickly and accurately?

If not, is it because of a lack of experience?

Can child handle money quickly and accurately?

Can he tender the correct amounts of money?

Can he give correct amounts of change?

Does he rely on others either to help with everything or to do things for him?

Have you ruled out the possibility that he may have been denied the necessary learning experience or may have other (physical and social) difficulties which prevent him from acquiring the above skills?

Are there any school reports of general retardation?

Do parents and others say child seemed to be having difficulty in coping with new situations, compared with other children?

Has child been described as a 'slow learner' or 'ESN'?

Are rest of the family reasonably bright or do they also appear slow?

Among other children, does child stand out as particularly dull?

Do other children treat him as if he were dull?

Can he play ordinary games with reasonable competence?

Does everything have to be explained to him more than once even when he is co-operative?

Are there school or other reports regarding child's poor verbal ability?

Does he come from a verbally unstimulating environment where high-level verbal skills are not emphasized?

Does he say he has difficulty in expressing himself?

Does child have difficulty in verbal reasoning or expression?

Any more than other children?

Are you sure he is not just being uncommunicative?

Are his vocabulary and reasoning powers restricted?

Does he ever get flustered with his attempts at communication?

Is child said to have had motor difficulties during early life?

Do reports speak of clumsiness, accident proneness, co-ordination difficulties and the like?

Are there reports of difficulties in doing practical tasks?

Does child say he has trouble doing things with his hands?

Does child have any noticeable gross motor difficulties?
Does he have difficulty in doing tasks which require relatively fine finger-work?
Does he show any frustration with such work?
How does he manage to do a reasonably easy jigsaw puzzle or other tasks that his age mates do fairly easily?
Does he have difficulty even when in a tranquil, co-operative mood?

Action
A retarded child is likely to be at a scholastic and social disadvantage. Appropriate stimulating and compensatory action should be taken to reduce its impact and potential impairment.

0202   Attention deficit disorder (ADD)

01	Fidgety and restless
02	Easily distracted
03	Difficulty in sustaining attention
04	Rapid shifting from one activity to another
05	Impulsive activity without thought for consequences
06	Passive, day-dreaming, bored
07	Other

Description
This attribute clusters around a child's difficulty in sustaining attention.
   This condition has been frequently described as 'hyperactivity' in the past. It has, however, become increasingly apparent that 'hyperactivity' or excessive movement, which may or may not be present, is only one aspect of this disorder. When present, it is mainly evident in childhood up to puberty. The disorder affects attending to, recognizing and responding to social and intellectual stimuli which are essential for normal development. The child is always 'on the go', finding it difficult to settle to any task or concentrate on instructions. Because of this the child bangs and bashes into things and does things that get him into trouble – even if he does not mean to. As the child gets older, the physical moving around may lessen and be experienced primarily in general fidgetiness, discomfort and irritability when inactive.

Associated features
Children suffering from this disorder usually perform badly at school; give parents problems of control; have no close ties with peers, are inclined to throw temper tantrums and generally disrupt organized activities; engage in a wide and generally indiscriminate range of anti-

social behaviours including offences against person and property. The clinical picture is one of an extroverted but not group-dependent child, impulsive, tense, unanxious, poorly developed moral comprehension and a fluid and negative self-concept.

Prevalence
The disorder is common and may affect 2–4 per cent of children with a moderate to severe condition. The prevalence of milder degrees is probably higher but the children are not identified or are routed and labelled differently. Boys are between 3 and 9 times more likely to present this condition than girls.

Onset and course
In severe cases, the onset for the majority is before the age of four. In milder cases, it may not be picked up until the child has to conform to organized activities at school or in many cases, beyond even that time. Most ADD children slow down as they grow older. However, in those with a low IQ, in disadvantaged families and when a pattern of anti-social behaviour has been established, the disorder is likely to continue in one guise or another, resulting in poor long-term prospects. About one third of ADD children continue with the explicit disorder into adulthood.

Predisposing factors
Currently available evidence does not suggest a genetic basis for this condition. There is a strong prevailing view that ADD is associated with general neurological damage or deficit, such as may result from 'minimal brain dysfunction'. The supportive neurological evidence is, however, scant. There is also some recent interest in and speculation about the relationship between poor, unbalanced or inappropriate diets and inattentive, hyperactive behaviour. Other than in the case of allergies and special vulnerability in a limited number of cases where elimination diets can be tried, this view also remains largely speculative. Poor, disadvantaged and otherwise chaotic families produce more of such children when a biological relative is also more likely to suffer from this disorder – particularly when accompanied by anti-social behaviour. In such cases, the children appear not to have learned to sit still and concentrate and are not generally interested in adult, organized activities. Indeed, to survive or get attention they may have to behave in a disruptive manner or otherwise ruminate on something more interesting.

Complications
None, unless there are other frank neurological signs present, or the child suffers accidents and causes adverse reactions in others. Some children may be subjected to drug or other treatments which may create their own difficulties. Differential assessment may, therefore, be difficult.

Impairment
The main casualties are likely to be poor school attainments, difficulties with parents and peers, a pattern of possibly deteriorating anti-social behaviour and other forms of conduct disorder.

Prompts
Is child easily distracted from tasks – more so than other children?
Is this true at home as well as in a formal setting?
Does this apply to both group and one-to-one situations?
Does he say there are things on which he can concentrate?
Does he lose concentration and interest after only a short while?
Does he lose concentration even when there are not significant distractions?
Do friends say he is scatterbrained?
Does he have difficulty in settling to games and organized activities?
Does he cut into speech before it is completed?
Does he have difficulty in following instructions to complete a task?
Does he often shift from one activity to another?
Does he often lose or misplace things?
Does he often get into scrapes or risky situations?
Does he often seem not to be 'with it'?

Action
ADD children cause a great deal of nuisance and disruption and will themselves suffer in the long term from inadequate scholastic and social learning. It may be possible to moderate their behaviour pharmaceutically or through psychological techniques. Referral via GP to a child psychologist or paediatrician is advisable.

0203 Specific learning disorders

01 Developmental reading disorder
02 Developmental writing disorder
03 Developmental arithmetic disorder
04 Other

Description
These conditions relate to specific difficulties in acquiring scholastic skills.
    Children with these disorders show some developmental deficit in the basic psychological processes which are involved in understanding and using spoken or written language and other symbolic representations. The deficit is not generally due to mental retardation or sensory impairment, such as blindness. Furthermore, the above difficulties must not be due to poor schooling and must have shown resistance to normal instructional measures. 'Dyslexia' – meaning literally 'disorder of reading' – is the most famous of these.

Associated features
Such children may suffer from one or more of a wide range of other disorders of more or less severity. These include hyperactivity, poor co-ordination, physical awkwardness, emotional instability, impulsiveness, poor memory and 'soft' neurological signs which may indicate possible brain dysfunction.

Prevalence
Estimates of prevalence vary widely, based on different definitions and measuring instruments. These suggest that, depending on the particular disorder and measures of its severity, prevalence ranges from 2 to 5 per cent 'hard core' (predominantly in the area of reading and writing) to 28 per cent for general estimates of learning disorders. Boys tend to outnumber the girls in excess of 2.5:1.

Onset and course
These disorders do not become fully manifest until second or third year of schooling, when an otherwise average or bright child fails to learn at the same rate as others. The course of the disorder depends on the intensity and success of remedial measures taken. If these are adequate, the disorder does not progress and the child gradually improves, although he may never reach the same level of attainment as in other areas. If the remedial measures are inadequate, the child falls further and further behind. Some children take their full learning disability into adulthood.

In the case of developmental reading disorder, a strong familial pattern is evident, although the mechanisms of transmission are not known.

Predisposing factors
Many children who suffer from learning disorders also suffer from attention deficit and may share with them possible neurological dysfunctions and other difficulties cited in ADD (please see **0202**). A specific dysfunction frequently cited in learning disorders is 'cerebral laterality', i.e. the preference for or prominence of functions associated with one rather than another side of the brain. None of these views is based on extensive or dependable research.

Complications
Majority of these arise from the fairly fundamental social skills of reading and writing. Such children, if *not* otherwise problematic, are likely to be very sensitive about their disability and may develop poor views of themselves and maladaptive behaviour patterns as a result.

Impairment
This is likely to be both social and intellectual, in terms of children's inability to participate in activities which demand reading and writing skills.

Prompts
Is child showing major problems in reading, writing or arithmetic?
Is this not associated with mental retardation or sensory impairment?
Not associated with emotional upset or undue stress?
Any other areas of functioning affected?
Not associated with poor schooling?
Have good remedial measures been tried?

Action
Because of its long-term impairing consequences, remedial action, after
rigorous and *specialist* assessment, is indicated.

0204 Memory

01	Short-term memory deficit
02	Long-term memory deficit
03	Auditory memory deficit
04	Visual memory deficit
05	Other

Description
This condition refers to specific difficulties related to memory.
    Children with deficient memory are often not specifically recognized,
but either ignored or mis-labelled. Disorders of memory usually come to
light in specialist assessment, although parents and teachers may readily
confirm that child is 'scatterbrained' or does not remember things seen,
heard or done. Disorder is only specified as such if not due to mental
retardation.

Associated features
Usually seen together with attention deficit disorder and the cluster of
other features which include poor attainments and anti-social behaviour.

Prevalence
Prevalence of this disorder and sex ratio are not known. Judged by
atypical clinic and institutional populations, the incidence is about 1 per
cent.

Onset and course
Onset is not known but becomes apparent during school years. Child, if
not suffering from ADD or adverse home circumstances, may well
develop compensatory measures. Otherwise poor memory is ignored.
Whether or not it improves in early adulthood is not known.

Predisposing factors
As in ADD, when associated with it. Otherwise not known.

Complications
None other than the potentially embarrassing consequences of not remembering something important.

Impairment
Memory is an essential component of all social and intellectual behaviour. A child with a memory disorder has difficulty in drawing upon past experience to cope with new situations, so learning is seriously impeded. Although such a deficit will undoubtedly impair certain aspects of intellectual functioning, it need not create a general impairment and may be compensated for by developments in other areas.

Prompts
Does child have difficulty in following instructions, especially when these relate to a sequence of actions?
Can child remember small lists of items?
Can child remember a sequence of digits, and up to what length?
Are there variations in the child's apparent capacity to memorize?
Is child said to be 'absent minded'?
Does child seem to forget past events easily?
Are instructions of a long-term nature forgotten?
Are all past events forgotten, or are some remembered quite clearly?
Does child seem unable to remember spoken instructions, yet can cope with written ones?
Does child have difficulty in memorizing rhymes and tunes?
Can child repeat words of several syllables accurately, when these are presented in spoken form?
Can child remember numbers given orally, such as telephone numbers?
Does child confuse or forget symbols such as geometric shapes and mathematical signs?
Does child seem to forget pictorial material quickly?
Does child remember spoken instructions much better than printed ones?

Action
Depending on the severity of condition and availability of specialist help, it may be worthwhile to give the child skills or 'tricks' of remembering important material.

0205 Reading

> 01 Inability to read
> 02 Severely retarded reading
> 03 Poor comprehension of written material
> 04 Inadequate vocabulary
> 05 Poor word-building skills
> 06 Other

Description
This condition concerns reading retardation not arising from a specific learning disorder.

Reading is the most fundamental of scholastic achievements. It is also a most complex cognitive task involving, as it does, general intellectual competence, perceptual acuity and co-ordination, memory, expressive ability, concentration, motivation, cultural and familial support. It is because of such complexity and the need for good functioning of so many interdependent factors that so many children have inadequate reading skills. These disorders of reading may also be due to developmental difficulties, or associated with mental retardation. Assessment must attempt to disentangle the possible form of disorder and its associated conditions.

Associated features
Children with poor reading are also likely to be retarded in other scholastic attainments and come from poor families who are not focally interested in their children's education.

Prevalence
It is estimated that as many as 20 per cent of school-age children are retarded in reading skills. Boys are usually poorer than girls. Their numbers are in the ratio of about 2:1.

Onset and course
The condition becomes evident usually in second or third year of school (or earlier) when child performs less well than others in the group. Reading usually improves with successive years but may well remain retarded in comparison with other attainments.

Predisposing factors
Children from disadvantaged families, where there is little stimulation to read and little encouragement from parents, and those with poorer intellectual potential, are more likely to be poor readers.

Complications
None, other than those arising from child not being able to read important signs and other communications.

Impairment
Mainly child's poor attainment at school, cumulative effects of possible criticism by teacher and, therefore, gradual formation of negative views of self. In extreme cases, serious social handicap results if child cannot read, with maladaptive compensatory responses emerging to hide and balance reading disability.

Prompts
Does child seem to guess at words from the first letter and bluff his way through?

Can he break a word down into its component syllables?

Does he recognize common words by their shape (i.e. 'look and say') or can he build them up phonically?

Does he fail equally with those 'regular' words which conform to phonic rules and the 'irregular' ones which do not follow a systematic rule?

Are there reports of any specific reading disorders such as 'dyslexia' in child's school reports?

Has child been subjected to psychological examination to determine learning disorders?

Does child appear motivated and intelligent enough to read, has had the opportunity to learn, but still cannot read?

Does child spend time struggling to read written material?

Is the child from the sort of impoverished background which you would expect would give him a poor vocabulary?

Are there comments from teachers and others about his poor vocabulary?

Is his vocabulary inadequate for his probable needs?

Does child stumble over many words while reading aloud?

Dos he ask often what a word is?

Are these words simple and common or complex and unusual?

Does he slide over a word he does not know or substitute another word for it?

Are there any previous (school) reports suggesting that the child's comprehension of written material is poor?

Does child say anything about his difficulty to understand?

Does he express concern?

Have there been any attempts to remedy the problem and with what results?

Does child talk about anything he has read?

Does he scowl, look puzzled or show other signs of incomprehension when presented with material that he can read?

How does he respond if you ask him to read a passage and tell you about it?

Do your sources of information suggest that the child has difficulty in reading?

Is there a school report to this effect?
Has severe reading retardation been hinted at or diagnosed?
Have sources of difficulty been identified?
Has there been any specialist remedial treatment?
Can child read simple material?
Can he read words of more than two syllables?
Does he attempt to read on his own?
Can you coax him to read?
How does he respond?
Does he appear to mind that he has a reading difficulty?
Are there reports suggesting that child cannot read or has reading
    difficulties?
Has child received remedial help, and if so, what type, for how long, and
    with what results?
How does he explain his difficulty to read? How do others?
What do the school reports say about his reading?
Does child avoid situations where reading skills are required?
Does he ask others openly or in a roundabout fashion to read to him?
Can he recognize letters and how many?
Can he copy letters and words?
Can he visually and orally distinguish between similar letters, e.g. b,d;
    p,q; n,u?
Can he read simple words?

Action
In view of importance of reading and availability of exceptionally good
remedial techniques, attempt should be made to ameliorate child's reading
difficulties.

0206 Spelling

01	Severely retarded spelling
02	Retarded phonic skills
03	Reverses letters/words in writing
04	Other

Description
This condition refers to difficulties of spelling.

This skill used to be accorded much greater importance in the past than
it is now. Not only were teachers better spellers themselves, but they also
insisted on correct spelling by their pupils. Nowadays many otherwise
well-educated and literate people make spelling mistakes, without much
opprobrium. This is because correct spelling has become non-essential for
the communication of written material – as is evident from the reading
of any daily paper. In its more serious forms, poor spelling can be an

impediment to a child's progress, but not much. The British government is trying to bring back good spelling as one of the lost virtues of an ideal (earlier) educational system.

Associated features
As for reading.

Prevalence
Depending on the measures used and the criteria of judgment, as many as 30 per cent of school-age children have persistent difficulties in spelling. Boys do less well in this area than girls.

Onset and course
Onset is associated with demands on children to write. However, children gradually improve with schooling, though some remain relatively poor throughout. Spelling difficulties usually get better with ageing, only if child continues writing and is encouraged to improve spelling on the basis of feedback received.

Predisposing factors
As for reading.

Complications
As for reading.

Impairment
This is the least essential scholastic skill, particularly in the English language, where even severely misspelt words can be understood.

Prompts
Has difficulty been confined to spelling or has it involved other basic attainments?
Does the problem prevent effective written communication?
Has he reversed letters and words ever since he started school?
Can he spell simple words? Up to what length?
Is there difficulty with all words or only the less common, 'irregular' words?
Do his errors bear any resemblance to the original word or are they bizarre?
Does he use a phonic approach even when the spelling is incorrect?
Does child reverse letters occasionally or regularly? Which letters?
Are whole words reversed and how often?
Does the child sometimes produce 'mirror writing' where whole sentences are reversed?
Are you satisfied he is not playing or being inventive?

Action
Worth noting and trying to remedy, if child is likely to want to take such examinations as English, where spelling is important.

0207 Written communication

01   Illegible handwriting
02   Poor written expression
03   Punctuation problem
04   Distorted grammar
05   Other

Description
This condition refers to children's difficulties in writing.

Children's writing difficulties do not give rise to the same concern as do their problems in other scholastic areas. This is partly because few children need to do much writing, other than at school. Even then, such difficulties as erroneous punctuation and grammar and poor handwriting are regarded as so common and culturally determined that correcting them usually comes low on the teacher's list of priorities, particularly in the secondary school. It is included here not just as a potentially 'unacceptable condition', but mainly for the sake of comprehensiveness.

Associated features
General scholastic difficulties, perhaps associated with poor intellectual functioning, a disinterested home and poor interest in school.

Prevalence
Not susceptible to estimation because of the highly subjective criteria for writing adequately. However, over 20 per cent of children, more boys than girls apparently, seem to have persistent difficulty in writing.

Onset and course
Usually becomes evident when child has to start producing written material towards the end of primary school and in secondary education. Although writing improves with practice, some people remain poor writers throughout their lives.

Predisposing factors
Poor intellectual competence, disadvantaged and disinterested home and poor schooling all play a part in producing poor writers.

Complications
None, unless child is required to write for some important outcome.

Impairment
None serious, unless the child has aspirations for academic progress or seeks a job in which writing is important.

Prompts
Has child been taught handwriting in a systematic way?
Are there previous reports of difficulties in writing?
Is child aware of and does he admit to having writing difficulties?
Does he understand what various punctuation marks are for?
Is he aware of his incorrect or idiosyncratic grammar?
Does his handwriting vary according to his mood and interest in the subject matter?
Is his handwriting consistently illegible?
Is he left-handed or ambidextrous?
Is there any hand tremor apparent?
Is his writing meaningless or of unclear meaning?
Does his expressiveness vary according to subject matter?
How does he respond when you ask him to write about a favourite subject?
Is his writing completely lacking in punctuation or is the punctuation wrong?
Is his writing so grammatically incorrect that it cannot be understood at all or only with great difficulty?

Action
Relatively easy to teach and improve, if considered important.

0108 Arithmetic

01	Severely retarded arithmetic
02	Cannot count
03	Cannot measure
04	Other

Description
This condition refers to difficulties in arithmetic.

Traditionally there seems to have been more emphasis on reading than on numeracy in schools, and there is some evidence that standards of numeracy have declined. And yet, on the other hand, employers in an increasingly technological society are demanding better standards of basic numeracy.

A particular characteristic of arithmetic is the cumulative nature of the subject matter. New information is frequently dependent upon previously learned material, more so than in either reading or spelling. Children who have not mastered the basic skills are, therefore, unlikely to make progress in more advanced areas of number work. Some children at the secondary level of education are unsure of their arithmetical tables and do not possess any alternative conceptual framework to substitute for them, and as a result progress in the subject is often halted.

Associated features
Mental retardation, other scholastic difficulties, more often than not a disadvantaged and academically disinterested home.

Prevalence
About 25 per cent of primary school children and 35 per cent of secondary children have some difficulty with arithmetic, particularly on standardized tests. There are contradictory and inconclusive views as to whether boys or girls do less well.

Onset and course
This difficulty becomes evident when child first starts arithmetic at school. It tends to suffer seriously as child gets older because of the essentially cumulative nature of arithmetical skills. With good teaching, however, children can improve significantly. Most, even the seriously retarded, acquire enough arithmetic to suffice for their social and leisure needs.

Predisposing factors
As in associated features, above.

Complications
None specific, unless child 'needs' the skills and is likely to react badly to not having them.

Impairment
Basic arithmetic skills are essential for normal social living. But many children who are deficient in formal arithmetic skills can lead a perfectly normal life and do what they want effectively – such as keep football scores and give and take change in transactions.

Prompts
Are there reports of mathematical difficulties from school or other sources?
Has he received remedial or other help with number work and with what results?
Is child aware of and does he report difficulties with number work?
Can child perform any or all of the four basic processes of addition, subtraction, multiplication and division?
Does he find specific difficulties in any particular area?
Has child received remedial help, and what type?
How does he respond to playing card games which involve recognition of numbers and counting?

Is he able to count aloud? Can he count money?
Is he able to measure length, volume and weight?
Can he tell the time?

Action
Simple remedial teaching to improve this skill would be worthwhile.

0209   Language disorder

01	Poor articulation of speech sounds
02	Poor expressive language
03	Idiosyncratic speech
04	Confused speech
05	Poor language comprehension
06	Other

Description
This condition refers to poor and inadequate verbal communication skills.

These disorders are characterized by marked impairment of the level of language functioning that might be expected of a child who is not mentally retarded and does not suffer from a pervasive developmental disorder, bad hearing or neurological disorder.

Poor articulation refers to child's inability to make the sounds (f, l, r, ch, sh, th) and more severe cases even such sounds as b, d, m, n, t. Poor expressive language refers to child's difficulty to talk at the level expected for his age and intelligence in such terms as vocabulary, length of sentence and specific content. Poor receptive ability refers to child's difficulty in understanding anything from basic vocabulary (in severe cases) to complex sentence structures (in mild cases). Idiosyncratic and confused speech are inevitably more bound up with prevailing cultural norms of what is good speech, though again in extreme cases this would make communication with child difficult.

Associated features
These disorders are usually present in a cluster including some motor difficulties and possibly enuresis. There is usually a history of delay in reaching developmental milestones. Sometimes ADD and behavioural difficulties may be present.

Prevalence
Estimates vary from about 3 to 10 per cent of school-age children suffering from these disorders. There is some suggestion that more boys than girls are prone.

Onset and course
Usually by age 3, one or more of these disorders have become obvious. This, however, depends on the level of language stimulation given to the child and the degree to which parents and caretakers engage the child in talking. Most children eventually catch up and sort out their speech disorder by early school years. More severe cases, particularly those with articulation disorders, may need speech therapy.

Predisposing factors
There is some evidence of chromosomal abnormality in some children with speech disorders. The incidence is also higher in families, but evidence on specific form of predisposition is light. Children with 'soft' neurological difficulties may be more likely to suffer from these, as would those from poorer families where there may be little talking or where speech is confusing, inadequate, or idiosyncratic.

Complications
None in particular, other than those which are likely to result from poor ability to communicate and other people's adverse reactions. Speech disorders must be distinguished from consequences of mental retardation or physical disorders.

Impairment
Given the central importance of speech in intellectual and social development, a child with speech disorders is likely to be seriously disadvantaged at school and in society. He is likely to be teased and develop maladaptive patterns of adjustment to his condition.

Prompts
Have any of these speech disorders been evident?
How young?
What sort of home?
Are there previous reports of idiosyncratic or confused speech? Are these independent of other reports concerning the child's poor scholastic performance?
Have his speech oddities attracted particular attention by teachers?
Has any attempt been made to correct them? With what results?
Does child give any evidence of being aware of or affected by his idiosyncratic or confused speech?
Does child make up his own words?
Does he commonly mispronounce words?
Is there any evidence of general confusion or disorder of thought?
Is this type of speech peculiarity or confusion a generalized occurrence, or is it specific to certain situations?
Does he have periods when his speech is lucid and normal?
If it is situation-specific, is it a response to stress?
Could he speak properly if encouraged to do so?

Do other children comment on his funny or peculiar speech?
Does his idiosyncratic speech make any special sense? What?

Action
If by age 5 child retains any of these disorders to a noticeable degree,
speech therapy and language enrichment programmes may be indicated.

0210   Interest in school or work

01	Avoidance of school
02	Embarrassed by poor skills
03	Disinterest in school
04	Expectation of failure
05	Other

Description
This condition refers to a child's poor interest in school or employment.

Although this is not strictly a cognitive skill, it is included here because
it is so intimately bound up with much of the earlier difficulties in this
area. Irrespective of a child's ability, he will not do well at school if he
is not interested in school work or finds school and matters associated
with it stressful. These may result from the absence of motivation for
school and work or counter-attractions of other activities.

The issue of attitudes has in the past often been played down or even
neglected. Although truancy has always been highlighted, many children
opt out of school by passively withdrawing *in* the classroom. They are
often overlooked, especially if they do not present overt management
problems within the school. Truancy is often only an overt and extreme
form of disinterest in or antipathy to school.

Thus, negative attitudes to school are manifested in a wider range of
behaviours, only some of which have been included here. These attitudes
reflect and in turn generate negative experiences at school. A child who
stands out or is ridiculed for scholastic incompetence is likely to avoid
school; one whose parents undervalue schooling will not see much reason
for persisting with difficult cognitive tasks; one who expects to fail will
avoid the test and one who becomes part of a delinquent group is likely
to find other activities more exciting and worth pursuing than persevering
with frequently 'boring' school work.

'School phobia' is a contentious topic and one which has come to be
used dubiously in all sorts of situations where there is no intense, irrational, debilitating fear of school, although undoubtedly some children
suffer from this condition. Because the diagnosis is frequently based on
an inadequate examination of alternative explanations, the descriptive
terms 'school avoidance' or school refusal are to be preferred. Any

phobias or intense anxieties will be dealt with under the appropriate heading in Chapter 13, Psychological problems.

Associated features   Such children *may* not be intellectually very bright. However, more often than not they come from seriously disorganized and disadvantaged families where their efforts are spent on simply surviving the physical and emotional trauma to which they are subject. The primary experience is one of failure and hopelessness, when not only does it take a lot of effort even to try, but there is little assurance that the effort will pay off. Associated difficulties can also include a wide range of conduct and anti-social disorders and wider clinical difficulties.

Prevalence
Difficult to estimate but said to affect over 20 per cent of the school and school-leaver population. Boys are apparently more affected than girls.

Onset and course
In severe cases, may be manifest from earliest school days. It is, however, more often a condition most apparent from the time of primary to secondary school transition, peaking around school-leaving time. In children from more disrupted backgrounds, the motivational difficulties carry well into early adulthood and probably beyond. They make up a significant proportion of marginal and unemployed people.

Predisposing factors
Poor intellectual potential and school experience feature strongly, as do disorganized families where parents (particularly father) either derogate school or are disinterested. Being involved in anti-social behaviour, or suffering from conduct or affective disorders, are also likely to predispose to this condition.

Complications
None by itself, apart from getting the child into trouble with school, failing to provide him with the necessary positive reinforcement of achievement and perhaps leading to drift into anti-social behaviour.

Impairment
Considerable, in an increasingly harder society where children must achieve economic independence. Likely to be denied chance of decent work, itself leading to other social and psychological problems.

Prompts
Do teachers and others comment on his poor work skills?
Has his inadequacy been made public by teachers or parents and with
    what results?
Does he say that he is embarrassed or worried about poor scholastic skills?
Have parents shown much interest in his school career?

Are they likely to devalue the school to their child?

Has child's attendance at school been spasmodic without other good reason?

Do school reports suggest general disinterest or only disinterest in certain subjects?

Are there school or other reports suggesting that the child expects to fail and, therefore, refuses to try or avoids school?

Are these expectations realistic? For what reasons?

Is child said to dislike or fear school?

Are there any obvious reasons for this problem?

Have other members of the family experienced similar problems?

What is the school's view of this problem?

Has child been referred to an Education Welfare Officer or been taken to court for persistent truancy? With what results?

Has he been referred to the Child Guidance Clinic or other specialists for his avoidance of school? What have they said about his problem?

Is problem so severe that it has been described as 'school refusal' or 'school phobia'?

What are his feelings about school and how does he express them?

Does child try to 'cover up' for his poor work skills by bluffing or opting out?

Does he fail to finish his work or hand it in in a manner others are not likely to notice?

Is he a passive observer rather than active participant in the classroom?

Does he grumble or more actively reject school work?

Are special efforts by teachers likely to produce a more interested response?

Is he more interested in some teachers' subjects than others?

Does child behave as if whatever he does he is likely to fail?

Does he give up easily in resignation or defiance?

Does he say anything to this effect?

Does child actively resist going to school?

Does he become tearful, sick or aggressive if his school attendance is enforced?

Is there anxiety, tension or severe unhappiness apparent when he is at school?

Does he stay away from school at the slightest reason such as being 'unwell' or problems at home?

How does he respond to attempts to make him more interested or welcome in school?

Do sanctions or threats make any difference to his reaction?

Action
As important as it is difficult, because remedy usually lies in creating fundamental personal motivation as well as changing family and social conditions.

Further reading

Albes, Z.M. (1982) *Child under Stress – Dyslexia? – a Practical Guide for Parents and Teachers*, Crawley: Granary Press.

Bakker, D.J. (1987) *Developmental Dyslexia and Learning Disorders: Diagnosis and Treatment*, Basel: Karger.

Banks, T.E. (1982) *Language and Learning Disorders of the Pre-academic Child – with Curriculum Guide*, Englewood Cliffs, Prentice Hall.

Barkley, R.A. (1990) *Attention Deficit Hyperactivity Disorder: a Handbook for Diagnosis and Treatment*, New York: Guilford.

Benton, A.L. and Pearl, D. (1981) *Dyslexia: an Appraisal of Current Knowledge*, New York: Oxford University Press.

Bernstein, D.K. and Tiergermann, E.M. (1989) *Language and Communication Disorders in Children*, New York: Merrill.

Blagg, N. (1987) *School Phobia and its Treatment*. London: Croom Helm.

Block, N. and Dworkin, G. (eds) (1977) *The IQ Controversy: Critical Readings*, London: Quartet Books.

Bloomingdale, L. and Sergeant, J. (eds) (1988) *Current Concepts and Emerging Trends in Attentional and Behavioural Disorders of Childhood*, New York: Pergamon.

Brown, B.B. and Beveridge, H. (eds) (1979) *Language Disorders in Children* London: College of Speech Therapists.

Bryant, P. and Bradley, L. (1985) *Children's Reading Problems*, Oxford: Blackwell.

Carrow-Woolfolk, E. (1988) *Theory, Assessment and Intervention in Language Disorders: an Integrative Approach*, New York: Allyn & Bacon.

Carrow-Woolfolk, E. and Lynch, J. (1981) *An Integrative Approach to Language Disorders in Children*, New York: Allyn & Bacon.

Chazan, M., Moore, T., Williams, P. and Wright, J. (1974) *The Practice of Educational Psychology*, Harlow: Longman.

Child, D. (1973) *Psychology and the Teacher*, London: Holt, Rinehart and Winston.

Clarke, A.D.B. and Clarke, A.M. (1973) *Mental Retardation and Behavioural Research*, London: Churchill Livingstone.

Cleland, C.C. (1978) *Mental Retardation: a Developmental Approach*, Englewood Cliffs: Prentice Hall.

Critchley, M. (1970) *Dyslexic Child*, London: Heinemann Med.

Darby, J.K. (1985) *Speech and Language Evaluation in Neurology*, New York: Allyn & Bacon.

Douglas, C.P. and Holt, K.S. (1972) *Mental Retardation: Pre-natal Diagnosis and Infant Assessment*, London: Butterworth.

Drew, C.J. (1988) *Mental Retardation: a Life Cycle Approach*, Columbus, Ohio: Merrill.

Eisonson, J. (1986) *Language and Speech Disorders in Children*, New York: Pergamon.

Gruneberg, M.M. et al. (eds) (1979) *Applied Problems in Memory*, London: Academic Press.

Grunwell, P. and James, A. (eds) (1985) *Functional Evaluation of Language Disorders*, New York: Grune & Stratton.

Gunzburg, H.C. (1975) *Progress Assessment Charts and Manual*, Birmingham: SEFA Publications.

Hersov, L.A. (1980) *Language and Language Disorders in Childhood*, New York: Pergamon.

Hynd, G. and Cohen, M. (1983) *Dyslexia*, New York: Allyn & Bacon.

Hynd, G. and Obrzut, J.E. (1981) *Neuropsychological Assessment and the School-Age Child*, New York: Allyn & Bacon.

Kahn, J.H. et al. (1981) *Unwilling to School: School Phobia or School Refusal – a Psychosocial Problem*, New York: Pergamon.

Kapur, N. (1988) *Memory Disorders in Clinical Practice*, London: Butterworth.

Kellerman, H. and Burry, A. (1981) *Handbook of Psychodiagnostic Testing*, New York: Allyn & Bacon.

Kirby, E.A. and Grimley, L.K. (1986) *Understanding and Treating Attention Deficit Disorder*, New York: Pergamon.

Knox, P. (1989) *Abuse of Care and Custody Orders and Understanding School Phobia*, Upton-upon-Severn, Worcs: Self Publishing Association.

Lees, J. and Urwin, A. (1990) *Children with Language Disorders*, London: Whurr.

McGinnis, D.J. (1982) *Analysing and Treating Reading Problems*, New York: Collier Macmillan.

McLaughlin, R.M. (ed) (1986) *Speech Language Pathology and Audiology*, New York: Allyn & Bacon.

Macmillan, D.L. (1982) *Mental Retardation in School and Society*, Boston: Little, Brown.

Matson, J.L. and Barrett, R.P. (eds) (1982) *Psychopathology in the Mentally Retarded*, New York: Allyn & Bacon.

Matson, J.L. and Mulick, J.A. (1983) *Handbook of Mental Retardation*, New York: Pergamon.

Mittler, P.J. (ed) (1970) *The Psychological Assessment of Mental and Physical Handicaps*, London: Methuen.

Moghadam, H. (1989) *Hyperactivity Revisited*, Canada: Detselig Enterprises.

Pavlak, S.A. (1985) *Informal Tests for Diagnosing Specific Reading Problems*, Englewood Cliffs, NJ: Prentice Hall.

Peters, E. (1978) *Reading Problems*, London: Heinemann Educational.

Peterson, H. and Marquardt, T.P. (1989) *Appraisal and Diagnosis of Speech and Language Disorders*, Englewood Cliffs, NJ: Prentice Hall.

Quinn, V. and Macauslan, A. (1991) *Dyslexia: what Parents ought to Know*, Harmondsworth: Penguin.

Reid, J. and Donaldson, H. (1978) *Reading: Problems and Practices*, East Grinstead, W. Sussex: Ward Lock Educational.

Rudel, R.G. (1988) *Assessment of Developmental Learning Disorders: a Neurological Approach*, New York: Basic Books.

Silver, A.A. and Hagin, R.A. (1990) *Disorders of Learning in Childhood*, Chichester and New York: John Wiley.

Snowling, M. (1987) *Dyslexia: a Cognitive-developmental Perspective*, Oxford: Blackwell.

Thomson, M. (1989) *Developmental Dyslexia: its Nature, Assessment and Remediation*, London: Whurr.

Thomson, M. and Watkins, B. (1990) *Dyslexia: a Teaching Handbook*, London: Whurr.

Wilson, B. and Moffat, N. (1984) *Clinical Management of Memory Problems*, London: Croom Helm.

Wodrich, D.L. (ed) (1986) *Multidisciplinary Assessment of Children with Learning Disabilities and Mental Retardation*, Baltimore, MD: P.H. Brookes.

Wolraich, M. (1987) *Practical Assessment and Management of Children with Disorders of Development and Learning*, Chicago: Year Book Medicine.

Wortis, J. (ed) (1986) *Mental Retardation and Development Disabilities*, New York: Elsevier.

Young, P. and Tyre, C. (1983) *Dyslexia or Illiteracy?*, Milton Keynes: Open University.

10

Home and Family Problems

Family is the central institution of all human societies. It is both the arena and the medium for turning primitive children into social beings. In the assessment of children's problems, the family background is almost the first area to be looked at and evaluated. It is by now part of the folk wisdom of Western society that most children's non-physical problems arise from difficult home circumstances. This is largely supported by research findings which show that practically every aspect of children's problems is to varying degrees associated with difficulties within the family unit.

From an assessment point of view, family problems present the most complex and heterogeneous area. To start with, a family is an integrated (even those which are disintegrating) functioning entity with a complex network of roles, controls, communications, affection and power relationships. These factors and others associated with them are diverse and operate at many levels. It is not always possible adequately to differentiate whether family problems 'cause' children's difficulties or are themselves reflections of difficulties presented by them. Additionally, family influences merge with those of peers, school and the wider society and are, therefore, difficult to disentangle. For this reason, it may be best to adopt a pragmatic approach and simply group together those factors which are involved in family functioning and generally associated with adverse circumstances, whether they affect the child directly or not. This is, in any case, the basis of official intervention in children's lives, whether the adverse family circumstances can be proved to be directly affecting the child's development or not.

Family disorders most fundamentally emanate from the failure of the family to fulfil and control its basic functions of providing physical, emotional and social care for its members. Other orientations to the family as a system of roles, network of relationships or medium for psychological and social development, would suggest other forms of dysfunction which may be regarded as worthy of assessment. Failure in any of these areas can be regarded as, at least, a passive contributor to the potentially disorderly development of the child and may be implicated in a child not receiving adequate 'care and control'.

Unacceptable conditions which may affect or be presented by the family range from its physical state, such as the physical and structural quality of the home and the neighbourhood, through relationships between the parents and their children, to aspects of emotional care, methods of control, and qualities and behaviour patterns presented to the child for modelling. Within this wide range only some of the problems are directly concerned with what a child does. The problems presented to and by the child's home include the impact of the community, the interaction between the community and the family, the relationship between the parents, interaction between parents and children and interrelationships of the children with one another.

These items are qualitatively different from those in other problem areas. Some of them, such as problems with the community, may have no direct impact on the child but because of their wider effects may be potential sources of adversity which should be considered in any comprehensive assessment of the child and his difficulties.

The assessment of family problems primarily involves the compilation of a factual catalogue of apparent and reported difficulties, a history of significant events within the family which are thought to have impinged on the child, and the making of inferences and judgments based on questions asked of or about the family and observations made of the behaviour of its members. Testing is largely inappropriate other than in determining some characteristics of one member of the family, although tests are available to evaluate members' perception of family relationships.

The family is the most close-knit and intimate unit of social interaction likely to come under the scrutiny of social agencies. It is the most difficult to penetrate and evaluate not only because of the intensity of its interrelationships but also because each community and subcultural setting manifests its influence on the family and the way it operates in different ways. It is not, therefore, always possible to be even moderately sure that what may be regarded as generally deviant and unacceptable in the wider society is necessarily so regarded in a particular family's case in relation to their subculture, or that it is having an adverse effect on the child. While it is possible to say that a family is problematic or is having an adverse influence on the child (in, for example, 'failing to thrive' cases), it may not always be possible to be specific about the sources of difficulty. Also, while some assessment agents are particularly insightful about family problems and can evaluate its difficulties comprehensively, others' evaluations are deficient and their judgments should not be treated as sacrosanct. These reservations are necessary as a corrective to the frequently glib and patronizing judgments made about a family's dynamics by professional workers. This caution is particularly important in dealing with families in trouble, who are powerless and incapable of countering negative value judgments passed on them. This is an area which is more susceptible to idiosyncratic judgments and the use of socially and ethically pejorative terms than any other.

Surprisingly, this area has not been a major focus of interest of those concerned with assessment of child and adolescent disorders. In the major diagnostic systems, it is regarded as being among a range of (undefined and unenumerated) 'psychosocial' stressors. In multivariate approaches, it does not even appear, and yet everyone agrees that child and adolescent disorders are frequently triggered off and maintained by home and family problems. One major concern of this book is to provide a possible checklist of problems and elaborate those where wider assessment may be relevant. The scheme adopted in this chapter is one of *pragmatic grouping* of adversities presented to or by the child within the home, ranging from the wider community to interactions with siblings. Although the term 'behaviour' as the third level of analysis is semantically inappropriate as a designation of social factors, it has nevertheless been retained for the sake of continuity with other chapters. Similarly, the usual format of the other chapters has been maintained in order to facilitate reference, even though some of them are not directly applicable.

0301   No home base

01	No parents or whereabouts unknown
02	Parents homeless/scheduled accommodation
03	Parents unwilling/unable/inappropriate to accommodate
04	No appropriate relative willing to accommodate
05	Other

Description

This condition refers to a child being literally or functionally homeless.

A child's home is the arena in which his basic requirements for survival and growth are met. The home provides the major source of perceptual stability in children's lives from which the first elements of identity begin to emerge. This does not appear to be any less important in adolescence than in childhood. Additionally, the absence of a constant home base indicates the possibility of other major adversities in the home which require special compensatory measures.

Associated features

Usually multi-generation adversity – economic, social and psychological – in the family. The children may not present any difficulties or alternatively any and many, from neurological disorders, mental and scholastic retardation, poor peer relationships, extensive conduct disorders and a range of psychological difficulties.

Prevalence

Roughly 3 per cent of the UK adult population are homeless at any given time. How many of these have children is not known. Even less is known about those children whose parents cannot be traced or who for some reason or other cannot or will not accommodate their own or relatives' children. Boys and girls are likely to be equally affected although more boys end up in care because of homelessness.

Onset and course
Divorce and break up of home is most common among couples 17–20 years old with very young children. A child can, therefore, be born homeless, although by law local authorities are required to house families with children. Homelessness can befall the child at any later age and has no specific course, although repeated homelessness is not uncommon in some families.

Predisposing factors
There are the usual conglomeration of impairments which befall the poor and disadvantaged in an otherwise affluent society – poverty, unstable marital relationships, alcoholism, poor health, persistent unemployment and many others.

Complications
A homeless child is likely to be subject to many other ills – likely to be boarded out in homes, sheltered accommodation or bed and breakfast 'hotels' of poor quality, with potentially serious consequences arising out of inconstant and stressed parenting.

Impairment
In a largely settled (as opposed to nomadic) society, the absence of a home base and all that is associated with it, such as break up, child abuse, parental death, is likely to leave the child seriously impaired – physically, intellectually and emotionally, as numerous studies of homeless parents and institutionalized children attest. A homeless child is, above all, more likely to develop a sense of profound insecurity and a 'worthless' self-concept that may, themselves, become the basis of serious subsequent maladjustment.

Prompts
Has child been in care because he has no parents?
If he has parents, how long have they been away and untraceable?
Have attempts been made to trace them?
Have any agencies attempted to find if child has relatives?
Have they been asked or encouraged to have the child?
Are parents homeless? Why?
Are they in scheduled or other temporary accommodation?
If yes, for how long?
Are parents unwilling to have the child?
Is this recent or long standing?
Is the refusal because of the child or changes in their own circumstances?
Are there any periods or circumstances in which they may be prepared to
   have the child?

Is the situation likely to change for better or worse?

Action
A parental home cannot be just created or changed sufficiently to be appropriate for the child. Effort must, therefore, be focussed on giving the child a 'permanent' place and countering the adverse effects of being homeless, through creating other permanencies – such as a good school.

0302   Locality

01	Development area
02	Poor amenities
03	Delinquent area
04	Culture contrary to family's
05	Other

Description
This condition refers to adversities associated with child's immediate environment.

From the moment children venture outside their own homes they come under direct and indirect influence of the wider social surroundings and the people who inhabit them. There is considerable research to show that particular parts of cities and regions are associated with greater incidence and prevalence of social and individual problems. The extent of social and educational provision within an area not only reflects its deficiencies but also the unwillingness or inability of both the inhabitants and administrators to make the necessary provision. This suggests other and deeper problems.

Associated features
Children from poor locales are likely to have a greater preponderance of neurological, intellectual, other home and family, conduct and emotional problems.

Prevalence
Well over 25 per cent of children are brought up in poor and disadvantaged environments. Some studies, using special indices (such as open space and amenities), put the estimate as high as 50 per cent. Boys and girls are equally affected.

Onset and course
Not applicable, although locality changes with child's address.

Predisposing factors
There is a long held belief, backed by some research, that downwardly mobile and otherwise disadvantaged citizens (for whatever reasons –

genetic, intellectual, social and economic) tend to gravitate to poor environments, because presumably these are the only ones available and affordable to accommodate them. Having reached there, their mere presence serves to exacerbate the locality's problems and make it difficult for them to escape.

Complications
There is likely to be a greater representation of all types of problems affecting children living in such localities. Sometimes these problems (such as accidents or family feuds) arise as a direct consequence of poor and stressful environments.

Impairment
Considerable – in intellectual, social and psychological terms, not only in terms of deficits but also of pushing the child into anti-social and psychologically damaging company. Children from such environments are much more likely to have fluid, unrealistic or negative sense of their own identity and to be judged to have poorer potential for development.

Prompts
Is area designated for slum clearance or development?
Is area derelict and run down?
Is dereliction so pervasive that the family is sucked into it?
Is there much sign of vandalism?
Are authorities not making adequate social and educational provisions for these reasons?
Do police and social services say the area is one of high level of problems?
Do parents accept their child's behaviour and contacts with his peers as normal?
Do they regard the law breaking and other problem behaviour by other youngsters as only to be expected?
Do they see themselves out of place in the locality?
Is this because they are better or worse than the rest?
Is this with good reason?
Is family distinctively different from other residents in the locality?
Is this difference based on origin, colour, religious pursuits, behavioural and economic standards or other matters?

Action
In an ideal world, transfer of child and family to a more benign and less benighted environment – not just physically but also with a change of culture, is highly desirable. Given the size and complexity of the problem, this remains an unattained ideal for most.

0303   Status in neighbourhood

01	Stigmatized
02	Ostracized
03	Victimized
04	Other

Description

This condition refers to a family's and child's difficulties in the neighbourhood.

Depending on the size, homogeneity and stability of a neighbourhood, a family may be more or less prominent. Prominence of a family arises either from the attribution of positive qualities (such as wealth, size of house, status of the parents), negative factors (such as poverty, mental and physical illness), or other dramatically visible differences between the family and the rest of the community (such as skin colour).

Both positive and negative factors can lead to conflict between the family and the neighbourhood and adverse reactions to the family by the rest of the community.

Stigmatization results from the attribution of particularly adverse characteristics to the family, which create social distance and conflict between it and others. The stigma can relate to the history of the family, the state of their home and current financial status, particular features of parents, or behaviour of the child.

Stigmatization can create social isolation and ostracism of the family and, in more extreme circumstances, their victimization by the rest of the neighbourhood. Ostracism is manifested through attenuated or severed social contracts between the family and neighbours and alienation from each other. Victimization is shown in negative acts, such as deliberate damage to the fabric of the house, exclusion of the family from the use of local amenities or deliberate targeting for hostile acts. Violent conflict takes the form of fights and destruction of property emanating either from members of the community or the family with one another.

Associated features

More likely to be associated with families from ethnic minorities and those who, by neighbourhood standards, are visibly deviant.

As this difficulty usually arises because of 'negative' features of the family, there are likely to be other problems. Ethnic minorities may have no difficulty other than that bestowed on them by the neighbourhood's prejudices.

Prevalence

Not known with any reliability. Small-scale studies of institutional children suggest that about 5 per cent of the families in poor neighbourhoods may have particular difficulties. Boys and girls are both affected but boys are more likely to be the 'cause' of adverse reactions by the neighbourhood, because of anti-social acts.

Onset and course

Prejudices – such as those against other races – may be endemic and predate a child's birth. Alternatively, the family may be stigmatized because of some event (e.g. revelation of sexual abuse by parents) or gradual change in their status (such as break up and mother's subsequent prostitution). Whether the condition improves or deteriorates depends on changes in the family and the neighbourhood, but circumstances usually improve when family move away to a more congenial environment.

Predisposing factors

None specific. As for previous condition.

Complications

None specific. As for previous condition.

Impairment

Considerable, bearing in mind that children have to survive and develop in an increasingly wider environment of school, play, peer relationships and acquisition of social identity. Stigmatized children are likely to be subjected to greater bullying, cruelty and abuse than others who are not. Whether they can cope or not, they will develop adaptive patterns which are likely to be unhealthy.

Prompts

Do family or any of its members have a reputation for any particular bad characteristics? According to whom?

Is this belief about family or its members widely shared by the community or only restricted to a small number?

How far are family shunned by the rest of the community, particularly neighbours?

How ready are the other members of the community to talk about or justify their ostracism?

Is family or any of its members are being victimized by a range of other community members?

Are family aware of this?

How do they react to it?

Is victimization justified on the basis of established facts or is family being unjustifiably scapegoated?

How extensive is the conflict between family members and others?

Are they general or only occur under specific circumstances?

Are they serious and likely to deteriorate?

Action
If possible, family should be moved away and/or attempt be made to mitigate the effects of experience on the child.

0304 Material condition

01 Substandard housing
02 Overcrowding
03 Gas and/or electricity cut off
04 Parents on Social Security benefits
05 Insufficient food/clothing
06 Lack of personal possessions
07 Other

Description
This condition concerns the material and financial state of the family.

There is by now considerable literature on the effects of poverty on social and psychological development of children. Poverty and its consequent material deprivation are a matter of degree within and between subcultures, perceived with various degrees of resignation by those affected and have, in turn, variable effects on people according to the presence or absence of other adversities. Any of the above conditions by itself is likely to result in adverse experiences both directly to the child (through, for example, hunger and cold) or indirectly (as in family distress).

Associated features
Poverty is fundamentally associated with numerous social adversities and is a major contributor to problems such as poor physical health and intellectual development, low achievement, considerable family conflict, high levels of delinquency and generally depressed and negative self-concepts. In developed societies where material standards are taken as indicators of social and psychological well-being, the absence of adequate physical provision creates tensions which have potentially severe consequences for the child and his family.

Prevalence
Roughly 25–30 per cent of British children live in impoverished conditions, though the prevalence varies, both up and down, according to the criteria used. What is more, the incidence changes according to economic and social conditions, which affect parents. Children of both sexes are equally affected.

Onset and course
Clearly a family can fall on hard times at any time – usually when parents break up or become unemployed. More usually, however, children are

born to poor families who remain on the margin of social improvements for the rest of their lives and pass the adversities on to their children. There may be ups and downs and occasional escapes upwards, but the family usually retain their relatively poor position in the hierarchy of material wealth.

Predisposing factors
Poverty itself is the major predisposing familial factor, going from one generation to the next, with minor breaks. Major disorders, such as alcoholism or mental illness in parents, may push them socially downwards, particularly when no adequate social or kinship support system is available.

Complications
Poverty is perhaps the single most consistent correlate of a wide range of physical, intellectual, social and psychological disorders. The more prevalent and serious the poverty, the more probable and intense the difficulties. Whereas being well off may not prevent problems, being poor makes them undoubtedly more likely.

Impairment
Considerable, dependent on how long standing or severe the poverty is and how well parents have succeeded in reducing its impact on their children.

Prompts
Is home structurally and decoratively in poor repair?
Are there more than one and one-half persons per room?
Does home lack an inside WC and hot water?
Are gas and electricity not readily available?
Are parents in receipt of social security or other special benefits? As much as they are entitled to?
Do any members of the family complain of lack of adequate food and clothing?
Is the amount of food and clothing available adequate and reasonable?
Do members of the family, particularly child, have personal possessions?
Are family members, particularly child, concerned with the lack of personal possessions?
Is there adequate space for privacy in the home?
Is this family worse off than the rest of the locality in any of the above respects?
Has it done anything to upgrade itself?
Are the parents and children aware of their status?
How do they feel about it?

Action
Both the fact and the implications of material deprivation for the parents

and the child must be ameliorated – infinitely more complex a task than most others in social or clinical practice.

0305   Child's status

01	Illegitimate
02	Adopted
03	Fostered
04	Does not know parents
05	Other

Description
This item refers to the legal status of a child in terms of parentage.

This condition remains important because many countries still legally recognize 'illegitimacy', believing that only children born in wedlock are legitimate. The stigma, though lessening, still remains, not only because of possible name calling but also the child's likely insecurity and difficulties in forming an appropriate identity which derives from having her own father. Adoption and fostering are increasingly frequent, particularly the latter, as an alternative to putting children in institutions. 'Not knowing parents' is only a problem if fostering or adoption have failed to give the child an appropriate identity and child articulates this as a difficulty.

Associated features
None specific. None of the above conditions need be a difficulty, unless other things have gone wrong.

Prevalence
Roughly 25 per cent of children are acknowledged now to be born out of wedlock. In many more cases parentage is accepted by the nominal father. Of children in public care, about 2.6 per cent are adopted and 57 per cent fostered. Fewer boys who have problems live with natural or foster parents.

Onset and course
A child may be adopted at any age but current practice attempts to achieve it well before child is five years old. Fostering can and does take place from birth until late adolescence. It is not known how many children do not know their own parents.

Predisposing factors
A child born to a mother who, for a variety of personal, physical, social and economic reasons cannot look after her child, or when father does not acknowledge paternity, or family break up.

Complications
None specific.

Impairment
None specific, but a range of difficulties may arise when child is not adequately parented by those who adopt or foster him. Given that parents are the major source of child's personal identity, difficulties experienced here are likely to have wide repercussions in terms of child's adjustment and social behaviour.

Prompts
The answers to the first three items are based on factual information and can be established from inspection of appropriate documents. The child's knowledge of his parents can be established by asking him the appropriate questions. Care should be taken to ascertain whether the child has already been asked that question and how he has reacted to it. The effect of further questioning on the child should be considered before proceeding.

Action
Little can be done but to reduce the impact of any difficulties that may have arisen in the course of child's adoption and fostering. Children now have a legal right to know who their natural parents are, though how the information is conveyed requires careful planning.

0306   Parents

01	Parent dead
02	Single-parent family
03	Divorced
04	Separated
05	Living apart
06	Child unsure which parent to live with
07	Other

Description
This condition refers to whether parents are together or not.

In most societies there is considerable delineation of parental roles in which parents undertake a set of overlapping but specific functions in relation to the child. Thus, both parents are regarded as necessary for the child's normal social and psychological development. The increasing attention to fragmented and one-parent families has brought to light the many adversities they suffer as a direct result of their state.

The causes and consequences of parental separation are diverse and complex. It is, however, important to ascertain the state of the family as an aid to evaluating its wider consequences.

When parents are alive and both retain a positive relationship with and responsibility towards the child, he may be unsure which one to live with. This is presumably because the positive and negative characteristics of the parents or their wider circumstances are in a state of balance. This may create anxiety, conflict of loyalties and a good deal of uncertainty in the wider functioning of the child, particularly as it may become difficult for the child to derive the full benefit of security of attachment and modelling from one particular parent.

Associated features
None specific. Parents die or break up for their own reasons and children have to adapt as best they can.

Prevalence
The statistics for this condition are unusually confusing. This arises because of the high rates of divorce as well as legal and informal separations. The children may be with one parent for different lengths of time. In the United Kingdom about one third of couples divorce in the first 17 years of marriage and another 20 per cent are separated at any given time. However, in the UK only about 6 per cent of all households seem to contain 'lone parents'. Of these, only a minority are widowed – the rest being divorced, separated or single. No one collects statistics of children's feelings about which parent to live with, if they have the choice. Boys and girls are likely to be equally affected, although the pattern of impact on them seems different in the long term.

Onset and course
Can occur at any time during child's life, although the longer the parents are together the less likely break up will be.

Predisposing factors
Parental youth, poor socioeconomic status and certain occupational groups are closely associated with parental break up.

Complications
None specific, but those which may arise from parental inability to provide adequate care and control.

Impairment
Potentially much, depending on the quality of substitute or compensatory parenting the child is given. Generally one-parent families or those where parents are divorced or separated but in conflict are more likely to be associated with difficulties for children. Even when there is a lot of trouble at home, or unless children have been brutally abused by one parent, they want their parents to be together. They suffer not only directly (because of financial difficulties, for example) but also indirectly when the remaining parent is upset. Serious anti-social behaviour and a range of clinical difficulties are disproportionately evident in such children.

Prompts
All the elements in this area can be established by asking specific questions or through inspection of documents and other social enquiry methods. All but the last are a matter of fact and can be stated as such. It may also be worthwhile to state the causes of the separation, if known, its duration and impact on the remaining parent and the child.

You are living with this parent? Why?
What would make you change your mind to live with the other parent?
Do you worry about your parents being apart?
Would you like them to be together again?

Both parents and other siblings or relations can be asked the same question about the child.

Action
It is important to reduce the impact of the above conditions on the child. This usually entails dealing with other related difficulties.

0307 Family instability

01   Parental separations
02   Short-term cohabitations
03   Other disturbing person in house
04   Other

Description
This condition refers to any aspect of parental 'movement' and changes of structure which make it difficult for the children to know where they stand in terms of adult figures.

It is generally believed that to fulfil its function in providing care and support for children, a family must be relatively stable in the composition of its members and their relationships. We would, therefore, look at the stability of the family so as to ascertain whether it is likely to have adverse consequences for the children. The depth and extent of family instability and its specific consequences for a particular child are a matter of individual detailed determination. The fact of family instability, however, can be fairly accurately established.

Associated features
Family conflict and parental promiscuity. In certain families, the difficulties of lone parents lead them to associations and partnerships which incur major costs to them and their children.

Prevalence

At any time about 20 per cent of couples are separated. How many have children is not known, nor is there any information on how many have other intimate relationships which impinge on the child. Boys and girls are likely to be equally affected.

Onset and course

The conditions may arise at any time during a child's life. It can develop in numerous ways and its impact on the child has to be measured at the time.

Predisposing factors

None specific, although it is now evident that children are at greater risk of neglect and wide-ranging physical, emotional and sexual abuse in unstable and unstably restructured families.

Complications

Difficulties arising from parental distress and preoccupation with other matters. Care and control is likely to suffer and children are at greater risk of abuse by the incoming (usually male) partner.

Impairment

Children from such families are likely to receive less parental attention than others. They are, therefore, more likely to suffer from physical, educational, social and emotional problems than other children. The child's sense of self-worth is likely to suffer in such a setting, particularly if there is grief for the absent parent which is not adequately dealt with.

Prompts

Have parents ever been separated and for how long?
Has parent with whom child has been living ever brought in another person to live with him/her in the house? For how long?
Has either parent had known extramarital affairs?
Are affairs known to the other parent and to the children?
Have partners in the affairs been brought into the home?
Have affairs been a source of conflict between the parents and/or them and the children?
Are there other persons in the house who aggravate the child?
What form of aggravation, and how deeply does it affect the family and child?

Action

If deemed serious, measures should be taken aimed at reducing impact of such conditions on the child.

0308   Adverse parental factors

01	Physical illness/defect
02	Mental disorder
03	Alcoholic/drug user
04	Gambler
05	Offender
06	Violent/cruel
07	Rigid/authoritarian
08	Anti-authority attitudes
09	Unemployment
10	Prostitution
11	Attempted suicide
12	Other

Description

This condition is essentially concerned with any major deficit, disadvantage or pathology that the parents may suffer from, which affects their lives and is, therefore, likely to affect their parenting, both directly and indirectly.

Parents have their own characteristics, over and above their qualities as parents. But their personal characteristics fundamentally affect the kind of parenting they can provide for their children. Parents' difficulties affect the impact they make on the family, though the quality of that impact is also dependent on the balance of other positive and negative influences in the home. In the evaluation of family problems, considerable weight should, therefore, be given to evaluating adverse parental factors and, where possible, determine their impact on the wider family and the child.

Associated features

Where any of these conditions exist, they are likely to be present in clusters with other adversities in themselves and in their children.

Prevalence

These are dramatically variable dependent on the special condition, its severity and the criteria used for evaluating it. It is not particularly helpful to cite figures for any of the conditions even where they exist reliably. Boys and girls are likely to be equally affected.

Onset and course

Any of these may appear at any time before, at or after the child is born. Each has its own course, which is also largely individual.

Predisposing factors

Being poor, coming from a disadvantaged family, being in a poor job, not having a great sense of self-worth, control over own destiny or hope for the future are likely to be as much precursors as consequences of these disorders.

Complications
Potentially numerous and massive, depending on the time-scale of the disorder, its intensity and its consequences for the parents and child.

Impairment
Variable but all potentially serious. Impairment arises not only from the long-standing social and psychological condition of the parent associated with the disorder, but also from the effects of the disorder on the stability and functioning of the family, its economic and social state and the adaptive mechanisms employed by the other parent and children for coping with the difficulties. The larger the number of difficulties, the more serious the presumptive impact on the child.

Prompts

Physical illness/defect
What ailment or defect does parent suffer from, if any?
How debilitating is it to the parent?
How adversely does it affect child and other family members?
What are the perceptible effects of parent's ailment or defect on other members of the family or child?

Mental disorder
What form of disorder is parent suffering from?
Who says so?
How insightful is parent about the disorder?
How well controlled is the disorder?
What is its impact on family and child?

The above questions form the basic observational frame in which the manifestations of the mental disorder and its effect on the child and the family can be gauged.

Alcoholic/drug user
Has either parent been diagnosed as an alcoholic? By whom?
Has either parent received treatment for alcoholism?
Is parent regarded as a heavy drinker, by himself, members of the family, or others?
Has parent been charged with behaviour under the influence of alcohol, lost a job, or suffered other adversities related to alcohol usage?
Is family's financial condition seriously affected by parent's alcohol usage?
Has drinking parent sought help from Alcoholics Anonymous or other agencies?
Is parent on medical or prohibited drugs?
With what effects?

The parent's frequency of drinking, state at the time of interview, his eagerness to get a drink by offering the interviewer one or by terminating the interview in order to go to the pub, can all be noted. The parent's treatment of their children when under the influence of alcohol can be observed.

Gambler

Is either parent known to gamble?
Is this associated with the more common horse racing and football pools gambling or the visiting of gambling clubs and meetings?
Has gambling caused serious disruption and conflict in the family?
Are there any offences associated with gambling?
Has parent sought help for gambling?

Offender

Has either parent a history of offences?
Are these offences against person or property?
How recent are they in origin?
What were the consequences of offending?
Is the parent currently on a charge, on probation, or in custody?

Violent/cruel

The other parent, children and others can be asked whether either mother or father resort to physical aggression and under what circumstances.
Do they physically hurt their victims by drawing blood and leaving marks?
Do they use any implements?
Do they have a favourite victim or is their violence indiscriminate?
Do they physically or verbally hurt 'for its own sake' rather than when in a temper or as a means of achieving another end?
Does this hurting go on even after the victim has submitted?
Are they cruel generally or do they have a favourite victim?
Is parental violence shown inside or outside the home?

There are no very good criteria regarding what constitutes violence. It is a matter of the interaction and intents of the 'violent' person and the perceptions of his victim. It should be evaluated in terms of its range, intensity and whether it is expressive and gratuitous, or instrumental, as a means of achieving another end. Parental violence is rarely observed when it is happening. It is usually seen in terms of its visible results, such as bruises or the terrified reaction of the child to the parent's presence or other acts which may presage violence. Particular caution should be exercised in (1) interpreting a parent's forceful acts as 'violent' and (2) not being aware of the subtler forms of cruelty and violence by either parent.

Rigid/authoritarian

Parental rigidity can be evaluated in terms of unswerving and inflexible adherence to moral and religious codes, close-mindedness, inability to accept the divergent behaviours under a variety of circumstances. Particularly skilful interviewing is required over a wide range of social and moral topics to elicit an accurate idea of rigidity. Additionally, however, the other parent and the child can be asked such questions as:

Do you find him a hard person?
Can you get him to change his mind?
Does he always strictly stick to what he says?

Authoritarianism is often associated with social and moral rigidity but in addition connotes a black-and-white idea of morality, considerable concern with power, punitiveness and tendency to interpret personal and social acts in terms of power struggles and obedience to superior power and contempt for the less powerful. Subtle and wide-ranging questions tailored to the particular situation are required to elicit evidence of parental authoritarianism.

Anti-authority attitudes
Parents can be asked:

What do you think of police, magistrates, social workers and others?
Do you find them helpful or not?
Have they been any use to you in the past?
Do you think they are against you?
If you were in trouble would you ask them for help?

The other parent and the child can be asked to project what the parent's feeling may be to particular authority figures.

Are parent's statements derogatory to authority figures?
Are they general or specific?
Does he give any particular reasons for his attitude?
Is parent willing to help social agencies with the management of child?
Does parent lie to social agencies? Is there any apparent reason for this?
Does parent refuse to meet or to carry out requests made by social agencies?
Does parent talk about social agencies in a derogatory manner in front of child?
Does he try to turn him against them?

Unemployment
Parental employment is the normal source of family income. Any major problems of employment are likely to result in family poverty and major tensions.
Do either or both parents have jobs?
Does father have a history of stable employment?
Is he described as a good worker?
If there is unstable employment, is this because of general unemployment problems or is he particularly susceptible to losing his job?
Does he get much satisfaction out of his job?
Is his job a major source of stress?

Does he, by virtue of his job, have to be away from the family for long
  periods?
Has this raised any problems?
Do his job problems spill over on to his family?
How do the family members, including child, see his employment?
Are there any problems associated with mother's employment?

Prostitution
There are diverse views among theorists and practitioners about the impact
on children of parental prostitution. Views range from those who regard
it as a pathological reaction and others who see it as a form of earning a
livelihood, which is no more damaging than many others. Regardless of
these views, however, no statutory agency can knowingly condone parental
(almost always mother's) prostitution and *has* to consider it as an adverse
factor in evaluating the child's family conditions.

Is the parent suspected of prostitution?
What is the evidence?
Does she have a police record for soliciting and 'immoral earnings'?
Does anybody else in the locality talk of her as a prostitute?
Is this an occupation or just a part-time activity?
Is activity carried out in the family home or elsewhere?
Are the other parent and children aware of it?
How do the rest of the family react to it?
Is activity conducted explicitly for money or for other reasons?
Is she open about her activities or are they denied?

Attempted suicide
Attempted suicide appears to be associated with serious personal pathology
or social and familial disorder. The reasons for it and its manifestations
are as diverse as the people who attempt it. Its effects on the family are
usually cataclysmic, generating intense anxieties and maladaptive patterns
of coping, particularly among the children. It is this latter factor which
frequently warrants close scrutiny of the child when a parent has attempted
suicide.

Has either parent attempted suicide?
How and with what immediate effect on the family?
How recent was the attempt?
How serious was it?
Has there been more than one attempt?
Did it require hospital treatment?
Did child witness it?
What reason does the parent give for it?
What reason do other family members give?
Has parent received psychiatric or other help for it?
Have there been long-term consequences?
Does the parent still threaten it?

Action
Depending on the severity of any of these conditions, action should be taken to reduce its impact on the child, which may include removing child from home.

0309   Parental coping ability

01	Physical difficulty
02	Intellectual difficulty
03	Coping with each other
04	Coping with children
05	Other

Description
This attribute is concerned with parents' ability to cope with demands of normal living, other than in those areas already cited elsewhere.

The quality of parents' adaptation to the normal stresses of living and bringing up children is determined by their ability to cope in a variety of circumstances. This is important to evaluate, not only in relation to their own stability but also in terms of the sorts of models they present for their children's social learning. A 'poorly coping parent' is more likely to produce a child who not only suffers because of parental inadequacy but one who may drift into trouble or become socially ineffective due to lack of countervailing models. 'Parental inadequacy' can arise from any of the factors mentioned in the previous attributes.

Associated features
Anything from the previous attributes, mental retardation, social disadvantage, anti-social behaviour and personal difficulties. It is not often that difficulties in coping present only in one area.

Prevalence
Not known, other than through children who become subject of formal intervention. On this basis, about 25 per cent of parents have difficulty in coping with one or more of these areas. Boys and girls are likely to be equally affected.

Onset and course
The fundamental parental characteristics, such as mental or physical handicap, are likely to predate child's birth. Others may be associated with a serious event such as accident, death or separation of a parent, or the onset of difficulties in the child. The condition can either deteriorate (if, for example, associated with a parent's degenerative disease) or improve (as when mother finds a stable partner).

Predisposing factors
Mental retardation, sensory or physical handicap and a background of adversity and inadequate preparation or capacity for coping with life's demands may predispose to or exacerbate this condition. Whether this is genetic or transmission of a culture of deprivation remains an unresolved issue. Both are likely to be factors in a person's own sense of competence which fundamentally underlies ability to cope.

Complications
Potentially considerable in terms of inadequate care and control, resulting in physical, intellectual and social difficulties in home, school and neighbourhood.

Impairment
From little to considerable, depending on its impact on the child in terms of extent, intensity and duration of particular elements of the condition, in response to demands placed on the child and family.

Prompts
These can be asked of either parent or children or others who have occasion to know of parents' difficulty to cope in a variety of areas.
Are there things parents cannot do because of physical infirmity or deficiency?
Are they said to be dull or slow and at a loss how to manage their lives because of this?
Is there any evidence for this?
Do they find it difficult to deal with demands made on them by official agencies and others?
Is there anyone in particular? Under what circumstances?
Do parents have trouble in coping with each other's demands and problems?
What particularly and how does it show itself?
Who controls the housekeeping?
Is the trouble with wasting the money on less essential items, inadequate planning, purchase of inappropriate goods or simply poverty?
Who complains of poor housekeeping?
Who has difficulty with which children and their problems?
How have they attempted to cope?
Is the admission of difficulty to cope made directly and without hesitation or is there some evidence of shame and unwillingness to admit?

Action
Depending on the area of coping difficulty and its severity, the impact on child may be reduced by parent training, psychological inoculation against stress or removal of child from the arena of parents' difficulties.

0310 Family harmony

01	Marital disharmony
02	Physical conflict
03	Parental conflict
04	Conflict between children
05	Other

Description
This condition is concerned with serious amount and quality of conflict within the home.

All families experience conflict but for many the difficulties are relatively transient and amicably resolved. However, for some, conflict within the family for whatever reason is long standing or serious enough to affect the children. Children from such families are known to suffer greatly, perhaps habituate to and develop maladaptive response patterns to both parental role models and the anxiety generated by the conflict.

Associated features
Conflict can and does take place in all families. Indeed, evidence suggests that even physical conflict is not confined to poor and otherwise disadvantaged families. But perhaps because such families are more frequently investigated by social agencies, a range of other difficulties, including parental adversities, coping ability, children's anti-social behaviour and affective difficulties also become evident.

Prevalence
Judged by applications for divorce and legal separations, as many as 50 per cent of families experience grave disharmony and in many cases a serious degree of physical conflict. Conflict with and between children may trigger or itself result from parental disharmony. Children of both sexes are affected, although the short- and long-term reactions and adaptations for boys and girls may be different.

Onset and course
The condition may predate the child's birth but often follows it. It can be sustained with some variations of intensity for years or may rapidly escalate to a final break. Rarely do these difficulties subside into insignificance.

Predisposing factors
The personality make up of parents, including their own family experiences, compounded by financial, social, emotional and personal pressures. These may be exacerbated by difficulties in bringing up the children and effectively communicating within the family and settling different demands.

Complications
None specific, but involving any difficulties which are created and sustained by problems in the family.

Impairment
Children from families in conflict tend to have a wide range of impairments. They may react with anxiety which may be manifested in difficulties such as psychosomatic disorders, school refusal, and emotional maladjustment. Alternatively, they may externalize the anxiety in the form of temper tantrums, aggressive behaviour, and other anti-social acts. Long-term impairment is likely to be serious, unless moderated by compensatory acts by parents and children's own resilience.

Prompts
Parents and others can be asked:
Do you often have arguments with each other?
What are these arguments about?
Do arguments get very heated?
Is there anything you agree on with each other?
How much can you predict your husband's or wife's views and behaviour?
Are you often wrong?
Does he often swear at you? Is this normal in your arguments?
Do you mind it?
Does he ever beat you or otherwise hurt you physically?
Does he often have disagreements or trouble with the child?
Are these about something in particular or about anything?
Who do you think is responsible for these problems?
Do the children often fight, scrap, argue with each other?
Are these about a particular topic or about anything?
Are they usually limited or do they spill into wider conflicts with the rest
    of the family?

In a home setting, observations of family conflict is likely to be difficult and incidental. All the above questions could be regarded as the basis of observing the interaction of members of the family with each other, perhaps in the setting of a 'whole family' assessment.

The ease and frequency of arguments between parents, the content and 'spread' of the arguments, whether their bodily stance to one another is belligerent or not, history or report of physical aggression and parents' arguments with the children, their content, extent and vehemence and similar aspects of children's conflict with each other, form a reasonable structure for commenting on the extent, intensity, duration and urgency of family conflict.

Action
Given the probable adverse consequences of serious family conflict, action should be directed at reducing its impact through psychological inoculation

exercises and remedial measures directed at parents. Difficult and time-consuming, with uncertain results.

0311 Family involvement

01 Parental over-protection
02 Parent–child indifference
03 Parent–child rejection
04 Sibling–child indifference or rejection
05 Other

Description

This condition relates to the extent and kind of parent/child involvement.

Children's sense of self-worth derives primarily and initially from the way they are treated by parents and others close to them. One aspect of such valuing is the degree and kind of parents' involvement with their child. This ranges from one positive (though by definition damaging) extreme of over-protection to the other of rejection. Involvement can best be seen in terms of the amount and kind of interest taken by each in the other's condition and how far what happens to one affects the other. Children who are over-protected are likely to be fearful of, and become incompetent in dealing with, difficulties that are within their physical and intellectual competence. Those who are unattached or rejected are likely to feel devalued and react either with anxiety or externalized anger and aggression.

Associated features

Anxious parents or those who have had unusually adverse experiences (involving children) are likely to be over-protective. Indifference is more likely in chaotic and badly integrated families, where, because of other serious stresses, either none of the children or this particular child does not count. Rejection is more 'active' and is usually associated with reactions to the particular child because of his attributed or assumed role in some unusual difficulty experienced by parents. As often as not, this is because of the child's unacceptable behaviour.

Prevalence

There is no reliable or general information about parental over-protection. Nor is there any about parental indifference or rejection, though some estimates may be gained by the number of children in care or other forms of accommodation than parental home and others subject to clinical intervention. On this basis approximately 2–5 per cent of children suffer from this condition. Boys and girls may equally suffer but more boys seem to act out and be subject to parental rejection and hostility.

Onset and course

Rejection and indifference may start from birth where, for example, a child is unwanted or has been cause of major trauma. More usually it sets in with parents' increasing experience of stress, either related to the child or wider problems of their own lives. The earlier the onset of indifference and rejection the more serious it is likely to be, because it suggests grave accumulation of difficulties which have led to such parental reaction.

Predisposing factors

More common when a child is not wanted and pleasurably anticipated. Also more common in families where there is a range of other disintegrative stresses.

Complications

None specific, other than arising from possible parental abuse or child's reaction to rejection.

Impairment

Over-protection may leave the children anxious and reduce their competence in the long run. Indifference and rejection are likely to create a deep sense of alienation, non-attachedness and drift in children, with serious consequences for their level of self-worth and, therefore, ability to care about the consequences of their behaviour. Severe affective and conduct disorders may ensue, mitigated by personal resilience and possible compensatory experience.

Prompts

Do the parents deny that child has any problems in order to protect him from the consequences? Do they express anxiety about these consequences?

Do parents become aggressively possessive and protective when it is suggested that their children may have problems and that they should receive some special form of help?

Do parents treat child as much younger than his years?

Do parents try to fight child's battles for him at school or with peers?

Is it felt that parents' attitude to the children's problems prevents the children learning that they have done wrong and that their acts have certain unpleasant consequences?

Do parents and child appear to coexist in parallel without making much impact on each other? Is there evidence of past or present lack of concern with each other?

Do either party claim that the other is indifferent?

Do either parents or children shun each other?

Do they express the wish to be parted or not to have anything further to do with each other?

Do parents refuse to have the child live with them or see them or write to them? Or vice versa?

Is there any history of the child having run away from home and/or expressing unwillingness to return home?

Is child's life style and his reasons for that life style in explicit negation of parental demands?

Do same considerations apply to the relationship of siblings with child?

In their physical encounter with child do they stand close to child, turn their body towards child or make any other gestures such as putting an arm around him which suggests protectiveness?

Is this protectiveness more than you consider warranted by the realistic demands of parenting, society or the circumstances?

Do they speak to each other in a manner as if the reaction of the other person did not matter?

Is their encounter devoid of excitement or any other normal sign of emotional significance?

In situations of physical encounter do they turn away from each other or make gestures of dismissal?

Is content of their verbal or physical encounter dismissive and uncaring?

Do any of the siblings behave towards child in this manner or vice versa?

Action

Intervention is as urgent as it is difficult, considering that it demands a fundamental change of attitude by parents.

0312 Emotional relationship

01   Loose emotional ties
02   Lack of emotional support
03   Emotional detachment
04   Other

Description

This condition refers to difficulties in expression and fulfilment of emotional relationships between parents and children.

The degree and quality of family life is both the basis and result of the quality of emotional relationship between the parents and their children. The two are frequently intertwined and inseparable. Emotional support given by parents is, however, distinct from the quality of their involvement. Parents may be closely involved, but in a hostile rather than supportive manner. The closer the degree of emotional support the more children will find it easy to cope with stress and overcome temporary disadvantage, because they are able to share this anxiety with and gain succour from parents. The degree and quality of emotional support can either be overpowering or alternatively too little to meet the needs of the child during growth.

The test of any emotional relationship is the degree to which parties are prepared to modify their behaviour for the sake of the other. Many parents and children say they 'love' each other, but on closer questioning can be seen not to be prepared to change their behaviour for the sake of the other person. The relationship is nominal and formal rather than one that is imbued with personalized caring.

Associated features
Many of the comments on parental involvement apply here. Additionally, when there are other major stresses, parents' emotional energies are diverted elsewhere. Children with poor emotional ties may suffer from ADD and serious conduct disorders.

Prevalence
Not known but frequently seen in clinic populations and those of children in care and otherwise away from home. Boys are more likely to suffer from this condition.

Onset and course
Parents and children have to learn to love each other beyond the conventional and 'normal' demands of parent–child relationships. This is now known to be affected by the children's early response to continuing interactions with parents. Emotional difficulties become manifest, therefore, after birth and may improve as, for example, in the case of a hyperkinetic child who slows down, or deteriorate, as in the case of an adolescent who becomes more seriously anti-social.

Predisposing factors
None specific, but associated with parents who have difficulties in relating or are subject to major stress which saps their emotional energies. Some parents are also emotionally cool and may have unwillingly become parents. In the case of children, pervasive developmental disorder, attention deficit disorder or anti-social behaviour and their emotional correlates may lead to difficulties in this area.

Complications
Potentially many, as so many of the normal hurdles of child and adolescent development place huge demands on emotional investment by the parents who, despite difficulties, are prepared to give their children unconditional love.

Impairment
Considerable to the child. A child who is not closely attached is likely to drift into serious difficulties more readily than one who is and is concerned about the consequences of his behaviour for people he loves.

Prompts
Parents should be asked:

How much do they speak of child having helped them cope with certain problems?

How much do they appear to rely on child to either fulfil any deficiencies in their life or to carry out tasks which should have been dealt with by other people?

Is either party known to have suffered in the absence of the other?

What does child say about his dependence on parents?

Do parents express intolerance of child's attitudes and behaviour?

Do parents express hostility to child?

Is the manner and content of speech suggestive of lack of love?

Is this different from other families you know in this social class and culture?

Do parents say that they will have nothing to do with child regardless of what is likely to happen to him?

Do they express a wish for child to be taken away or to be locked up or to die? Or vice versa?

Does either party complain of lack of love and caring on the other's part?

Do either parents or child become tearful or otherwise emotional when possibility of their separation is mentioned?

Do parents and child speak in warm and sympathetic terms about each other?

Do either parents or children speak or behave in dismissive or hostile manner towards the other?

Do they say or do things to each other which are hurting or undermining?

Are their actions obvious or subtle?

Are they used to this or do they still react strongly?

Action

As with so much else in the area of home and family, the need to do something about this condition is as urgent as it is difficult. To change this condition demands intensive, long-term, expert intervention, with parents and child who *want to* or can be led to want to become closer.

0313   Parental guidance

01	Inadequate
02	Inconsistent
03	Deviant
04	Other

Description

This condition is concerned with deficient or deviant direction given by parents to children in the course of their development.

In order to turn a randomly growing child into a socially competent individual, parents must provide intensive guidance and correction over a prolonged period. This guidance involves not only demonstration of what is expected and acceptable within the family setting but also highlights and enforces the wider social boundaries. There is considerable literature to show that delinquent and disordered children have frequently received inadequate or inconsistent guidance. Such guidance is not only preventive but is also parental acknowledgment that the child's behaviour may be unacceptable and, therefore, in need of correction. Many parents do not give their children adequately detailed or consistent guidance, or what they give is deviant, thus hindering and distorting child's development. The conditions must have prevailed for over a year to be so identified.

Associated features
These parents are unlikely to have planned or thought through the demands of parenthood. They are likely to have their own difficulty in coping and a range of personal adversities, and be loosely attached to their children.

Prevalence
Judged by the number of children and adolescents who experience avoidable difficulties, more than 30 per cent of the population may be affected. Clinical experience suggests that boys suffer more from this than girls.

Onset and course
This difficulty usually becomes apparent from age five onwards when child starts school. Parents fail to rehearse and debrief the child about daily activities and difficulties he may face. Unless the process starts when the first difficulties become apparent, the condition is likely to deteriorate as child grows older and his need for guidance becomes more complex.

Predisposing factors
Families who have long standing, inter-generational difficulties in coping and behaving prosocially are more likely to give their children inadequate guidance.

Complications
Children who *grow up* passively are much more likely to drift into difficulties than those who are actively *brought up* or parented. These may range from physical accidents and substance misuse through school difficulties to anti-social behaviour and psychological difficulties.

Impairment
The severity and quality of pulls and pushes on the child will determine how far he is likely to be impaired by the absence of adequate or appropriate parental guidance.

Prompts

Do parents acknowledge that the child has any problems?

Do they express the belief that child's problems will sort themselves out?

Do their expressions regarding child's problems appear feeble, irrelevant or inappropriate?

Do their accounts of the content and quality of their guidance tally with each other's or with their actions?

Are they known to have taken any measures to curb child's problems?

Do parents suggest that it is someone else's job – teachers, the police or others – to provide such guidance?

Do parents' attitudes and actions suggest that they may be inculcating deviant views and norms in their child?

If parents are themselves deviant, do their expressions of how they want their child brought up significantly differ from their own actions?

Does child's account of parental guidance suggest that either parent or both are inadequate, inconsistent or deviant?

Are parents known to have inculcated deliberately deviant views and forms of action in their children?

Do parents speak as if they approve of children's deviant or problematic behaviour?

Action

This is a *relatively* easy area of intervention, to encourage and teach parents to take a more guiding role with their children, provided there is basic stability and interest in the family.

0314 Family communications

01	Inadequate
02	Superficial
03	Deviant
04	Other

Description

This condition refers to the difficulties of family members, but particularly parents and children, in conveying to each other feelings, thoughts and intentions effectively and efficiently. The condition is intimately bound up with involvement, support, guidance and control features cited earlier.

Communication is the core medium through which parents and children convey everything that is important to each other. Given that communication takes place through verbal and non-verbal exchanges, it encompasses expressions of involvement and affection, as much as thoughts and intentions about mutually affecting behaviours. Inadequate and deviant communication is likely to distort and undermine all other aspects of parenting, however competent or well meaning they may be.

'Inadequate' communication refers to parents and child not talking to each other enough or about enough subjects that concern them. It also encompasses the condition when each party may convey just thoughts, or feelings and information when the three facets are separated rather than conveyed together. 'Superficial' refers to the unwillingness or inability of parents and children to convey to each other detailed thoughts, feelings and information about issues and events that really matter to them. Characteristically, they each keep a lot of 'secrets' from each other or for whatever reason do not attempt to discover what and how things matter to the other person. 'Deviant' communication concerns the deliberate, systematic or involuntary and random distortion of thoughts, feelings and information, usually by parents to children, and usually with a view to bringing about a particular outcome. The tendency to lie, not to reveal real intentions, make ambiguous statements or loaded communications are examples of this.

Associated features
Children from such families are likely to be emotionally unexpressive or alternatively show deviations in their communication pattern. Suggestions that 'expressed emotions' are characteristic of adolescent schizophrenic families need much greater support.

Prevalence
Not known and immensely difficult to estimate because of the variability and contextual definitions of what is effective and efficient communication. It is, however, a pervasive feature of many families in which children present and experience difficulties. Boys and girls are likely to suffer equally.

Onset and course
These difficulties are primary features of the people who eventually become parents. They are, therefore, likely to be present from the time parents start to communicate with the newborn. The condition becomes more apparent as children grow older, the need for more extensive and complex communication increases and they notice the level of communication between parents.

Predisposing factors
Strongly bound up with cultural patterns of whether it is appropriate or not to engage with children (or, indeed, other adults) in open communications about thoughts and feelings. This arises from the views both that the children cannot understand or should not be made party to full communications as well as a tendency – particularly British and male – not fully to communicate or express emotions. Many parents also do not recognize the need to modulate or vary the content and quality of their normal adult communications to the susceptibilities of their children.

Complications
None specific, apart from the probable reactions of other non-family people to the child's learned communication patterns. There may also be occasional 'desperate' acts by children (such as attempted suicide) who feel parents do not 'hear' them.

Impairment
Considerable, pervasive and probably lifelong. A child who has been brought up in a poor or deviant communicating environment is likely to adopt similar communicating style or maladaptive reactions to it. Bearing in mind the fundamental and central role of communication in making and maintaining appropriate social relationships with age mates and adults, such a child is likely to be significantly handicapped.

Prompts
Is there much talking among family members?
Does any member complain of not being able to talk to (any) others?
Is inadequacy because of quantity or quality of communications?
Do members complain/state that they do not usually know what is happening to other family members?
Do members share secrets with each other?
Does anyone say/complain that they do not know what is going on in the others' minds?
How far and with what kind of information would they trust each other?
Do members make statements which are ambiguous or double-edged?
Do they often lie to each other? White lies?
Do they deliberately mislead each other?
Do they say one thing and do another?
Are their expressed thoughts discrepant with their feelings and information otherwise available?
How far has child started showing these features?

Action
As important as it is fundamentally difficult to do something about this problem. With appropriate family therapy and parent training there is hope, provided parties are prepared to work at it.

0315   Parental control

01	Inadequate
02	Inconsistent
03	Harsh
04	Through bribes
05	Through collusion against other parent/authority
06	Other

Description

This condition entails difficulties and distortion in parents exerting control over the child. It is intimately bound up with such other conditions as involvement, support, guidance and communication.

In the course of normal growth, every child behaves, from time to time, in a manner which is unacceptable either from the parents' point of view or judged by the wider norms of society. Most children grow up and out of this with minimal intervention. Parental response to such behaviour is indicative not only of the qualities earlier discussed but also of the kind and extent of control they exert and the methods they use to do so.

The extent and closeness with which parents supervise their children's behaviour in and out of the home determines how much they notice deviant behaviour which, if not corrected, may become persistent. Parental control can be exerted to correct unacceptable behaviour which is manifested in any setting, from the family to the school and the wider society. It is the parents' acknowledgment and ability to exert such control which is eventually internalized and reflected in the degree of self-control manifested by the child. If the extent and quality of parental control is inadequate, then the child is likely to get caught in an ascending spiral of social and psychological difficulties. This is so serious as to have been included as a major legal test of whether a child should be taken into care.

Associated features

Almost all parents have occasional difficulties in controlling their children. Here concern is with those in whom this is a persistent feature. Such parents are likely to present and experience a range of physical, intellectual, marital, financial and emotional difficulties. Children who are 'out of control' are likely to be poor achievers at school and be involved in a range of anti-social and other disordered acts.

Prevalence

Based on the number of children in care, under supervision or otherwise subject to substitute or compensatory interventions at any given time, the prevalence may be as high as 5 per cent or more at the more serious end and higher in the milder forms. Boys are much more likely to suffer from this. There is in general a wider array of social control filters affecting girls, but at the 'heavy end', girls seem to experience similar problems.

Onset and course

This condition becomes manifest around school entry age when suddenly the greater demands placed on the child and the greater opportunities for misbehaviour begin to test parental ability to control. It is likely to deteriorate as child grows older and becomes able to resist parental attempts to control. On the other hand, those who acquire the necessary skills may be able to stop such deterioration before child reaches secondary school.

Predisposing factors
As the features above indicate, parents who present persistent difficulties or deviances in this area are likely to have received similar parenting. They are also likely to be subject to serious current stresses.

Complications
A child who is out of control or is controlled by deviant means is likely to provoke social reactions (e.g. being taken into care) which are likely to exacerbate and further undermine parental difficulties in this and other areas. Such children are also more likely to suffer from abusive parental attempts to control.

Impairment
A child who is not adequately controlled or controlled in a socially acceptable way is likely to be deficient or deviant in *internal controls*. He is, therefore, likely to behave in a socially unrestrained and damaging fashion, so that external sanctions are imposed. Given that parents can and often do undermine the application of such controls, the child is likely to remain at risk for an extended period, with ever increasing social sanctions correlated with damage to others and personal suffering.

Prompts
How closely do parents and child say he is supervised? Just in the home or outside it as well?

How much do they know of where he is, who his companions are and what they are doing? Have you checked that this knowledge is accurate?

Do parents know of any undesirable association the child has and have they done anything to curb the contact?

Do parents say that they cannot control their child? What methods have they used and with what results?

Do they speak as if they have given up or are likely to give up controlling their child?

Are views expressed by parents about the control of the child's behaviour inconsistent either internally or with one another?

Do they express disapproval of each other's methods of control?

Do they express approval of one form of control while exercising a different one?

Are parental expressions of control disproportionately harsh?

Do they speak of their child's behaviour as if it were most seriously problematic than it is and therefore justifies their preference for more punitive methods of control?

Do parents talk as if they feel that giving their children more of their own way is likely to alleviate the problem? Does anyone else say that parents have attempted to control their child through harsh measures or bribes?

Do parental expressions suggest that one parent attempts to control the child's problem behaviour by disguising it or denying it to the other?

Do parents ignore some behaviours but attend to others?

Do they ignore some behaviours at one time but pick them out at another?
Are parents known to have used harsh physical punishment as a means of
controlling their child's behaviour?
Have either parents or child complained of harsh punishment?
Does child behave in a frightened manner when speaking of parental
punishment?
Is there any evidence that parents have given in to all child's demands
within their means in order to control his behaviour?
Does child or anyone else say that he was 'bribed' to stop the trouble?

Action
Because of probable damage to the child and others, it is urgent to achieve
or normalize control over child's behaviour through parent training and
imposition of external boundaries.

0316   Child abuse

01	Pawn between parents
02	Scapegoat
03	Physical abuse
04	Sexual abuse
05	Emotional abuse
06	Other

Description
This condition refers to a range of unacceptable behaviours by parents/
adults or other youngsters towards children which are either aimed at or
result in hurting the child.

The public have become increasingly shocked at the number of children
and adolescents who are subjected to physical and mental cruelty by
parents. This is sometimes accidental and an unfortunate result of inept
parental attempts to control a child's behaviour, such as quieten a
persistently crying baby. Often the physical hurt of the child and its consequences so frighten the parents that the form of control is not exerted
again. In some instances, however, punitive over-reaction to the child's
problems becomes habitual and in still more serious cases it becomes a
ritual of torture almost for its own sake. But overt physical hurt is only
one form of abuse to which children can be subjected.

Emotional abuse has more subtle effects but, in the long term, is even
more likely to impede normal physical and psychological development of
children and leave a deeper scar. Sexual abuse is now also seen as a
widespread activity, usually (though not invariably) by the male figure(s)
in the home. The form of sexual abuse may change with children's age.

Assessment of parental abuse of adolescents is more difficult than that
of young children. This is because adolescents' own deviant behaviour,

such as prostitution, may bear the same consequences, such as physical hurt, as abuse. Also, they have no close network of agencies to oversee their development, and do not present the same linked clues about maltreatment as do younger children.

Parents who are at odds sometimes get at each other through the children, using them as emotional weapons. Equally, some families displace major difficulties with a parent (the literature on schizophrenia frequently cites a 'sick mother') or other stresses on to the child, thus concealing or disguising other difficulties. An example would be a daughter who is groomed to take on a sick or absent mother's full duties, including the sexual one.

Associated feature
Child abuse in all its ramifications is likely to be associated with a range of inadequate and deviant family dynamics. These may entail not only parental problems (though they may be well disguised) but also substantial difficulties for the children. These difficulties include physical disorders (such as enuresis or 'not thriving'), intellectual (school refusal, poor attainments), home and family difficulties of the type described in earlier attributes, poor social relationships, anti-social behaviour and serious psychological difficulties.

Prevalence
Estimates vary widely depending on the kind and severity of the abuse – from over 5 per cent for sexual abuse to over 10 per cent for physical abuse and over 20 per cent for emotional abuse. All estimates are likely to be widely out because of severe under-reporting, particularly of sexual abuse and the culturally determined fashions in focussing on others. There are no good defining criteria for abuse, unless physical marks are present or child makes an appropriately detailed statement. Emotional abuse is not even systematically evaluated, despite immense strides in this area. In many ordinary families where the marital relationship is disintegrating, children may become pawns between parents. Girls are more frequently subject of both physical and sexual abuse, although this may be because of severe under-reporting of abuse of and by boys.

Onset and course
Children can become subject of physical abuse from birth onwards. Sexual abuse can also start before child is one year old. The incidence of both goes up as child grows older, with physical abuse peaking by age five although it continues in some cases into adolescence. Sexual abuse, on the other hand, seems to go on, with some ups and downs, well into adolescence and adulthood, particularly where the family dynamics have locked the child into an abusive relationship with parent or sibling. Other forms of abuse increase with age and some take the place of physical abuse.

Predisposing factors

Contrary to earlier views, it is now accepted that all social classes and types of families engage in abuse of children, although severe physical abuse remains *largely* the preserve of the poorer and more disadvantaged families. This is perhaps because other families do not report it or have better ways of dressing it up and coping with it. All deaths of children as a result of abuse have been from poor or disorganized families. In such families mother is usually young, with poor social support, living with a partner who may or may not be the child's father. The child is usually unwell and cries a lot.

Attempts to isolate or develop a profile of sexually abusive families have so far failed. The only constant factors are men (usually, though there are also abusive women) and disturbed family dynamics, in terms of intimate relationships, though even this latter is suspect. In general terms, abusers are people who have relative power but inadequate or deviant internal controls and ideas about who should be the subject of their power and how it should be expressed.

Complications

Potentially numerous. Severe forms of physical abuse are deadly – as so many enquiries into deaths of abused children have testified. Short of death, abuse can result in serious physical injuries. Abused children do not thrive well, do badly at school, have difficulties in social relationships, may behave in seriously anti-social fashion and present a range of affective and other personal disorders. It is often difficult to distinguish the cause and effect relationships in such cases, since not all abuse has such consequences.

Impairment

Short of death, results are at worst catastrophic, pervasive and lifelong. Given the protective role of parents and the fundamental need to develop trust and security, a child who is hurt is likely to suffer profoundly from insecurity and lack of trust in adults. Physical impairment is usually repaired or remits spontaneously. In sexual abuse (which is essentially made up of physical and emotional) the personal distress and damage is likely to be considerable, depending on the extent, duration and recency of abuse as well as the particular circumstances surrounding it. Clearly these are in turn a function of the resilience or vulnerability of the victim, as increasing evidence from adult abused populations show. The other forms of abuse would follow the same basic outline.

Prompts

Are parents in conflict?

Is one more attached to child than the other?

Is child or her welfare used as mediator, impediment or link by one to the other?

Are there major problems in the family displaced on to child?

Is child the 'only one' to have a problem?

Does child bear inadequately explained marks, bruises or fractures?

Is child withdrawn, anxious or weepy?

Does child show particular anxiety in home or other setting?

Is child failing to thrive?

Is child doing badly at school despite apparently adequate ability?

Does child suddenly start wetting or soiling?

Does child show an inappropriate knowledge of sexual language or acts?

Does she behave in a sexual way towards other children or adults, when inappropriate for age or setting?

Does child suddenly start running away from home?

Does child suddenly start to solicit?

Does child behave with abnormal aggressiveness when this not part of a general delinquent pattern?

Do parents say that in their conflicts the child takes one side rather than the other? Is child closer to one than the other? Do parents say anything which suggests that they use the child as a way of controlling or affecting their partner's behaviour?

Does either parent speak of leaving home or sending child away?

Does either parent appear to frighten child inappropriately about the effects of his behaviour on either parents or other members of the family?

Do parents readily place the blame on child for their troubles with one another, with other children or with wider society?

Is this untrue and inappropriate?

Does child appear to 'pay' for the aggravation caused by either parents, other siblings or problems with the community?

Does child or anyone else accuse parents and siblings of wrongly blaming her for the problems of the family?

Does either parent or child speak of physical hurt inflicted on the child?

Is there any evidence of child having been hurt in the home?

Is parent's explanation of injuries inadequate, discrepant, or excessively plausible?

Do any social agencies suspect that parents are likely to inflict injury on child?

Is there a history of violence in the family or injury to other children?

Does child have a history of violence and destructiveness to other children, animals or property?

Has child ever attempted self-destructive acts at behest of the family?

Has either parent or child ever accused a parent of sexual abuse?

Is child known to have been sexually assaulted or engaged in (damaging, forced) sexual acts with either parents or siblings?

Action

This problem has now the highest priority profile of any difficulty experienced by children, where stringent laws demand intervention at the first sign of abuse.

0317   Adverse sibling factors

01	Physical defect
02	Mental disorder
03	Alcoholism/heavy drinking
04	Prostitution
05	Special education
06	Offender
07	In alternative care
08	Penal establishment
09	Other

Description
This condition refers to difficulties associated with other children of the family.

Although the parents are regarded as the main source of influence on their children, there is considerable evidence to suggest that siblings are also powerful shapers of each other's behaviour. For this reason, it may be worthwhile to look at the other children and any adverse factors that may affect them. Such adversities may also point to the existence of probable difficulties in the home which may not yet have manifested themselves in the case of the particular child under scrutiny.

Associated features
As for 'adverse parental factors'.

Prevalence
Not known, but substantial when above conditions are aggregated.

Onset and course
Any of the problems can start at any time before or after a child's birth and may progress as appropriate to the problem and effectiveness of interventions.

Predisposing factors
Other than in the case of physical and mental disorder, these arise from and compound parental adversities and poor patterns of upbringing.

Complications
Potentially many, depending on the specific factor. The child is likely to suffer both directly and indirectly from sibling adversities.

Impairment
As for complications, dependent on the range, intensity and duration of sibling problems.

Prompts
As for parental adversities. Usually factual questions or records concerning the other children are the source of information.

Action
Usually aimed at mitigating impact on child by a range of measures, including removal of child from home, if appropriate.

Further reading

Abidin, R.R. (1982) *Parenting Skills – Workbook*, New York: Human Sciences.
Blagg, H. (ed) (1989) *Child Sexual Abuse: Listening, Hearing and Validating the Experiences of Children*, London: Longman.
Bond, T. (1986) *Games for Social and Life Skills*, London: Hutchinson.
Brooks, J. (1987) *Process of Parenting*, New York: Mayfield.
Chasnoff, I.J. (ed) (1988) *Drugs, Alcohol, Pregnancy and Parenting*, Lancaster: MTP.
Clark, E. (1989) *Young Single Mothers Today: Qualitative Study of Housing and Support Needs*, London: National Council for One Parent Families.
Connolly, K. (1985) *Lost Children: Poverty and Human Development*, Exeter: University of Exeter.
Covitz, J. (1986) *Emotional Child Abuse*, San Francisco: Sigo.
Creighton, S.J. (1980) *Child Victims of Physical Abuse, 3rd report*, London: NSPCC.
Diamond, S.A. (1985) *Helping Children of Divorce: a Handbook for Parents and Teachers*, New York: Shocken.
Dibb, J. (1991) *Wherever I Lay My Head: Young Women and Homelessness*, London: Shelter (National Campaign for the Homeless).
Dowling, E. and Osborne, E. (eds) (1985) *Family and the School: Joint Systems Approach to Problems with Children*, London: Routledge.
Fagg, C. (1982) *Homelessness: Training Pack*, London: National Association of Youth Clubs.
Faller, K. (1989) *Child Sexual Abuse: an Interdisciplinary Manual for Diagnosis, Case Management and Treatment*, London: Macmillan Educ.
Finkelhor, D. (1985) *Child Sexual Abuse: New Theory and Research*, New York: Collier Macmillan.
Finkelhor, D. (1986) *Source Book on Child Sexual Abuse*, Newbury Park, Calif: Sage.
Gaffney, M. et al. (1991) *Parenting: a Handbook for Parents*, London: Town House.
Gelles, R.J. (1987) *Violent Home: Study of Physical Aggression between Husbands and Wives*, Newbury Park, Calif: Sage.
Gil, D.G. (1971) *Violence against Children: Physical Child Abuse in the United States*, Cambridge, Mass.: Harvard University Press.
Glaser, D. and Frosh, S. (1988) *Child Sexual Abuse*, London: Macmillan Educ.
Group for Advancement of Psychiatry (1978) *Treatment of Families in Conflict: the Clinical Studies of Family Process*, New York: J. Aronson.
Hammer, T.J. and Turner, P.H. (1990) *Parenting in Contemporary Society*, Englewood Cliffs: Prentice Hall.
Health and Social Security, Dept. of (1988) *Diagnosis of Child Sexual Abuse: Guidance for Doctors*, London: HMSO.
Hoghughi, M.S. and Hipgrave, T. (1986) *Towards a Discipline of Fostering*, London: NFCA.
Hope, M. and Young, J. (1986) *Faces of Homelessness*, Lexington: Lexington Books.
Howells, J.G. (ed) (1971) *Theory and Practice of Family Psychiatry*, Edinburgh: Oliver & Boyd.
Inglis, R (1978) *Sins of the Father: London Study of the Physical and Emotional Abuse of Children*, London: P. Owen.
Jones, D.P. and McQuiston, M.G. (1988) *Interviewing the Sexually Abused Child*, London: Royal College of Psychiatrists/Gaskell.

Kagan, R. and Schlosberg, S. (1989) *Families in Perpetual Crisis*, New York: W.W. Norton.

Kennedy, S. (ed) (1987) *Streetwise: Homeless among the Youth in Ireland and Abroad*, Dublin: Glendale Press.

Kersten, L. and Kersten K.K. (1988) *Marriage and the Family: Studying Close Relationships*, New York: Harper & Row.

Krementz, J. (1985) *How it Feels when Parents Divorce*, London: Gollancz.

Law Commission (1986) *Illegitimacy*, 2nd report, London: HMSO.

Lees, D. (1987) *Successful Parenting for Stressful Times*, New York: R & E Publishing.

Lerner, R.M. and Spanier, G.B. (eds) (1979) *Child Influences on Marital and Family Interaction: a Life-span Perspective*, London: Academic Press.

McConville, B. (1988) *Family Life: Children in Conflict*, London: Macdonald.

McNay, M. and Pond, C. (1980) *Low Pay and Family Poverty*, London: Study Commission on the Family.

McWhinnie, A.M. (1966) *Adoption Assessments*, London: Association of British Adoption Agencies.

Marsden, D. (1969) *Mothers Alone*, Harmondsworth: Pelican.

Millar, J. (1989) *Poverty and the Lone Parent Family: the Challenge to Social Policy*, Aldershot: Gower.

Milner, J. and Blyth, E. (1989) *Coping with Child Sexual Abuse: a Guide for Teachers*, London: Longman.

Mitchell, A.K. (1986) *When Parents Split Up: Divorce explained to Young People*, Edinburgh: Chambers.

Mrazek, P.B. and Kempe, C.H. (1981) *Sexually Abused Children and their Families*, New York: Pergamon.

National Council for One Parent Families (1983) *Single Mothers and Illegitimacy – Selected Reading List*, London: NCOPF.

Noller, P. and Callan, V. (1991) *The Adolescent in the Family*, London: Routledge.

Nye, F.I. (1982) *Family Relationships: Rewards and Costs*, Beverly Hills, Calif: Sage.

O'Brien, M.J. (1989) *Characteristics of Male Adolescent Sibling Incest Offenders*, New York: Safer Society Press.

O'Hagan, K. (1989) *Working with Child Sexual Abuse: a post-Cleveland Guide to Effective Principles and Practice*, Milton Keynes: Open University Press.

Open University (1989) *Social Problems and Social Welfare – Units 6–7: Family Gender and Welfare*, Milton Keynes: Open University Press.

Open University (1989) *Social Problems and Social Welfare – Units 8–9: Family, Gender and Welfare – Masculinity, Homophobia and Sexuality – Women, Work and the Family*, Milton Keynes: Open University Press.

Open University (1989) *Social Problems and Welfare – Unit 12: Family, Gender and Welfare – Review*, Milton Keynes: Open University Press.

Patterson, G.R. (ed) (1990) *Depression and Aggression in Family Interactions*, Hillsdale, NJ: L. Erlbaum.

Powers, D.F. (ed) (1985) *Adoption for Troubled Children: Prevention and Repair of Adoptive Failures through Residential Treatment*, New York: Haworth Press.

Quinton, D. and Rutter, M. (1988) *Parenting Breakdown: Making and Breaking of Intergenerational Links*, Aldershot: Gower.

Richards, M. (1985) *Key Issues in Child Sexual Abuse: Some Lessons from Cleveland and Other Inquiries*, London: NISW.

Rickell, A.U. (1989) *Teen Pregnancy and Parenting*, New York: Hemisphere.

Riem, C. (1990) *Adopted Child: Family Life with Double Parenthood*, New York: Transaction Publishers.

Rutter, M. and Madge, N. (1976) *Cycles of Disadvantage*, London: Heinemann.

Schaefer, C.E. (1979) *How to Influence Children: a Handbook of Practical Parenting Skills*, New York: Van Nostrand Reinhold.

Sgroi, S. (1982) *Handbook of Clinical Intervention in Child Sexual Abuse*, Lexington, Mass.: Lexington Books.

Shaw, M. and Hipgrave, T. (1986) *Teenagers in Care: Seminars on Fostering Adolescents*, London: NFCA.

Smith, C.R. (1984) *Adoption and Fostering*, London: Macmillan.

Triseliotis, J.P. (ed) (1980) *New Developments in Foster Care and Adoption*, London: Routledge.

Walker, C.E., Bonner, B.L. and Kaufman, K.L. (1988) *The Physically and Sexually Abused Child*, New York: Pergamon.

Wallerstein, J.S. and Kelly, J.B. (1980) *Surviving the Breakup: How Children and Parents cope with Divorce*, Oxford: Grant McIntyre/Blackwell.

Watson, S. and Austerberry, H. (1986) *Housing and Homelessness: a Feminist Perspective*, London: Routledge.

Wiggans, A. (1983) *Housing, Homelessness and the Process of Leaving Home*, London: National Council for Voluntary Youth Services.

Williamson, P.R. (1989) *Family Problems*, London: Oxford University Press.

11

Social Skills Problems

Social skills are concerned with making and maintaining social relationships. A child has a problem when her dealings with other people, whether adults or children, are fraught, full of conflict or devoid of satisfaction, for her or others. Most of these difficulties can be and still often are construed under the rubric *relationships*.

'Relationship', however, is a confused and confusing term invested with wide-ranging emotional overtones. It is so frequently used and in such diverse circumstances that it has become almost devoid of any clear meaning. For this reason it is avoided in a book which advocates the clear description of children's problems.

In any case, relationships are the *end product* of the exercise of social skills. Any attempt to improve the social interaction of a child with those around her must seek to put right those individual elements which may be responsible for the child's and others' dissatisfaction with her social functioning.

Of all the problem areas described in this book, problems of social skills are, at least overtly, given the lowest priority both by referral and treatment agencies. This is in part because social skills problems are mainly manifested in small group settings when the members are, for a variety of reasons, close enough to be affected. Members of small groups do not complain about each other's social skills unless these are severely deficient or deviant and then manifested in obnoxious or destructive behaviour. For the same reason, hard information of the type available on some other conditions in this book is seriously lacking. However, normative information is also less important in this section where the perceived difficulties of the child, rather than empirically established reference points, are necessary for the definition of abnormality.

Social agencies are not particularly concerned with children's interpersonal problems unless these are associated with or thought to cause other problems such as running away, fighting or deliberate self-harm.

Social skills difficulties are also deeply culture-bound. Some individuals and groups are more intolerant of unusual social behaviour than others. On the whole, middle-class people appear to be more concerned with and prone to evaluating others in terms of their social skills than are other classes. Although 'airs and graces' are sometimes pejoratively regarded as 'bourgeois', basic social 'manners' are necessary for peaceful and rewarding coexistence within almost any group of people, however disordered, regardless of class. We have, therefore, concentrated on those social skills deficiencies and peculiarities which create problems for children and people around them in otherwise tolerant settings. The same cultural biases and filters may be the reason why more boys than girls are seen as suffering from social skills difficulties.

In Western countries, 'social skills' and 'social training' have become associated with 'social problem solving', such as experiencing normal sexual relations or successfully completing a job interview. But these situations encapsulate and test and are a culmination of many different social skills. For this reason, we have brought together such situations as apply to children and young people as 'specific situational problems'.

Characteristically, difficulties in this area arise from deficient or deviant socialization experiences in the course of children's growth. A child who has been brought up in a culturally alienated and disordered family is likely to acquire skills for survival within that family which may place her at odds with those from more 'normal' (in this sense meaning 'usual' rather than 'correct') families.

Other children may develop social skills problems because of some personal oddity such as a badly scarred face or tendency to withdrawal, and yet others because they lack the necessary intellectual or linguistic competence to understand or learn from social interactions.

In the assessment of social skills, because of the probability of cultural biases, it is particularly important to be specific about the circumstances in which children have a problem, in order to draw valid conclusions about their difficulties. Depending on the importance to be attached to the assessment and certainly before any treatment commences, it may be necessary closely to follow the format of questions set out earlier in Chapter 5.

The assessment of social skills relies more on observations than any of the other problem areas. When the opportunity is not available the framework of observations can be translated into a series of questions which those close to the child – parents, teachers and other children – may answer. The opinion of peers regarding a child's specific problem behaviours are particularly noteworthy and may be elucidated by a range of techniques and games.

This problem area does not receive any attention from the other major approaches to assessment. Diagnostic systems do not even have a vague 'axis' other than perhaps the 'psychosocial' which may cover it. Multivariate analyses do not identify it as a major constellation of difficulties, perhaps because the interest in this area is recent and not many research data are available on it.

0401   Presentation

01	Dirtiness, smelliness
02	Odd body movement or posture
03	Odd facial features
04	Odd speech rate/volume
05	Poor eating habits
06	Other

Description

This condition refers to the difficulties of the first impression the child makes on others.

First impressions are significant determinants of how people react to each other. Children who present badly are more likely to be made the subject of intervention than those who do not, whether because they are deemed to be 'in need of care' or suffering from some disorder.

Associated features

Children who present poorly are likely to have a range of other difficulties from perhaps physical and intellectual to anti-social and personality problems. Above all, however, they are likely to come from disadvantaged families or others who, by virtue of their other difficulties, have not inculcated or been able to support high-level personal habits in the child.

Prevalence

Not known with any certainty, but between 10 and 20 per cent of clinic and other groups of children with other difficulties present some of the above features. Boys and girls seem to present this condition equally.

Onset and course

Usually condition applies to children from two onwards, becoming most noticeable when child can be seen in context of peers, as in school. Condition usually improves towards adolescence as child becomes more integrated in groups, though relatively scruffy looks and habits can continue into adulthood. Girls mature earlier and seem to take an earlier interest in improving their looks.

Predisposing factors

None specific, but coming from a materially poor and otherwise stressed home where little attention is paid to the children is likely to be prominent.

Complications

Potential hygiene problems may occur. Also child is likely to be stigmatized by others, therefore shun company and develop maladaptive response and habit patterns.

Impairment

Considerable in social terms because of the potential of poor presentation to isolate the child from peers and adults. People's attitudes and attributions to a child are significantly affected by how the child looks and their attitudes are likely to affect their behaviour accordingly.

Prompts

Do parents and others comment on his presentation?

Are there any suggestions or reports that others may have found him offputting?

Does the child notice anything odd about himself?

How does he appear to feel about it?

Do people shy away from him because of his smell, looks or manner?

Are there any oddities of posture, co-ordination, muscular control (including tics and twitches) or walking gait?

If so, do they restrict his physical activities only or games and other social activities as well?

Is there anything offputting about his facial features – usually open mouth, drooling or sores?

Is his speech aggressive and querulous?

Are eating habits properly formed? Do other people object to his eating habits?

Does he take notice of any feedback given to him in these areas?

Action

Important to do something about the child's presentation, for which effective, low-cost techniques exist.

0402   Interaction skills

```
01   Odd visual contact
02   Misuse of facial expression
03   Inappropriate use of gesture
04   Staning too close/too far
05   Touching people inappropriately
06   Other
```

Description

This attribute refers to one or more basic difficulties the child may have in making social contact with others.

Eye contact, facial expression, gestures and bodily distance are all involved in even the most basic social contact. In the course of their growth and according to cultural patterns, children learn to adopt the appropriate use of these means of expression. They become a form of implicit body language to which other people respond.

Their 'correct' use is necessary not only in order to make and maintain normal social contact, but also to convey accurately any emotional information which may or may not be communicated verbally. If the verbal and bodily messages are incongruent or inappropriate, this may give rise to conflict with adults and lead to the labelling of the child as 'peculiar', 'odd' and socially inept.

These interaction skills are so basic that any deficiency is usually indicative of either very poor social training or alternatively of other functional disorders.

Associated features
Children suffering from pervasive developmental disorders, mental retardation, those from damaging home and institutional experiences and, less commonly, serious conduct disorders are likely to present some or all of these problems. Possibility of serious visual or hearing defect should be ruled out.

Prevalence
Given their potential seriousness, less than 5 per cent of all children seem to present the more severe forms of these difficulties. Considerably greater numbers present one or more in mild forms. Boys seem more prone to these difficulties than girls.

Onset and course
From two years onwards these difficulties become noticeable. Where they are associated with pervasive developmental disorders they are likely to deteriorate until pre-puberty, from which point they stabilize and gradually improve, although some difficulties will continue to be evident throughout. With mentally retarded and other groups of children, these features gradually improve until at adolescence most will be reasonably normal. The exception is 'touching people inappropriately' which with the awakening sexuality of adolescents may take on a new intensity during this period.

Predisposing factors
In the case of children with pervasive developmental disorders the same predisposing features as that condition apply. In mental retardation and other conditions, these features seem to be associated with poor social and familial modelling and inadequate social teaching.

Complications
None specific, other than potentially adverse peer and adult attitudes which arise whenever a child is seen as 'odd' or 'different'.

Impairment
Significant in the area of social relations because the skills which these indicate are fundamental building bricks of more complex social relationships.

Prompts
Are there any reports from school or other sources speaking of the child's oddness? Do they give instances?
Do the parents notice any difference between this child and others? In what terms? Do they relate the 'oddness' to any particular factors?
Does the child show any awareness of how others regard him?
Do the parents and others comment on any of the above behaviours?
Does the child stare? Is the stare blank? Is it always there or does it vary with his mood and circumstances?

Does child look you in the eye when talking? Does he avert gaze whenever eye contact is made? Does the contact shift and flicker rapidly? Are facial expressions appropriate to the mood and matter of the moment?
If relatively unvarying, what emotion does it indicate?
Is facial expression marked by a habitual tic or grimace?
Does child use a lot of gestures? Are they appropriate to what he is talking about or are they pervasive and relatively unvarying?
Does child have a characteristic gait and body posture? Are these adopted for effect?
Does child stand so close or so far as to make others uncomfortable?
Does child touch people too often? Is the touch suggestive?
Of what? Does child maintain contact for long?
Is the child a 'fidget'? Does fidgeting impair interaction or communication?
Does it follow a stereotyped pattern?

Action
Important to try to improve these skills through a variety of available techniques to ease child's social relationships and avoid more serious difficulties.

0403   Conversation skills

01   Making noises while others speak
02   Interrupting
03   Persistent, irrelevant questioning
04   Constantly whining
05   Other

Description
This attribute concerns child's difficulties in making and sustaining conversation, when these are not attributable to hearing, speech and language difficulties.

Conversation is the chief medium of social interaction. Even in young children, speaking to each other is the chief form of gaining information and co-ordinating actions. It is, therefore, important that as well as learning the language which permits communication, children master the skill of conversing. The subjects children talk about must interest others if they are to gain enjoyment in the conversation and they, in turn, are to gain social acceptance. A child whose conversation is boring or offensive will have difficulty in making friends.

Associated features
Making noises may be associated with pervasive developmental disorders or mental retardation. As often and like other difficulties in this area, it

is associated with children who come from disadvantaged homes or from institutions, where the level and quality of parenting may not have been very high. More often than not the conditions are associated with anti-social conduct and related disorders.

Prevalence
In their milder form, teachers say about 30 per cent of the school population shows some of these features. In the more severe form, however, the prevalence is likely to be of the order of 5–10 per cent, with disproportionately greater numbers among clinic and institutional populations. Apart from making noises, girls seem to be more prominent in this area.

Onset and course
This difficulty becomes evident usually in the early school years and, unless corrected, continues to escalate as the child grows older. It begins to tail off in late adolescence, although some residual (and in some instances worse) features may remain.

Predisposing factors
Mainly poor parenting and general socialization, where the condition does not arise from more serious physical or personality disturbance.

Complications
Unpopularity with both peers and adults and bullying may be complicating features.

Impairment
Depending on severity and persistence, this condition may be potentially serious in handicapping the child scholastically, socially and in employment opportunities.

Prompts
Do people complain that the child cannot hold a sensible conversation?

Does she complain that no one ever listens to her?

Does she either irritate others in the way she starts conversation or fails to gain attention when she appears to want it?

Do people seem to take an interest in talking to the child?

Have people said that the child is a nuisance in discussion groups or impossible to talk to?

Has she been referred to as 'stupid' or 'immature' on the basis of what she says rather than what she does?

Does child start conversations by hanging round aimlessly until spoken to; grabbing people physically; shouting across the room; just barging in?

Does child wander off while still being spoken to?

Does child habitually make a noise or go on chattering while others are speaking?

Does she interrupt frequently?

Does she reply when people are talking to her? Does she seem to ignore what people are saying? Is there any suspicion of hearing loss?

Is child verbose, does she take hours to reach her point, repeat herself, gabble away without giving others a chance to speak?

Is her speech monosyllabic or over-curt?

Are her comments usually related to what is being talked about?

Does she wander off the topic frequently?

Does she persistently ask inane questions?

Is her silliness amusing or irritating? Does she acknowledge that she is being silly or does she seem to be in a world of her own?

Does child frequently tell lies? Are these small lies or fantastical tales? Is it done to the extent where no one believes a word she says? Does she insist they are true when challenged?

Is child forever complaining or whining? What about? Is it justified?

Action
If not severe, action is not warranted as maturation will sort it out. If it is, good techniques exist for correcting the child's difficulty and nuisance, unless a more fundamental difficulty is present.

0404 Assertiveness

01	Not making demands or requests
02	Giving in quickly when challenged
03	Generally pushed around
04	Making demands petulantly or incompetently
05	Making demands aggressively
06	Shyness and uneasiness
07	Easily embarrassed
08	Avoiding social contact
09	Showing anxiety in interaction
10	Inept attempts at making friends
11	Other

Description
This condition refers to the child's difficulty in making demands or requests, whether they are her 'right' or not, in an appropriate manner.

'Appropriate' in this context means neither putting up with being pushed around nor making demands in an aggressive or incompetent manner. These difficulties suggest that the child's social relationships are not satisfactory or that she is uncomfortable in social settings. They include fears concerning social contact and complaints of dissatisfaction. These can, in themselves, further reduce social acceptability by making others feel ill at ease. Similarly, constant inept attempts at making friends may indicate that the child is lonely and socially unskilled and such failures may further promote unease and unhappiness in relationships.

Associated features
Children suffering from pervasive developmental disorders or mental retardation may not make demands at all and be subject to bullying and pushing around by others. Others may be emotionally withdrawn, fragile and frightened. Those who try to get their way in petulant, incompetent or aggressive manner are likely to suffer from a range of conduct and anti-social disorders.

Prevalence
This is one of the most pervasive difficulties among all children but particularly those who come from disadvantaged and insecure backgrounds. Between them the conditions are claimed to be found in as much as 30 per cent of the school children, though much higher in clinic and institutional populations. Condition seems more associated with personality type than gender, with girls predominating in the earlier conditions and the boys in the more externalized and aggressive behaviours.

Onset and course
Evident in early school and becoming gradually more prominent as child grows older. Both extremes of the condition reach their peak in adolescence and seem to continue into adulthood and lifetime behaviour patterns, unless corrected.

Predisposing factors
Poorly socialized, abused and badly parented children are much more likely to present these conditions than those brought up in environments where they have not either taken flight from distress or adopted aggressive patterns of social adaptation.

Complications
More likely to be associated with unusual personality patterns, particularly of a withdrawn type. There may, therefore, emerge other affective difficulties, anorexia and similar conditions. Aggressive patterns may result in strong social reactions which may in fact exacerbate child's condition.

Impairment
Considerable in its more serious reaches. Society is not so eternally attentive or forgiving that it will go on giving appropriate fulfilment to unassertive or aggressively demanding children. The children are, therefore, likely to be deprived of much social reward or be subjected to painful sanctions.

Prompts
Do reports from school suggest social unease or other difficulties in this area?

What would the teachers say if questioned about this area?
Do parents say anything about their child's difficulty in social settings?
Does child himself complain?
Can he relate his difficulties to particular settings or types of company?
Does he say whether he has tried to do anything about it?
Does he spend most of his time alone?
Does he stay at home most of the time?
Does he seem anxious or worried in social situations?
Does child seem quiet and shy?
Does he seem suspicious of other children's approaches?
In his approach to others is he tentative and ready to withdraw?
Does he seem to fear being in the limelight?
Is he easily flustered by people?
Does he appear muddled and confused about what to do in company?
Is this true of a particular type of company?
Does he try to work by himself when possible?
Does he ignore the fads or crazes of the group?
Is he reluctant to take part in group activities?
Does he rarely initiate speaking?
Does he avoid break or free time activities in school?
Does he join groups then leave quickly (scouts, youth clubs)?
Does child try to make friends but fail?
Does he try to make friends mostly with younger or less able children?
Does he try to 'buy' friendships with gifts or promises?
Does he swamp newcomers with attention?
Does he pester other children?
Does he get over-excited when friendship seems to be developing?
What do other children think of him?

Action
Crucially important to teach appropriate assertiveness skills to reduce the probability of very unhappy life. Fortunately, good techniques exist, but they demand prolonged patience.

0405 Sensitivity

01	Undersensitivity to cues
02	Misinterpretation of cues
03	Ignoring cues
04	Not altering behaviour to fit social environment
05	Other

Description
This area concerns difficulty in picking up and responding to social cues.

Sensitivity is used here to refer to perception of the feelings, mood and reaction of others particularly as expressed by physical signals of facial expression, voice tone and gesture.

Some environments (such as courts, libraries, classrooms, assemblies) have an atmosphere either because of the mood of the people in them or because of their function. These require certain responses. Some children fail to respond to these and, therefore, behave in socially inappropriate ways.

In order to co-ordinate his action to the feelings of the others in any situation, a child must first notice the cues they give (such as facial expression), understand the meaning of cues and then alter his behaviour to fit the situation. Problems of how a child reacts to others' feelings rather than how he perceives them are dealt with in the last chapter.

Associated features
Children suffering from pervasive developmental disorders, mental retardation and attention deficit disorders are likely to be seriously deficient in this area. Otherwise, children with this difficulty are likely to come from chaotic and poorly integrated environments where little attention has been paid to the finer details of their behaviour. Conduct and anti-social disorders are particularly prominent. Deficient sensitivity is evident in many clinical conditions.

Prevalence
The difficulty of estimation lies in the complex nature of social sensitivity and definitional preferences. No general estimates are available. Clinic and institutional children show this feature in about 30 per cent of cases. Boys are more likely to present this condition, though even here halo and other filtering effects may be responsible for this impression.

Onset and course
Usually noticed in early school years but condition usually gets worse towards a peak in adolescence and persists into adulthood, when demands on social sensitivity grow apace.

Predisposing factors
Apart from the physically based disorders such as pervasive developmental disorders, children with this difficulty are likely to come from poorly caring environments or those in which the dominant models have also been insensitive. Particular personality types (such as highly extroverted) may be more prone to this condition than others.

Complications
Only those that result from the child's inability to behave with enough sensitivity towards age mates and adults, including potentially serious anti-social acts.

Impairment

Potentially grave, depending on the severity of the condition and the circumstances in which child is likely to find himself. An insensitive child is fundamentally handicapped and does not even arouse the charity and protectiveness that may be extended to other children with serious physical or mental disability.

Prompts

Do parents and others speak of tactless or unfeeling behaviour?

Is there any suggestion that child is not aware of the feelings of others?

Does child constantly behave in a way which is opposed to the mood of the group as a whole?

Does child describe people's reactions or feelings towards him in a way that suggests he has misunderstood what is happening?

Would you call him 'tactless' or 'thick skinned'?

Does child frequently behave in a way which is inappropriate to his environment?

What does child do?

How does child describe other people's reactions to him?

Is child good at judging other people or does he seem constantly surprised or indignant at their reactions to him?

Does child respond to frowns and other cues of annoyance or does he have to be ordered verbally to stop what he is doing?

Is there any particular mood to which child seems oblivious – tired, cheerful, irritable?

Does child ever apologize or show contrition when he has annoyed or hurt someone?

Does child comment on others' moods or feelings?

Does child respond to the atmosphere of different social environments, or is his behaviour constant?

Is child aware of the need to behave differently according to others' moods or the place he is in?

Is child in these respects very different from other children in a normal setting? And those in current setting?

Action

Urgently necessary to do something about this condition. Techniques are available for 'shaping' sensitive behaviour but they are onerous and time consuming.

0406   Fellow-feeling

01	Failing to help others
02	Not saying kind things about others
03	Not showing appreciation
04	Not showing affection
05	Unsupportive when others are troubled
06	Showing no interest in others
07	Not sharing things
08	Not conceding
09	Not co-operating
10	Other

Description

This condition refers to the difficulty in dealing with others in a sympathetic manner.

Sympathy or fellow-feeling is essential for social and biological survival of both the individual and the species. To help another human being in trouble and to provide support when someone is distressed are qualities regarded as fundamentally human. This is so basic that anyone who is deficient in this area arouses deep anxieties and misgivings in fellow human beings. Sympathy can be regarded as a collection of skills and personal *qualities* which include the correct reading and response to social cues, warmth and sensitivity.

Some of these qualities, such as warmth, appear to be based on inborn potential and related to wider aspects of personality. Others, such as sensitivity, appear to require not only certain cognitive and perceptual aptitudes but also a reasonably stimulating, caring and consistent social background. Children who are inadequately endowed with any of these may, as a result, show poor fellow-feeling.

The consequence of poor sympathy is that other people feel unwanted, superfluous and 'object-like' in the company of the child. A further cause of concern is that children deficient in these skills, particularly those caught up in anti-social acts, are more likely to inflict serious hurt because they are incapable of gauging the effects of their behaviour on others' feelings.

Associated features

As with sensitivity, this characteristic is likely to be found in an extreme form in children with pervasive developmental disorders, mental retardation and, to a lesser extent, in attention deficit disorders children. Otherwise, the condition is associated with poor and disadvantaged backgrounds where children have been so devalued that they find it difficult to value others and 'feel with' them. The condition will be particularly prevalent among children with anti-social, oppositional and other conduct disorders.

Prevalence
Not known in the general population. In clinic and institutional children seen in its unacceptable form with three or more of the above conditions in about 15 per cent of the children, more in boys than in girls.

Onset and course
Usually first evident in school. Dependent on measures taken, usually becomes more noticeable as child grows older, reaching a peak in early adolescence, when unsympathetic behaviour and its consequences are socially more 'visible'.

Predisposing factors
Physiologically based disorders cited in associated features will lead to deficient learning in this area. Otherwise disadvantaged and abusive homes where the behaviour patterns are self-centred and where parents provide poor role models are more likely to produce children with this difficulty.

Complications
None specific. Child is likely to get into trouble for other specific anti-social or disordered behaviour of which this is a feature.

Impairment
Considerable in making and maintaining satisfactory social relationships with peers and adults. An unsympathetic child, like an insensitive one, is likely to be shunned or actively targeted for hurt.

Prompts
Do school and other reports suggest that child is unfeeling toward or unconcerned with others?
Do parents say child was unaffected by distress in the family or that things did not seem to touch him?
Do adults use the adjectives 'selfish', 'uncaring', 'cold', or 'careless' when talking of child?
Do other children refer to him as 'selfish' or 'greedy'?
Does child possess a reasonable fund of information about people with whom he has daily contact?
Does child complain that people make him do more than his fair share of helping?
Does child complain unjustifiably that he always has to share or never gets his own way?
Does what child has to say about others suggest much depth of feeling?
Does child show any insight into what it might be like to be distressed?
Does child speak of others as if their feelings might guide his actions?
Does child help other people?
Does child complain or hinder when asked for help?
Does child ever remark kindly on others' appearance or achievement?
Does child notice or show pleasure at gifts or kindness?

Does child seem grateful for help when in difficulties?

Does child seem pleased to see people?

Does child muddle people's names or use stereotyped titles (Sir, Miss) even when he knows people well?

Does child show any conventional, physical sign of affection?

Does child smile at people or is his face always glum or blank?

Does child express positive feelings about anyone? What sorts and about whom?

Does child show any interest in people by watching them, talking and asking questions?

Does child keep sweets and possessions to himself?

Does child ever give something he values to others?

Does child take more than his fair share of food at meals or equipment in the classroom?

Does child do anything which shows he knows how others are feeling? Is the impression he gives that he does not know or does not care?

Does child insist on having his own way in spite of others' needs?

Does child simply conform to adult requirements without being 'touched' by them?

Does child co-operate with other children in work or play without bossing or quarrelling?

Does child apologize for hurting or offending others? Does he show any sign that the realizes when he has done so?

Action
Important to help child acquire the necessary skills in order to have a nicer time. Techniques are available but demand consistent work over a longish period.

0407   Social integration

01	Ignoring by others
02	Disliking by others
03	Bullying by others
04	Scapegoating or taunting by others
05	Social isolating
06	No friends
07	Other

Description
This condition refers to the degree the child is part of a peer group, and more rarely, an integral part of an adult group.

Human beings operate in relatively small groupings of family members, peers and sometimes others. Social behaviour is about 'give and take' in such groups, to which all the social skills mentioned so far contribute. A child who is not socially integrated does not 'belong' and has, therefore, no good or adequate points of reference for regulating his own life. He is, to that extent, adrift and at the mercy of any pulls and pushes which may arise from his own internal impulses, 'temptations', or external stimuli. An unintegrated or poorly integrated child is unlikely to desist from behaviour because of its consequences for other people or himself. This is one of the most general and pervasive indicators of a child's difficulty in a social group. It does not only indicate the probability of other difficulties, but is a problem in its own right, because it seriously undermines a child's ability to draw pleasure from social contact.

Associated features
Children with pervasive developmental disorders, mental retardation or attention deficit disorders are likely to suffer from this condition. Otherwise the condition is associated with under-socialized, aggressive, conduct-disordered children or those with anxiety or other affective disorders.

Prevalence
There are various estimates, ranging from 15 to 40 per cent of school children, recognizing the constantly shifting patterns of popularity and group integration and varying degrees of severity. In the more serious forms, as seen in clinic and institutional children, the condition applies to about 10 per cent, with apparently equal spread of boys and girls, in relation to own sex groups.

Onset and course
Evident from about four years when children start to play together but becomes more noticeable as children grow older and more likely to form groupings. No particular course, continues more or less with some children throughout adolescence and beyond.

Predisposing factors
Apart from physically based disorders, this is more likely to be a feature of badly brought up or aggressive, anti-social children, who even in a group of similar peers, stand out for their poor integration. Small physical size and physical marks as well as certain personality features such as coldness or withdrawal make this condition more probable.

Complications
A poorly integrated child may become hostile, withdrawn or willing to do anything to gain approval and integration. Anti-social behaviour and its consequences may, therefore, complicate the picture of poor integration.

Impairment
This is potentially considerable depending on severity, the child's resilience and perceived 'need' for social integration. Given the amount of time children are forced to be in groups, the difficulty is also likely to impede scholastic and social maturation.

Prompts
Does child have difficulty in finding people to play with outside school?
Do other children call for him?
Are his siblings unwilling to go out with him because of others' reactions?
Is child friendless?
Does child lay claim to friends who do not act like friends?
Do parents say child is taunted or picked on?
Do parents and others say child is unpopular or friendless?
Does the child himself complain of isolation and unpopularity?
What reasons does he give?
Does child have difficulty in making and keeping friends?
Is child usually forgotten or the last to be chosen for teams, games, etc?
Does child leave classes or school all by himself?
Does child approach others far more often than they approach him?
Do other children seem reluctant to work or play with him?
Do other people ignore him when child talks?
Does child seem to be disliked by most other children?
Does child seem to be disliked by most adults?
Do others seem to avoid him?
Do others complain about him?
Is child bullied?
What forms of bullying is used: verbal, physical or extortion?
Is child subjected to excessive teasing?
Do other children play practical jokes on him that could really hurt?
Does child have derogatory nicknames?
How does child react to the teasing?
Does child ever appear tearful, bruised or unhappy on return from a
  gathering of age mates?

Action
Necessary or advisable, depending on its severity and importance to the
child. Being bullied demands focal attention. Difficult and time consuming.

0408 Attitude to other children

01	Antagonism to others
02	Domineering tendencies
03	Manipulatoriness
04	Over-dependence
05	Submissiveness
06	Other

Description
This condition refers to prominent patterns of behaviour towards other
children.

How children get on with other children will determine how happy or miserable they are going to be for the major part of their social lives.

Children's attitudes to their peers, like all other attitudes, are acquired in the course of their growth. They are shaped by the outcome of their cumulative experiences with others and the influence of significant models in their lives.

All children show elements of negative attitudes, depending on the circumstances. It would be inappropriate to regard these as problematic. However, when children appear to adopt a primary mode of response to others and this mode of response is not altered to suit the circumstances and leads to conflict with other children or adults, it becomes maladaptive. Such modes of response, here called *attitudes*, are essentially behavioural and may or may not be associated with expressions of appropriate beliefs and feelings.

Associated features

These depend on the particular form the attitude takes. Those who are habitually negative towards their peers are likely to show a range of aggressive and probably other conduct disorders. The generally withdrawing and submissive behaviours are more likely to be associated with anxiety and other emotional difficulties.

Prevalence

At the extreme end of this dimension, somewhere between 10 and 20 per cent of children (depending on the criteria used) present this difficulty, probably in equal proportions of boys and girls. In milder forms the prevalence rate would be higher in a normal population and much higher in clinic and institutional populations. Boys and girls appear to present equal difficulties, relative to prevailing norms in the age and gender group.

Onset and course

Difficulties may become apparent from the earliest days of child's social play, particularly in the extreme forms. However, more often mild difficulties in primary school are seriously exacerbated at the time of transfer to secondary school. If not properly handled, they are likely to deteriorate further until the end of schooling. There is little information about subsequent development but the basic established pattern of interaction with peers is unlikely to change suddenly.

Predisposing factors

Abnormal neurological features, associated with extremes of extroverted or introverted behaviour; features associated with pervasive developmental disorders or attention deficit disorders; growing up in an aggressive or very insecure home; abuse of all sorts or living in a severely stressful school or other environment may all predispose to extreme forms of such behaviour.

Complications
A child who behaves negatively towards others is likely to provoke strong reactions and suffer for it. One who is submissive or over-dependent is likely to be bullied and used by others. Both may get into trouble for anti-social behaviour whose repercussions may exacerbate their condition.

Impairment
Given the amount of time children have to spend with each other, difficulties in this area are likely to have serious repercussions for their adaptation to peer company. This will, in turn, affect their scholastic and social adjustment.

Prompts
Do school reports suggest that child is unattached to any grouping?
Are there any other reports which speak of child's loyalty and attachment to others?
Do parents speak of their child's lack of attachments?
Does child try to get children to do things which profit her?
Do other children believe child 'uses' them?
Is child said to be 'bossy' or 'domineering'?
Have such words as 'antagonistic', 'provocative' or 'disruptive' been used about her? Are they based on any reported instances?
Do parents and others describe her as a 'follower', 'meek', 'gullible', 'easily led' or other such things?
Is there any evidence that she has previously done what others have suggested without much resistance or thought for the consequences?
How does child describe her own attitude to other children?
Is this much at variance with their descriptions of her?
Does the child tell tales or divulge 'secrets' about other children ('grassing') without much persuasion?
Do her dealings with other children suggest the absence of emotional ties?
Is child 'crafty' in her dealings with other children? To her own benefit and their distress?
Does child set about organizing others against their will?
Does child taunt or bully others into accepting her status? What are the consequences?
What does child do with those children who resist her attempts to dominate?
Do her dealings with the other children frequently end in conflict?
Do the other children complain of her as a tease or a bully?
Is her teasing cruel or beyond reasonable fun?
Is child involved in more squabbles than other children?
Do most children react to her in this way or only a touchy minority?
Is child the butt of other children's teasing?
Is child an early choice for anyone who wants a follower or a 'fall guy'?
Do other children take advantage of her?

Is child easily taken in, dared to do silly things or tricked into doing others' work?

Does child complain of being mistreated?

Does child resist others' attempts to dominate her?

Action

Little can be done other than in closely structured settings and only with great effort and ingenuity.

0409   Attitude to adults

01	Hostility
02	Defiance
03	Untrustingness
04	Over-familiarity
05	Over-dependence
06	Other

Description

This condition concerns the broad thrust of child's dealings with authority figures.

As children grow older and go to school they come into increasing contact with adults other than parents. The children's attitudes to adults, it is believed, are shaped by and are an extension of attitudes to their own parents or their surrogates. If the attitude is trusting, open and controlled, children are likely to act in a similar manner to the adults they encounter outside home. If not, they will generalize to the adults whatever negative experiences they may have had with their own parents.

But adults are not just passive recipients of the children's attitudes. They also have specific response modes to children according to their own perceived roles and experiences. Their consequent response to children will, in turn, elicit reactions which are likely to generate self-reinforcing patterns. Because adults have the power to decree that certain of children's conditions are unacceptable, problem children's contact with and attitudes to adults are likely to be negative. This is particularly true of authority figures who are able to make powerful judgments (such as teachers and magistrates) about children with consequences that the latter do not like. Because assessment agents are also adults, it is important to guard against the possibility of personal reactions and biases to a child who, by virtue of past experiences, may react to them in a manner they do not like.

Associated features

Children who present these features are likely to have been brought up in aggressive, inconsistent homes and to have had broadly negative and hurtful experiences with adults, such as teachers, police and carers.

Prevalence
Despite frequent claims by adults to the contrary, most young people behave in a courteous and compliant manner with adults most of the time. Research studies show prevalences of 5–12 per cent of 'serious' forms of such behaviour among adolescents. The prevalence among younger children is likely to be lower, as is the ratio of girls to boys at about 1:4. In institutional settings, however, girls' difficulties in this are of the same order as the boys', if not worse.

Onset and course
This problem becomes manifest initially in primary school and progressively gets worse, peaking in late adolescence and early adulthood. It is not known whether and how attitude to authority changes in adulthood.

Predisposing factors
Children from poor homes who have been badly parented or damaged by institutional experience and who are prone to conduct disorders are more likely to behave in this manner.

Complications
None specific, apart from various negative adult reactions to child's behaviour.

Impairment
Considerable in its severe forms. This condition seems to be like a 'degenerative' disorder if for no other reason than adverse adult reactions to child's behaviour are likely to exacerbate the very condition. A child who is at odds with adults is likely to suffer a great deal at their hands both actively and as a result of their avoidance and indifference.

Prompts
Have previous reports from schools and other authority figures suggested any difficulties of the above kinds?
If yes, do they specify difficulties with particular type of person?
Do parents speak of difficulties with a particular person?
How does child express his attitude to adults?
Does child say he gets a rough deal from adults?
Is child's response legitimate in the circumstances?
What does child say about the reason for or experiences associated with his reactions?
Does the child look or behave warily towards adults?
Does child believe what you tell him or check it out with other children if the opportunity arises?
Does child keep out of adults' way? Does the length of his acquaintance with or the gender/position of the adult make any difference?
Does child come into frequent conflict with adults because he does not do what he is asked?

Does child openly question or defy adult authority?

Does child challenge adults to carry out threatened sanctions?

Does child behave similarly to most adults regardless of age, position or ability to deal with him?

Are his challenges pursued to a showdown or does he retract? Under what conditions?

Does child do anything to 'get at' any adults?

Is this for an obvious reason? How generalized is this reaction?

Are his actions public or covert?

Do the tone and content of his conversations with adults betray any hostility?

Does child use adults' first names even if they object?

Does child quiz them on their personal lives?

Are the jokes child exchanges risqué? Does he banter and make supercilious comments?

Is child constantly asking adults for help?

Does child hang round them?

Is there any obvious sign of anxiety at their departure or delight at their return?

Action

Important to do something about the condition to improve child's chances of making out with adults. Effort and unconditional caring and tolerance needed more than techniques, which are available.

0410 Specific situational skills

01	Getting service in shops and cafés
02	Using the telephone
03	Relating to opposite sex peers
04	Joining clubs and organizations
05	Interviews
06	Seeking and getting jobs
07	Other

Description

This condition concerns a young person's difficulties in particular circumstances.

As can be seen from this list these problems do not usually arise until adolescence and this attribute usually applies only to older children although they encapsulate and put to the test many different social skills. Problematic behaviour can arise in specific situations for two main reasons: either children have not learned the signals and/or rituals necessary to ensure smooth passage in these particular circumstances or they have notions about the situation which cause anxiety and discomfort.

The range of situations a child may have to cope with varies with cultural and socioeconomic factors. Therefore, the list in which behaviour may be problematic is only intended as a guide and assessors should compile lists appropriate to the children they are assessing. For instance, some adolescents may need to know how to behave in youth clubs while others need to know how to behave in a job setting.

Associated features
Children with mental retardation, later stages of mild pervasive developmental disorders, those with sensory impairment, serious anxiety and others with long institutional history may experience these difficulties.

Prevalence
Over 10 per cent of adolescent population may suffer from difficulties in one or more setting with higher prevalence for clinic and institutional populations. Boys seem to experience more of these difficulties than girls.

Onset and course
These are usually evident first in puberty and gradually get worse towards adolescence and beyond into early adulthood. Early corrective training is likely to halt such deterioration.

Predisposing factors
Neurological and sensory difficulties, mental retardation, being brought up in many and poor institutions, other major social skills difficulties, an introverted, shy personality and very poor self-concept are likely to predispose to these difficulties.

Complications
None specific, apart from the consequences of not being able to fulfil normal social demands.

Impairment
Level and quality depends on severity of condition and youngster's needs and circumstances. Those associated with the opposite sex and employment are likely to pose serious difficulties.

Prompts
These arise from gentle questioning of youngster regarding above situations and any others that seem important. The pervasiveness and severity of condition are of particular interest.

Action
Relatively simple to remedy once a youngster feels secure in the relationship with the concerned adult and corrective training has been undertaken.

Further reading

Argyle, M. (1979) *Social Interaction*, London: Methuen.

Argyle, M. (1983) *The Psychology of Interpersonal Behaviour*, 4th edn, Harmondsworth: Pelican.

Argyle, M. and Trower, P. (1979) *Person to Person*, London: Harper & Row.

Cartledge, G. and Milburn, J.F. (1986) *Teaching Social Skills to Children*, Oxford: Pergamon.

Chenevert, M. (1983) *Special Techniques in Assertiveness Training for Women in the Health Professions*, London: Mosby.

Douglas, T. (1986) *Group Living*, London: Tavistock.

Hargie, O. (1986) *A Handbook of Communication Skills*, London: Croom Helm.

Hersen, M. and Bellack, A.S. (eds) (1976) *Behavioural Assessment: A Practical Handbook*, Oxford and New York: Pergamon.

Holland, S. and Ward, C. (1991) *Assertiveness: a Practical Approach*, London: Winslow.

Hollin, C. and Trower, P. (1986) *Handbook of Social Skills Training, Vol. 1*, Oxford: Pergamon.

Hollin, C. and Trower, P. (1986) *Handbook of Social Skills Training, Vol. 2*, Oxford: Pergamon.

Hopson, B. (1988) *Assertiveness: a Positive Process*, Leeds: Lifeskills Associates.

Liberman, R.P., King, L.W., DeRisi, W. and McCann, M. (1975) *Personal Effectiveness: Guiding People to Assert Themselves and Improve Their Social Skills*, Illinois: Research Press.

Liss, M.B. (ed) (1983) *Social and Cognitive Skills: Sex Roles and Children's Play*, London: Academic Press.

McGuire, J. and Priestley, P. (1981) *Life After School: Social Skills Curriculum*, New York: Pergamon.

Matson, J.L. and Ollendick, T.H. (1988) *Enhancing Children's Social Skills: Assessment and Training*, New York: Pergamon.

Michelson, L., Sugai, P., Wood, R.P. and Kazdin, A.E. (1983) *Social Skills Assessment and Training with Children*, New York: Plenum Press.

Richards, M.P.M. (ed) (1974) *Integration of a Child into a Social World*, Cambridge: Cambridge UP.

Roland, E. and Munthe, E. (eds) (1989) *Bullying*, London: David Fulton.

Stone, R. et al. (eds) (1990) *Learning to be Strong: Developing Assertiveness with Young Children*. Corby, Northants: Pen Green Family Centre.

Stott, D. (1974) *The Social Adjustment of Children: the Manual of the Bristol Social Adjustment Guide*, 5th edn, London: Hodder and Stoughton Educational.

Trower, P., Bryant V. and Argyle, M. (1978) *Social Skills and Mental Health*, London: Methuen.

Wilkinson, J. and Canter, S. (1982) *Social Skills Training Manual: Assessment, Programme Design and Management of Training*, London: John Wiley.

12

Anti-social Behaviour

Of all the problem areas tackled in this book, anti-social behaviour arouses the deepest social concern. This is because law breaking and disruptive acts are public and visible and affect a wide range of people. Anti-social acts are endemic and pervasive, and legitimize much official intervention in children's lives, in part because of the risk they are thought to present to the social fabric.

Whereas most other problems encountered in this book result in personal difficulties and private sorrow, anti-social acts directly threaten the safety of other people and their property, as well as some of the most cherished notions of what makes for an orderly, civilized society. Indeed, a child's other problems frequently come to light when he is identified as an offender. This is particularly so in the case of working-class children who constitute the majority of young offenders and who are the focus of much formal assessment.

Although the criminal justice system is primarily concerned with offences against person and property, these are not the only forms of anti-social behaviour, or, in the long run, necessarily the most serious. Others include victimless offences such as drug taking and soliciting. Yet other socially disruptive and proscribed behaviours include truancy, running away, temper tantrums, uncommon sexual interests and general aggression, which may not result in offences at all.

Also included in this area are self-destructive or 'parasuicidal' acts which, at their extreme, result in suicide. At first sight, it may seem peculiar that self-injury should be included in the category of anti-social behaviour. After all, suicidal acts are thought to be the result of such intense private sorrow or distress that self-destruction may be the only way out of an unbearable life. But extensive research and wide clinical experience shows that deliberate self-harm, particularly prevalent among young people, is qualitatively different from 'genuine' suicidal acts. Although such acts may result in death, they are more often thought of as socially disruptive, maladaptive, manipulatory acts which are intended to make their major impact not on the attempter but on her social surroundings. This is often evident among the more disturbed and disordered young people who are referred for assessment. A genuine, persistent wish to die is usually associated with other conditions, such as depression, which are dealt with under other headings.

The common characteristic of the wide gamut of behaviours covered in this area is that they make their major impact on the wider social setting. This warrants society's intervention, referral for assessment, and frequently the eventual restriction of liberty or other forms of sanction. Much of the evidence regarding past disruption and anti-social behaviour is gained through normal social enquiry methods of reading the available documentation and asking appropriate questions from such agencies as the police, probation, social services and others.

In very general terms, research evidence has tended to emphasize that much law-breaking behaviour is a normal, 'socialized' response of disadvantaged working-class youngsters during a particular phase of their development. However, some youngsters possess certain genetic, intellectual, familial and personality characteristics which make them vulnerable to particular forms of social stress and lead them to develop an anti-social response pattern. Depending on one's political and empirical point of view, either explanation may be emphasized. There are few indicators which point *unambiguously* one way or the other, although the existence of an underlying 'anti-social personality' seems increasingly probable.

Because both social disadvantage and personal vulnerability tend to persist, the longer the history of anti-social acts, the more likely it is that the child will continue to present further anti-social risk in the future. Assessment is, therefore, aimed at discovering the extent and intensity of both social disadvantage and personal vulnerability as an aid to assessing current condition and predicting further risk potential.

In assessment, social enquiry reports, complemented by interview material and observations, provide much of the necessary information. The state of testing in the assessment of anti-social potential, for research purposes, is highly developed though of questionable practical utility in the majority of settings in which assessment is likely to be carried out. The high-level pervasiveness of anti-social disorders is acknowledged by other approaches to assessment, as identified in Chapter 3. Diagnostic systems pay special attention to it, seeking to infer special sub-categories (such as 'unsocialized aggressive') which are not particularly helpful in treatment. Multivariate systems show that such behaviours constitute the single largest category of disorders in child and adolescent psychopathology, more pervasively than any other. In the present context, given the descriptive orientation, a range of anti-social acts are described, allowing the clinician to carry out a detailed assessment of the behaviour, minimizing the need for inferences about underlying conditions by augmenting the assessment with other conditions that appear under other headings, as for example in the next chapter.

0501 Disruptiveness

01	Stirring up trouble
02	Making allegations
03	Temper tantrums
04	Disturbing others
05	Making odd/inappropriate noises
06	Other

Description
This condition refers to the child's propensity to interrupt other people's activities without good reason.

In the previous chapter, comment was made on the skills required for adequate social functioning. Either because a child is inadequately skilled in this area or because he particularly wishes to upset a group, he may engage in a variety of disruptive acts. In group settings, children can be seen to fall on a continuum from the meek, submissive and compliant, to the dominant, aggressive and disruptive. This condition assumes major importance for anyone who has to deal with children, particularly in groups, because it raises problems of management which, unless tackled, can lead to fragmentation and considerable discomfort for the individual and the rest of the group. Disruptive acts can be analysed as *instrumental*, a means of achieving another end, or *expressive* – undertaken for their own sake. A child may switch from one to the other depending on the circumstances. Although it may not be sensible to speak of a general quality of disruptiveness in children, a child who engages in such acts under one set of circumstances is likely to do so in another context, more than one who is not disruptive. The degree to which this is a general characteristic of the child rather than his response to a particular set of circumstances can be determined by removal from one setting to another, such as from a general class group, to a 'sanctuary' unit, or from an open setting to a more structured one.

Associated features
Children with some disorder of the nervous system, attention deficit disorders, those from poor and disorganized families and with other conduct disorders are more likely to behave in a disruptive manner.

Prevalence
At the mild end, almost *all* children are disruptive from time to time. The more seriously persistent seem to constitute about 2–5 per cent of school population. Boys are generally more disruptive than girls, although the latter's behaviour is often more spectacular.

Onset and course
This condition presumes organized activities, such as classwork, in which child's disruptiveness usually becomes evident. Fairly common in primary school until the children learn 'rules' of group activities, the condition normally subsides by the time of secondary school. If it continues, it is usually the more serious kind which is likely to get worse into and beyond adolescence, unless corrective measures are taken.

Predisposing factors
Neurological disorder, hyperactivity, undisciplined upbringing and child's tendency to extroverted and attention-seeking behaviour are likely to conduce to this.

Complications
These usually arise from the adverse and sometimes punitive reactions of other children and adults who dislike their activities being disrupted. Child's suspension or exclusion from school is likely to create pressures on parents which may lead to punitive action by them. Such children are also likely to become isolated and engage in other anti-social acts.

Impairment
Variable, to the extent that it interferes with child's ability to benefit from schooling and the socializing benefits of co-operative group play and other activities. The wider unpopularity of the child is likely to have long-term negative consequences. A disruptive youngster is likely to become a social isolate and engage in acts which provoke punitive sanctions and lead to further maladaptive responses.

Prompts
Does child have a history of troublesome behaviour at home?
Is there a history of conflict with siblings?
Do the parents say that he has caused trouble between them and/or between the family and others?
Is there a history of troublesome behaviour, particularly with other children at school or in other group settings?
Does child say that he frequently gets into trouble with peers?
Do other children regard him as troublesome?
Do adults consider him ready to stir up trouble?
Is child said to make allegations and tell tales from one party to another?
Do these serve a particular purpose or seem to be for their own sake?
Are other people, both children and adults, disturbed by his presence?
Do either parents, members of the family or others, say that he has thrown temper tantrums?
Are these tantrums thought to be for particular ends or just general reactions to frustration?
Do these tantrums date from early childhood or relate to a particular period of child's life?
Are temper tantrums said to have occurred in any particular setting, such as home or school, or generally?
Are the tantrums brought to an end by any particular outcome or method?
Does child verbally or physically aggravate others?
What particular ploys are used to get others irritated?
Are these acts generally successful?
Does child pick particular types of children and adults with whom to make trouble or from whom to seek attention?
Can any particular aspects in the situation, such as other people, setting and the child's state, be identified as associated with such acts?
Does child behave in a fidgety, over-active, unsettled manner?
Does he upset other people's activities? Is this believed to be deliberate?
What happens when victims react angrily?

Does child seem to learn from consequences and reduce the acts, remain unaffected, or increase them?
Does child run around, make odd noises and inappropriate gestures?
Does child make allegations? Against whom? Are these obvious ploys or subtle?
Does he goad others into retaliating?
What consequences do his disruptive acts produce?

Action
Because of its significance in child's development, it is important to bring disruptive behaviour under early control. Techniques are available for shaping such behaviour, though some deterioration, at least in the early stages, should be anticipated.

0502 Response to control

01	Defying adults
02	Testing out limits
03	Forcing confrontation
04	Unreasonably seeking attention
05	Demanding counselling/medication/ services for no good reason
06	Provoking frequent conflicts
07	Wearing out adults
08	Other

Description
This attribute concerns those aspects of child's behaviour, usually in a school, clinic or institutional setting, which have a particularly negative effect on child/adult carer relationships.

Although for society at large a child's offences against person and property are the most important, to those who actually have to handle the children, such acts are much less serious than child's response to management.

A child is in a particular setting (including own home) for a particular purpose. Whatever the task undertaken – care, education, assessment or treatment – an essential prerequisite is the drawing and enforcement of boundaries of acceptable behaviour and some degree of stability without which none of the other aims can be achieved. Depending on the condition of the children, adults expect to spend a certain amount of effort and resource in achieving adequate control over their behaviour. When the children fail to respond to what is regarded as 'normal effort', they are regarded as 'management problems' requiring special resources or handling skills which may not be readily available.

This arouses apprehension, anxiety, anger and, occasionally, fear among the adults involved. This not only has repercussions for the children and their future, but is also likely to lead to stigmatization warranting more serious forms of intervention. This may lead to rejection by one service after another. Under these circumstances children soon *learn* that they are 'uncontrollable', and, thus reinforced, continue to test out to the limits any new service which attempts to cope with them. There comes a point at which fairly dramatic steps have to be taken to exert control over their behaviour.

It is crucial to recognize that the management difficulties presented by a child are not only indicative of past history and response potential but also a direct reflection of the coping competence of particular environments. This problem supremely illustrates the 'interactive' nature of many of children's social difficulties.

Associated features
This condition does not seem to be particularly associated with physiological, intellectual or personality differences. It is manifested usually by children who come from homes where they have received inadequate control, guidance, communication or affection. Social skills are usually very poor, in the context of an immature, sometimes explosive, tense and perhaps anxious personality. These children have often little or no sense of control over their lives, associated with history of many and inadequate previous interventions.

Prevalence
In normal home or school settings, between 10 and 15 per cent of young people present one or more of above difficulties relative to the rest of the group. In institutional and clinical settings, the proportion may be higher, depending on the intake and whether the criteria of judgment are absolute or relative. In co-educational school settings, more boys present these difficulties. In mixed clinic and institutional populations, girls are more prominent by the dramatic nature and often frequency of their response to control. This may be because of the many social filters diverting girls from formal interventions, so that only the most disordered come to light. This phenomenon may be relevant to most of the prevalence figures in this (and perhaps the next) chapter. Girls *seem* to be more often prone to such behaviour.

Onset and course
Difficult behaviour can be manifest from the earliest days of children's interaction with authority – usually first evident in school. Unless corrected, condition is likely to deteriorate with fits and starts, if for no other reason than that adverse adult reactions and other stressors on the child create a self-enforcing cycle.

Predisposing factors
Children with neurological and metabolic difficulties, attention deficit and

a history of disorganized, harsh and inconsistent parenting and poor social integration are more likely to present problems of control.

Complications
None, other than increasingly adverse adult reactions to the child. This condition may mask a range of other difficulties in all the other problem areas.

Impairment
Considerable. A child who is seen as difficult, demanding and defiant is likely to be stigmatized and rejected by the very adults who are entrusted with duties of care and treatment.

Prompts
Did parents and/or teachers find child difficult to manage and why?
Did they find that some styles of management were more successful than others?
Has child been regarded as particularly difficult in any facility?
If so, how many facilities have attempted to cope and how?
Why did they find her difficult?
Was child regarded as difficult generally or only under particular circumstances?
Was this difficulty experienced by everyone or just by particular persons?
Does a pattern of age, sex and authority relationship seem to account for this?
Did other children find her difficult and, if so, what were their reasons?
Are management difficulties experienced in response to the adults' expectations or self-generated?
What form do management difficulties take?
Are the difficulties not a reasonable response to unreasonable pressures?
Is child more or less difficult to manage under particular circumstances?
Was child excluded from any setting because of the management difficulties she presented?
Is she a drain on adult patience, tolerance, sympathy and courage?
Would adults be happy to get rid of her?
Does child believe she is difficult to manage?
What are her reasons for saying so?
Are statements 'factual' or tinged with sorrow or boasting?
What does she believe to be the effects of her behaviour on others? On herself?
How does she see her future? Is she concerned?

Action
It is important to do something about this condition for the sake of both child and her carers and to forestall serious and damaging deterioration. Nothing else can usefully be done with child until this is achieved.

0503   Truancy

01	School refusal
02	Not attending school – persistent
03	Not attending school – occasionally
04	Other

Description

This condition concerns children's failure to attend school without publicly legitimate reasons.

Both normal demands of socialization and the law require that children should be educated. The State spends a vast proportion of its resources on setting up an educational system to educate children and realize their academic potential. If children do not participate in educational activities they are likely to be handicapped in achieving their potential. Also, research confirms the existence of a strong association between truancy and offending. Over and above the acquisition of scholastic skills, attending school brings children under the (usually) beneficial influence of their educators and provide opportunities for appropriate social modelling.

Children who stay away from school, therefore, are regarded as a cause for concern and become subject to early intervention by the State. This is in part to determine whether there are any special adverse reasons that *push* or drive the child from school (such as bullying and inappropriate pressure towards scholastic attainment) or there are factors in the environment (such as parental dependence for company or shopping, or the excitement of peer group escapades) that *pull* the child away.

These reasons are explored in the relevant chapters such as those relating to cognitive functioning, family, social skills and personal problems and will come to light in a comprehensive assessment. In this chapter, only the problem of non school attendance, its extent and intensity rather than its 'causation', is discussed. The reason for non-attendance may range from persistent sickness through staying home to look after mother, school phobia to staying out to go fishing with mates.

Associated features

Children from poorly organized homes, where they are out of control and do not closely communicate with or receive guidance from parents are likely also to truant. The condition is also strongly associated with anti-social behaviour, as it is with withdrawing, shy and anxious children who avoid school as a source of unbearable stress.

Prevalence

Almost all children truant some time in their school careers. Furthermore, this condition has been shown to be closely related to the atmosphere of the school and its 'hold' on the child – for positive (such as liking the teachers) or negative (such as fearing the Head) reasons. It is, therefore, difficult accurately to estimate truancy, particularly as it can be disguised, often with parental and school knowledge, in a variety of ways. Nevertheless, studies show that at any given time about 10–15 per cent (in some schools many more) of students may be truanting, though this varies with the time of the year, age and other factors. Boys are more likely to truant than girls.

Onset and course
By definition, this condition becomes apparent when children start school. Early difficulties are apparent with over-anxious or otherwise poorly socialized children, but with sensitive and firm handling the condition improves in most cases. Major impetus to truanting occurs at the time of transfer to secondary school and it continues to grow until school leaving age. Some children hardly ever go to school in their later years.

Predisposing factors
There may be occasional association of truancy with mild neurological disorder or hyperactivity. More often than not it is one aspect of disorganized and inadequate parenting of children from poor families who go to unsympathetic and (to them) 'boring' schools. Search for excitement, often in anti-social behaviour, is the most common reason given for truanting. The other major group is of children who are introverted, have poor social integration skills and are generally anxious or are fearful of large groups of other youngsters and their own ability to cope. Although the concept 'school phobia' is a questionable one, some children have undoubtedly fearful reactions to school and are likely to become truants.

Complications
Physical accidents, substance misuse, difficulties with parents and teachers, strong probability of drifting into a range of anti-social behaviours, and becoming subject of sexual abuse, are all probable complications of truancy, to a greater or lesser degree. This is not to say that some children do not occupy their time away from school with wholesome activities, such as wandering in the country, train spotting or earning a meagre living.

Impairment
Depending on child's intellectual prowess and level of compensatory education, child may not suffer greatly from strict intellectual consequences of not attending school. However, he is likely to be severely impaired, depending on the level of truancy, from not acquiring the many subject attainments which are built up cumulatively. There are also likely to be social and group skill deficits and difficulties in much rule-following behaviour which characterizes school programmes.

Prompts
The most appropriate form of establishing the extent and intensity of

truancy is through examining school records and questioning school staff. Children, when relaxed, are also reasonable respondents, particularly in relation to their motives for truancy and associated activities.

Action

This is a potentially degenerative behaviour, recognized in law and care practice, which must be curbed lest it should lead to further difficulties.

0504　Running away

01　Running away from adults
02　Planning and executing attacks on property to escape
03　Hanging around doors and attempting to run out
04　Encouraging others to run away
05　Running away from home and other placements
06　Other

Description

This condition applies to those children who run away from places where they are required to be by law or custom.

Running away only arises as a result of children being placed in a setting which they do not, however momentarily, like to be in. It involves either *running away* from something, *running to* another, or the continuation of a habit of running as an *end in itself*. Children in the latter group are likely to continue running away from any placement, including their own home, simply as part of a habit. If the pattern is curbed by placement in security or other forms of close care, such as fostering, the habit *may* break or subside. Different forms of running away are associated with different circumstances and almost invariably result from an interaction of the state of children at a particular time with their perception of the particular environment and payoff of running away.

'Absconding' applies strictly to children who are removed from their natural homes to another setting because they have presumably presented or experienced one or another serious problem. As such, these children are already either subject to or a source of risk. Because of this, and the fact that absconding puts them beyond the reach of the agents of control, absconding arouses deep anxieties in those responsible for the management of children in non-parental care. For this reason, running away has always been prominent as a major source of disruption and received some research attention. It is also known to be strongly associated with the commission of anti-social acts both as a means of keeping alive while on the run and as part of a wider pattern of deviant behaviour.

Associated features

The condition is likely to be associated with milder forms of attention deficit disorder, being a habitual substance abuser, and disorganized homes, where quality of parental guidance and control are poor. Abused children may also run away from home or institutions, if old enough. Solitary absconders may also have social skills deficits as well as a strong propensity to anti-social behaviour. Absconders are likely to be impulsive and tense, with poor tolerance of frustration and insight and generally negative views of themselves and their prospects.

Prevalence

Many children aspire to or have short periods of absence from home, but these are not seen as problematic until absences become persistent. About 1 per cent of children run away from home at some time or other, some persistently. In institutions, absconding can involve as many as 50 per cent of children, though rates vary depending on season, age of children and a variety of other factors. More children engage in absconding type behaviour than actually carry it out – wandering away and coming back. There is little apparent difference between boys and girls either in running away or absconding.

Onset and course

Very young children often wander away from home but not sufficiently to be deemed a problem. The earlier such behaviour starts, the more frequent it is likely to be, and the longer the episodes the more persistent it is likely to become. 'Persistent' running away or absconding applies when there are more than three episodes in a month, though an average of one a month over a period of several months would also qualify for this description.

Predisposing factors

Children with poor concentration and attention span, who are not very bright, as well as those from disadvantaged and inadequately parenting families, those with poor social skills and others who seek excitement in anti-social acts, are likely to constitute the majority of runners. Unhappy, stressful and oppressive environments, *as well as* therapeutically beneficent facilities which seek to engage and confront the young people with their difficulties are also likely to produce disproportionately higher levels of runners.

Complications

Children who run away are likely to be at substantially greater risk of personal injury, sex resulting in pregnancy for girls, transmitted diseases and serious physical and psychological damage for both them and boys, school difficulties, conflict with adults and of drifting into a wide range of anti-social acts from survival offences to drug taking and robbery. Such consequences may either reinforce or inhibit further running.

Impairment
None direct, unless by being absent child fails to benefit from available scholastic, social and emotional opportunities.

Prompts
Is there a history of running away from home and other similar places?
Have there been abscondings from previous residential placements?
Has child run away from adults in open settings?
Is there a history of damage to property or attacks on other people in the furtherance of absconding?
Has absconding taken place solo or with others?
Have there been any particular factors associated with these abscondings, such as personal upset or unhappiness?
Are abscondings thought to have been planned or impulsive?
Are they thought to have been running away *from* something or running *to* something else?
What have been the past official and other reactions to absconding?
Does child talk about absconding?
Does child give the impression of 'casing the joint' in an attempt to abscond?
Are attempts overt and easily detectable or subtle?
Does child appear preoccupied with the thought of and activities associated with absconding?
Are these easily discernible?
Are there any particular factors associated with the rise and fall of this preoccupation?
If put in a situation apparently unsupervised, will child attempt to abscond?
Does child encourage others to abscond?

Action
If the child has to be where he is, then presumably there are good reasons for it. Because of significant attendant risks, it is important to curtail this behaviour. More difficult and demanding to remedy than many other problems.

0505 Deliberate self-harm (DSH)

01	Serious attempted suicide
02	Taking overdoses or poisons
03	Inflicting wounds on self
04	Attempting to obtain harmful materials
05	Tattoos
06	Other

Description

This condition concerns any deliberate act which is intended to inflict significant harm on the child.

The sanctity and continuity of life is the fulcrum around which all other social interests revolve. A person who puts his own or others' lives in danger arouses the most intense reactions. All acts of aggression against self are regarded with pity and horror because such acts, particularly in a child, arouse deep guilt feelings in the adults concerned with the child because they question whether they could or should have done something (more) to make life less intolerable. These acts are frequently associated with serious forms of social pathology and personal disturbance which warrant decisive intervention. Over and above placing a young life at risk, however by default, self-destructive acts are regarded as particularly deviant modes of communication and gaining ends which may not be obtainable by other means. They cause severe disruption in any social setting whether the family, school, clinic or other facility.

This is despite the weight of a good body of evidence suggesting that deliberate self-harm or 'parasuicide' is aetiologically and clinically different from genuine suicide attempts. In the extreme reaches, however, it is not very easy to distinguish genuine self-destructive acts from persistent attention-seeking attempts. In any case, it is not prudent to be very confident that a person is an attention seeker rather than genuinely intending to kill herself. Death by default or serious unintended injury are not improbable. Under this rubric are included all acts such as tattoos, which involve the infliction of physical hurt on the self.

Associated features

Many clusters of abnormality have been noted in relation to DSH children. Perhaps the most useful distinction is between (1) those whose attempts are serious and potentially lethal and (2) those who make frequent but less dangerous attempts. The first group are usually older adolescents of both sexes but particularly boys who are subject to severe affective stress, perhaps exacerbated by illness, sexual abuse or drug misuse, who see no way out of their difficulties. The second group are youngsters from the more disadvantaged and chaotic families where a great many other chronic difficulties, including marital strife, parental breakdown and attempted suicide, persistent abuse of the children, as well as a range of anti-social behaviour and affective disorders may be present.

Prevalence

In clinic or institutional populations this condition affects anything between 6 and 30 per cent of youngsters. The more disordered the population the more probable such behaviour is. The prevalence in the general population is likely to be significantly lower than this, but often DSH goes unreported unless serious or frequent. In general terms, girls are likely to engage more frequently in milder forms of DSH and boys less often but more seriously.

Onset and course
Acts of deliberate self-harm are very uncommon before puberty although
there are occasional reports of such behaviour in even very young children.
Post-pubertal DSH gradually gathers pace, range and intensity towards
late adolescence. The more serious acts of self-harm are likely to persist
into adulthood.

Predisposing factors
Ideas of suicide and acts of self-harm resulting in specialist attention are
more common among the parents of such children than in other groups of
disordered adolescents. Whether this indicates a genetic predisposition, in
keeping with propensity to affective disorders, has not yet been
established. However, in clinic and institutional populations, the
probability of such predisposition seems higher, given the wide range of
intergenerational difficulties. Adolescent psychotic states, heavy substance
misuse, a seriously disorganized family in deep strife, poor support for and
criticisms of the child, absence of good peer relationships, pronounced
propensity to a wide range of anti-social and aggressive acts, shy,
withdrawn personality make up and susceptibility to tension, anxiety and
depression can all, in different clusters, predispose to DSH in vulnerable
  lividuals.

Complications
Depending on the method used, DSH can result in serious physical damage
to child, such as impact of poisoning on the central nervous system. Also,
given the seriousness of the act, intervention measures may be taken with
the youngster (such as forcible admission to hospital or residential treatment facility) which may create new difficulties and exacerbate the
youngster's condition.

Impairment
Depends on mode and severity of the attempt. Poisoning may leave
residual neurological damage. Cutting, scratching and tattoos all leave
permanent marks and scars which are likely to be source of future embarrassment. More importantly, even if child survives intact, the history and
memory of such behaviour is likely to distort or impede subsequent
development, unless good alternative coping skills have been acquired.

Prompts
Is there a history of child having talked about taking his own life?
Has child ever attempted or succeeded in taking overdoses or poisons?
Are these thought to have been impulsive or premeditated?
Has child attempted to obtain offensive weapons or poisons for which
    there are no adequate alternative explanations?
Has child been involved in other self-destructive acts such as running in
    front of a bus, jumping from a high point, or self-strangulation?
Has child received hospital or other specialist treatment for these acts?

Are these acts thought to have been reactions to a particular set of circumstances or not?

What was the outcome of the previous acts?

Did child receive much positive attention or other desired ends?

Is setting in which the child attempts such an act so intolerable as to justify it?

If child does not have a history of self-destructive behaviour, does he do anything that causes concern?

Does child threaten to kill herself?

Does child do so only under particular circumstances or as a ready response whenever frustrated?

Does child do so in adult hearing or does this come to adult ears via other sources?

Are there any other indications such as notes, diaries or gestures which indicate possible self-destructive intentions?

Are these acts and gestures made with bravado or quietly?

Does child open wounds or scars?

Does child pick scabs or other parts of body so as to produce damage?

Is child on the lookout for potentially dangerous instruments?

Is child ready to use such instruments or turn others into weapons for this purpose?

Is this done quietly when child cannot be observed or publicly and when readily discoverable?

Does child appear to be impervious to painful physical stimulation?

Is child so despondent and unhappy he may seek to injure himself?

Action

No act of DSH in a young person should be taken lightly, because of risk to life, even if unintended and by default. Urgent action must be taken to identify the triggers and associated conditions, place the young person in a safe and protective environment and attempt to give better coping skills.

0506 Verbal aggression

01 Criticizing
02 Antagonizing
03 Threatening
04 Swearing
05 Gesturing/snarling
06 Screaming abuse
07 Other

Description

This condition concerns a distinct and persistent tendency on the child's part to attempt to hurt others verbally.

Aggression is a generic term indicative of the use of force, verbal or physical, which is used either to ventilate frustration or to inflict deliberate hurt. In social encounters, verbal aggression not only indicates the mood but also the intent of the aggressor and as such provokes retaliatory action. It arouses anxiety, defensiveness and hostility and is, therefore, liable to provoke similar behaviour from others.

The significance of verbal aggression lies in its potential for antagonizing others and spiralling into further conflict. It is not necessarily associated with physical aggression though those who are ready to be verbally aggressive also appear to be more ready to use physical force.

Associated features
Verbally aggressive children are more likely to suffer from epilepsy and other neurological conditions; engage in substance misuse; come from poor families where there is a great deal of hurt and conflict; have poor social relations; engage in a wide range of anti-social acts; be extroverted, impulsive and intolerant of frustration; suffer from tension and have negative views of themselves.

Prevalence
The above behaviours in their milder and less persistent forms are so widespread across cultures, social classes, ages and condition of people that they do not warrant citing as a 'problem'. In its more serious reaches also the condition affects all children from time to time, depending on whether they are angry, frustrated or otherwise need to ventilate tension or swear out of habit. In the more serious *and* persistent form, however, such behaviour affects up to 15 per cent of the normal age group and about 30 per cent or more of clinic or institutional children. Boys more commonly engage in verbal aggression, although in the more serious reaches there do not appear to be any differences between boys and girls. Indeed, girls seem to be louder and use more dramatic and graphic language than boys.

Onset and course
Such behaviour usually emerges in school years and builds up towards late adolescence. There are peaks and troughs in response to the stresses on youngsters and the prevailing atmosphere in which they are likely to find themselves.

Predisposing factors
Neurological damage; substance misuse; low intelligence; coming from a poor home, poor social skills particularly in assertiveness; an extroverted personality, poor impulse control; becoming easily frustrated; tension; generally negative self-concept and poor moral standards are all likely to increase the probability of verbally aggressive behaviour in the young.

Complications

These are predominantly social. A youngster whose verbal interchange with others is aggressive and unpleasant is likely to be shunned or actively targetted for bullying and retaliatory actions, which may, in turn, exacerbate the original condition.

Impairment

As above. Such a child is likely to grow up with poor social relations and, therefore, develop other maladaptive responses to people.

Prompts

Is child regarded by parents, siblings and peers as verbally aggressive?
Which of above behaviours particularly characterize him?
Is there a particular target?
Do they regard him as generally like this or only under particular circumstances?
Is the same thing said of him at school and by other people who know him?
Has child been cautioned, or disciplined by his teachers and others, for using abusive language?
Do peers regard him as verbally aggressive?
Does child antagonize, threaten, swear and engage in other such acts that you would regard him as aggressive?
How does he compare with others of the same cultural background?
Does child frequently get into conflict with peers and adults because of bad language?
Does child use such language habitually or only when aroused to anger?
Does child use aggressive language habitually or as a means to an (obvious) end?
Does he have the ability to control his language if he wants to?
Is it easy to bring such language under control?
Is this the sort of behaviour which is likely to antagonize others so that they might retaliate?

Action

Depending on severity, action is warranted. Good techniques exist for controlling such behaviour and gradually shaping it but this takes a great deal of effort and control over triggers.

0507 Physical aggression

01	Nipping/biting
02	Hitting/punching/kicking/head butting
03	Using objects to hurt
04	Bullying
05	Injuring others deliberately
06	Violence to animals
07	Other

Description

This condition refers to the persistent and serious aggressive acts by child against others.

Sanctity of the person is the crux of social order in Western societies. Any threat directed against others arouses strong feelings of anxiety and hostility. Because of this, it is the single most critical form of social behaviour.

In any grouping of children and, indeed, in the course of a child's growth, aggressive acts are normal and occur from time to time in the course of establishing group relationships and a social hierarchy. Whether this is done in play or in earnest depends on many circumstances. Such 'normal' aggression, which is, indeed, essential for normal social development, is accepted until the child grows away from the need and opportunity to exercise it. There is, additionally, a latitude of social tolerance which can accommodate a good deal of episodic aggression. This human characteristic, like many others, ranges from the minimal and negligible to the persistent and gravely serious. When aggression becomes either habitual or serious, it becomes the subject of severe social sanction aimed at curbing its escalation into grave acts of violence.

Even more than verbal aggression and other forms of anti-social behaviour, physical aggression appears to be a response to personal anxiety, frustration and anger. It acts as a safety valve which releases tension and allows a person to regain some equilibrium. It is also frequently used instrumentally as a means of escape, gaining dominance in a peer group, or in the furtherance of other acts, such as extortion. To a lesser extent, it is sometimes employed as the basis of personal identity or 'machismo' and its equivalent in girls.

Western societies are currently experiencing a dramatic surge in offences of violence. Although statistics on this issue are hard to interpret, it appears nevertheless that the public's awareness of physical violence is vastly increased and reflected in portrayal of this problem by the media. The evaluation of aggressive potential of a child is, therefore, likely to become a matter of increasing concern to people in judicial, health, educational and social agencies who have to handle aggressive children.

Associated features

Aggressive children are more likely than non-aggressive children to suffer one or more of the following conditions: neurological damage; substance misuse; low intelligence; attention deficit disorders; pathological family conditions including severe strife, inconsistent, abusive, harsh parenting and poor relationships; poor social skills (though whether as cause or effect is not certain); wide-ranging anti-social behaviour; poor emotional maturity and control; poor tolerance of frustration, tension and perhaps anxiety; unrealistic and negative self-concepts and poor moral development.

Prevalence

Very difficult to estimate because of different criteria used in terms of behaviour/offence, age, persistence and association with other conditions. Most aggressive acts in peer groups never come to light. Accordingly, seriously aggressive behaviours (such as associated with overt bullying 'lager louts', 'football hooligans', or 'mugging') can be seen to affect up to 30 per cent of the adolescent population, lessening as age goes down. In clinics the prevalence goes down to about 10 per cent. In institutions for adolescents, depending on the base criteria, the prevalence may be as high as over 30 per cent, suggesting that a subculture of aggression may be prevalent.

Boys outnumber girls in the ratio of 5:1 in both the general and special populations, although at the more serious end the ratios are less dramatically different.

Onset and course

Aggressive behaviour is 'interactive' and 'attributed' – it depends very much on the circumstances and who is 'naming' the behaviour. However, some children are reported as 'unacceptably' aggressive from a very young, pre-school age. This seems to subside in early school years and rise again towards the end of primary school. It is again lower in the early secondary school years but rises to a peak in late adolescence and early adulthood. The ups and downs very much depend on the environment of the youngster and how far it facilitates and/or fails to curb such behaviour either actively or by its prevailing atmosphere.

Predisposing factors

All the elements cited under 'Associated features' above have been cited at one time or other as predisposing to aggression. The question of 'chicken and egg' has not been satisfactorily settled. However, it appears that certain 'personality types' emerging from particular types of families and subcultures, are more prone to aggressive behaviour, exacerbated by glandular changes and cultural pulls and pushes in adolescence.

Complications

Predominantly social, in the reactions and attempts at curbing they provoke. The measures themselves (such as removal to an ill-run facility for similarly aggressive adolescents) are often likely to reinforce the behaviour by providing both stresses and opportunities for such behaviour. Such behaviour may mask a range of other serious difficulties.

Impairment

Considerable, depending on severity and wider context of aggressive behaviour. Social reactions resulting in stigmatization, incapacitation and punishment are all likely to make it more difficult for the young person to fit easily into 'gentle' and 'normal' environments, thus affecting further his wider social and psychological development.

Prompts

Does child have a history of what parents and siblings would describe as 'aggressive' behaviour?

What particular form have such aggressive acts taken: nipping, biting, spitting, kicking, hitting, punching, throwing objects, head butting or injury to animals?

How young was child when first showing such behaviour?

Has behaviour continued unabated or been periodic?

If periodic, are these said to have been associated with particular events or phases in child's life?

If continuing, has the problem become better, worse or remained the same?

Has this behaviour been manifested at school, in the playground and similar settings with other children?

Are the same things said of it as they were at home?

Is the aggression said to have been directed mainly at other children or adults? Was there any sex preference?

Is there any evidence that it was triggered by particular acts or situations?

Is child said to have engaged in such behaviour for its own sake or in order to gain a particular outcome?

Is he said to have been sorry and to have tried to make amends, to have been unaffected or to have derived positive enjoyment from his acts?

Is he said to have been deterred at any particular period or from tackling a particular type of person by the effects of any retaliation?

Does child describe himself as aggressive?

Whether 'yes' or 'no', what are his reasons and bases for comparison?

What feelings does he express regarding his acts?

Is there any warmth, contrition or guilt?

What does he say about personal and social consequences of being aggressive?

Has he ever been severely beaten? By whom? What are his recollections and feelings about it?

Does child engage in any of the aforementioned behaviours and others like them?

Is he particularly aggressive compared with the other children?

Is his aggressiveness a general response characteristic or only something he shows when provoked or in a tight spot?

Is there any pattern in terms of targets, how and under what circumstances?

Does he use aggression as a way of gaining particular social or material ends?

How is he affected by the outcome of his aggressive acts?

Does he seem exhausted and sad after an aggressive act, indifferent or flushed and excited?

Does he really hurt others or are his aggressive acts superficial assertions and acts of bravado?

How well does he appreciate that he is hurting his victim?

Does child do anything which suggests ability to inflict grave violence on other people? If so, what is the evidence?

How would the aggressive acts be judged in terms of range, severity and duration?

Is the condition deteriorating?

Action

Urgent action is required to curb and shape out such behaviour at its earliest persistent manifestation to save considerable subsequent hurt to child and others, without destroying child's ability to respond with 'normal' aggression when under threat. Good techniques exist but demand considerable patience and resilience.

0508 Sexual disorder

01	Cross-dressing
02	Fetishism
03	Exhibitionism/public masturbation
04	Homosexuality under age
05	Interest in little children
06	Sex with hurting or being hurt
07	Attempting non-consenting sexual activity
08	Soliciting
09	Unusual interest in pornography
10	Other

Description

This condition concerns seriously deviant or uncommonly persistent forms of sexual behaviour or ideas on part of the young person.

The main features of such disorders (referred to as 'paraphilias') are intense urges, fantasies or behaviour associated with (1) non-human objects, (2) infliction or suffering of pain, (3) imposing sexual behaviour on non-consenting sexual partners.

Increasingly in the course of the present century, it has been recognized that sex play and sexual exploration are part of normal development of children and adolescents. Evidence shows that many 'normal' youngsters engage in a variety of sexual behaviours which, although still frowned upon by adults and viewed with concern, must be regarded as the 'normal' base against which any evaluation of sexual misbehaviour should be made.

Many children are still referred for assessment by a variety of agencies because parents and other people are worried about their sexual behaviour. Such behaviour ranges from the tendency of the child to talk a lot about sex through collecting pornographic and sex-related materials to engaging in public sexual behaviour which is, nevertheless, not a breach of the law.

It is such behaviours, defying as they do adults' and often other children's sexual strictures, that raise the possibility that the child may be in danger either of putting others at risk or being himself put at risk from 'moral danger'.

Since greater prominence has been given to sexual abuse, it has become apparent that many children are sexually 'traumatized' or gain deviant sexual knowledge and skills, probably as a result of their own victimization. It is now widely accepted that sexual disorders detailed above are unlikely to remit spontaneously and that the more 'active' and aggressive types (such as interest in little children, hurting and being hurt and exposure to 'heavy' pornography) are likely to lead to enactment of these interests via deviant fantasies and other cognitive distortions and related behaviours.

It is critical in this area to ensure that the personal morality of the assessment agent does not become the standard by which the child's problems or the problems he presents to others are judged. Even more than some other areas in the totality of a child's problems, this attribute should be based on evidence.

Associated features
Predominantly pathological circumstances in the home, associated child abuse, poor parental supervision, guidance, communication and affection, poor social integration, either solitary or domineering social relationships, a range of other anti-social behaviours, as well as tension, poor or confused identity and poorly developed moral standards, are likely to be associated with such behaviours.

Prevalence
Estimates vary widely and there are no reliably usable statistics for conditions cited above. Even when they become manifest in offences, the deviant imagination and behaviour pattern are not often separately evaluated. Judging, however, by reported usage of pornography by adolescents, some tentative studies of school children and adolescents' assertion about the prevalence of such behaviour, estimates for the 'normal' population would be up to 10–15 per cent and rather more for clinic and institutional populations. These are almost exclusively male disorders. When they appear in girls they are usually associated with more serious pathological conditions.

Onset and course
Most of these disorders arise in the transition from puberty to adolescence and continue into adulthood. However, there is increasing evidence that pre-pubertal children in primary school, either as a result of exposure to sexual acts (most commonly as victims of abuse) or greater availability of sexual material in the environment, may be picking up deviant ideas and behaviour patterns in these areas. The condition usually gets worse with increasing age, well into late adolescence and adulthood.

Predisposing factors
None identified, apart from exposure to deviant material and experiences, probably in the course of suffering or being witness to sexual acts, abusive or otherwise.

Complications
None, apart from persistent acting out or expression of fantasies in above areas which are likely to provoke social sanctions. Children caught up in or searching for sexual rewards (monetary and otherwise) may suffer physical damage, sometimes serious, including death.

Impairment
Likely to result mainly from social sanctions against such behaviour. Social contact is likely to be affected by people shunning the adolescent or using him in damaging ways.

Prompts
Has child ever been referred for sexual problems?
If yes, have they occurred at home and/or in other settings?
What form is it said to have taken?
Have parents complained of or shown concern about such behaviour?
Has he collected pornographic material or other sex-related objects?
Has he been known to have exposed or publicly masturbated?
Has he attempted to masturbate others without their consent?
Is there a history of soliciting or engaging in sexual activities?
For money, goods or other reasons?
Is this unusual in the child's family or cultural setting?
Does the child talk a lot about sex?
Is the talk exaggerated or is it about the present reality?
Is the talk suggestive of what he wishes to do or be done to?
Is it accompanied by gestures and illustrative acts?
Does he engage in subtly or overtly suggestive acts?
Is this directed at others without their consent?
Is this behaviour triggered off and maintained by any obvious aspect of his
    surroundings, including other people?
Does his behaviour embarrass, anger or amuse others?
What is his reaction?
Does he flaunt his sexuality? Mainly to adults or other children?
Is this more than can be regarded as a 'normal' search for sexual iden-
    tity?
Does child use sex as a bargaining or bartering counter?
Are these behaviours thought to be deliberate or beyond the child's
    control? What is the evidence for either conclusion?
Do parents complain of or comment on any unusual sexual behaviour or
    interests?
What form is this interest said to take?
When did such behaviour first become apparent?

Did child show this interest openly or did he hide it?

Are/were there any other members of the family or immediate acquaintances of the child known to have engaged in such behaviour? Did the parents regard this matter with serious concern or only as mildly unusual?

Do teachers and others recollect or express concern about the child's wearing of clothing belonging to the opposite sex, particular sexual response to specific articles, exposure and flashing, or abnormal interest in members of the same sex?

Were these manifestations readily discernible or only discovered by accident?

Does child express preference for dressing in clothes of the opposite sex?

Is this over and above what would be regarded as normal 'unisex' style of clothing? Has this preference existed over a period?

Does he seem to derive particular (sexual) pleasure from handling and touching an object or a particular item of clothing?

If given the opportunity will he steal or secrete away an item of clothing belonging to the opposite sex?

How much do particular strictures and styles of management inhibit or facilitate overtly sexual behaviour?

Is child called a 'poof' or similar names by age mates?

Is this because of certain characteristics – soft voice, manner and style of walking – or because of more suggestive acts?

Can he be observed to seek proximity to or handhold, touch and engage in more overt sexual acts with a member of his own sex?

Action
If sexual misbehaviour in a child reaches a point when it is identified publicly, it is already likely to be well established. Urgent treatment is, therefore, required. Likely to be a long, difficult and demanding job.

0509   Sexual offences

01	Indecent exposure
02	Indecent assault
03	Buggery
04	Unlawful sexual intercourse
05	Attempted rape
06	Rape
07	Other

Description
This attribute refers to a range of what are regarded as illegal sexual behaviours in most contexts.

Even ten years ago in the earlier edition of this book, sexual offences were regarded as rare and not warranting extended coverage. Since then, however, this range of behaviours has achieved unprecedented prominence as its extent, seriousness and significance, particularly in relation to the abused–abuser cycle, has become more evident, particularly in the young.

The offences range from one extreme of indecent exposure associated with mental handicap and immature, anxious youngsters, to the other extreme of rape as a grave, aggressive act against another person. In between, different offences indicate different degrees of behavioural pathology and cognitive abnormality. For one thing is now clear – sexual offences are both a legal and clinical deviation suggesting a more serious problem, in extent, intensity, impact and clinical complexity than recognized so far.

These offences result from deviant beliefs and feelings about sex, compounded by wide availability of pornographic and other stimulating material. Sexual liberalism and preoccupation of adults seem to have reached down to young children and adolescents, without any adequate attempt to define and enforce boundaries of what may and may not be appropriate to each age. The above behaviours, however, constitute offences in all who are held criminally responsible. There is considerable evidence, at least in the UK, that police and social agencies are reluctant to charge young people under age 14 with any of these acts and often unwilling to act when the offence has been committed with another young person of the same age.

Associated features

Young sex offenders have rarely any physical abnormalities. Most are of average or low average intelligence and are usually not very good at school. There are often a range of family difficulties including parental conflict, poor communication, guidance, control and inconsistent expressions of affection. There is also a probability of abuse of the offender by a male person and his abuse of siblings, which parents usually deny they knew about. Social skills are usually poor, from unintegrated or isolated child abuser to the domineering rapist. Anti-social behaviour presents a mixed picture with little or none for some (usually the anxious child molesters) and considerable for the more aggressive and calculating offender. The clinical picture may present extremes on the personality dimension of introverted-extroverted, social and emotional immaturity, considerable egocentricity, variable pictures of impulsivity and frustration tolerance, considerable tension, anxiety in some correlated with offence but not otherwise, hardly any neurotic features or affective disorders, negative or unrealistic self-concepts and usually primitive moral development.

Prevalence

Sexual offences are the most under-reported of serious anti-social acts. Even at the severe end of rapes, only about 10 per cent of all serious offences are apparently reported. In the case of adolescents, particularly those who molest siblings or other children, the known incidence is recognized as being a gross under-estimate. Evidence shows that every known or freely admitted offence represents many more. Even so, such offences are thought to involve 0.5–2 per cent of all young people, with boys almost always as perpetrators.

Onset and course
Until very recently, major sexual offences were thought to occur only from 14 years onwards, which is why the law would not allow prosecuting those under 14. However, accumulating information suggests that although such offences among adolescents are predominantly committed between 14 and 17 years, many start their careers earlier, some as young as 8 years, even though pre-pubertal youngsters are normally thought to be incapable of penetrative sexual offences. Sexual offending usually becomes more frequent and serious, because of the highly rewarding outcomes for an unsuspected and undetected youngster. However, it may remain on a reasonably flat opportunistic plateau, for those who do not actively plan such offences. For the latter, however, it is thought gradually to get worse until it becomes a preoccupation, with supportive fantasy life and associated behaviours.

Predisposing factors
Evidence suggests that experience of sexual abuse as a victim, emotional abuse at the hands of cold and ineffectual parents, repeated exposure to pornography and sexual acts, availability of opportunity and poor alternative social networks and activities, may make such offending more probable. Increasingly, however, it is also becoming evident that certain cognitive styles – distorting, denying, projecting and deviant fantasy stimulation are closely associated with offending, whether as predispositions or concurrent triggers and consequences is not wholly clear. Offence-specific assessment of cognitive, affective and behavioural features of the offence should clarify the picture.

Complications
Parental denial, projection and denial of guilt frequently mar attempts at assessing true extent and ramifications of such offending in a young person. Youngsters' poor intellectual equipment and social skills and support networks (as well as deviant personality features) may adversely affect the clinical picture. Complications will include the adverse social reaction to offending.

Impairment
Primarily depends on and is result of social sanctions against offending – usually removal from normal setting for non-specialist intervention. Such a setting may not only provide considerable peer or young adult reinforcement of deviant cognitive and behavioural patterns, but also provide a further arena for sexual abuse – as victim, perpetrator, or both.

Prompts

Has child committed any sexual offences?

Has there been only one episode or have there been others even if not legally processed?

Are they of recent origin or spread over a period?

Have they become 'worse'? In what sense?

Has offence been committed against a particular category of victim, or does it appear to have been relatively indiscriminate?

Was offence committed solo or jointly?

Was offence planned or apparently committed on impulse?

Are there any particular circumstances that could account for it?

Was offence associated with another act or an end in itself?

Was it committed in a relatively public place or a secluded area?

How is youngster said to have reacted during and after the commission of the offence?

Is the act regarded as totally unexpected and out of character or something that might have been expected?

Is there any history of such offences in the family?

How did those in chid's immediate environment react to his behaviour when it became known?

What are youngster's views and feeling about the offence?

Does he show any appreciation of or insight in the seriousness of his behaviour?

What does he say about his victim's feelings?

What does he say about sex offences generally?

How deviant or distorted are his beliefs and feelings about sexual acts in general and unwilling victims in particular? Are there any signs of guilt or contrition? Are these more than 'crocodile tears'?

Is blame projected on to the victim or others?

How does he rate the chances of a repetition of the offence?

How does he react to the probable consequences?

Does child force or draw attention to his own sexuality?

Does he force sexual contact on others of opposite or same sex?

Do children or adults of the opposite sex feel uncomfortable or threatened in his presence? Do they try to avoid him?

Is his behaviour manifested only under specific circumstances or fairly generally?

Is it particularly affected by outcome or reactions of others?

Does he engage in a lot of sex talk?

Does he brag about sexual activities?

Do you feel he is capable of committing a serious sexual offence?

Does he feel he needs treatment?

Action

Urgent intervention to stop further offending and its escalation in quantity and quality is imperative. Treatment is complex and long-term but good outcome is claimed and sometimes demonstrated.

0510   Property offences

01	Aiding and abetting
02	Theft
03	Taking and driving without owner's consent
04	Burglary
05	Robbery
06	Robbery with violence
07	Destroying/damaging property
08	Other

Description
This condition refers to activities aimed at removal of or damage to property without owner's consent.

Next to offences against the person, property offences attract the most hostile public reaction. The 'territorial imperative', of which possession of property is a major part, is regarded as almost a biological principle necessary for the survival of species and any acts against it are treated harshly. This is particularly so in Western societies where property ownership is closely tied with power and social standing. There is some acceptance of mild, petty thieving, particularly by children. This is because children are regarded as morally ignorant until they reach a particular age. In any case, the courts could not deal with all thefts, even if the police knew about and managed to apprehend all the thieves. But persistent and serious property offending is a different matter.

Delinquency primarily concerns group participation of boys in acts of theft. As such it is an international phenomenon and something most children grow out of as they move towards adulthood. However, there are wide variations in the rate and quality of property offences not only between countries but also among different social classes and different areas of the same country. Persistent thieving occurs mainly as a means of obtaining goods which are not otherwise available to the relatively impoverished working-class youth who engage in it, and it is they who are seen as an intolerable threat and a nuisance by the rest of society and dealt with accordingly. There is extensive legislation and a complex structure of judicial and quasi-judicial response to this form of behaviour.

Associated features
Persistent crime against property has spawned a huge research literature where pretty well everything has been claimed as an associated feature. The most consistent of these are propensity to substance misuse, low intelligence, poor school attendance and attainments, a greater extent and intensity of family problems of all sorts, reasonably good social relationships with peers and adults (unless the offender is 'unsocialized aggressive'), a range of other anti-social acts, an extroverted, socially

immature personality, with not much affective disorder but generally negative or fluid self-concepts and poor moral development.

Prevalence
Wherever there is property, there is also property theft. Adolescents between 14 and 18 are thought to constitute the largest group of property offenders from casual, opportunistic theft from shops to highly planned and intricately executed burglaries, both solo and in groups. Given the considerable under-reporting of much smaller thieving, such offending is a regular feature of about 5–20 per cent of all adolescents and considerably more of clinic and institutional populations. Boys account for much greater rates of property offending, about 6:1.

Onset and course
Knowingly taking someone else's property, without permission and often without intent to return it, happens from early childhood years. Taking things is as normal as parental correction that the child should not. The pattern of thieving is usually established by about eight years and continues to escalate by fits and starts until late adolescence and in the serious cases, into an adult career. The earlier the onset the worse the prospects, although typically the most serious offences, including those involving motor cars, start in the middle adolescent years in boys. Focal intervention, bringing about changes in both social circumstances of child and his cognitive/behavioural patterns, are likely to halt the deterioration of the condition, though this rarely happens.

Predisposing factors
There is now some evidence that persistent anti-social behaviour is more prevalent in certain families and that genetic concordance rates are higher for biologically related family members. Whether this is transmitted in the child's neurological condition or otherwise is not known. Poor intellectual equipment and scholastic achievement, coming from a low income, large family where father or elder brother have been in trouble, as well as social and emotional immaturity and poor moral development, are likely to predispose to such offending. The odds seem to increase dramatically if mother is an offender. The differential availability of opportunities, the mass of social and contextual factors which turn exploratory behaviour into habitual patterns must not be discounted, even if they are part of the environment rather than the youngster.

Complications
Few, apart from those which result from social sanctions if the youngster is caught and adequately dealt with, or the exacerbation of the behaviour pattern if he is not. The picture may be complicated by a range of clinical conditions from neurological and substance misuse difficulties to affective disorders, though they are not a direct consequence of offending. Serious physical injury in the course of offending, including deaths from motor accidents, are not uncommon.

Impairment
Usually inflicted on the victim rather than the perpetrator. However, some sanctions against persistent property offenders are likely to limit their social and scholastic achievement and stigmatize them for future opportunities. Stealing from home and siblings and peers is a particularly poor prognosticator, suggesting that the behaviour may blight future, even close, relationships.

Prompts
Has child committed any property offences?
What did this entail?
Were the offences committed jointly, solo or both?
Does he have a long history of offending (more than two years) or a relatively short one?
Does pattern of offending suggest that they have become more extensive and serious in the course of time?
Can offences be seen as means of fulfilling material needs or do they appear indiscriminate?
Were offences premeditated and planned or impulsive?
What was done with child when offences were first discovered and how did this affect him?
Is there any evidence that child had been forced into offending?
Do parents speak of child stealing from home and other places?
How did they react?
Was there any stealing at school?
How ready is child to talk about offences?
Is there any evidence of guilt, shame or remorse?
Are accounts of the offences accurate, underplayed or exaggerated?
What does he say about his offence history?
Why does he say he committed them?
Does he try to exonerate himself? How? Does he shift the blame?
What does he say about chances of committing further offences?
What feelings does he express regarding the probable outcome?
Does he seem to derive much self or public esteem from his accounts of his offences?
Is readiness to steal indiscriminate or are his victims well chosen?
Are there any particular circumstances associated with thefts?
Is his theft for something he badly wants, or does it seem to be an act of taking for its own sake?
Does he steal as a way of taking 'revenge' on another child or adult?
Is he ready to receive what he knows to have been stolen from others?
Does he incite others to steal in order to give him the property?
Is there evidence that he may become a more serious and determined property offender?
If yes, what?

Action

Depending on the severity and persistence of offending diversion is best, provided it focally alters factors associated with the offending. Otherwise the task of treatment is likely to be long, arduous and often ineffective. The earlier the rigorous intervention, the better the long-term outcome will be.

0511   Fire setting

01   Lighting fires
02   Setting fires to destroy
03   Preoccupation with fire and fire setting materials
04   Other

Description

This condition refers to established acts of arson or child's unusual preoccupation with fires and fire setting.

In terms of gravity, arson falls somewhere between serious property offences and physical violence against persons. Indeed, arson, though directed at property, has potential for the infliction of severe hurt on people. For this reason, offences of arson are regarded as 'grave crimes' and treated as such. Whether an act of fire setting is designated as one of 'arson' or treated otherwise, such as 'malicious damage', depends on the circumstances of the offence, the child's situation, and the particular police officer's views and the policy of the prosecution service.

Fire seems to have a profound and almost mystical significance for all human beings. Its importance for children is probably no less but not as well understood. It is commonly observed that most children, at some time in the course of their growth play with fires, engage in fantasies about it, experiment with its properties and take delight, mixed with fear, in its obvious destructive properties, warmth and beauty. It is difficult to distinguish between a child who lights fires accidentally or for fun and one who sets them deliberately either as a means of destruction or in order to satisfy some yearning. Because of the potentially serious consequences, not only for the fire raiser but also of property damage and severe injury to others, all acts of fire raising are treated seriously.

It is suspected both by the police and insurance companies that most fires are associated either with criminal arson by adults or fire setting by youngsters as acts of revenge or as a means of gaining some other satisfaction. As with other offences, the evaluation of the child's past history of fire raising is achieved through normal social enquiry methods and the perusal of official records, as well as clinical interviews, observation and specialized measures.

Associated features

The most consistent feature of fire raisers is that they come from poor homes where poor parenting (and often paternal absence) is compounded by parental drug misuse, violence to child and other family members. Younger fire raisers are often solitary, anxious and neurotic and present a range of other anxiety-related disorders. This group often and only raise fires at home. The older group show the same family conditions but are often caught up in a range of other anti-social and disordered activities. They are more likely to be considered conduct disordered than anxious or neurotic.

Prevalence

As with all anti-social acts, this is also under-reported. However, studies of clinic populations show a range of 0.25–1 per cent, the latter being particularly prominent in treatment facilities for disordered adolescents and among those found guilty of gravest crimes. Boys are much more likely to be fire raisers, by a ratio in excess of 4:1.

Onset and course

Fire *lighting* is an early source of fascination and fear to children. Fire *raisers* have been found as young as 4 but the largest group seem to engage in this activity around 8 years, usually lighting fires in their own homes. Most seem to grow out of it if the usual insecurity about home and related conditions is treated. The next onset occurs around age 13, when this activity is part of a more generalized and serious pattern of anti-social behaviour both solitary and in groups. If not treated and in pathological (rather than accidental or opportunistic) cases, the condition deteriorates into adulthood.

Predisposing factors

Seem to be different for the two groups: in the younger child, experience of and exposure to abuse and violence at home, unhappiness, poor and insecure relationship with parents leading to an ill-articulated sense of vengefulness seem to be significant factors. In the older group, poor parenting and socialization, being abused and socially unintegrated, poor intellectual and scholastic attainment, drifting with a group of other anti-social youths and having an immature, tense personality and particularly negative and helpless views of self seem to predispose to such behaviour. These are also factors that are associated with conduct disorders of an aggressive and anti-social kind.

Complications

None specific for assessment or treatment. Anything that requires additional attention beyond this specific problem (and there are usually a great many) is likely to complicate the condition. Possible physical damage to the child in the course of fire setting should not be discounted.

Impairment

Primarily a consequence of social sanctions. If not quickly controlled, child is likely to be coercively removed to a facility where he can be kept out of harm's way. Thus educational and social development may suffer and unless special measures are taken, child may acquire other deviant modes of adaptation.

Prompts

Has child committed any offences of fire raising?

Was this offence of recent origin (within two years) or does it go back earlier than that?

Are there reports of other acts of fire raising not dealt with by the police?

Were these committed jointly or solo?

Do they appear to have been premeditated or impulsive?

Is there any evidence that they were aimed at gaining particular ends (such as destroying a disliked school) or for no particular apparent reason?

Was the fire raised at night or during the day?

Was it of public or private property, secluded or open to view?

Was it deserted or occupied and was this condition known to the child?

What were the consequences of the fire raising?

How did parents and others react to the fire and the consequences?

How did child react to the fire and the consequences?

Are there any parental and other reports about child's preoccupation with fire?

What form did this take?

What does child have to say about the fires?

Why did he say they were raised? What feelings does he express?

Does he try to exonerate himself?

What does he say about the possible consequences? For others? For himself?

Does child talk about fire and fire raising?

Is he more ready to talk about it than other children?

Is he seen to be drawn to fires, lights or materials which could be used for this purpose?

If such materials are 'accidentally' left around does he pick them up?

Does he hide them or use them openly?

Does he volunteer for making a fire or doing something which involves the use of fire, heating or lighting materials?

Action

Requires urgent and *focussed* attention to change child's behaviour, given the grave risks involved; likely to require intensive and prolonged effort.

0512 Offences against person

01	Aggravated robbery
02	Bodily harm, actual or grievous
03	Attempted murder
04	Manslaughter or murder
05	Other

Description
This condition refers to a range of the more serious offences against the person, excluding the sexual.

Sanctity of life and limb is the cornerstone of Western civilization and social structure. Offences against the person negate this and put people at risk. Social response is the most consistently punitive and restrictive of any against anti-social acts. There is considerable evidence that offences against the person are being increasingly committed by young people, as witnessed by the sharp rise in convictions for such offences. The facts of the case are usually known.

There are major cultural determinants of aggression. Some societies and cultures within them are more aggressive and prone to regarding life more cheaply than in others. Some young people in some parts of the country 'earn their stripes' through actual commission of daring and often gratuitous anti-social acts, including violence. They should be distinguished from the rarer and usually more serious solo offenders against the person. Specific assessment concentrates on identifying the cognitive, affective and behavioural sequences with a view to establishing whether child's behaviour is likely to persist and, therefore, estimating risk.

Associated features
As with non-offending, aggressive acts to which these offences are closely related, a huge range of possible conditions apply: neurological damage or abnormality, psychotic state, hypoglycaemia and other abnormal physical states, including substance misuse; poor intellectual potential and school achievement; high level of family disorder, parental instability, absence and violence, experience and witness of physical and other abuse; poor social skills and network; involvement with other anti-social youngsters and general features associated with immature, tense 'borderline personality' youngsters with poor impulse control, deviant self-image and poorly developed moral sense.

Prevalence
Mild forms of assault and aggressive acts against other people are grossly under-reported, well under 10 per cent. Taking Actual Bodily Harm (but not common assault) into account, well under 1 per cent of the general population of young people perpetrate such acts. The prevalence in clinic and institutional populations rises considerably beyond this, to as much as

30 per cent in some. Murders and manslaughters remain rare. Boys vastly outnumber girls, although the rise in violent offences by girls seems to be sharper than that for boys.

Onset and course
These offences (other than 'out of the blue' murder) are, in the case of persistent offenders, usually an extension and development of earlier aggressive acts which may start before school. More commonly, however, they start around change of school from primary to secondary and the greater likelihood of the youngster being caught up with an anti-social peer group. In repeated acts, offences are likely to become more serious, if for no other reason than young person's increasing physical strength and the well-established cognitive and emotional distortions about other people as victims.

Predisposing factors
As set out in the description of associated features. It is often difficult to separate 'cause and effect' relationship in this area. There is, however, some evidence suggestive of intergenerational transmission of aggressive behaviour which may be genetic or psychological. Particular cognitive and affective styles, tendency to hostile domineering and explosive reactions are likely to be associated with persistent forms of such condition (please also see **0507** and **0605**).

Complications
These are usually consequences of harsh social sanctions, which may result in strong build-up of anxiety or anger. Removal of young person from home or being placed on medication both have side-effects which may complicate and exacerbate the condition.

Impairment
If aggressive offending continues, youngster is likely to be subjected to increasingly restrictive social sanctions. Both in this context and the immediate response of family, peers and other adults, the youngster is likely to suffer the consequences of his act in emotional and social isolation. Unless focally and adequately treated, the young person is likely to acquire a range of further maladaptive responses.

Prompts
Very much as for fire raising, including:
What type of offending – how serious and whom did he assault?
How serious were the injuries?
Joint or solo?
Involved the use of a weapon?
Opportunist attack or premeditated?
Victim known to him?
Vengeance attack?

Over what sort of period? Have attacks become worse?
What response to outcome? Level of insight into or anticipation of
    outcome?
What response to social and legal reaction?
What ideas and feelings expressed?
What feelings about the victim?
What feelings about probable repetition?
Does he believe he needs help?

Action
Early response and *focal* treatment to reduce probability of further acts is
urgently indicated.

0513   Attitude to anti-social acts

01	Denial
02	Distortion of reasons for acts
03	Projecting blame
04	Lacking or poor insight
05	Boasting or uncaring
06	Other

Description
This condition relates to children's response to their anti-social behaviour,
in terms of thoughts, feelings and expressions of intention to avoid further
acts, insight into reasons for such behaviour, as well as expressions of
shame, guilt or remorse.

All the elements of this condition are varieties of cognitive distortions
from one extreme of denial to the other of boasting of the act as an
achievement. Denial only applies if it has been established beyond
reasonable doubt that the young person committed the offence. Distortion
can be judged by what appear to be probable and reasonable explanations.
When youngster exculpates himself or seems not to see that there is a
problem at all, then the condition could be seen as serious, as it is also
when he positively boasts about the acts or shows no concern for their
consequences.

Associated features
Coming from a disorganized and criminal family in a deprived environment, being poorly integrated into prosocial peer and adult networks and
having a strong anti-social and negative identity are usually associated with
such attitudes. The most serious and consistent condition is that of conduct
disorders of an aggressive kind where no insight, remorse or shame are
apparent and criminal behaviour is driven by a range of positively
construed outcomes.

Prevalence
By definition this condition applies to those young people whose anti-social behaviour is known and may be subject to assessment. In general and in the milder forms, over 50 per cent of young people who behave anti-socially show one or more of these features, at least temporarily. About 30 per cent of the more seriously anti-social youngsters show these attitudes consistently and over a protracted period. Boys and girls seem to be similar in this regard.

Onset and course
These ideas and feelings about anti-social behaviour may predate but usually accompany or follow anti-social acts. If behaviour continues, these activities harden through adolescence and are further reinforced and continue into adulthood.

Predisposing factors
Coming from a family and 'subculture' where such attitudes and associated anti-social behaviours are prevalent.

Complications
None specific, apart from the anti-social acts which usually coexist with them.

Impairment
This arises primarily from society's response to the youngster's anti-social behaviour which may, depending on its mode and impact, in fact exacerbate and solidify the youngster's attitude. Because such attitudes are precursors of anti-social behaviour, further offending becomes likely.

Prompts
Does child deny commission of acts?
Is this general or only for specific acts?
What reasons does he give?
Are these sensible or blatantly unconvincing?
Is distortion of reasons systematic or haphazard?
Is it intended to put blame on others?
Is projection of blame on to someone/something specific or general?
Is it apparently intended to make him look guilty, when he may not be?
Does child show any insight into gravity of acts or their consequences, for himself or others?
Can he reason cause and effect and show appropriate reaction?
Can child reason what the long-term consequences of his behaviour may be?
Does child show insight into the pattern and trend of his acts?
Does he seem concerned?
Does child appear to derive pleasure or status from acts?
Can he suggest what might stop him?

How realistic is this reasoning?
Is there any suggestion of dislike of authority figures such as the police, courts and others?
Do the attitudes to anti-social acts seem to be related to dislike of authority?
Is there any element of 'squaring' or revenge in the acts?
Does child appear resigned and fatalistic about anti-social acts?

Action
Changing such attitudes is an essential component of any programme for changing anti-social behaviour. Techniques exist but demand strong motivation and control over the outcome of anti-social behaviour. Motivation is the main problem.

Further reading

Allen, C.V. (1991) *Running Away*, London: Severn House.
Bandura, A. (1973) *Aggression: a Social Learning Analysis*, Englewood Cliffs, NJ: Prentice Hall.
Belson, W.A. (1975) *Juvenile Theft: the Causal Factors*, London: Harper & Row.
Berkowitz, L. (1962) *Aggression: a Social Psychological Analysis*, New York: McGraw Hill.
Besag, V.E. (1989) *Bullies and Victims in Schools*, Milton Keynes: Open University Press.
Coe, T. (1990) *Murder among Children*, Harpenden: No Exit Press.
Cohen, L. and Cohen, A. (eds) (1987) *Disruptive Behaviour: a Sourcebook for Teachers*, London: Harper & Row.
Farrington, D. and Gunn, J. (1985) *Aggression and Dangerousness*, Chichester: John Wiley.
Faulk, M. (1988) *Basic Forensic Psychiatry*, Oxford: Blackwell.
Feldman, M.P. (1977) *Criminal Behaviour: a Psycho-Analysis*, Chichester: John Wiley.
Frude, N. and Gault, H. (1984) *Disruptive Behaviour in Schools*, Chichester: John Wiley.
Gane, C.H.W. (undated) *Sexual Offences*, London: Butterworth.
Goldstein, A.P. and Keller, H. (1987) *Aggressive Behavior – Assessment and Intervention*, New York: Pergamon.
Green, R.G. (1989) *Human Aggression*, Milton Keynes: Open University Press.
Grimshaw, R. and Pratt, J. (1986) *Pastoral Care and Truancy: an Investigation of Theory and Practice*, Sheffield: University of Sheffield.
Hamer, J. (1985) *Running Away from Home*, Manchester: Gatehouse Project.
Hawton, K. (1986) *Suicide and Attempted Suicide among Children and Adolescents*, London: Sage.
Hawton, K. and Catalan, J. (1987) *Attempted Suicide: Practical Guide to its Nature and Management*, London: Oxford University Press.
Herbert, M. (1981) *Behavioural Treatment of Problem Children: a Practice Manual*, London: Academic Press.
Herbert, M. (1987) *Conduct Disorders of Childhood and Adolescence*, 2nd edn, Chichester: John Wiley.
Hersov, L.A. and Berg, I. (1980) *Out of School: Modern Perspectives in Truancy and School Refusal*, Chichester: John Wiley.
Hersov, L.A. and Berger, M. (eds) (1978) *Aggression and Anti-social Behaviour in Childhood and Adolescence*, Oxford: Pergamon.
Hoghughi, M.S. (1978) *Troubled and Troublesome*, London: Burnett Books/André Deutsch.
Hoghughi, M.S. (1983) *The Delinquent: Directions for Social Control*, London: Burnett Books.
Hollin, C.R. (1990) *Cognitive Behavioral Interventions with Young Offenders*, New York: Pergamon.

Hollin, C.R. and Howells, K. (eds) (1978) *Clinical Approaches to Aggression and Violence*, Leicester: British Psychological Society.

Holman, P. and Coghill, N. (1986) *Disruptive Behaviour in Schools: Causes, Treatment and Prevention*, Bromley: Chartwell-Bratt.

Home Office (1988) *Schools, Disruptive Behaviour and Delinquency: a Review of Research*, London: HMSO.

Janus, M.-D. et al. (1987) *Adolescent Runaways*, Lexington, Mass.: Lexington Books.

Keith, C.R. (1984) *The Aggressive Adolescent*, Glencoe, Ill.: Free Press.

Knopp, F.H. (1982) *Remedial Intervention in Adolescent Sex Offenses*, New York: Safer Society Press.

Kreitman, N. (1977) *Parasuicide*, London: John Wiley.

Kreitman, N. and Platt, D. (1989) *Current Research on Suicide and Parasuicide*, Edinburgh: Edinburgh UP.

Lamson, A. (1982) *Psychology of Juvenile Crime*, New York: Human Sciences Press.

Leyton, E. (1991) *Sole Survivors: Children who Murder their Parents*, Harmondsworth: Penguin.

Morgan, H.G. (1979) *Death Wishes? Understanding and Management of Deliberate Self Harm*, Chichester: John Wiley.

Newman, C. (1989) *Young Runaways: Findings from Britain's First Safe House*, London: Children's Society.

Parens, H. (1980) *Development of Aggression in Early Childhood*, New York: J. Aronson.

Parens, H. (1988) *Aggression in our Children: Parents Coping with it Constructively*, New York: J. Aronson.

Paterson, F. (1989) *Out of Place: Public Policy and the Emergence of Truancy*, London: Falmer.

Pepler, D.J. and Rubin, K.H. (eds) (1991) *Development and Treatment of Childhood Aggression*, Hillsdale, NJ: L. Erlbaum.

Reid, K. (1985) *Truancy and School Absenteeism*, London: Hodder Educ.

Scherer, M. and Gersch, I. (eds) (1990) *Disruptive Behaviour: Assessment, Intervention Partnerships*, London: Macmillan Educ.

Scottish Child and Family Alliance (1990) *Young Runaways: a Scottish Review*, London: HMSO.

Tattum, D.P. (1986) *Management of Disruptive Pupil Behaviour in Schools*, Chichester: John Wiley.

Tattum, D.P. (1989) *Disruptive Pupil Management*, London: D. Fulton.

Tollison, C.D. and Adams, H.E. (1980) *Sexual Disorders: Treatment, Theory and Research*, New York: Gardner Press.

Tyreman, M.J. (1968) *Truancy*, London: University of London Press.

West, D.J. and Farrington, D.P. (1973) *Who Becomes Delinquent?*, London: Heinemann.

West, D.J. and Farrington, D.P. (1977) *The Delinquent Way of Life*, London: Heinemann.

Zillman, D. (1984) *Connections between Sex and Aggression*, Hillsdale, NJ: L. Erlbaum.

13

Psychological Problems

This area encompasses the individual characteristics and ways of functioning that determine a person's unique adjustment to the environment. It includes personality structure, motives, habits, attitudes, feelings and value systems. Psychological or personal problems are not exclusively problems of personality, even if personality factors contribute massively to a person's failure to cope successfully with the demands of life. Although personality is involved in everything a person does, including physical, intellectual, family and social behaviour, this section deals primarily with those aspects which other people would regard as distinguishing features of a person's behaviour. In that sense, they are the most fundamental, persistent and pervasive features of a person's *style* of adaptation.

Historically, people experiencing psychological problems have been the concern of psychiatrists and clinical psychologists who have employed various classifications and diagnostic terms to describe them. Many of the traditional terms and labels, therefore, are retained here, partly because no better terminology is currently available, and partly to act as a communication bridge between traditional nosology and the problem approach advocated here. What is not retained is any theoretical presumption or inference about the probable nature and bases of these disorders. Although much is known about the disorders in this chapter, both the amount and quantity of information are such that no one theoretical allegiance is justified.

Psychological problems are mainly manifested in maladaptive behaviour patterns and seem to arise from three main sources:
(1) Deviations in personality structure and trait. Personality is the cluster of distinctive characteristics of an individual. Without excluding those features which are universal human traits, personality emphasizes those qualities, or combinations of qualities, which set one person apart from another. A person's personality is not defined by being human, or possessing speech, or being gregarious, but more by how personal 'mix' operates to identify one as an individual in a social context. Problems can arise if the individual's characteristics deviate massively from what is generally regarded as normal.
(2) Variations of response to others, emotional tone, adaptation and control make up another group and include those disorders traditionally classified as conduct disorders and neurotic reactions, in which distortions of interpersonal perception, anxiety and mood disturbances occur, often accompanied by maladaptive patterns of behaviour, such as phobic reactions.

(3) Personal identity and self-concept refers to the individual known to oneself: our conception and appraisal of the kind of person we perceive ourselves to be. Moral concerns also fall in this group. The whole area is, therefore, something of a mixture. Pragmatically, however, its unifying core is that these are all manifestations of the fundamental personality and psychological difficulties a person experiences or presents to others.

In diagnostic approaches to assessment, primary focus is on mood and affective disorders. Impulse control is covered in the context of attention deficit, although there are many children who are impulsive but do not suffer from attention deficit. The same may be said of frustration tolerance. Egocentricity and what here has been called 'conduct disorders' are normally considered, if at all, as an adjunct to offending. Personal identity and moral development are not covered at all, other than in relation to 'gender identity disorder' in DSM. Multivariate approaches also primarily emphasize mood and affective disorders.

The above attributes are covered separately here, because they constitute major variables in the comprehensive assessment of children with problems.

0601 Maturity

01	Preferring company of younger children
02	Emotional reactions inappropriate for age
03	Social reactions inappropriate for age
04	Engaging in behaviour appropriate to a younger child
05	Engaging in behaviour appropriate to an older child
06	Other

Description
This condition refers to the children behaving in a manner inappropriate to their chronological age.

Immaturity refers to the presence in a child of bodily and mental biases, attitudes, modes of expression and patterns of responses usually associated with a younger child. Levels of maturity involve behavioural, cognitive and social aspects.

Deviations in emotional development suggest that the child's behaviour and attitudes are not commensurate with those usually seen in someone of the same chronological age. His behaviour, therefore, tends to place him at odds with peers and adults, who label the behaviour 'childish', or, on the other hand, accuse him of trying to 'behave like an adult'. Either pattern of behaviour causes problems for the child, though more in the former than the latter. Level and style of maturation appear to reflect primarily the way a child has been brought up.

Despite frequent usage, it is evident that 'immature' is much more an evaluative than a descriptive term unless the condition is extreme. It is, as such, deeply bound up with cultural and individual biases regarding what constitutes mature behaviour. This is because there is little consistent information available about the attitudes, values and behaviours of youngsters in different age groups against which judgments of maturity can be made with any great confidence. Caution should, therefore, be exercised in making such judgments.

Associated features

Almost any condition can be associated with immaturity, from neurological and other physical disorders to mental retardation, attention deficit, coming from disordered and unsupportive, or over-protective and anxious homes, poor social skills, anti-social behaviour and a range of clinical conditions.

Prevalence

Maturity is likely to be a 'normally distributed' characteristic in the general population, with equal numbers of mature and immature children. Therefore, about 15 per cent of children would behave in a manner judged inappropriate for their age, although all children do so at some time or other. Though there seems little good reason for it, boys seem more frequently to be described as immature than girls.

Onset and course

This judgment can be made at any time after the first two years of life but rarely is until the middle school years and into adolescence. Some children's maturation accelerates in the secondary school but others remain immature well into adolescence and beyond.

Predisposing factors

Neurological disorder or deficit, chronic sickness and corresponding social isolation and emotional over-protection, mental impairment, inconsistent handling, susceptibility to social pressure and presence of affective disorders may all conduce to this condition.

Complications

This condition is a hallmark of pervasive developmental disorder and mental retardation, both or neither of which may be present. The child may also be responding to acute or chronic stress by resorting to earlier, habitual modes of behaviour. The judgment would only be worth making if condition is chronic and seriously impairing. Immature behaviour may land the child in social difficulties.

Impairment
Considerable, depending on severity, pervasiveness and social pressures for age-appropriate behaviour. Not a major problem in tolerant environments but everyone has limits of tolerance. Child is likely to be scapegoated and called names, which may lead to other maladaptive behaviour and social disadvantage.

Prompts
Is child described as 'immature' or 'babyish' by parents and others?
Is child said to spend most time with younger or duller children?
Is child said to be able to do things without relying on other people, or without supervision?
Do parents and others express concern about the rate at which child is growing up?
How does child see himself in relation to age mates – more or less grown up?
Does child seek company of younger/older children most of the time?
Is he happy with his choice?
Does he respond to praise and criticism in a manner usually seen in a much younger or older child?
Does he share things with his friends?
Is child very independent?
Are demands on adults and other children very different from those of age mates?
Has child a sense of give and take?
Is child reasonably aware of his physical, social and intellectual limitations and capabilities?
Does child's imagination fall within the limits of reality?
Are interests and behaviours appropriate for a child of his age?

Action
Depending on severity, intensive stimulation and encouragement may be needed to promote maturation.

0602   Self-centredness

01	Interest primarily in self
02	Using others for own ends
03	Seeking to achieve personal superiority
04	Greediness, over-demanding
05	Enviousness
06	Not helping others
07	Indifference to others' feelings
08	Other

Description

This condition refers to an abnormal degree or persistence of selfish behaviour by the child.

A major mark of social growth is altruism or at least enlightened self-interest, manifest in a degree of give and take even in young children. Egocentric children are so narrowly preoccupied with their own concerns that they regard themselves as 'number one' in all situations, often to the detriment of the welfare of others. Other people are regarded mainly as means to their own ends.

In its extreme form, egocentricity functionally prevents children from engaging in a harmonious social life. Emphasis on 'take' and neglect of 'give' exposes them to others' resentment and may lead to early rejection and social isolation. It should be stressed that all children, particularly in their earlier years, have periods or areas of selfishness which gradually lessen in the course of growing up.

Associated features

A stressful home, where child's survival depends on predatory and acquisitive behaviour; threatening, stressful or domineering peer relationships, a range of anti-social behaviours and features associated with conduct disorders are likely to be found together with this condition.

Prevalence

No statistics are available for the general population. In clinic and institutional populations, this condition is present in up to 20 per cent of children, more often in boys than girls. In its extreme forms, the condition applies to between 2 and 5 per cent of such populations.

Onset and course

Usually evident from an early age when child first starts in social groups or with siblings. Most grow out by middle school years, but some continue in either steady or worsening condition into and beyond adolescence. In its extreme form, egocentricity and using people as objects is strongly associated with adult personality disorders of an aggressive and anti-social kind.

Predisposing factors

Clustered with other components of conduct disorder, this condition is more prevalent in parents and other biologically related relatives, thus suggesting possible genetic predisposition. Even more probably, cold and unsupportive parents, resorting to harsh and inconsistent discipline, are more likely to produce such children, particularly when alternative sources of succour, such as grandparents, are not available.

Complications

Primarily home and peer environments which may have shaped and be maintaining such behaviour, which may well be adaptive, even though abnormal. Persistence of behaviour in 'normal' environments must thus be established before the judgment can be made. The behaviour is likely to provoke serious and potentially punitive sanctions from others.

Impairment

Very considerable. Social give and take is a cornerstone of satisfactory living with other people. An egocentric child is likely rapidly to be singled out for ignoring or worse, unless too powerful for such treatment. Even then adults' views and behaviour are likely to be seriously negative and restrictive, so that the child is likely to be a significant loser in the long run.

Prompts

How does he feel when his favourite team or friend loses?

Does child very much mind losing in any games or competitions?

Does child ever give presents, bought or found, to others?

Does he ever do favours for others unasked?

Does child ever give up some thing or opportunity to someone else who may seem to need it more?

Does child express appreciation of other people's points of view?

Is child affected by them?

Do relationships with others tend to be superficial and ephemeral?

Does child invariably thrust himself forward when 'goodies' are distributed?

Does he ever offer anything to others, such as food on the table, before helping himself?

Is child easily roused to envy or jealousy?

When given choices, does child take the lion's share?

Is child generally unmoved by the misfortune of others?

Does child frequently seek to manipulate situations to suit own ends?

Does child offer assistance when others are struggling?

Does child open a door, place chairs, etc. for others?

Does child tend to put own interests before those of others?

Does child give any sign that behaviour is affected by considerations of others?

Action

As urgent as it is likely to be unproductive, certainly in the short run and without complex ploys to make altruistic behaviour worthwhile for child.

0603 Frustration tolerance

01 Lacking patience
02 Inability to tolerate delay of gratification
03 Showing tantrums/aggression if does not get own way
04 Easy to disappoint
05 Giving up on tasks easily
06 Other

Description
This condition applies to abnormal degree or persistence of inappropriate response to blocked goals.

Frustration tolerance is the ability to postpone or delay the reaching of a goal, or to respond reasonably to a thwarted wish or desire. In the nature of society, not all goals, needs or wants can be immediately satisfied. Young children have little appreciation of possible impediments and demand immediate fulfilment. As they grow older they learn increasingly to control demands and to accept delayed gratification. In the course of growing up children also have to learn that daily living is a mixed bag of pleasant and unpleasant events. Early explosive responses to unpleasant experiences have to be gradually moderated if children are to find an acceptable place in society.

There is some evidence that frustration tolerance may be a basic and inborn personality feature. Even so, like other personality traits, frustration tolerance is fundamentally shaped by experiences of growing up. Demanding, petulant and self-willed children have usually been brought up by parents who seem to have been unable to set and enforce boundaries for their children and have given in to all their demands as a means of gaining compliance.

Associated features
This condition is a prominent hallmark of attention deficit although it often exists without this, but in the context of other features such as neurological disorders, particularly epilepsy, intoxication, intellectual impairment, poor upbringing, poorly integrated social relationships, conduct disorders, anti-social behaviour or affective disorders.

Prevalence
Not known reliably in the general population of children, although figures of up to 10 per cent have been cited. In clinic and institutional populations, the condition is prevalent – often as high as 20 per cent – though severe cases are relatively rare – no more than about 3 per cent. There seems to be little difference between boys and girls, although the latter behave in a more cataclysmic fashion.

Onset and course
The condition can be apparent from a very early age. Depending on adult response, it may well subside by early school years. If it does not, and again dependent on severity and consistency of adult response, it may well continue to become more severe and disruptive as child passes puberty into adolescence. Typically and given appropriate treatment response, the condition settles down with maturation.

Predisposing factors
This condition seems to be more prevalent in biologically related persons. Equally, however, inadequate and inconsistent parental boundary setting and enforcement seem to predispose to this condition.

Complications
Likely to be predominantly neurological or a family and social environment which provokes and maintains such behaviour, thus rendering it reasonably adaptive.

Impairment
Potentially considerable, given other children's and adults' intolerance of the more disruptive forms of such behaviour. The child is likely to be singled out for adverse treatment and will suffer the long-term consequences of inadequate social learning.

Prompts
Do reports suggest that the child has always been demanding?
What do they say of response to frustration?
Did child always try to get his own way immediately?
Did child give up easily if he hit snags in anything he was doing?
Have the parents and others tried to do anything about the child's poor tolerance and with what results?
How does child rate his own tolerance?
Does child say he would be annoyed if he had to wait for something he wanted?
Does child accept that he is bound to have frustrating experiences?
Does child say his ability is changing? For better or worse?
Does child see himself as having conflicts because of his poor tolerance?
Is poor tolerance restricted to a particular area?
Can child wait for something he wants?
How does child react if he has to wait? Is there a pattern of reaction relating to particular forms of frustration?
Do these involve particular people or child's moods?
Are the reactions in any way unusual or extreme compared with other children's?
Does child generally lack patience?
Does child make unnecessary mistakes due to impatience?
Does child give up easily when success is not immediate?

How noticeable are these characteristics compared with other children?
Does child get into trouble with adults and other children because of this
  tendency?

Action
Fairly good techniques exist for making rapid impact on the more florid
aspects of this condition, given close and rigorous input, but relative long-
term tendency is likely to remain.

0604   Impulse control

01   Acting without apparent thought, volition or deliberation
02   Not trying to control self
03   Bored easily
04   Poor resistance to temptation
05   Other

Description
This condition refers to child's unusual difficulty in behaving in a thought
out and deliberate fashion.

Impulsivity is characterized essentially by sudden urge to act, without
apparent deliberation or volition, on the mere presentation of a stimulus
or situation. Poor impulse control embroils children in numerous and
varied troubles. The sudden translation of ideas or impulses into overt acts
does not allow children to consider the ramifications of their actions.
Further, such disinhibited behaviour is disliked in cultures which value
serenity and caution. The process of socialization is seen by many to be
primarily aimed at increasing self-control, to guide one's actions after due
weighing up of pros and cons, to resist temptation to do wrong and to take
an ever longer view of the consequences of one's actions.

These cultural ideals are largely manifested by the majority of adults
who are valued in society. The fact that practically everyone behaves
impulsively from time to time, that 'spontaneity' is the name we give to
the same characteristic in the people we like, and that we distrust people
who are always well controlled, does not diminish our anxiety about
impulsive behaviour.

Associated features
This is the chief feature of attention deficit disorder without hyperactivity.
However, it can and does present with a range of other conditions, such
as neurological damage or deficit, serious drug misuse, mental impairment,
deviant parenting, tendency to serious and persistent anti-social behaviour,
conduct disorder and sometimes acute anxiety.

Prevalence
In its mild form, this condition affects most children at some time or other. In the more serious or persistent form the disorder affects about 5 per cent of children, the prevalence being higher among clinic and institutional populations, younger children and boys.

Onset and course
The condition can be evident from two years onwards and may remit by the time of going to school. If it has not, it is likely to continue into late adolescence and beyond, though becoming less prominent as child grows older.

Predisposing factors
Biologically related family members are more susceptible to this condition. Neurological damage, drug use, intellectual impairment, poor parenting and extroverted personality make up may all predispose to the condition.

Complications
Neurological abnormality, poor intellectual equipment, effect of food and other allergies, consequences of taking drugs may all complicate the assessment of impulse control. Poorly controlled impulses are also likely to result in accidents and other problems for the child.

Impairment
Child can become involved in serious accidents or damage affecting himself and others as a result of impulsive behaviour. Such a child is also unlikely to derive full benefit from schooling and social education. Emotional ties are likely to be strained and the child is much more likely to become involved in serious anti-social behaviour.

Prompts
Do parents and others refer to child as impulsive or thoughtless?
Do they say he has been in trouble because of it? What trouble?
Do they say he is like any other member of the family?
What particular aspects of impulsiveness have worried them?
What have they done about it?
Is child noticeably different from other children in this respect?
Does the child say he tends to do things on the spur of the moment?
What does he say he would do if another child cheated him during a
    favourite activity?
Does child say he would fight first and ask questions afterwards?
What would he do if he found himself in a shop and the assistant was in
    the back room?
Is child easily bored? Flits from one activity to another?
Does child regard himself as quick tempered?
What does child say about the consequences of being impulsive?
Does child take long chances?

Are verbal and behavioural reactions quick or slow and deliberate?

Does child admit to thoughtlessness? Does this affect his subsequent behaviour?

Does child give in readily to temptation?

Is child more susceptible to some temptations than others? Are these affected by circumstances?

Is he easy 'bait' for the other children?

Does he quickly lose his temper when provoked? Does he show any insight into his responsiveness?

Do other children regard him as unpredictable?

Action

If serious enough to warrant action, considerable patience and flair is required to use the limited range of relevant techniques, with uncertain results.

0605   Conduct disorders

01	High level self-centredness
02	Emotional coldness
03	Lacking feeling for others
04	Calculating and manipulatory behaviour
05	Callousness and cruelty
06	Little or no remorse or guilt
07	Not learning from mistakes
08	Abnormal searches for excitement and variety
09	Difficulty in delaying gratification
10	Lacking inhibition
11	Becoming hostile easily
12	Cheating/lying
13	Viewing others as enemies or objects to be used
14	Other

Description

This condition refers to a fundamental distortion of personality features associated usually with serious anti-social behaviour and response to other people. In diagnostic classifications, the term 'conduct disorder' designates a range of anti-social *behaviours* such as theft, lying and fire setting. In this book, however, these behaviours are assigned to the category 'anti-social behaviour' or elsewhere, as is appropriate to a descriptive classification.

The term 'conduct disorder' in the present context is used as the equivalent of 'personality disorder' in the over 18s, where the more persistent, deviant characteristics of behaviour are identified as having been established over a long period. Thus, although such personality features come to light when child breaks the law, they are also evident in other contexts. There are, indeed, such children who, coming from middle-class and protective families, usually do not get caught up in offending, but nevertheless, present a range of other difficulties. In an important sense, this condition describes the *quality* of interaction of the young person with others – which is the major source of differentiating a habitual but 'socialized' anti-social youngster from the cold, hostile and 'unsocialized' youngsters who may or may not be 'offenders'.

Many of the above features, characteristic of anti-social personality disorder in adults, can be readily seen in the more seriously disordered young people from about 12 years onwards. Nevertheless, as is evident from the range of features included, this is a rag-bag or dustbin category of characteristics, some of which are also included in other disorders. It includes many features which usually cluster together and often present a clear picture of disturbed and disturbing conditions that demand clinical and other responses.

The underlying and inevitably inferential premise is that no one can present the above difficulties without suffering from some form of pathology. And yet, frequently, such people are free of other obvious clinical disorders. The social basis of clinical diagnosis, subject of so much recent debate, is nowhere more clear than in the category of anti-social or 'dissocial' personality disorders. Almost all the behaviours in this area are severely or persistently anti-social and remorseless. No 'normal person' is assumed to behave in this way. The child is, therefore, thought to suffer from a form of psychopathology – a kind of fundamental 'kink' in personality trait or structure. This form of pathology has been variously referred to as 'moral insanity', 'psychopathy', 'sociopathy' and, in the case of children, 'character disorder', 'conduct disorder' and a number of other exact-sounding names, particularly when associated with persistent or grave anti-social acts. This diffuse set of disapproved behaviours has been elevated to the status of a disease with the diagnostic feature of 'disorder of the mind'.

Despite their usefulness as means of communicating negative value judgments or administrative shorthands, the scientific and clinical status of such terms as 'psychopath' and 'personality disordered', even with qualifications like 'aggressive' or 'inadequate', remain seriously doubtful. The groups so termed have as many dissimilarities as likenesses. The findings regarding their characteristics and origins remain either inconsistent or insignificant. This is not to say that there are no common features among sub-groups, but that these shift according to the criteria employed and the criteria do not remain constant. Nevertheless, in the case of young people, the above constellation of items seems worthy of assessment.

Associated features
The above behaviours may be found in the context of youngsters with retarded intellectual level (though not the most seriously retarded),

attention deficit and lower than expected educational attainments; disordered and inconsistent, cold, abusive and punitive homes, where father–child relationships are poor or disrupted. Social skills are usually poor, relationships with peers are predatory and those with adults manipulatory and instrumental. There is usually a wide range of anti-social behaviours and negative attitudes to authority, which often bring such a child to attention. The child may be normally outgoing and mature but frustration tolerance and impulse control are likely to be poorly developed, accompanied by an inflated or unrealistic self-concept and ill-developed moral sense.

Prevalence
Many of the characteristics are difficult to measure with any degree of reliability though teachers estimate about 5 per cent of children as manifesting such behaviour. In clinic and institutional populations, as much as 20 per cent of the young people may manifest noticeable degrees of these characteristics. Boys are significantly over-represented in this condition, perhaps as a result of more being identified as anti-social.

Onset and course
This condition can become apparent from middle childhood onwards, gradually causing more concern as child grows towards adolescence and beyond. Some young people (usually girls) do not manifest such characteristics until about thirteen, and long-term prospects for them are better. Given young people's physical strength in peak adolescence, this is also when the above characteristics in the context of serious anti-social behaviour can cause the most damage. Short-term outcomes of intervention are very poor.

Predisposing factors
Harsh, inconsistent family background, with inconstant father figures, disrupted or institutional life in early years, extroverted personality and impulsive egocentricity are likely to predispose to this condition if for no other reason than adaptation to abnormality and modelling. Genetic predisposition is also suggested by greater prevalence of these characteristics among biological relatives – particularly when this condition is taken as a general and persistent form of malfunctioning involving social relationships and behaviour.

Complications
Likely to include substance misuse, injury from accidents and fights, pregnancy, poor school performance, exclusions or suspensions, removal from home and custodial treatment and public reactions which may exacerbate the condition. From an assessment viewpoint, the complication lies in the inferential nature of the condition and the need for considerable observational and interviewing acuity to support such a conclusion.

Impairment
Dependent on degree, potentially considerable. A young person with these characteristics is unlikely to be able to engage in socially acceptable two-way relationships with peers and adults. Interpersonal response is, therefore, likely to be rejecting and isolating, reducing the opportunity for socially acceptable pleasures and creating tensions which may lead to future restrictive treatment.

Prompts
Has child been described in any of the above terms by others?
Are such judgments relatively uniform across parents, teachers, friends or others, or do they vary?
Do descriptions suggest a relatively persistent pattern?
How do people describe child in current setting?
Are similar remarks made by adults and other youngsters?
Are there any serious incidents or acts which illustrate particular features?
Can the evidence be interpreted any other way, such as 'normal' response to abnormal conditions?
Are these characteristics discernible in how child presents at interview?
Does child show insight into or otherwise account for such reactions?
Are these features associated with anti-social acts?
Is there a trend/deterioration in such acts and/or child's view of them?
Most seriously, can child be regarded as seeking hostile dominance, disregarding others' feelings?
Is there any sign of guilt, shame, remorse or contrition?
Is there much likelihood that any of these could develop?
Is there much chance of child's wider circumstances changing significantly and modifying such features? For better or for worse?

Action
As urgent as it is likely to be unproductive in the short term. Usually maturation of child combined with considerable freedom from adverse experiences and positive shaping is required if any perceptible shift is to occur.

0606   Emotional response

01	Crying/laughing easily
02	Getting over-excited inappropriately
03	Sulkiness, petulance
04	Over-reacting to stress
05	Pronounced mood swings
06	Bland or rare emotional expressions
07	Superficial or shallow emotions
08	Other

Description

This condition refers to abnormalities in child's level and quality of emotional responsiveness, expression and control. It should not be confused with 'affective disorders' which, traditionally, refer to anxiety and depression.

Changes in emotions reflect variations of experience, both internally and externally stimulated. Some variation in emotional expressions is normal and to be expected. When such changes are dramatic and beyond what is acceptable, or, alternatively, when they do not occur at all, they provoke an uneasy, worried or suspicious response from other people.

Emotional lability is characterized by instability or quick changeability of feelings, their probable biological bases and their expressions in behaviour. The emotionally unstable or labile child often becomes a management problem because of unpredictable behaviour. Adults, for example, say that they 'don't know where they stand' with such a child. Such unpredictability of response also leads to isolation from peers.

Emotional depth (or shallowness) is a more difficult quality to define because it is so bound up with children's relationships with the people to whom they are reacting. Many children, because of the hurt and damage they have sustained, become emotionally shallow, cold or bland as a defence against further hurt. Whether for this reason or others, some children are more shallow or bland with both peers and adults than is warranted by the immediate circumstances.

Associated features

This condition can exist by itself but is frequently associated with others, including neurological difficulties, sometimes pervasive developmental disorder, significant levels of mental impairment, attention deficit, seriously deficient or deviant family experiences, poor social relationships, anti-social behaviour or affective disorders.

Prevalence

Estimates suggest that 3–5 per cent of the population of school children suffer significant degrees of mood disorder. The prevalence in clinic and institutional populations is sometimes as high as 50 per cent. In the more pathological form, about 15 per cent of such children suffer from mood disorders. Girls seem to show more moodiness and extremes of response than boys.

Onset and course

These difficulties are common in early childhood but usually settle down by middle school years. Those who have not improved, or become noticeable at this age, are likely to continue with this difficulty into adolescence and beyond. The intensity of reactions seems to peak in late adolescence or early adulthood, exacerbated by the unique stresses of this stage of development.

Predisposing factors
Allowing for ambiguities of judgment in this area, biologically related family members, particularly the nearer ones, seem to share these features. Given the fundamental nature of this area of response, it is likely to be heavily influenced by inherited or perhaps peri- or postnatally affected physiology.

Complications
Neurological features, serious mental impairment, effects of drugs, food and other allergens and immediate or chronic stresses and determinants of behaviour, must be considered in arriving at this judgment.

Impairment
Potentially considerable, dependent on the severity, form and pervasiveness of the disorder. It is likely to affect child interactions with and enjoyment of experiences, particularly those involving other people. Abnormalities of emotional response can be alarming or offputting to others and effectively rebound on the child.

Prompts
Do parents and others recount a history of noticeable moodiness?
Can they associate these with particular periods or events?
Did they become evident in different settings?
Was (is) moodiness a problem at school?
Do adults usually know 'where they are' with the child?
Is child's reaction like other members of family?
Does child see herself as moody?
Does child admit to laughing or crying easily?
How does child rate her emotional self-control?
If not well, does child mind it? Does child say she tries to control mood and temper?
Is child aware of things or events that excite or depress her mood?
Is child concerned about emotional tone?
Do the other children describe her as 'moody' or 'cold'?
Does child lose control easily when under pressure?
What does she do?
Is child subject to mood swings? Are these precipitated by particular events?
Are they periodic or cyclical? Is mood better in the morning or later in the day?
Is child emotionally over-sensitive? Is she easily hurt, or pleased?
Does child show little emotional response, even under adverse conditions?
Do other people, including children, regard her as a 'cold fish'?
Does it appear as if she is trying to control her emotions or that she experiences none?
Do people feel as if she is emotionally distant and beyond reach?
How does this distance manifest itself?

Do children and adults express unease about her?
Do they avoid her?

Action
Little evidence that much can be done about such a fundamental
characteristic, if it well established. If disorder is recent and reactive, treatment for associated condition(s) is likely to improve it.

0607   Anxiety

01	Tension or inability to relax
02	Restlessness
03	Overactivity
04	Apprehensiveness
05	Indecisiveness
06	Needing constant reassurance
07	Irritability, jumpiness
08	Tics and tremors
09	Feelings of impending disaster
10	Sleep disturbance
11	Palpitations or pallor
12	Excessive perspiration
13	Nausea or other bodily discomfort/ pain
14	Constipation or bedwetting
15	Apparent imperviousness to stress
16	Other

Description
This condition refers to unrealistic or unnecessary worry or apprehension
on the part of the child, manifest in any combination of above behaviours,
over a period of three months or more.

Anxiety may be defined as an unpleasant subjective emotional
experience, varying in degree from mild unease to pain and intense dread.
It leads to physiological and behavioural changes, very similar to those of
fear. It also shares certain features of depression. Levels of anxiety are
influenced by personality traits (trait anxiety), as well as personally significant stresses (state anxiety). Anxiety may be general and all-pervasive (free-
floating) or alternatively, reactive to circumstances (focal).

In assessing anxiety in children, several considerations seem pertinent.
Above all, anxiety may be a normal or an appropriate response to a whole
range of circumstances, from examinations and changes of school to
parental break up. Anxiety has considerable biological significance for
survival in terms of increased alertness and awareness and as a response
to threat and unfamiliarity. Anxiety is often a sign and symptom of other

psychiatric, psychological and physical disturbance and may, therefore, indicate other disorders which should be investigated. Further, anxiety levels and responses are protean, with different children showing different reactions to ostensibly the same anxiety-inducing situations.

Although low anxiety levels may be regarded as a blessing, an abnormally low level of anxiety will deprive the child of that aspect which acts as an early warning system and indicator of undue stress. A child who does not react with appropriate anxiety is likely to get into scrapes and other forms of trouble which are avoided by a person with a normal complement of anxiety.

Associated features
Children suffering from anxiety are also likely to suffer from other conditions arising from or otherwise associated with it. These include neurological and drug-induced conditions, physical illness or impairment, distractibility and poor school performance, a wide range of adverse home and parenting experiences, a tendency to withdraw from new situations or people, irrational fears, difficulty in resting, sleeping or concentrating. Depressive features may be present as may persistent ideas about personal inadequacy.

Prevalence
Depending on the criteria used, anxiety disorders occur in about 2.5–5 per cent of the child and adolescent population. The prevalence rate rises with age. In clinic and institutional populations, prevalence rate can be as high as 30 per cent, though most such reactions are of a transitory nature. Persistent anxiety reactions affect about 5–10 per cent of such populations. Boys and girls are equally affected. In later adolescence, anxiety disorders are more common in girls than boys. In clinic and institutional populations, however, the difference in prevalence between the sexes is not marked, though there are variations when other difficulties are also present.

Onset and course
Depending on the form and focus, anxiety disorders can be evident from pre-school years. They gradually grow in spread and intensity as child grows older. In part associated with stresses of adolescence, anxiety disorders also become more serious in this stage of development and into adulthood.

Predisposing factors
Children with neurological disorders, such as epilepsy, and those with a serious physical illness or disability, are more likely to suffer anxiety. The role of the home is unclear in that apparently both 'good' and 'poor' homes produce children with this disorder. Much more likely is recent experiences of loss – significant person, pet, move of house or school. Anxious parents are also more likely to produce anxious children, though whether for biological or social reasons is unclear.

Complications
Physical complaints may demand lengthy investigations and possible adverse consequences for the child. The child may also adopt modes of coping with anxiety, such as deliberate self-harm, substance misuse, excitement-seeking with peers and other activities which may provoke negative sanctions. Identifying a general anxiety reaction from a reactive one can be complicated by the presence of other difficulties.

Impairment
Potentially considerable, given the unpleasant subjective experience of anxiety and the personal drive to remove or channel it. A seriously anxious child is likely to experience more physical difficulties, do less well at school and be more buffeted by normal rough and tumble of life and adolescent development. Serious anxiety may presage or mask depression and other functional breakdown.

Prompts
Do parents and others speak of the child as anxious and worried?
Has child always been like this or only recently? Do any events account for this?
Has child been referred to anyone for this problem and with what consequences?
How does child describe herself in this context?
Does child often have 'the shakes' in hands?
Does child sweat a lot, even when sitting quietly?
Does her heart often 'thump' for no good reason?
Does she have difficulty going to sleep?
Is there something worrying her? Is she afraid of something? Does she know what it is?
Does she often feel something terrible is going to happen?
Does she worry a lot? Does she try to reduce her anxiety? Does she have what she considers good reasons for her state? Does she think she needs help?
Is child excessively fidgety?
Does she appear to be 'on edge'?
Is she often indecisive even over small matters?
Does she often complain of feeling sick?
Does child complain of difficulty in going to sleep?
Is she edgy and over-sensitive? Is this regardless of time, place and events?
Is she 'always on the go'? Is this with a purpose or does it appear to be just time filling?
Does she seem to lack confidence? Is this better or worse with particular people and situations?
Does she often seek help, company and counsel for small matters?

Action
Depending on its severity, anxiety demands early intervention. Good

treatments are available, provided attention is also paid to the circumstances which may trigger and sustain it.

0608 Anxiety-related disorders

Hypochondriasis
01 Exaggerated concern with physical and/or mental health
02 Frequently complains of minor ailments
03 Frequent demands for medical attention

'Hysteria'
01 Loss or disorder of sensory or motor functions
02 Loss of voice
03 Sleepwalking
04 Loss of memory

Obsessive-compulsive disorder
01 Rigid conformist and orderly behaviour
02 Intolerance or inflexibility
03 Doing the same things over and over again
04 Complaining of persistent, irrational thoughts, impulses and actions
05 Other

Description

This even more than usually conglomerate condition refers to a range of quite different abnormal reactions all of which are thought to be maladaptive responses to persistent or high-level anxiety. The features cited above are only the more frequently seen. Many other behaviours may be associated with anxiety. They are banded together here because of their relatively low prevalence in either normal or clinical populations of young people.

Hypochondriasis is the name given to a collection of behaviours characterized by persistent and exaggerated worry about bodily health, when there is nothing demonstrably wrong with the child. In spite of reassurance, the child remains convinced that he is suffering from a disability or disease.

'Hysteria', in spite of its popular usage as a specific condition, remains another clinical dustbin. Speculations as to its nature are legion and have abounded for centuries among diagnosticians, although there is little to suggest that such a condition exists as a discrete disorder. For the purpose of this book, although the term will be retained, its behavioural components will be emphasized. Exaggeration of emotional expression characterizes the 'histrionic' type of personality. Hysterical symptoms (behaviours) can occur in numerous clinical conditions and often stem from the person's inability to cope with life, or as reactions to some unbearable stress, often spilling over into conversion of symptoms or 'dissociation'. These are when anxiety reaction takes the form of some bodily malfunction (such as 'hysterical blindness'), thus overlapping with psychosomatic disorders.

Compulsions usually occur with obsessions (persistent, unpleasant beliefs and thought patterns) but they involve specific, repetitive acts (such as hand washing and getting out of bed to check things for safety), which child knows are irrational and unnecessary. 'Obsessive-compulsive' behaviour should not be confused with habit patterns. Many children rigidly adhere to their own ways of doing things, particularly when younger and, indeed, display much checking and other compulsive behaviour. Clinically compulsive behaviour can be distinguished by the child's slavish adherence to behaviour patterns which may be unpleasant, maladaptive and not pleasurable. Much of this behaviour is normally related to particular levels of individual development and unlikely to cause severe distress.

Associated features
These are as for anxiety but exacerbated by unusually long exposure to stressors and patterns of similar behaviour in members of family or the child's reference group, either real or imaginary.

Prevalence
The confusion of anxiety-related complaints about the body with adequately diagnosed, 'true' physical conditions is so great that no sensible prevalence estimates can be made in cases of hypochondriasis. The incidence of 'true hysteria' is said to be less than 1–2 per cent in clinic populations and almost non-existent in the general population. In institutions the prevalence of such behaviour is about 2–3 per cent. Compulsive behaviour is quite common among children up to secondary school age. Obsessions are likely to be even more common but are less observable. Both conditions in a clinically intense form are, however, very rare, occurring in less than 1–2 per cent of the population. These conditions are, however, kept 'private' and estimates are likely to be grossly unreliable, particularly if the focus of thoughts and behaviour are seen by the child as unusual. Insofar as any reliable estimates can be made, 'hysterical' behaviour occurs more often in girls but hypochondriasis and compulsive behaviour in boys.

Onset and course
Tendency to complain about injuries or other bodily problems can be evident from an early age and is likely to continue, with ups and downs in individual cases, throughout life. Hysteria is much less common among young children. The tendency to 'convert' anxiety to a serious sensory/

motor loss of malfunction becomes usually evident in adolescence and grows from then onwards. The same pattern occurs in obsessive-compulsive behaviours. Unless the behaviours are manipulation attempts with a temporary, definable gain, and shown to be so by focussed treatment, they are likely to continue into adulthood largely unabated.

Predisposing factors

Similar difficulties in parents of children with these disorders have been found, thus raising the possibility of genetic predisposition to anxiety, as well as shaping by parental or other significant models. Other family difficulties and poor ability to relate to peers or behave assertively in anxiety-producing circumstances are likely to predispose to this condition.

Complications

All these behaviours may in fact mask a 'real' difficulty – physical or mental – in the child. Thus, the child may be suffering from a true physical disorder which may or may not be revealed by examination – given errors in medical investigations. However, the very examinations may also exacerbate the condition and generate their own ('iatrogenic') difficulties. Unusual intensity of emotional reaction to these conditions by some adolescents may also raise the possibility of a schizophrenic process. The condition is rarely presented in a simple form.

Impairment

This depends on both the severity of condition and the response to it. Any of these disorders is likely to impair the child's functioning in physical, intellectual and social areas.

Prompts

Do parents and others say that the child has been a worrier about his state?
Are parents worried about the child's health?
Have they sought frequent help to sort out the ills?
Do parents' and child's worries have a good foundation?
Does child worry about his health?
Does he often think he is ill more than other people?
What does he do when 'not well'?
Does child frequently request to see doctor or nurse?
Does he make a fuss if he is suffering from some minor ailment?
Is he described as 'always having something wrong with him?
Is he considered a pest because of his complaints?
Are there any reports of loss of function without good physical reasons?
Have parents and others sought help for it? If yes, with what results?
Does child say he loses the sensation in or use of an arm or leg for no apparent reason?
Does he say he has 'fits' or has difficulty keeping his balance?
Does he sometimes suffer from blurred vision, or feel that there is something wrong with his eyes?

Does he often get pains in his chest or back?

Does he ever do things in a sort of 'dream' without remembering afterwards what he did?

Does he sometimes lose his memory?

Does he sometimes find himself in places without quite knowing how he got there?

Does he appear lost at times?

How does he explain and feel about his difficulties?

Does he appear indifferent and seem to be content to let others get on with solving his problem?

Does the child stumble, limp, or faint without any discernible physical cause?

Does he complain of deafness or being unable to speak?

Does he engage in exaggerated emotional expressions and behaviours of the type called 'histrionic'?

Are there other family members with the same behaviour patterns?

Does he say he checks over and over again things he has already completed?

How does he feel if he has not rechecked something?

Does he like to touch or count things over and over again?

Does he avoid certain routes or paths? Does he say he tries to stop himself from doing things but cannot?

Does he say he gets lots of awful thoughts coming into his head?

What are these thoughts? Why does he regard them as awful?

Does he try to push the thoughts out of his mind? How and with what results?

Does child repeat things over and over again? Both words and actions?

Does he engage in precise and predictable behaviour patterns repeatedly? What?

Are these related to what is required of him? How frequently does he do these?

How does he respond to a change in established routines?

Is he preoccupied with always doing things in a strict, orderly manner?

Does he have very regular habits?

Does he have stereotyped expressions and mannerisms?

Is child meticulously slow when doing something?

Does he often appear scowling and preoccupied? Does he take the opportunity to snap out of these thoughts?

How does child react to minimal failure?

Do the other children regard him as odd?

Does he think his state is unusual?

Is he worried about his state?

Does he think he needs help?

Action

If not severe, the condition can be safely ignored. If severe, treatment is as necessary as it is likely to be difficult.

0609 Phobic reaction

01	Abnormal fear of animals and insects
02	of situations
03	of persons
04	of places
05	of objects
06	of injury
07	Other

Description
This condition refers to an unusually intense fearful reaction by child to a range of objects or experiences.

Fear of dangerous or unfamiliar objects and situations is biologically necessary for survival. Fear or apprehension associated with a wild animal or a potentially hazardous situation is not a neurotic reaction. Neither is an isolated, specific fear of, say, heights, dogs or air travel – these are idiosyncratic reactions or personal preferences. To be called a phobia, a fear must be irrational, intense, persistent, and characterized by a high level of anxiety which is *debilitating*. Many children experience fears, some of them intense, in the course of growing up. They eventually grow out of these and do not require any particular help, especially if the fears do not impede normal living.

An intense fear becomes maladaptive when it so disturbs the individual that he is unable to lead a normal, healthy life. For example, if a young person is so seriously disturbed about being in groups that he is unable to use public transport, go to school or enter shops, then a phobic reaction is indicated. His irrational and intense fear will be reflected in his anxiety and persistent attempts to avoid anything to do with the feared stimulus. Phobias are regarded as instances of 'overlearning' associated with an intense reaction to a particularly fearful or traumatic experience.

Associated features
Such reactions may be present in the context of physical disorders, such as anorexia, stressful and possibly abusive home environments, recent traumas, including the fear-arousing event and possibly conduct and perhaps other emotional disorders.

Prevalence
Estimates suggest that this condition may exist in up to 7 per cent of adolescents but that in only about 2 per cent is it likely to produce a debilitating reaction. The prevalence in clinic populations is somewhat higher, though the rates vary with age and particular focus of phobia. Though particular phobias may differentially affect boys and girls, overall incidence does not seem to be noticeably different.

Onset and course

Some intense fears, such as those of animals and insects, occur very early – from about three years onwards. Others, such as 'social' phobias (as of groups), become evident in mid adolescence and grow beyond late adolescence into adulthood. With treatment, any of the phobias may be sorted out at any age.

Predisposing factors

Insofar as fearfulness may be related to anxiety, there may also be a genetic predisposition. More probably, fearful children come from distressed families, which are sometimes apparently whole on the surface. In general terms, being in a 'system' which either exposes to or fails to comfort children against fearful experiences is likely to predispose to this condition.

Complications

None specific, though phobias may be mixed with other personality and emotional disturbances, including psychoses.

Impairment

Depending on severity, potentially considerable. Fear of open spaces, meeting people, going to school or participating in group leisure activities are likely significantly to restrict a child's movement. The intense anxiety associated with possibility of encountering fearful situations is also likely to drain the child's energies from school and other learning environments and lead to a range of maladaptive avoidance behaviours.

Prompts

Are there reports of particular fears?
Were these regarded as unusual either in kind or degree?
How did the fear manifest itself?
Was child ever referred for help?
Are there any other members of family with intense fears?
Does child say she has strange fears?
Does she avoid certain things or places because she knows they will make her feel uneasy?
Is she abnormally afraid of the dark?
Can she think of anything that gives her the 'jitters'?
Is she unhappy about the fear? How does she explain it?
Does she try to cover it up? How?
How does she rate herself in relation to other children?
Does the child show signs of high anxiety in specific places, at certain times, or when in the presence of certain people or animals?
Is the avoidance or fear reaction obvious or subtle?
Does the reaction interfere with her normal life?
Do other children know of her fear?
Is she likely to suffer because of it?

Does she think she needs help?

Action
Depending on intensity, intervention is well warranted. In any case, good techniques exist for relatively uncomplicated and fruitful applications.

0610 Depression

01	Excessive and continual unhappiness
02	Lack of attention to others
03	Self deprecation and pity
04	Sleep or appetite disturbance
05	Preoccupation with self
06	Persistent lethargy and apathy
07	Weeping with little or no provocation
08	Guilt feelings
09	Suicidal ideas
10	Depression alternating with periods of exaggerated, elevated mood
11	Other

Description
This condition refers to a child's persistent, severe unhappiness and emotional disturbance for no less than two weeks, or a moderate form over a longer period.

Depression is defined clinically as an emotional state with retardation of psychomotor and thought processes, a flattened or apathetic emotional reaction, feelings of guilt, hopelessness and unworthiness. It can refer to a physiological mood state, a subjective feeling, a collection of clinical signs or a disease entity. To tell these apart and separate a deep and appropriately depressed reaction from a possible physiological, morbid change, requires high levels of clinical experience and is, even then, often difficult. The difficulties are exacerbated by the changing and different patterns of symptoms for boys and girls and at different developmental stages, with frequently atypical responses, marked by other difficulties. In certain circumstances, young people subject to severe and prolonged stress develop a mode of protective adaptation which might be regarded as 'existential' rather than clinical depression, sharing some of the above features but in a mild form.

Clinical depression should not be confused with the normally occurring state of being 'fed up', which is a transient and expected part of day-to-day living. A genuine clinical depression is an intense and almost palpable state that has a debilitating effect on the individual which, to all intents and purposes, isolates her from the mainstream of life. Clinical depressions, though they occur, are rare in very young children, but recent events, such as separation, bereavement, may induce a transitory or longer term depression which warrants management, care and attention. Risk of suicide in adolescent depression is significant.

Associated features
Where identifiable, these concern primarily recent experiences of loss or other serious adversity. Brain damage, epilepsy, anorexia, substance misuse and sleep disturbance may be present. More recently, abuse in home or school have been cited as associated factors and these warrant investigation. Attention deficit, headaches, bedwetting and conduct disorder are all possible correlates of depression in children. The child's personality profile before the depressive episode is likely to have been introverted and shy with a tendency to anxiety reactions.

Prevalence
Estimates in the general population range from about 1.4 per cent in very young children to about 4 per cent in adolescents, although the variation depends on who does the estimating. The prevalence of bipolar or 'manic-depressive' condition in adolescents is extremely rare. In clinic and institutional populations the prevalence of depression ranges from about 14 to over 30 per cent, depending on criteria for referral. Up to about age 11, prevalence for boys seems to be greater than for girls, but as they move into adolescence, so the rate for girls begin to outstrip that for boys until in late adolescence the ratio is 2+:1 in favour of girls.

Onset and course
Clinical depression requiring specialist help is extremely rare in early childhood but not unknown. It usually becomes evident around eight years and gradually becomes noticeable as the child fails to mix with others and shows other evidence of depression. The condition is usually exacerbated by change of school and the greater demands of reciprocal peer group and family relationships. Depending on whether depression is reactive to immediate experiences which can be relieved with treatment, early depressive reactions are likely to presage recurrence of more serious episodes in adulthood.

Predisposing factors
The status of genetic predisposition to this condition remains uncertain even though families where a biological relative is depressed are more likely to produce depressed children. But then so are those which are punitive, chaotic, harsh, abusive and emotionally cold. Loss of a parent, usually through death but also by break up, is also more likely to be associated with depression in adolescence and beyond, particularly in girls.

Complications
Sleep and eating disorders and substance misuse are likely to confuse the clinical picture. More importantly, however, serious or parasuicidal

attempts may result in institutional admission which is likely to create its own difficulties, including reactions to psychotropic medication or ECT which is rarely used with adolescents. Resort to anti-social behaviour is not very common but such behaviour may mask an atypical depressive picture. Difficulties of assessment are additionally encountered in determining the type of depression as well as potential for committing suicidal and other serious acts.

Impairment
Depending on severity, potentially catastrophic and life-threatening through suicide attempts. Less dramatically, anorexia, sleep disturbance and drug misuse may reduce the young person's ability or wish to respond to others and this will affect scholastic achievement and peer relationships.

Prompts
Have the parents or others commented on the child's depression? Have equivalent words been used to describe her?
Has she previously been referred to a GP, clinic or psychiatrist for any of the above behaviours?
Is parental worry and behaviour long standing or of recent origin?
Is the behaviour associated with any recent events? If so, what?
Has child's deterioration been slow or rapid?
Does child comment on her own mood?
Does she recognize it as unusual?
Does child go around with a hangdog expression?
Can she be induced to laugh or smile easily?
Does child seem sad and miserable? Does she seem so even when apparently unobserved?
Does child withdraw from company?
Are child's self-descriptions indicative of guilt or worthlessness?
Does child speak as if unable to alter her state on matters that adversely affect her?
Is she aware of the source of her misery?
Does child complain of loss of sleep? What is the pattern of waking?
Does child express feelings about her body being diseased or falling to pieces?
Has child committed acts of deliberate self-harm?
What? How long ago? How persistently? The same act or different ones?
How serious were these? Did they provoke specialist attention?
They were not manipulatory acts?
Is child's depression episodic or continuous?
Does it appear to be response to known adverse circumstances?
If so, of sufficient severity to warrant such a reaction?
If episodic, do depressions alternate with periods of 'normality' or exaggerated good cheer and expansiveness?
Are there any delusional or other psychotic features present? Does child show any insight into her condition?

Does she think she needs help? Does she think she will improve with help?

Action
If condition is serious enough to be noticed and lasts beyond two weeks or so, then it is likely to demand urgent intervention through a range of available ameliorative measures. Attention should also be paid to factors that may maintain the condition. Estimation of suicide risk and appropriate response is an urgent priority.

0611   View of self

01	Disagreement with others' view of self
02	Unrealistic
03	Inflated
04	Confused
05	Controlled by outside events
06	Negative or deviant
07	Other

Description
This condition refers to a child's negative or inappropriate self-concept.

Identity concerns the totality of individuals' thoughts, feelings and behavioural intentions about themselves, as well as their needs, fears, aspirations and expectations. It can best be construed as children's answers to such questions as 'Who am I?' or 'Who cares for me and whom do I care for?', 'What am I worth?', 'What is my place among the people I know?'

Quite obviously not many children (nor many adults for that matter) pose such explicit questions to themselves and try to answer them. But self-concept is thought to emerge from children's interactions with their human environment and will determine their perception of who they are, how much they are loved and cared for and, therefore, how much they are worth. Their attitudes to themselves will largely reflect those of others. This is the main reason why children who are unloved believe themselves to be unlovable and eventually turn out unable to love others.

All purposive behaviour has to be mediated by the self-concept. Such behaviour is likely to suffer and result in being at odds with the environment if the self-concept is negative or deviant. Although a child's 'ideal' self may be different from his 'actual' self, both must be sufficiently clear and 'realistic' to facilitate socially and personally satisfactory behaviour. Any of the above difficulties may be associated with a young person's confusion about his gender or sexuality as part of a wider disturbance of self-concept.

Associated features
May be associated with any adversity or negative condition in the physical, intellectual, educational, home and family, social relationships, anti-social behaviour and other clinical conditions. Self-concepts are inadequately formed or distorted in stressful, devaluing, abusive and insecure environments, particularly in the case of children who have been subject to long-term special intervention in justice, health, educational or social services settings. The brighter the young person, the more corrosive the effect of such adversity on the development of self-concept seems to be.

Prevalence
In the nature of the condition, it is not possible to have generally acceptable estimates of difficulties in this area. It is likely, however, that about 15 per cent of the 'normal' population of adolescents have more or less serious problems of self-concept. The prevalence in clinic and institutional populations may be as high as 60 per cent, showing the high interrelation of poor views of self with other disorders. There does not seem to be any difference between boys and girls in this disorder.

Onset and course
Ideas of self emerge only gradually from middle childhood onwards, becoming explicit in the more articulate youngsters in adolescence. Difficulties in this area are likely to take the same course, exacerbated by awakening sexuality and uncertainties about gender, sexual preferences and position in family and peer groups. In the case of chronically sick or educationally retarded, those from disordered families, with poor social relationships and conduct disorders, the gradual fusing of difficulties in self-concept accompany the course of the particular difficulties. Effect of distortions and difficulties in self-concept are cumulative and increasingly difficult to modify with age.

Predisposing factors
None specific; as set out in associated features.

Complications
None specific, apart from separating the 'cause and effect' order when other difficulties are present.

Impairment
Pervasive and considerable, depending on the negativeness or distortion of self-concept, as it underlies and mediates *everything* that a young person purposively undertakes.

Prompts
Are there any reports to the effect that the child seems to live in a fantasy world?
Is child's view of self particularly confused or negative?

What does she think of herself?

What does she say about her difficulties, her hopes, fears and aspirations?

How does she describe her ideal person in terms of personality characteristics, behaviour towards others, and pursuits?

What would she choose if allowed to have any three wishes?

How would she describe herself in relation to her idea?

Does she have difficulty in answering such questions as the above?

Is the difficulty more than expected for a child of her ability?

Are her accounts beyond anything that might be regarded as reasonably realistic?

Are they confused, contradictory and frequently changing?

Does she emerge from her statements as a purposive youngster, in control of what is happening to her, or at the mercy of events?

Does she see herself as inexorably progressing into more difficulty?

Does she express concern about the consequences?

Action

Just as negative views of self develop as a result of cumulative life experiences, so considerable positive engagement and empowerment of the young person is necessary to ameliorate the condition over a long period. Intervention is as urgent as it is difficult.

0612 Moral development

01	Inability to identify right and wrong
02	'Wrong' defined by probable punishment
03	Minimal concern for the impact of behaviour on others
04	Ignoring rules/obligations
05	Identifying with and emulating delinquent standards
06	Anti-authority attitudes and proclivities
07	No guilt or shame
08	Other

Description

This condition refers to inadequate or deviant moral development of the child.

Moral development refers to progressive changes in the degree and manner individuals are able to resist temptation to do what is pleasurable or profitable, even if regarded wrong. In this case, an 'immoral' person is one who fails to inhibit such impulses but pursues the immediate gratification of his desires. Morality may also refer to the control of one's behaviour by reference to 'internalized' standards, rather than the possible external consequences of the behaviour. Motives and intentions of the actor must be considered, because taking action solely on the basis of its consequences is not deemed 'moral', whereas actions taken because of moral prescriptions or prohibitions are. Finally, moral behaviour follows a 'moral decision', and the behaviour is carried out because it is considered to be 'the right thing to do'.

Moral development implies that the child has 'internalized' concepts of differences between right and wrong, and the degree to which he subscribes to dominant principles and rules. It also includes the child's ability to understand and observe the rights of others, the manner and the degree of resisting temptation, and how far actions correspond with verbal intentions. Clearly, moral development is a matter of degree, with children being more or less developed. Also, perhaps in more than most other areas covered in this book, judgments of this condition are likely to be subjective.

Associated features
Inadequate and deviant moral development may occur in children who abuse substances, with mental retardation, those from criminal and otherwise deviant and chaotic families, those with seriously disordered social relationships and others who engage in anti-social behaviour and show evidence of conduct disorder.

Prevalence
Not susceptible to accurate and useful estimation. In statistical terms, 15 per cent of young people would be expected to be morally immature or deviant. The prevalence in clinic populations is higher and those in institutions considerably more so. Boys seem to present more of this difficulty, perhaps as a result of more being identified for anti-social behaviour.

Onset and course
Moral development progresses through identifiable stages from middle childhood onwards. It is a cumulative process and, therefore, difficulties and deviances are likely to grow with age, continuing well beyond adolescence.

Predisposing factors
As for associated conditions, with particular emphasis on quality of family, parenting and social environment. In reality a society's moral standards are a patchwork quilt of quite different norms with some degree of consensus, reflected in the law. Social experience is the only medium for such development.

Complications
None other than mainly anti-social behaviour associated with inadequate and deviant moral development.

Impairment

Dependent on the extent and severity of correlated behaviour and public response to it. Such responses are likely to be more or less negative. The child is likely to be stigmatized in this regard, harshly treated and, therefore, develop further maladaptive responses.

Prompts

These are either direct or couched in situations with a 'moral' element which the child is asked to explain or interpret.

What would you do if you found £1 in the street?

Which is worse – someone who deliberately smashes a glass or one who accidentally drops a whole trayful of glasses? Why?

Which is worse – a father breaking a promise to his son, or the son breaking a promise to his father? Why?

Who are your favourite book or TV characters?

Do you try to copy them?

Can you put yourself in someone else's place and understand their point of view?

Do you ever think about your own behaviour? In what way?

Do you ever feel sorry for anyone else? If so, who and when?

Do you care if other people are very pleased or disappointed by your behaviour?

Do you ever think about the consequences of your behaviour? Why? How?

Do you think of other people's behaviour in terms of right and wrong?

What kinds of things do you think are right and what wrong? List five of each.

Do you have some rules of your own that you always stick to, no matter what happens? What are they?

Do you keep your word? Do you do what you say you will do?

What do you feel and do if you have done something wrong or harmed somebody?

Does the child usually admit to being wrong or acting badly?

Does he attempt to minimize the severity of his undesirable behaviour?

Does he usually blame someone or something else for his misdemeanours?

Does he ever spontaneously talk about 'right' and 'wrong'?

Can he put himself in someone else's shoes?

Does he ever comment on his own (mis)behaviour in moral terms?

Does he sympathize with or comment sympathetically upon another person's misfortune?

Does he appear to have any personal rules or principles?

Is he trustworthy?

Does he tell tales on other children?

How well can he resist temptation? Does this vary in different situations?

Does he express sorrow, remorse or guilt after doing something wrong?

Do these appear to be sincere or are they demanded by the circumstances?

Does he do anything to remedy whatever wrong he has done?

Action

Normal maturation may ameliorate the condition. The alternative is exceedingly laborious and costly work, with uncertain payoff.

Further reading

Agras, W.S. (1985) *Panic: Facing Fears, Phobias and Anxiety*, Oxford: W.H. Freeman.

Allen-Meares, P. and Shore, D.A. (eds) (1986) *Adolescent Sexualities*, New York: Haworth Press.

Apter, S.J. and Conoley, J.C. (1984) *Childhood Behaviour Disorders and Emotional Disturbance: Introduction to Teaching Troubled Children*, Englewood Cliffs: Prentice Hall.

Bannister, D. and Mair, J.M.M. (1968) *The Evaluation of Personal Constructs*, London: Academic Press.

Burns, R.B. (1979) *The Self Concept*, London: Longman.

Cantwell, D.P. and Carlson, G. (eds) (1983) *Affective Disorders in Childhood and Adolescence: an Update*, Lancaster: MTP.

Chiles, J. (1988) *Teenage Depression and Suicide: Encyclopaedia of Psychoactive Drugs*, New York: Chelsea House.

Cochrane, D.B. and Casimir, M. (eds) (1980) *Development of Moral Reasoning*, New York: Praeger.

Davison, G.C. and Neale, J.M. (1974, 1982, 1986) *Abnormal Psychology*, New York: John Wiley.

Duska, R. and Whelan, M. (1975) *Moral Development: Guide to Piaget and Kohlbert*, New York: Paulist Press.

Feldman, P. (1987) *Sex and Sexuality*, London: Longman.

Flapan, D. (1978) *Assessment of Early Child Development*, New York: Aronson.

French, A.P. and Berlin, I.N. (1980) *Depression in Children and Adolescents*, New York: Human Sciences Press.

Gelfand, D.M. and Peterson, L. (1985) *Child Development and Psychopathology*, Newbury Park, Calif.: Sage.

Gilbert, P. (1984) *Depression*, London: L. Erlbaum.

Graham, P. (1986) *Child Psychiatry – a Developmental Approach*, London: Oxford University Press.

Hare, R.D. (1970) *Psychopathy – Theory and Research*, New York: John Wiley.

Herbert, M. (1974) *Emotional Problems of Development in Children*, London: Academic Press.

Herbert, M. (1987) *Conduct Disorders of Childhood and Adolescence*, 2nd edn, Chichester: John Wiley.

Herbert, M. (1991) *Clinical Child Psychology*, Chichester: John Wiley.

Horne, A.M. and Sayger, T.V. (1990) *Treating Conduct and Oppositional Defiant Disorders in Children*, New York: Pergamon.

Howells, J.G. (1965) *Modern Perspectives in Adolescent Psychiatry*, Edinburgh: Oliver & Boyd.

Hunt, J.M. and Endler, S. (eds) (1985) *Personality and the Behavioural Disorders*, Vol. 1, Chichester: John Wiley.

Kazdin, A.E. (1987) *Conduct Disorders in Childhood and Adolescence*, Newbury Park, Calif.: Sage.

King, N.. (1988) *Children's Phobias: a Behavioural Perspective*, Chichester: John Wiley.

Klein, R.G. and Last, C.G. (1989) *Anxiety Disorders in Children*, Newbury Park, Calif: Sage.

Kroger, J. (1989) *Identity in Adolescence*, London: Routledge.

Lawson, R. (1965) *Frustration: Critical Issues in Psychology*, New York: Collier Macmillan.

Lickona, T. (ed) (1976) *Moral Development and Behavior*, New York: Holt, Rinehart & Winston.

Maas, J.W. (ed) (1987) *Affective Disorders*, Cambridge: Cambridge University Press.

McKnew, D.H. et al. (1985) *Why isn't Johnny Crying? Coping with Depression in Children*, New York: W.W. Norton.

Maier, N.R.F. (1982) *Frustration: The Study of Behaviour without a Goal*, London: Greenwood.

Marks, I.M. (1969) *Fears and Phobias*, London: Heinemann.

Marks, I.M. (1987) *Fears, Phobias and Rituals*, New York: Oxford University Press.

Matson, J.L. (1989) *Treating Depression in Children and Adolescents*, New York: Pergamon.

Medinnus, G. (1978) *Child and Adolescent Psychology: Behaviour and Development*, Chichester: John Wiley.

Millon, T. (1981) *Disorders of Personality: DSM-III – Axis II*, New York: John Wiley.

Mischel, W. (1968) *Personality and Assessment*, Chichester: John Wiley.

Mittler, P. (ed) (1970) *The Psychological Assessment of Mental and Physical Handicap*, London: Methuen.

Montgomery, S.A. et al. (1990) *Obsessive Compulsive Disorder*, Southampton: Duphar Medical.

Morris, R.J. and Kratchowill, T.R. (1982) *Treating Children's Fears and Phobias: a Behavioural Approach*, Oxford: Pergamon.

Nunnally, E.W., Chilman, C.S. and Cox, F.M. (1988) *Mental Illness, Delinquency, Addictions and Neglect*, Newbury Park, Calif.: Sage.

O'Byrne, S. (1976) *Moral Development and Logical Reasoning of Adolescents: a Experimental Research Study with Adolescent Girls comparing Different Techniques*, Dublin: Frederick Press.

Oldham, J.M. (ed) (1990) *Personality Disorders: New Perspectives on Diagnostic Validity*, Washington: American Psychiatric Association.

Open University (1985) *Personality, Development and Learning – Units 15–16: Personality and Change: the Self Concept*, Milton Keynes: Open University Press.

Oster, G.D. and Caro, J.E. (1990) *Understanding and Treating Depressed Adolescents and their Families*, New York: John Wiley.

Page, J.D. (1971) *Psychopathology*, Chicago: Aldine Atherton.

Patros, P.G. and Shamoo, T.K. (1989) *Depression and Suicide in Children and Adolescents: Prevention, Intervention and Postvention*, Boston: Allyn & Bacon.

Paykel, E.S. (1982) *Handbook of Affective Disorders*, London: Churchill Livingstone.

Pope, A.W., McHale, S.M. and Craighead, W.E. (1988) *Self-Esteem Enhancement with Children and Adolescents*, New York: Pergamon.

Poppen, R. (1988) *Behavioral Relaxation Training and Assessment*, New York: Pergamon.

Purkey, W.W. (1986) *Self Concept and School Achievement*, Englewood Cliffs, NJ: Prentice Hall.

Rachman, S. (1974) *The Meanings of Fear*, Harmondsworth: Penguin.

Rest, J.R. (1986) *Moral Development: Advances in Theory and Research*, New York: Praeger.

Rosenberg, M. and Kaplan, H.B. (eds) (1982) *Social Psychology of the Self Concept*, New York: H. Davidson.

Roy, A. (1982) *Hysteria*, Chichester: John Wiley.

Russell, G.F.M. and Hersov, L.A. (eds) (1984) *Handbook of Psychiatry, vol. 4, Neuroses and Personality Disorders*, Cambridge: Cambridge UP.

Sarason, S.B. et al. (1978) *Anxiety in Elementary School Children: a Report of Research*, London: Greenwood Press.

Saul, L.J. (1979) *Childhood Emotional Pattern: Key to Personality, its Disorders and Therapy*, New York: Van Nostrand Reinhold.

Schlebusch, L. (1979) *Conduct Disorders in Youth*, Johannesburg: Butterworth.

Seifert, K. and Hofnung, R. (1987) *Child and Adolescent Development* Boston, Mass.: Houghton Mifflin.

Shamoo, T.K. and Patros, P.G. (1990) *I Want to Kill Myself: Parent's Guide to Understanding Depression and Suicide in Children*, Lexington, Mass.: Lexington Books.

Sigman, M. (ed) (1985) *Children with Emotional Disorders and Developmental Disabilities*, New York: Grune & Stratton.

Slavney, P.R. (1990) *Perspectives on Hysteria*, Baltimore: Johns Hopkins University Press.

Sperling, M. (1978, 1982) *Major Neuroses and Behavior Disorders in Children*, New York: Aronson.

Stewart, A. and Friedman, S. (1987) *Child Development: Infancy through Adolescence*, New York: John Wiley.

Tickel, A.U. and Allen, L. (1987) *Preventing Maladjustment from Infancy through Adolescence*, Newbury Park, Calif.: Sage.

Turkat, I.D. (1990) *Personality Disorders: a Psychological Approach to Clinical Management*, New York: Pergamon.

Varma, V.P. (ed) (1984) *Anxiety in Children*, London: Croom Helm.

Williams, J.M.G. et al. (1988) *Cognitive Psychology and Emotional Disorders*, Chichester: John Wiley.

Wright, D. (1971) *The Psychology of Moral Behaviour*, Harmondsworth: Penguin Books.

Appendix 1
Child and Adolescent Problem Profile

The Child and Adolescent Problem Profile (CAPP) sets out in summary form the assessment of a child or adolescent's problems. Of the six problem areas only anti-social behaviour and psychological problems are reproduced here. They give some idea of the comprehensiveness of problem profile and its ease in use.

Name	
D.o.B.	
Age	
Ref No.	

CAPP
Child & Adolescent Problem Profile

Instructions

1. The Child and Adolescent Problem Profile (CAPP) is completed when adequate relevant information about the child is available. Alternatively, it may be used as a preliminary checklist of possible problems to be evaluated.

2. The problem areas correspond to those expounded in Assessing Child and Adolescent Disorders: a practice manual by Hoghughi (Sage, London 1992). The definitions of the attributes and major features of each condition and prompts for assessment are provided in that book.

3. The major attributes in each of the six problem areas are presented in columns. Other attributes may be added according to the specialist requirements of particular client groups.

4. The presence of each condition in a child is indicated with a tick in the "Presence" column. The severity of each problem is indicated in the "Severity" column on a scale 1-3, with 1 denoting *"mild"*, 2 *"moderate"* and 3 *"severe"* conditions.

5. Space is allowed to highlight notable features of problem areas and particular strengths. Further space is provided for recording priorities for action which will be based on the judgement of need for treatment.

6. A 'Profile' may be drawn of the number and severity of the child's problems in the space provided opposite, by adding number and ratings of problems in each area.

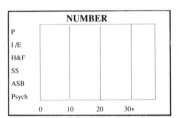

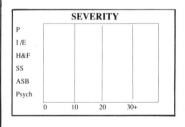

05 Anti-social Behaviour

	pres.	sev.

0501 Disruptiveness
01 Stirring up trouble
02 Making allegations
03 Temper tantrums
04 Disturbing others
05 Making odd/inappropriate noises
06 Other

0502 Response to Control
01 Defying adults
02 Testing out limits
03 Forcing confrontation
04 Unreasonably seeking attention
05 Demanding counselling/medication/services for no good reason
06 Provoking frequent conflicts
07 Wearing out adults
08 Other

0503 Truancy
01 School refusal
02 Not attending school - persistent
03 Not attending school - occasionally
04 Other

0504 Running Away
01 Running away from adults
02 Planning and executing attacks on property to escape
03 Hanging around doors and attempting to run out
04 Encouraging others to run away
05 Running away from home and other placements
06 Other

0505 Deliberate Self Harm (DSH)
01 Serious attempted suicide
02 Taking overdoses or poisons
03 Inflicting wounds on self
04 Attempting to obtain harmful materials
05 Tattoos
06 Other

0506 Verbal Aggression
01 Criticising
02 Antagonising
03 Threatening
04 Swearing
05 Gesturing/snarling
06 Screaming abuse
07 Other

0507 Physical Aggression
01 Nipping/biting
02 Hitting/punching/kicking/head butting
03 Using objects to hurt
04 Bullying
05 Injuring others deliberately
06 Violence to animals
07 Other

0508 Sexual Disorder
01 Cross dressing
02 Fetishism
03 Exhibitionism/public masturbation
04 Homosexuality under age
05 Interest in little children
06 Sex with hurting or being hurt
07 Attempting non-consenting sexual activity
08 Soliciting
09 Unusual interest in pornography
10 Other

	pres.	sev.

0509 Sexual Offences
01 Indecent exposure
02 Indecent assault
03 Buggery
04 Unlawful sexual intercourse
05 Attempted rape
06 Rape
07 Other

0510 Property Offences
01 Aiding and abetting
02 Theft
03 Taking and driving without owner's consent
04 Burglary
05 Robbery
06 Robbery with violence
07 Destroying/ damaging property
08 Other

0511 Fire Setting
01 Lighting fires
02 Setting fires to destroy
03 Preoccupation with fire and fire setting materials
04 Other

0512 Offences against Person
01 Aggravated robbery
02 Bodily harm, actual or grievous
03 Attempted murder
04 Manslaughter or murder
05 Other

0513 Attitude to Anti-social Acts
01 Denial
02 Distortion of reasons or acts
03 Projection of blame
04 Lacking or poor insight
05 Boasting or uncaring
06 Other

Notes

06 Psychological Problems

	pres.	sev.

0601 Maturity
01 Preferring company of younger children
02 Emotional reactions inappropriate for age
03 Social reactions inappropriate for age
04 Engaging in behaviour appropriate to a younger child
05 Engaging in behaviour appropriate to an older child
06 Other

0602 Self-Centredness
01 Interest primarily in self
02 Using others for own ends
03 Seeking to achieve personal superiority
04 Greediness, over demanding
05 Enviousness
06 Not helping others
07 Indifference to others' feelings
08 Other

0603 Frustration Tolerance
01 Lacking patience
02 Inability to tolerate delay of gratification
03 Showing tantrums/aggression if not getting own way
04 Easy to disappoint
05 Giving up on tasks easily
06 Other

0604 Impulse Control
01 Acting without apparent thought, volition or deliberation
02 Not trying to control self
03 Bored easily
04 Poor resistance to temptation
05 Other

0605 Conduct Disorders
01 High level self-centredness
02 Emotional coldness
03 Lacking feeling for others
04 Calculating and manipulatory behaviour
05 Callousness and cruelty
06 Little or no remorse or guilt
07 Not learning from past trouble
08 Abnormal search for excitement and variety
09 Difficulty in delaying gratification
10 Lacking inhibition
11 Becoming hostile easily
12 Cheating/ lying
13 Viewing others as enemies or objects to be used
14 Other

0606 Emotional Response
01 Crying/laughing easily
02 Getting over-excited inappropriately
03 Sulkiness, petulance
04 Over-reacting to stress
05 Pronounced mood swings
06 Bland, or rare emotional expressions
07 Superficial or shallow emotions
08 Other

0607 Anxiety
01 Tension or inability to relax
02 Restlessness
03 Overactivity
04 Apprehensiveness
05 Indecisiveness
06 Needing constant reassurance
07 Irritability, jumpiness
08 Tics and tremors
09 Feelings of impending disaster
10 Sleep disturbance
11 Palpitations or pallor
12 Excessive perspiration
13 Nausea or other bodily discomfort/pain
14 Constipation or bedwetting
15 Apparent imperviousness to stress
16 Other

	pres.	sev.

0608 Anxiety Related Disorders
Hypochondriasis
01 Exaggerated concern with physical and/
   or mental health
02 Frequent complaining of minor ailments
03 Frequent demands for medical attention
'Hysteria'
01 Loss or disorder of sensory or motor functions
02 Loss of voice
03 Sleepwalking
04 Loss of memory
Obsessive-compulsive disorder
01 Rigid conformist and orderly behaviour
02 Intolerance or inflexibility
03 Doing the same things over and over again
04 Complaining of persistent, irrational thoughts, impulses
   and actions
05 Other

0609 Phobic Reaction
01 Abnormal fear of animals and insects
02 Of situations
03 Of persons
04 Of places
05 Of objects
06 Of injury
07 Other

0610 Depression
01 Excessive and continual unhappiness
02 Lack of attention to others
03 Self deprecation and pity
04 Sleep or appetite disturbance
05 Preoccupation with self
06 Persistent lethargy and apathy
07 Weeping with little or no provocation
08 Guilt feelings
09 Suicidal ideas
10 Depression alternating with periods of exaggerated,
   elevated mood
11 Other

0611 View of Self
01 Disagreement with others view of self
02 Unrealistic
03 Inflated
04 Confused
05 Controlled by outside events
06 Negative or deviant
07 Other

0612 Moral Development
01 Inability to identify right and wrong
02 'Wrong' defined by probable punishment
03 Minimal concern for the impact of behaviour on others
04 Ignorings rules/obligations
05 Identifying with and emulating delinquent standards
06 Anti-authority attitudes and proclivities
07 No guilt or shame
08 Other

Notes

Appendix 2

An Assessment Report

This appendix shows the application of the problem profile approach in the assessment of an actual young person's condition. The format of the report is the latest version used at Aycliffe. Only the anti-social behaviour section is reproduced in some detail to indicate how complex, comprehensive and yet easily digestible the information is. The concluding section (pp. 38–40) also shows that the whole purpose of assessment is to provide a rational and publicly accountable basis for deciding what should be done about a young person's problems.

Patron: HRH The Duke of York

Aycliffe

Centre for Children

Director: Dr MASUD S. HOGHUGHI

Copelaw,
Newton Aycliffe,
Co. Durham,
DL5 6JB.

Telephone: Aycliffe (0325) 300101
Fax 300101 ext 256

CONFIDENTIAL

REPORT ON	:	**Jane E.**
DATE OF BIRTH	:	16.1.74
NAMES AND ADDRESSES OF PARENTS OR PEOPLE RESPONSIBLE	:	Mr. & Mrs. M. E.
RESPONSIBLE AUTHORITY	:	G. COUNTY COUNCIL
SOCIAL WORKER	:	Miss H. A.
ADDRESS	:	
TELEPHONE	:	
ADMITTED TO AYCLIFFE ON	:	22.10.90
ADMISSION NUMBER	:	
BASIS FOR ADMISSION	:	

ABSTRACT

Jane was admitted to the secure facilities at Aycliffe, following an act of criminal damage to the value of £2,000, during which, it is alleged, she presented a danger to both herself and others.

Jane is fostered and is in care on a voluntary basis. She has been involved in intense substance misuse and deliberate self-harm and she continues to threaten that she will kill herself.

She has received regular psychiatric and psychological oversight and is currently undergoing cognitive therapy. She presents as a depressive character.

It is alleged by Jane that she was subjected to a sexual assault by a stranger some three years ago.

1

Date of last routine medical examination: October 1990

Result: G. General Hospital contacted for details of Jane's
          hospital admissions there. No reply has yet been received.

Current physical state: Satisfactory, although limping slightly from an
                          injury sustained to her left foot on 1.12.90.

Height: 5'6"   Weight: 109lbs

Comment: 75th Centile for height, but just beneath 25th for weight, for her
          age.

Medication at present: Beconase nasal spray and Fibogel in sachets
                         once daily.

Treatment in course: Bulking agent for constipation and nasal spray for
                         blocked nose, night and morning with effect.

Treatment/Investigations planned: Bulking agent to be discontinued and
                                     replaced by a high fibre diet.

Outstanding Medical appointments:

Record of examinations & findings, following restraints, absconds, etc:-

Date	Reason for Examination	Clinical Findings
23.10.90	Fight with another child.	No injuries identified.

Record of illness & notes on other injuries and medical examinations:-

30.10.90   Self-inflicted laceration to left wrist upper aspect and to
             right shoulder. Neither required treatment.

6.11.90   Dental check up and filling applied to complete treatment.

15.11.90   Numerous self-inflicted superficial cuts to left forearm.

19.11.90   Jane lost her filling and another dental appointment was
             arranged for 21.11.90, when this was replaced by a temporary
             filling. All treatment eventually completed by 3.12.90.

1.12.90   Jane landed awkwardly during an activities session,
             sustaining injury to the base of her left foot.

3

PHYSICAL

HISTORY	CURRENT STATE

Birth Circumstances

Jane was born at Moorfield
General Hospital, G.,
following a normal delivery.
Her birth weight was 7lbs. 4ozs.

Developmental Milestones

Whilst at ------ Nursery,
episodes of rocking and head
banging were reported. These
behaviours gradually diminished and
no further problems were recorded.
She was described as quick to walk
and talk. Child developmental
records indicate that Jane
achieved other milestones
within normal limits.

Physical Condition

It is reported in a letter,
dated 25.4.90, from Dr. -
Consultant in Child and
Adolescent Psychiatry to the
family's G.P. that Jane had
been rather small in comparison
to her class peers.

(Current State)

Jane appears gaunt in appearance,
and tall and thin. She maintains an
acceptable standard of personal
hygiene.

Upon admission, she presented with
numerous self-inflicted scars to her
hands, arms and shoulder. She display
no tattoos.

Pervasive Developmental Disorders

There is no evidence of behaviour
normally associated with such
disorders.

(Current State) No evidence.

Psychoses

Although there is no evidence to
suggest behaviours normally
associated with psychoses, it
is reported by Dr. A. M.,
Principal Clinical Psychologist,
that whilst a patient in the secure
ward at -------- Hospital,
Jane began to mimic other
severely disturbed patients.

(Current State) No evidence.

4

COGNITIVE

History of Schooling

1979 - 84	Kirklam Primary School
1984 - 86	St. John Middle School
1986 - 88	Crown School, G.
Jan 89 - Nov 89	----- School, G.
Nov 89 - March 90	O. Hospital) Home and Hospital
May 90 - June 90	Ashwell House F.G.H.) Teaching Service

STORY   CURRENT STATE

sic Personal Knowledge

evidence of difficulties.

ital Retardation

ere is no evidence to indicate
ital retardation. Recent formal
sting based on WISC-R scores
licates that Jane was
erating within the high average range
ability. It is suggested that at the
ne of testing, Jane had been on
ne anti-depressant medication which
y have affected her overall perfor-
ice.

- High School reports indicate
it Jane achieved average G.C.S.E.
ainments.

ention Deficit / Hyperactivity

-- School reported that Jane's
ention and concentration gradually
lined. She had a tendency to
dream which, at times, developed
o vacant glazed expressions which
e reportedly attributed to her
blems outside the school setting.

is stated in an educational report
mitted by --- Assessment Centre
it Jane was easily distracted from
sks and worked well for short
iods only. She was also easily led
o following any silly behaviour
ibited by other pupils.

9

HOME AND FAMILY

Changes in Home Setting

Birth - Feb 75	Maternal grandparents' home.
Feb 75 - May 75	Foster placement.
May 75 - Dec 75	------- Nursery.
Dec 75 - 1979	Foster parents Mr. & Mrs. E.
1979 -	Current Address ------

Family List

Father	A. E.	51	Solicitor
Mother	T. E.	49	Part-time Nurse.
Brother	C. E.	20	Casual employment.
Sister	N. E.	19	Shop Assistant Living in ------.
Subject	Jane E.	16	

HISTORY	CURRENT STATE

Home Base

A constant home base has been provided for Jane since her fostering by Mr. and Mrs. E.

Environment

The family home for the past eleven years has been a converted farmhouse situated in a commuter village on the outskirts of G.

The immediate neighbourhood consists of a mixed, predominantly, white population.

Status in Locality

According to the local authority social worker, Mr. and Mrs. E. impress as a professional, middle class, respectable and conventional couple. They are both respected members of the local community where Mrs. E. plays an active role in the local Church. Mr. E. attends church but is not an office bearer.

Material Condition

There is no evidence of problems associated with material or physical deprivation within the home.

SOCIAL SKILLS

History of Residential Placements

May 1990   Ample House
June - Sept 90   Malling Assessment Centre
24-27 Sept 90   O. Secure Unit, M., B.

HISTORY	CURRENT STATE
Self-presentation	
A decline in Jane's general appearance was noted whilst at ----- School when she arrived at school, having slept out overnight.	Jane's haunted look, coupled with her self-inflicted scarring makes her overall appearance rather awesome to others. She is cleanly presented though she wears ill-fitting garments. Her eating habits are of an acceptable standard. She adopts a stooped posture on occasions.
Basic Interaction Skills	
No information.	Jane has a blank stare. She tends to avert her gaze whenever eye contact is made.
Conversation Skills	
No information.	Jane does not initiate conversation, and tends to join in others' discussions. Once entrenched however, she is articulate and can offer a clear account of herself and her life.
Assertiveness	
It is stated in a psychological report that her attempts at increasing her assertiveness and expressions of feelings whilst at O. Hospital often resulted in Jane "falling foul of the ward staff and being put in seclusion".	Jane does not freely express her opinions and emotions. She tends to adopt submissive gestures, such as shrugging of her shoulders, or appears embarrassed when she has been criticised or teased by her peers.
Sensitivity	
No information.	Jane is good at judging other people and responds appropriately to given social situations.

Child's Views

Jane notices nothing odd about her self-presentation. She is uncomfortable in unfamiliar company and "never knows what to say". When asked about friends she claimed she had two different types. Some of her friends, she felt, were not so respectable, and she, therefore, did not allow them to call for her. Those whom she felt were more acceptable and "boring", she invited into her home. She claims that her parents disliked her choice of some of her friends and she was, therefore, careful not to upset them (in any way) by inviting them in.

She tends not to trust adults and states she feels uneasy in their presence. She is polite and nothing more. Jane dislikes some male figures and prefers female adults or older men.

Jane spoke warmly of one particular male pensioner, who had befriended her in the past. The man tended to sit and talk with her in a local pub, and Jane often confided and discussed problems with him.

When questioned about her social assets, Jane claimed she is very tolerant of other children and usually sympathetic towards those who are "worse off" than herself.

Jane admits to feeling uncomfortable with boys. She has been involved in several social activities in the past, though most have been church related. These include choir singing and the Brownies. Jane admits she has no long-standing leisure pursuits and easily becomes bored.

ANTI-SOCIAL BEHAVIOUR

HISTORY	CURRENT STATE
Disruptiveness	
Occasional disturbances were noted whilst at --- Assessment Centre which took the form of running around the premises, climbing roofs and breaking windows. One particular occasion warranted police intervention and she was subsequently charged with a Breach of the Peace. She is said to have unreasonably sought attention on occasions and attempted to "wind up" staff by hiding.	Jane generally keeps herself to herself and stays well clear of any troublesome antics exhibited by others.
Within the school setting, Jane reportedly engaged in "silly" behaviour with other pupils. According to her parents, Jane was "naughty" whilst at --- School, and had a tendency to shout at teachers or "going into a class when she should not be there".	

HISTORY	CURRENT STATE
impulsive in nature and which have not been dealt with by the police. There is one brief reference to an incident which occurred at G. Hospital when Jane set fire to her sheets, after an adult male patient climbed into Jane's bed with another woman who had initially approached Jane. The other incident occurred during an episode of petrol sniffing with another girl in a garage, when Jane had attempted to burn off some spillage and her friend's dress had caught fire as a result. During a subsequent interview, the girl suggested that Jane had said "bye bye" just before it happened. There is yet another report which would question her intent to cause a fire. When asked why she was building a model of her local parish church for her mother on one occasion, it is reported by Dr. A. M., Clinical Psychologist, that Jane replied, "so she'll have something to remember when I burn it down".	

Special Comments

It is alleged by Jane that she was subjected to a sexual assault involving some force by a stranger in the local community just after her thirteenth birthday. She also reported that she inflicted a wound to her shoulder following the assault. Jane made the disclosure in early 1990, after which a number of "counselling sessions" were conducted.

Child's Views

At interview, Jane claimed she engaged in troublesome behaviour as a means of drawing attention to herself. She states she was only "difficult" with those teachers whom she felt were picking on her at the time. She punched the head teacher only after she herself was subjected to a physical attack.

She states she ran away because she enjoyed the freedom to be able to acquire drink and other substances when she chose to.

With regard to her self-harm, Jane claims she has felt suicidal on occasions when she "did not care" about anything or anyone. She claims the last occasion she felt desperate enough to kill herself was approximately two months ago when she cut herself with a razor blade. During her period of assessment, Jane claims she is encouraged to harm herself, by peers, and for fear of "losing face" she occasionally makes remarks to the effect that she would like to kill herself. On the two occasions she has superficially cut herself, she had been reminded indirectly of the sexual assault she alleges she was subjected to. Jane wanted to really harm herself on these occasions but the objects she had used were not entirely effective.

Jane finds it very difficult and painful to discuss her previous sexual experiences. She talks about "this man" who did "things" to her. Whilst in London, she states she had no choice but to "do things" with men in order to survive and keep her job in a bar. She related several occasions when female patients had attempted to "get into bed" with her and she expressed her fear at the time.

Jane denies any pre-occupation with fire in general. She set fire to her sheets out of sheer desperation with a match she "found" on the floor. At the time, she wanted to "escape" and did not fully realise the possible consequences of her actions. Again, Jane admitted she "did not think" when she lit a match in the garage. She wishes now that she had "gone up in flames" rather than her friend. With regard to her intent to burn the church down, she claims she made the threat purely in jest.

Jane will not or cannot discuss her most recent offence, but simply states she is unable to remember the evening in question. Further examination of the events surrounding the offence has not been conducted in view of the fact that the case is sub judice.

PSYCHOLOGICAL CONDITION

HISTORY	CURRENT STATE
Maturity	
There is no evidence of difficulties.	Jane's behaviour and attitudes are generally commensurate with her chronological age. She behaves independently without constant adult supervision. She appears embarrassed on occasions, however, when praised by staff.
Self Centredness	
No evidence.	There is no evidence of ego-centricity. She is helpful, not greedy and offers assistance when she sees others struggling. She accommodates others in her actions.
Frustration Tolerance	
When thwarted in her attempts to run away from --- Assessment Centre, on occasions, she has been described as agitated and uncontrollable. On one occasion, she was reportedly in	In terms of material gratification, Jane does not lack patience nor is she easily disappointed. She can methodically follow a task through until completed to a high standard.

Psychological Report

Jane was admitted to Aycliffe on 27th September 1990, following increasing
behaviour problems and self-inflicted injuries and solvent misuse. She was interviewed by the psychologist during November 1990.

Jane is of above average ability. Her verbal skills are especially well developed
even though this may not be evident in conversation, because of her general
reticence. Her ability in practical areas is also above average, the only weakness
being areas requiring especially good conversation.

Jane is fairly competent at the three basic attainments. Her reading skills are
above average for her age, though spelling is slightly less than average. At
number work she experiences no significant problems in any of the basic processes
and understands fractions and decimals.

Although Jane is now sixteen years of age, she has thought little about her future
career. She is interested in landscape gardening, and is especially interested in
vehicles of all types, and would like to consider work in this area.

Jane briefly discussed her family, an area covered in depth elsewhere. She stated
that she would hope to return home to live, adding, "they want me home".

Jane is a rather solitary individual who finds it difficult to form meaningful
relationships with peers. She is rather reticent and guarded in discussion and has
an introspective outlook upon life.

Jane's behaviour problems are long-standing in origin and latterly have
increasingly featured aggression directed inward towards herself, in the form of
self-injury, mainly cutting her arms. This appears to have proved a very
successful attention seeking ploy, at least as far as Jane herself is concerned.
Eventually Jane was admitted to a psychiatric hospital ward where the attention
seeking took the form of setting fire to sheets in the hospital. Other anti-social
behaviours appear to have had the function of attention seeking. Jane has
increasingly sniffed solvents and gas, and has even drunk petrol. She has posed a
great danger to herself in terms of even her survival. Jane is self-centred
insofar as she often acts impulsively, following her own urges, and not stopping to
consider the effects of her actions on other people. Her behavioural responses
have been learned over a long period of time, and have now become habitual in
nature.

An in-depth personality evaluation using specialised psychometric tests was carried
out, given the nature of Jane's problems. A personality screening test
suggested that Jane is introverted in nature, generally preferring a quiet
routine and her own company to that of peers. She appears to have the emotional
capacity to consider the needs and feelings of others, although in terms of actual
responses this is not always apparent, since Jane presents as an emotionally
shallow individual. The problem area would appear to be one of not communicating
feelings, rather than actually not having the feelings. Jane's anxiety level
appears to be above average, and she admits to worrying about things. An
evaluation of feelings of hostility was carried out, and the results indicate that
Jane has quite strong feelings of hostility, and that these are mainly directed
inwards. Thus, Jane is very self-critical and has a poor "self-image"; she
experiences strong feelings of guilt for past life events; and she feels that other
people are constantly "getting at" her. She is not generally critical towards
other people nor hostile towards them, in general terms. Looking back at her life,
Jane feels that it has been "horrible", but she has no idea about how to resolve
things in the future. Indeed, Jane has a depressive outlook upon life, which it
was decided to evaluate in more detail. Components of hostility were also

examined, and these include strong feelings of resentment, suspicion and
irritability.

On a psychometric test specifically designed to measure levels of depression in
children, Jane scored at extremely high levels, indicating a very high level of
depression, and a low capacity to experience pleasure. This objective measure
confirms more subjective conclusions, and the high level of depressive feelings
indicates that, in treatment terms, Jane's depression should be viewed as a
central personality trait.

In treatment terms, Jane needs a specially designed individual programme with
intensive, ideally daily input, using ingredients such as positive feedback, life
plan construction, target goals and dates, experiencing success in specific chosen
areas, cognitive behaviour change, and stability of place and person. Jane
needs to set goals and feel that she is reaching them. Beyond her treatment
placement, she needs to feel "wanted" and part of a family. These are her primary
life needs; beyond this are secondary needs, all part of her life plan, including
her future career at work, leisure interests, relationships, and fulfilment of
goals. Behaviour 'shaping' could be a useful technique in achieving some of these
goals. Psychiatric oversight is also recommended.

Psychiatric Report

I saw Jane in Royston on 15th November. The interview was conducted 'blind' as
the notes were not immediately to hand. I was subsequently able to peruse the
notes containing the background information and history of previous psychiatric and
other professional input. For the sake of brevity I will refer to the background
information only where relevant.

Jane was admitted on 27th September 1990, under Section 21a. She told me she is
facing a charge of criminal damage but was unable to give me further details
regarding the charges though she gave me the impression that she might consider
pleading guilty. Jane claims that when she was approximately aged 13, on her way
home in the evening, she was grabbed by a man who raped her. She did not
immediately report the incident to anyone and has only disclosed it to
professionals, and her parents, in recent times. Jane is unsure whether she is
believed, particularly by her parents. At about the same time, Jane began to get
into severe behavioural difficulties which manifested within as well as outside the
home. She recalls that she was often in trouble at school for getting drunk: she
also began to truant and abscond from home, and started experimenting with drugs.
She claims that she smoked marijuana on numerous occasions and took magic mushrooms
and LSD. During this phase she also started sniffing gas and petrol. Some of the
drug abuse was in the company of her peer group but quite often when she was alone.
She claimed that she enjoyed it and found the illusions particularly thrilling.
She has occasional flashbacks in which she often sees a man dressed in a woman's
clothes.

Given the severity of her behavioural problems, Jane's family were unable to cope
with her. This led to her admission to a children's home, and the local
psychiatric facility, for almost a year: six months this time was spent in a secure
unit. She was prescribed psychotropic medication and, for a while at least, it
seemed to control her level of anxiety and feelings of unhappiness. The medication
was discontinued.

In April/May 1990, Jane, yet again, returned to live with her family but felt
unable to cope. Re-admission to a children's home did not work as Jane started
absconding again, and experimenting with drugs. She has had a couple of admissions
to the Intensive Care Unit as she collapsed after sniffing a massive amount of gas
and/or petrol. The most recent crisis which led to her admission is said to be due

to Jane having sniffed petrol and provoking others to do the same. I gather she spilled a considerable amount of petrol in the unit leading to concern about the physical safety of other children, and the building itself. The charges of criminal damage are possibly connected with this incident.

Jane is a tall, attractive girl, who was not particularly anxious or depressed and was fairly forthcoming. She implied that most of her difficulties were subsequent to the episode of her abuse; a trauma which she initially failed to, or was unable to, share with anyone. She claims that she feels generally sad and unhappy and wonders where she will end up. The suicidal thoughts she has are in response to her sense of frustration and are rarely persistent. She misses her family but, above all, her liberty as in the last few years she has found instant gratification is the only thing that satisfies her, albeit temporarily. My attempts to judge her feelings towards her parents and family was not particularly successful though I got the impression that there is some degree of repressed anger towards her parents and a desire to project blame on to them.

The social background needs further clarification which might benefit Jane.

My initial interview raises more questions than it answers. During the assessment period we need to clarify and obtain more details regarding developmental factors, learn more about the strength of the bond she developed with her parents and siblings, and perhaps question the accuracy of the suggestion that Jane was no bother at all prior to the age of 12 or 13. On the basis of one interview, I am not persuaded to see Jane as a clinically depressed girl who will respond to psychotropic medication, although there is no doubt she feels sad and unhappy.

Personal History

27.10.74.	Jane was born at Moorfields General Hospital, G. Initially cared for by her mother at her parents' home.
Jan 1975	Mother "disappeared" leaving Jane in her parents' care.
20.2.75.	Jane placed in a short term foster home.
2.5.75.	Jane transferred to --- Nursery.
13.12.75.	Placed with her current foster parents, Mr. and Mrs. E., at ---
Sept 1979	Began formal education at Primary School, G.
Sept 1984	Transferred to --- School.
1986	Transferred to Crown School, G.
Mar 1986	Foster mother's mother died of cancer at the age of 83.
June 1987	Foster father's father died of old age at the age of 94.
19.1.89.	Transferred to --- School.
Nov 1987	It is alleged by Jane that she was sexually assaulted by a stranger in the local community. She reportedly inflicted a wound to her shoulder on the same day but did not reveal the facts until 1990.

11.9.90.   Absconded and apprehended by police after stealing cigarettes from a newsagent. Absconded again with two other residents.

12.9.90.   Apprehended in Gloucester.

13.9.90.   Received treatment at Casualty Department following substance misuse.

14.9.90.   Absconded, claiming she was going to London. Apprehended by a member of staff. Returned of her own accord. Interviewed by police and absconded again later.

20.9.90.   Jane absconded with another resident and returned later intoxicated with petrol and with their clothes saturated in petrol. Both girls splashed a large quantity of petrol onto the walking link between the old and more recent parts of the premises. As a result of fire risk, the Fire Brigade was summoned and Jane and the other resident were transported to --- District Hospital. It is understood that the ambulance men questioned whether Jane's heart had stopped beating and she reportedly had convulsions after her admission.

24.9.90.   Jane charged with criminal damage (£2,000) and returned to --- Secure Unit, ---, ---.

27.9.90.   Admitted to Aycliffe, Centre for Children, under conditions of security.

8.11.90.   **--- JUVENILE COURT**
Charged with criminal damage and case adjourned.
21a Secure Accommodation Authority was granted for three months.

CONCLUSIONS

Summary of Condition

1.   **Physical**

Despite a history of quite serious substance misuse, Jane is currently a fit and healthy girl. She is, however, lean and underweight for her age.

2.   **Intellectual/Educational**

Jane is a girl of probably high to above average intelligence. However, she does not seem to have operated up to this level for some time. Despite a number of changes of schools, her educational attainments are satisfactory.

3.   **Home and Family**

On the basis of the information available, there does not seem to be any major problems in the home and family. However, the information available is highly superficial and unenlightening. Given both Jane and her sister's difficulties, the conclusion must be that there have been stresses and turbulences in the family over a long period. Jane is a fostered girl and is aware of this status. The whereabouts of her family of birth and condition do not seem to have been talked through with her with a view to resolving her conflicts of identity. Although foster parents remain intensely

---

interested in Jane and express affection for her, it is uncertain that Jane is very confident of their sentiments or that she has received adequate guidance, expression of affection or opportunity to communicate her feelings with them for a long time. She certainly has not felt confident enough of her relationship with them to share her distress about a range of adverse experiences.

4. Social Skills

Jane has a good repertory of social skills and is adept at getting on with others. However, she is relatively shy, somewhat ill at ease in social situations and quick to withdraw when under stress.

5. Anti-social Behaviour

Jane has an extensive history of escalating anti-social behaviour, including disruptiveness, truancy, running away and verbal aggression. Her most serious form of anti-social behaviour, however, have been wide ranging acts of deliberate self harm and absconding. She is not overtly anti-social in attitude.

6. Psychological

Jane is a relatively introverted, though socially mature girl. Her major problem is quite serious unhappiness, apparently bordering on depression. This is associated with a highly negative and fluid view of herself, coloured by strong feelings of helplessness and hopelessness. She is not mentally ill and her behaviour, as recorded in the past, should not have resulted in being sectioned under the Mental Health Act.

Treatment Recommendations

1. Physical

Jane requires a rigorous programme of physical activities aimed at making her physically stronger, to give her confidence to stand up for herself. She might also pursue one or two activities to friendly competition level as a means of building up her self confidence. Given her history of substance misuse, she should receive specific treatment in this area to reduce the probability of her further recourse to substance misuse.

2. Cognitive

Jane is bright enough to pursue high level academic activity with a view to going into further or higher education. There should, therefore, be considerable emphasis on increasing her educational competence and enabling her to take examination-based subjects sufficient to get her into an institution of higher education by the time she is 18 or 19. Giving her some vocational skills would be part of her normal curriculum rather than an area of emphasis.

3. Home and Family

Given the complexities of family relationships, intensive and probably prolonged work with the family is a high priority. Equally, Jane must become fully aware of her parentage and this aspect of her identity should be the focus of detailed, planned work. Given the importance of the family to her, every attempt should be made to maintain closest contact between her and her family.

4.   Social Skills

Jane would benefit from intensive assertiveness training aimed at enabling her to cope with rougher, more powerful peers and adults in authority.

5.   Anti-social Behaviour

Given the high level of risk Jane presents to herself, her initial treatment should be under conditions of security. She requires focused and intensive treatment to divert her from deliberate self harm and teach her alternative methods of coping with distress. Crown Prosecution Service should be strongly advised not to proceed with her prosecution if that is the main associated factor because of its impact on her mental condition.

6.   Psychological

Jane requires intensive personal and emotional care from a male and female pair who will establish a relationship of trust with her and help her towards achieving a greater sense of self worth. She also requires clinical oversight to ensure that her condition improves in an appropriate manner.

Treatment Venue

There are four broad treatment venues available in justice, health, education and social services sectors. Treatment in the justice service is irrelevant because she is not currently on a serious enough criminal charge. Although Jane's condition warrants mental health intervention, the history so far is a most unhappy one and it is unlikely that her current condition would respond to treatment in a mental health setting. Educationally, Jane could be 'statemented' but it is unlikely that her wider problems could be treated in an educational setting. Of social services facilities, return home immediately is inadvisable, and further fostering is inappropriate because she will not receive the necessary treatment. Placement in children's homes, hostels and community homes would similarly fail to provide for her treatment needs and may invoke the past pattern of behaviour. She, therefore, requires a hybrid facility where intensive, focused treatment can be provided, initially under conditions of security, and subsequently under open conditions.

Treatment Placement

Aycliffe, Centre for Children, Secure Facilities.

Signed _____
                              Director

Dated _____10th January, 1991_____

/SM/SG

Index

Main references to disorders are indicated by **bold** type.
PPA = Problem Profile Approach.